French Harpsichord Music
of the 17th Century

Studies in Musicology, No. 11

Other Titles in This Series

French Harpsichord Music
of the 17th Century

A Thematic Catalog of the Sources with Commentary

VOLUME ONE
Commentary

by
Bruce Gustafson

umi
RESEARCH PRESS

Produced and distributed by
University Microfilms International
Ann Arbor, Michigan 48106

Library of Congress Cataloging in Publication Data

Gustafson, Bruce, 1945-
   French harpsichord music of the 17th century.

   (Studies in musicology ; no. 11)
   Includes bibliographies and index.
   1. Harpsichord music—Thematic catalogs. 2. Music,
French—Thematic catalogs.   I. Title. II. Series.

ML128.H35G9   016.7864'04'210944   79-23567
ISBN 0-8357-1069-6 (set)
ISBN 0-8357-1066-1 v.1

For
Arthur Lawrence

CONTENTS

COMMENTARY

CONTENTS

CATALOG

ix

LIST OF COMMENTARIES AND INVENTORIES

LIST OF EXAMPLES

LIST OF FIGURES

LIST OF ABBREVIATIONS

Abbreviations: General

anon	anonymous	meas	measure
app	appendix	ms	manuscript
arr	arranged, arranged by	mss	manuscripts
attr	attributed to	n	note
b	born	n b	*nota bene*
c	century	n d	no date
ca	*circa*	n p	no publisher
cf	*confer*	p, pp	page, pages
chap	chapter	p *l*	preliminary leaf
cm	centimeters	q v	*quod vide*
CO	concordance	r	*recto*
d	died	rev	revised
ed (ED)	edition, edited by	r h	right hand
e g	*exempli gratia*	S	Schmieder, *Bach-*
etc	*et cetera*		*Werke-Verzeichnis*
et seq	*et sequens*	s s	*senza segnatura*
ex	example; exemplar	s v	*sub verbo*
facsim	facsimile	T	Taylor (see
ff	following		Bibliography)
fl	flourished	tr	transcribed,
i e	*id est*		transcribed by
intro	introduction	trans	translated
K	Kirkpatrick, Ralph,	v, vols	volume, volumes
	Domenico Scarlatti	v	*verso*
	(see Bibliography)	Z	Zimmerman, *A*
l, ℓ	leaf, leaves		*Thematic Catalog*
l h	left hand		(see Bibliography)
m	married	#	number

Abbreviations: Sources, Editions, Literature

Add-16889   London: British Library, Reference Division [British Museum], Department of Manuscripts; Additional 16889. Lute tablature, ca. 1615-1618.

Add-22099   Ibid.; Additional 22099. Keyboard ms, 1704-1707.

Add-52363   Ibid.; Additional 52363. Keyboard ms, 1704.

Adler-I
Adler-II
Adler-III   Adler, Guido, ed. *Johann Jakob Froberger, Orgel- und Klavierwerke,* Denkmäler der Tonkunst in Österreich. Graz: Akademische Druck- u. Verlagsanstalt, 1896; reprint ed., 1959.

Anglebert, d'   See Inventory 68.

Anglès   Anglès, Hygini, ed. *Musici organici Iohannis Cabanilles, Opera omnia.,* vol. 1. Barcelona: Biblioteca de Cataluña, 1927.

Apel-HKM   Apel, Willi. *The History of Keyboard Music to 1700.* Translated and revised by Hans Tischler. Bloomington: Indiana University Press, 1972.

Apel-R   _____, ed. *Adam Reincken, Collected Key-board Works,* Corpus of Early Keyboard Music: no. 16. N.p., American Institute of Musicology, 1967.

Arkwright catalog   Arkwright, Godfrey Edward Pellen. [Thematic Catalog of Anonymous Pieces in the Christ Church Library, Oxford.] MS, 1935.

Arsenal-410/24   Paris: Bibliothèque de l'arsenal; s.s (*olim* M 410/24). Unlocated "méthode de clavecin."

Aubert   Aubert, Pauline, and Brigitte François-Sappey, ed. *Jean-François Dandrieu, Trois Livres de Clavecin.* Paris: Schola Cantorum, 1973.

Babell   See Inventory 24.

Babell-T	Chicago, Newberry Library, Special Collections, Case MS VM350 B113t. Instrumental trio ms part books, ca. 1700.
Ballard-1611	Ballard, Robert. [*Premier Livre de luth.* Paris: P. Ballard, 1611]
Ballard-1614	Ballard, Robert. *Diverses Piesces mises sur le luth par R. Ballard.* Paris: P. Ballard, 1614.
Bang	Bang, Claus Hansen. *Med lyst vil jeg begynde* [broadside]. n.p., 1639.
Bangert	Bangert, Emilius, ed. *Dietrich Buxtehude, Klavervaerker.* 2nd ed. Copenhagen: Hansen, 1944.
Banquet-2	*The Second Book of The Ladys Banquet.* London: Walsh & Hare, 1706.
Basel	Basel: Öffentliche Bibliothek der Universität Basel, Musiksammlung; Ms F. IX. 53. Lute tablature, 17th c.
Bauyn	See Inventory 35.
Beatrix	Brussels: Bibliothèque royale Albert 1er, département de manuscrits; MS III 900. Ca. 1660?, keyboard ms.
Benoit	Benoit, Marcelle. *Musique de Cour, Chapelle, Chambre, Écurie, 1661-1733, Documents recuillies,* La Vie musicale en France sous les rois Bourbons: no. 20. Paris: Picard, 1971.
Berlin-8551	West Berlin: Staatsbibliothek der Stiftung preussischer Kulturbesitz, Musikabteilung; Mus. Ms. 8551. Ca. 1725?, keyboard ms.
Berlin-30206	See Inventory 15.

Berlin-30363	East Berlin: Deutsche Staatsbibliothek, Musikabteilung; Mus. Ms. 30,363. Post 1723, keyboard ms.
Berlin-40147	Unlocated. Ca. 1660-1680, keyboard ms.
Berlin-40623	See Inventory 3.
Berlin-40624	Unlocated. Post 1715, keyboard ms.
Bernoulli-Moser	Bernoulli, Eduard, ed. *Heinrich Albert, Dritter Theil der Arien oder Melodeyen* (1640). Revised by Hans Joachim Moser. Denkmäler deutscher Tonkunst: vol. 12. Wiesbaden: Breitkopf & Härtel, 1958.
Besard	Besard, Jean-Baptiste. *Novus Partus, sive Concertationes Musicae.* Augsburg: 1617.
Bod-220	Oxford: Bodleian Library; Ms. Mus. Sch. D. 220. 1654, instrumental bass part.
Bod-393	Ibid.; Ms. Mus. Sch. E. 393. 1700, vocal ms.
Bod-425	Ibid.; Ms. Mus. Sch. E. 425. Post 1708, keyboard ms.
Bod-426	See Inventory 25.
Bod-576	Oxford, ibid.; Ms. Mus. Sch. F. 576. Post 1679, mixed ms (lute, vocal, harpsichord).
Bonfils-13	Bonfils, Jean, ed. *Henri Dumont, L'Oeuvre pour clavier,* l'Organiste liturgique: no. 13. Paris: Schola Cantorum, 1956.
Bonfils-18	_____. *Les Pré-classiques français,* l'Organiste liturgique: no. 18. Paris, Schola Cantorum, 1957.
Bonfils-25	_____. *Anonyme français du 17e siècle, le livre d'orgue de Marguerite Thiéry,* l'Organiste liturgique: no. 25. Paris: Schola Cantorum, n.d.

Bonfils-29   _____. *Clém. de Bourges et N. de Grotte, fantaisies; Ch. Racquet oeuvres complètes; Denis Gautier, tombeau,* l'Organiste liturgique: no. 29. Paris: Schola Cantorum, n.d.

Bonfils-31   _____. *Les Pré-classiques français (supplément),* l'Organiste liturgique: no. 31. Paris: Schola Cantorum, n.d.

Bonfils-58   _____. *Les Pré-classiques français, La Barre, Gautier, Ballard, et anonymes, 8 courantes extraites du ms. Lynard A1 de Lübbenau,* l'Organiste liturgique: no. 58-59. Paris: Schola Cantorum, 1967.

Bonfils-LP   _____. *Livre d'orgue attribué à J. N. Geoffroy,* Le Pupitre: no. 53. Paris: Heugel, 1974.

Borren   Borren, Charles van den. "Einige Bemerkungen über dem handschriftlichen Klavierbuch (Nr. 376) der Königlichen Bibliothek zu Kopenhagen." *Zeitschrift für Musikwissenschaft* 13 (1930-31): 556-558.

Brade   Brade, William. *Newe lustige Volten, Couranten, Balletten, Padoanen, Galliarden, Masqueraden, auch allerley arth Newer Französischer Täntze.* Berlin, 1621.

Breig   Breig, Werner. "Die Lübbenauer Tabulaturen Lynar A1 und A2." *Archiv für Musikwissenschaft* 25 (1968): 96-117, 223-236.

Briquet   Briquet, Charles M. *Les Filigranes, dictionnaire historique des marques du papier.* Paris, 1907. Facsimile ed., with supplement, ed. by Allan Stevenson. 3 vols. Amsterdam: The Paper Publication Society, 1968.

Brown   Brown, Alan, ed. *William Byrd, Keyboard Music,* Musica Britannica 28. London: Stainer and Bell, 1971.

Brunold-Co Brunold, Paul, ed., *Louis Couperin, Oeuvres complètes.* Paris: Oiseau Lyre, 1936.

Brunold/Dart-Co _____. *Louis Couperin, pièces de clavecin.* Revised by Thurston Dart. Monaco: Oiseau Lyre, 1959.

Brunold-D _____. *Dieupart, six suites pour clavecin.* Paris: Oiseau Lyre, 1934.

Brunold-Tessier _____, and André Tessier, ed. *Jacques Champion de Chambonnières, oeuvres complètes.* Paris: Senart, 1925; reprint ed., New York: Broude Brothers, 1967.

Brussels-926 See Inventory 28.

Brussels-24.106 Brussels: Conservatoire royal de musique, bibliothèque; cf XY 24.106 [unlocated]. 18th c., Philidor ms.

Brussels-27.220 Brussels, ibid.; cf XY 27.220 [unlocated]. 17th c. harpsichord ms.

Bull See Inventory 26.

Burette-407 Unlocated. 1695, harpsichord ms.

Burette-408 Unlocated. 1695, harpsichord ms.

Burette-409 Unlocated. 1695, harpsichord ms.

Burette-410 Unlocated. N.d., harpsichord ms.

Caldwell Caldwell, John. *English Keyboard Music Before the Nineteenth Century.* New York: Praeger, 1973.

Campbell Campbell, Pauline M. "A New Chapter in the History of the Clavecin Suite: Jean Nicolas Geoffroy." M.M. thesis, University of Illinois, 1967.

Cassel See *Écorcheville.*

Cecilia	See Inventory 30.
Celle	Celle: Boman Musik Bibliothek; MS 730. 1662, keyboard ms.
Chamb-I	See Inventory 62.
Chamb-II	See Inventory 63.
Ch-Ch-378	See Inventory 20.
Ch-Ch-1113	Oxford: Christ Church Library; Mus. Ms. 1113. 17th c., harpsichord ms.
Ch-Ch-1177	See Inventory 22.
Ch-Ch-1236	See Inventory 18.
Cherbury	Cambridge: Fitzwilliam Museum; ms 3-1956. Ca. 1608-1640, lute ms.
Chigi	See Inventory 29.
Chigi-27	Rome: Biblioteca Apostolica Vaticana; Ms. Chigi Q IV 27. Ca. 1650?, keyboard.
Choice	*A Choice Collection of Ayres for the Harpsichord or Spinet.* London: Young, 1700.
Churchill	Churchill, W. A. *Watermarks in Paper in Holland, England, France, etc., in the XVII and XVIII Centuries and Their Interconnections.* Amsterdam: Menno Hertzberger, 1935.
Clark-D173	Los Angeles: University of California at Los Angeles, William Andrews Clark Library; D. 173 M4 H295 1690Bd. 1690, harpsichord ms.
Clark-M678	Ibid.; M. 678 M4 H295 1710. 1710, harpsichord ms.
Cofone	Cofone, Charles J. F., ed. *Elizabeth Rogers Hir Virginall Booke.* New York: Dover, 1975.

Cohen

Cohen, Albert. "A Study of Instrumental Ensemble Practice in Seventeenth Century France." *Galpin Society Journal* 15 (March, 1962): 3-17.

Collection

A Collection of Lessons and Aires for the Harpsichord or Spinnett compos'd by Mr. J. Eccles, Mr. D. Purcell and Others. London: I. Walsh and I. Hare, [1702].

Copenhagen-376

See Inventory 1.

Copenhagen-396

See *Lundgren.*

Cosyn

See Inventory 16.

Cummings

South Bend: private collection: Bruce Gustafson. Ca. 1700, 3 instrumental part books.

Curtis-Berkeley

Curtis, Alan. "Musique classique française à Berkeley; pièces inédites de Louis Couperin, Lebègue, La Barre, etc." *Revue de musicologie* 56:2 (1970), pp. 123-164.

Curtis-Co

_____, ed. *Louis Couperin, pièces de clavecin,* Le Pupitre 18. Paris: Heugel, 1970.

Curtis-D

_____, ed. *Jean Denis, Traité de l'accord de l'éspinette* (Paris, 1650). New York, 1969.

Curtis-MMN

_____. *Nederlandse Klaviermuziek uit de 16e en 17e eeuw,* Monumenta Musica Neerlandica: no. 3. Amsterdam: Verenigung voor Nederlandse Muziekgeschiedenis, 1961.

Danckert

Danckert, Werner. *Geschichte der Gigue.* Leipzig: Kistner & Siegel, 1924.

Dandrieu-1

Dandrieu, Jean-François. *Livre de clavecin composé par J. F. D'Andrieu dédie à Monsieur Robert.* Paris: author, Ribon, Foucault, [ca. 1704].

Dandrieu-2   _____. *Livre de clavecin composé par Monsieur Dandrieu, organiste de St Merry.* Paris: author, Foucault [ca. 1704].

Dandrieu-3   _____. *Pièces de clavecin courtes et faciles de quatre tons différents composé par le Sieur d'Andrieu, organiste de St. Merry et gravées par Claude Desvogue.* Paris: author, Foucault [ca. 1704].

Dandrieu-4   _____. *Premier Livre de pièces de clavecin.* Paris: author, 1724.

Dandrieu-5   _____. *Second Livre de pièces de clavecin.* Paris: Boivin, 1728.

Dandrieu-6   _____. *Troisième Livre de pièces de clavecin.* Paris: author et al., 1734.

Darmstadt-17   Darmstadt: Hessische Landes- und Hochschulbibliothek, Musikabteilung; Mus. ms. 17. 1672, keyboard ms.

Darmstadt-18   Ibid.; Mus. ms. 18. 1674, keyboard ms.

Darmstadt-1198   Ibid.; Mus. ms. 1198. 16??, score in German organ tablature.

Dart   See Inventory 45.

Dart-BI   Dart, Thurston, John Steele and Francis Cameron. *John Bull, Keyboard Music: I*, Musica Britannica 14. London: Stainer and Bell, 1960.

Dart-BII   _____. *John Bull, Keyboard Music: II*, Musica Britannica: no. 19. London: Stainer and Bell, 1963.

Dart-Ch   _____. *J.C. de Chambonnières, les deux livres de clavecin.* Monaco: Oiseau Lyre, 1969.

Dart-Co   _____, rev.; Paul Brunold, ed. *Louis Couperin, pièces de clavecin.* Monaco: Oiseau Lyre, 1959.

Dart-HI	_____. *The First Part of Musick's Hand-maid Published by John Playford.* London: Stainer and Bell, 1969.
Dart-HII	_____. *The Second Part of Musick's Hand-maid, Revised and Corrected by Henry Purcell.* 2nd ed. London: Stainer and Bell, 1962.
Dart-L	_____. *Matthew Locke, Keyboard Suites.* 2nd ed. London: Stainer and Bell, 1964.
De Lafontaine	De Lafontaine, Henry Cart. *The King's Musick.* London: Novello, 1909; reprint ed., New York: Da Capo, 1973.
Denis	See Inventory 57.
Dickinson	Dickinson, Alis. "Keyboard Tablatures of Seventeenth Century in the Royal Library, Copenhagen." Ph.D. Dissertation, North Texas State University, 1974.
Drallius	Lüneburg: Ratsbücherei der Stadt Lüneburg, Musikabteilung; Mus. Ant. Pract. KN 146. 1650, keyboard ms.
Drexel-5609	New York City; The New York Public Library and Museum of the Performing Arts, Music Division; Ms. Drexel 5609. Late 18th. c., copied from earlier mss by Sir John Hawkins.
Dufourcq-L	Dufourcq, Norbert, ed. *Nicolas Lebègue, oeuvres de clavecin.* Monaco: Oiseau Lyre, 1956.
Dufourcq-O	_____. *L'Orgue parisien sous le règne de Louis XIV.* Copenhagen: Hansen, 1956.
Dumont-1652	See Inventory 58.
Dumont-1657	See Inventory 59.
Dumont-1668	See Inventory 61.

Écorcheville	Écorcheville, Jules, ed. *Vingt Suites d'orchestre du XVIIe siècle français.* 2 vols. Paris: L.-Marcel Fortin, 1906.
Egerton-814	London: British Library, Reference Division [British Museum], Department of Manuscripts; Egerton 814. 1744, chanson ms.
Egerton-2514	Ibid.; Egerton 2514. 17th c., chanson ms.
Egerton-2959	Ibid.; Egerton 2959. Late 17th or early 18th c., English keyboard ms.
Eitner	Eitner, Robert. *Biographisch-bibliographisches Quellen-Lexikon der Musiker und Musikgelehrten der christlichen Zeitrechnung bis zur Mitte des 19. Jahrhunderts.* Leipzig: Breitkopf & Härtel, 1898-1904.
Elling	Elling, Catharinus. "Die Musik am Hofe Christian IV. von Dänemark." Vierteljahrschrift für Musikwissenschaft 9 (1893): 62-98.
Epstein	Epstein, Ernesto. *Der französische Einfluß auf die deutsche Klaviersuite im 17. Jahrhundert.* Würtzburg-Aumühle: Triltsch, 1940.
Eyck	Eyck, Jacob van. *Der Fluyten Lust-Hof, Vol Psalmen, Paduanen, Allemanden, Couranten, Balletten, Airs, etc.* 2 vols. Amsterdam: Paulus Matthysz, 1646, 1654.
Eÿsbock	Stockholm: Kungliga Musikaliska Akademiens Bibliotek; Tabl. 1. Ca. 1600, keyboard ms.
Faille	Unlocated. Ca. 1625, keyboard ms. Copy in papers of Charles van den Borren, "ms Vincent de la Faille." Brussels; Conservatoire royale de musique, Bibliothèque; s.s.
Fasquelle	*Encyclopédie de la musique.* 3 vols. Paris: Fasquelle, 1958-1961.

Ferguson	Ferguson, Howard, and Christopher Hogwood, eds., *Complete Harpsichord Works, William Croft.* 2 vols, London: Stainer & Bell, 1974.
Ferrard	Ferrard, Jean, ed. *F. Roberday, fugues et caprices pour orgue,* Le Pupitre: no. 44. Paris: Heugel, 1972.
Fétis	Fétis, François J. *Biographie universelle de la musique.* 2nd ed., 8 vols. Paris: Didot, 1866-1870.
Finspong	Norrköping: Stadsbiblioteket; Finspong 9098. 17th c., violin ms.
François-Sappey	François-Sappey, Brigitte, ed. *Jean François Dandrieu, trois livres de clavecin,* Publications de la société française de musicologie 1:21. Paris: Heugel, 1975.
Frotscher	Frotscher, Gotthold. *Geschichte des Orgelspiels und der Orgelkomposition.* 2 vols. Berlin: H. Hesse, 1935-1936.
Fuhrmann	Fuhrmann, Georg Leopold. *Testudo Gallo-Germanica.* Nuremberg: Norici, 1615.
Fuller-Maitland	Fuller-Maitland, J.A., ed. *The Contemporaries of Purcell.* 7 vols. London: Chester [n.d.].
Gaultier	Gaultier, Pierre (de Marseilles). *Symphonies de feu Mr. Gaultier de Marseille.* Paris: Ballard, 1707.
Gen-2348/53	See Inventory 38.
Gen-2350/57	See Inventory 54.
Gen-2354	See Inventory 43.
Gen-2356	See Inventory 47.
Gen-2357[A]	See Inventory 34.

Geoffroy — See Inventory 37.

Geraklitov — Geraklitov, A. A. *Filigrani 17 veka* [Watermarks of the Seventeenth Century in Paper of Manuscript and Printed Documents of Russian Origin]. Moscow: Publishing House of the Academy of Sciences, 1963.

Gigault — See Inventory 67.

Gilbert — Gilbert, Kenneth, ed. *Jean-Henry d'Anglebert, pièces de clavecin*, Le Pupitre: no. 54. Paris: Heugel, 1975.

Gillier — Gillier, Pierre (l'Ainé). *Livre d'airs et de symphonies meslez de quelques fragments d' opéra.* Paris: author, Foucoult, 1697.

Gresse — See Inventory 27.

Grimm — Vienna: Österreichische Nationalbibliothek, Musiksammlung; MS 16,798. 1699, keyboard ms.

Grove-5 — Grove, Sir George, ed. *Grove's Dictionary of Music and Musicians.* 5th ed., edited by Eric Blom. 9 vols. London: Macmillan, 1954.

Grove-5-S — Ibid., *Supplementary Volume.* London: Macmillan, 1961.

Grove-6 — Ibid. 6th ed., edited by Stanley Sadie. London: Macmillan, [forthcoming]. Citations to "Grove-6" reflect information in articles as of November, 1975 to January, 1976, in the offices of *Grove-6*.

Haas — Haas, Arthur. "The Chaconne and Passacaille in French Baroque Harpsichord Music." M.A. Thesis, University of California at Los Angeles, 1974.

Hamburger — Hamburger, Povl. "Ein Handschriftliches Klavierbuch aus der ersten Hälfte des 17. Jahrhunderts." *Zeitschrift für Musikwissenschaft* 13 (1930): 133-140.

Handmaide	See Inventory 59a.
Handmaide-2	See *Dart-HII.*
Harpsichord-1	See *Petre.*
Harpsichord-2	*The Second Book of the Harpsichord Master.* London: Walsh, 1700.
Harpsichord-3	*The Third Book of the Harpsichord Master.* London: Walsh & Hare, 1702.
Hawkins	Hawkins, Sir John. *A General History of the Science and Practice of Music.* 5 vols. London: Payne and Son, 1776.
Heardson	See Inventory 19.
Heawood	Heawood, Edward Ard. *Watermarks, Mainly of the 17th and 18th Centuries.* Hilversum: The Paper Publication Society, 1950.
Heawood-I	_____. "Papers Used in England After 1600; the Seventeenth Century to c. 1680." *The Library* 11 (March, 1930): 263-299.
Heawood-II	_____. "Papers Used in England After 1600; c. 1680-1750." *The Library* 11:4 (March, 1931): 466-497.
Heawood-III	_____. "Further Notes on Paper Used in England After 1600." *The Library* 5:2 (1947): 119-149.
Hendrie	Hendrie, Gerald, ed. *Orlando Gibbons, Keyboard Music,* Musica Britannica: no. 20. London: Stainer and Bell, 1962.
Hexachordum	See *Moser.*
Hintze	See Inventory 8.

Honegger	Honegger, Marc, ed. *Dictionnaire de la musique.* N.p.: Bordas, 1970.
Howell	Howell, Almonte Charles Jr., ed. *Nine Seventeenth-Century Organ Transcriptions from the Operas of Lully.* Lexington: University of Kentucky Press, 1963.
Hunt	Hunt, Edgar. "Tuning and Temperament." *The English Harpsichord Magazine* 1:7 (October, 1976): pp. 201-204.
Ihre-284	See Inventory 9.
Imhoff	Vienna, ibid.; MS 18491. 1649, keyboard ms.
Inglis	Edinburg: National Library of Scotland; Inglis 94 MS 3343. Ca. 1695, keyboard ms.
Jacquet	Jacquet (de la Guerre), Elizabeth. [*Pièces de clavessin*]. Paris, 1691. No ex. located.
Jurgens	Jurgens, Madeleine, ed. *Documents du Minutier central concernant l'histoire de la musique (1600-1650).* 2 vols. Paris: SEVEPEN, 1967 (vol. 1); La Documentations française, 1974 (vol 2).
Kabinet	'T Uitnement Kabinet vol Pavanen, Almanden, Sarbanden, Couranten, Balletten, Intraden, Airs, etc. Amsterdam: Paulus Matthysz, 1646, 1649.
LaBarre-1	Berkeley: University of California at Berkeley, Music Library; MS 765. Post 1682, vocal ms.
LaBarre-2	Ibid.; MS 766. Post 1685, vocal ms.
LaBarre-3	Ibid.; MS 767. Post 1686, vocal ms.
LaBarre-4	Ibid.; MS 768. Post 1688, vocal ms.
LaBarre-5	Ibid.; MS 679. Post 1693, vocal ms.

LaBarre-6	See Inventory 48.
LaBarre-7	Berkeley, ibid.; MS 771. Post 1699, vocal ms.
LaBarre-8	Ibid.; MS 772. Post 1703, vocal ms.
LaBarre-9	Ibid.; MS 773. Post 1718, vocal ms.
LaBarre-10	Ibid.; MS 774. Post 1719, vocal ms.
LaBarre-11	See Inventory 51.
Lange	Lange, S.F., ed. *Apparatus musico-organisticus [1690] von Georg Muffat.* Leipzig: Rieter-Biedermann, 1888.
LaPierre	See Inventory 44.
Lebègue-I	See Inventory 64.
Lebègue-II	See Inventory 65.
LeBret	Paris: Bibliothèque Sainte-Geneviève; MS 2382. 18th c., harpsichord ms.
Leningrad	Leningrad: Library of the Academy of Sciences; MS QN 204. 1650, keyboard ms.
Lesure	Lesure, François, ed. *Marin Mersenne: Harmonie universelle.* Paris: Centre national de la recherche scientifique, 1963.
Lincoln-I *Lincoln-II* *Lincoln-III*	Lincoln, Harry B., ed. *Seventeenth-century Keyboard Music in the Chigi MSS of the Vatican Library,* Corpus of Early Keyboard Music: no. 32, vols. 1-3. 3 vols. N.p., American Institute of Musicology, 1968.
Linz	Linz: Oberösterreiches Landesmuseum; MS 16 Inc. 9467. 1611-1613, keyboard ms.

Lüneburg-147	Lüneburg: Ratsbücherei der Stadt Lüneburg, Musikabteilung; Mus. Ant. Pract. KN 147. 17th c. keyboard ms.
Lüneburg-207:6	Ibid.; KN 207:6. 17th c. keyboard ms, probably partly Weckmann autograph.
Lüneburg-1198	Ibid.; Mus. Ant. Pract. KN 1198. 1687, keyboard ms.
Lundgren	Lundgren, Bo, ed. *Johann Lorentz, Klavierwerke.* Lund: n.p., 1960.
Lynar	See Inventory 4.
Lynar-A2	East Berlin: Deutsche Staatsbibliothek, Musikabteilung; Lübbenau Tabulaturen, Lynar A-2. Ca. 1615-1650, keyboard ms.
Maas	Maas, Martha, ed. *English Pastime Music, 1630-1660*, Collegium Musicum: Series 2, vol. 4. Madison: A-R Editions, 1974.
Madrid-1357	Madrid: Biblioteca nacional; Ms 1357. 1706, keyboard ms.
Madrid-1360	See Inventory 31.
Marais-RI	Marais, Roland. *ler. Livre de pièces de viole.* Paris: author, 1735.
Massip	Massip, Catherine. *La Vie des musiciens de Paris au temps de Mazarin (1643-1661)*. Paris: Picard, 1976.
Menetou	See Inventory 46.
Mersenne	See Inventory 56.
MGG	Blume, Friedrich, ed. *Die Musik in Geschichte und Gegenwart.* Kassel, Basel: Bärenreiter, 1949-1968.
MGG-S	Ibid. [supplementary fascicles], 1969- .

Minkoff	*Manuscrit Bauyn* [facsim. ed.]. Preface by François Lesure. Geneva: Minkoff, 1977.
Minorite	Vienna: Minoritenkonvent, Klosterbibliothek & Archiv; MS 743. 1708-17??, keyboard ms.
Möllersche	See Inventory 13.
Moser	Moser, Hans Joachim, and Traugott Fedke, ed. *Johann Pachelbel, Variationswerke, Hexachordum appolinis*, 1699. Kassel: Bärenreiter, 1958.
Munich-1503k	Munich: Bayerische Staatsbibliothek, Musiksammlung; Mus. Ms. 1503k. 17th c. organ ms.
Munich-1503l	See Inventory 5.
Munich-1511e	See Inventory 6.
Munich-1511f	See Inventory 7.
Newberry	Chicago; Newberry Library, Special Collections, Case MS Vm350 B113t. Ca. 1700?, instrumental.
Nicolai	Nicolai, Alexandre. *Histoire des moulins à papier du sud-ouest de la France, 1300-1800.* 2 vols. Bordeau: G. Delmas, 1935.
Noske	Noske, Frits, ed. *Klavierboeck Anna Maria van Eijl,* Monumenta Musica Neerlandica: no. 2. Amsterdam: Verenigung voor Nederlandse Muziekgeschiedenis, 1959.
Nostitz	*The Nostitz Papers,* Monumenta chartae: no. 5. Hilversum: The Paper Publication Society, 1956.
Nuremberg	Nuremberg: Germanisches Nationalmuseum, Bibliothek; Hs. 31781. 1699-1721, keyboard ms.

Oberst Oberst, Günther, ed. *Terpsichore (1612)*, Gesamtausgabe der Musikalischen Werken von Michael Praetorius, Friedrich Blume, general editor: vol. 15. Wolfenbüttel: Georg Kallmeyer Verlag, 1929.

Oldham See Inventory 32.

Oldham-2 See Inventory 53.

Ottobeuren Ottobeuren: Benediktiner-Abtei, Musiklarchiv und Bibliothek; MO 1037. 1695, keyboard ms.

Oude *Oude en niuwe Hollantse Boeren-Lietes en Contradansen.* 12 parts. Amsterdam: Roger, n.d.

Oxford-IB Unlocated. 1652, keyboard ms.

Paignon See Inventory 50.

Parthenia *Parthenia or the Maydenhead of the First Musicke that Euer Was Printed for the Virginalls.* London: Evans, [ca. 1613].

Parville See Inventory 36.

Perrine See Inventory 66.

Philidor Versailles: Bibliothèque municipale; Ms. Mus. 139-143. Instrumental mss, 18th c.

Piccard Piccard, Gerhard. *Die Turmwasserzeichnen*, Wasserzeichnenkartei Piccard im Hauptstaatsarchiv Stuttgart: Findbuch 3. Stuttgart: W. Kohlhammer, 1970.

Pidoux Pidoux, Pierre, ed. *G. Frescobaldi, Orgel- und Klavierwerke.* 5 vols. Kassel: Bärenreiter, 1948-1953.

Pierront Pierront, Noëlie, ed. *Chacones et passacailles*, Orgue et liturgie: 22. Paris: Schola cantorum, 1954.

Pirro	Pirro, André, ed. "Huit Pièces inédites," *Revue musicale,* supplément, Feb., 1921.
Playford	See Inventory 60.
Pohlmann	Pohlmann, Ernst. *Laute, Theorbe, Chitarrone.* Bremen: Deutsche Musikpflege, 1968.
Prunières	Prunières, Henri, ed. *Six Airs et une passacaille de Luigi Rossi.* Paris: Senart, 1914.
Pulver	Pulver, Jeffrey. *A Biographical Dictionary of Old English Music.* London: Paul, Trench, Trubner & Co., J. Curwen, 1927.
Quittard-H	_____. [Hardel]. *Revue musicale,* supplément, Nov. 15, 1906.
Rave	Rave, Wallace John. "Some Manuscripts of French Lute Music," Ph.D. dissertation, University of Illinois, 1972.
Rameau-1706	Rameau, Jean-Philippe. *Premier Livre de pièces de clavecin.* Paris: author, 1706.
Rameau-1728	_____. *Nouvelles Suite de pièces de clavecin.* Paris: author, [1728].
Rastall	Rastall, Richard, ed. *Complete Keyboard Works: Benjamin Rogers.* London: Stainer & Bell, [1969].
RCM	London: Royal College of Music Library; ms 2093. 17th c., keyboard ms.
Redon	See Inventory 55.
RésF-933	See Inventory 49.
Rés-Vma-ms 7/2	Paris: Bibliothèque nationale, département de la musique; Rés Vma ms 7 (1-2). 1731, chanson ms.
Rés-89ter	See Inventory 33.

Rés-476	See Inventory 40.
Rés-819-2	Paris, ibid., fonds conservatoire; Rés 819 (2). Post 1661, German keyboard ms.
Rés-1184	Ibid., exemplar of *Parthenia*; see Inventory 16.
Rés-1186bis	See Inventory 22.
Rés-2671	See Inventory 52.
Roberday	Roberday, François. *Fugues et caprices à 4 parties.* Paris: Sanlecque, 1660.
Roche	Roche, Martine. "Un Livre de clavecin français de la fin du XVIIe siècle." *Recherches 7* (1967): 39-73.
Rodenegg	West Berlin: Staatsbibliothek der Stiftung preussischer Kulturbesitz, Musikabteilung; Mus. Ms. 40,068. 1656, lute tablature.
Röntgen	Röntgen, Julius, ed. *Oud-nederlandsche Muziek uit het Muziekboek van Anna Maria van Eijl.* Amsterdam: Alsbach; Leipzig: Breitkopf & Härtel, 1918.
Roesgen-Champion	Roesgen-Champion, Marguerite, ed. *Pièces de clavecin composées par J. Henry d'Anglebert.* Paris: Droz, 1934.
Rogers	See Inventory 17.
Rollin	Rollin, Monique, and Jean-Michael Vaccaro, eds. *Oeuvres des Mercure.* Paris: Centre national de la recherche scientifique, 1977.
Roper	See Inventory 22a.
Rossi-Palazzo	Rossi, Luigi. *Il Palazzo incantato.* Facsim. ed. New York: Garland, 1977.

Rost	Paris: Bibliothèque nationale, département de la musique; Vm7 1099. 17th c. instrumental ms.
Rudén	Rudén, Jan Olof. "Ett nyfunnet Komplement till Dübbensamlingen." *Svensk Tidskrift för Musikforskning* 47 (1965): 51-58.
Ryge	See Inventory 11.
Sargent	Sargent, George, ed. *Elizabeth Roger's Virginal Book, 1656*, Corpus of Early Keyboard Music: no. 19. N.p., American Institute of Musicology, 1971.
Saizenay-I *Saizenay-II*	Besançon: Bibliothèque municipale; N° 279152, 279153. 1699, lute tablature.
Schmidt	Schmidt, Jost Harro, ed. *J. P. Sweelinck,* [selected works], Exempla Musica Neerlandica: 2. Amsterdam: Verenigung voor Nederlandse Musiekgeschiedenis, 1965.
Schwerin-617	See Inventory 10.
Schwerin-619	See Inventory 14.
Shindle-I *Shindle-II* *Shindle-III*	Shindle, W. Richard. *Girolamo Frescobaldi, Keyboard Compositions Preserved in Manuscripts,* Corpus of Early Keyboard Music: 30. 3 vols. N.p., American Institute of Musicology, 1968.
Skara	Skara, Sweden: Stifts- och landsbiblioteket, Högre Allmänne Läroverks Musiksamling; Skara 493b (nr 31). 1659-post 1661, keyboard ms.
Sloane-1021	London: British Library, Reference Division [British Museum], Department of Manuscripts; Sloane 1021. 17th c. lute tablature.
Sloane-2923	Ibid.; Sloane 2923. Ca. 1683, lute tablature.

Souris-BaI   Souris, André, and Sylvie Spycket, ed. *Robert Ballard, premier livre (1611)*. Introduction by Monique Rollin. Paris: Centre national de la recherche scientifique, 1963.

Souris-BaII   _____, and Jacques Veyrier, ed. *Robert Ballard, deuxième livre (1614) et pièces diverses.* Introduction by Monique Rollin. Paris: Centre national de la recherche scientifique, 1964.

Souris-Be   _____. *Oeuvres pour luth seul de Jean-Baptiste Besard.* Introduction by Monique Rollin. Paris: Centre national de la recherche scientifique, 1969.

Souris-C   _____. *Oeuvres de Chancy, Bouvier, Belleville, Dubuisson, Chevalier.* Introduction by Monique Rollin. Paris: Centre national de la recherche scientifique, 1967.

Souris-D   _____. *Oeuvres de Dufaut.* Inroduction by Monique Rollin. Paris: Centre national de la recherche scientifique, 1965.

Souris-G   _____. *Oeuvres du vieux Gautier.* Introduction by Monique Rollin. Paris: Centre national de la recherche scientifique, 1966.

Souris-M   _____. *Oeuvres de René Mesangeau.* Introduction by Monique Rollin. Paris: Centre national de la recherche scientifique, 1971.

Souris-V   _____, Monique Rollin and Jean-Michel Voccars, ed. *Oeuvres de Vaumesnil, Edinthon, Perrichon, Raël, Montbuysson, La Grotte, Saman, La Barre.* Paris: Centre national de la recherche scientifique, 1974.

S.Saëns   Saint-Saëns, Camille, ed. *Jean Philippe Rameau, pièces de clavecin.* Paris: Durand, n.d.

Starter   Starter, Jan. *Friesche Lust-Hof.* Amsterdam: Dirck Pieterszoon Voscuyl, [1624].

St-Georges	Paris: Bibliothèque nationale, départment de la musique; Vm⁸ 1139. Post 1724?, harpsichord ms.
Stockholm-2	Stockholm: Kungliga Musikaliska Akademiens Bibliotek; Tabl. 2. Ca. 1680?, keyboard ms.
Stockholm-176	Stockholm: Kungliga Biblioteket; S. 176. Post 1681, keyboard ms.
Stockholm-228	Ibid.; S. 228. Post 1685, keyboard ms.
Stoss	Paris: Bibliothèque nationale, département de la musique; Vm7 1818. Post 1684, German harpsichord ms.
Strizich	Strizich, Robert W., ed. *Robert de Visée, Oeuvres complètes pour guitare.* Le Pupitre: no. 15. Paris: Heugel, 1969.
Tenbury	See Inventory 23.
Terburg	Unlocated. 17th c. ms.
Tessier-F	Tessier, André. "Une Pièce inédite de Froberger." *Festschrift für Guido Adler zum 75. Geburtstag*, Studien für Musikgeschichte. Vienna: Universal, 1930; pp. 147-152.
Tessier-G	_____, ed. *La Rhétorique des dieux et autres pièces de luth de Denis Gaultier.* 2 vols. Paris: Droz, 1932-1933.
Thiéry	Paris, ibid., fonds conservatoire; Rés 2094. 1677-1683, organ ms.
Thomelin	See Inventory 41.
Thott	Copenhagen: Det kongelige Bibliothek, Haandskrift Afd.; Thott 292 8o. 1699-1702, keyboard ms.

Tilsen	Tilsen, Herta. "Eine Musikhandschrift des Benediktinerklosters Ottobeuren aus dem Jahre 1695." Ph.D. Dissertation, Munich, 1922.
Trios-1 *Trios-2*	Babell, Charles, ed. *Trios de differents autheurs.* 2 vols. Amsterdam: Roger [1697, 1700].
Uppsala-409	Uppsala: Universitetsbiblioteket, Carolina Redivia; MS 409. Ca. 1650-1662, instrumental score.
Uppsala-134:22	Ibid.; IMhs 134:22. Ca. 1650-1662?, instrumental score.
Valerius	Valerius, Adriaen. *Nederlantsche Gedenck-Clanck.* Haarlem: Valerius, 1626.
Van-Eijl	Amsterdam: Toonkunst-Bibliotheek; 208 A 4. 1671, harpsichord ms.
Vat-mus-569	Rome; Biblioteca Apostolica Vaticana; Ms. Vat. mus. 569. Italian keyboard ms, ca. 1660-1665.
Veron	Paris: Bibliothèque nationale, département de la musique; Vm6 5. 1691, violin ms.
Vm7-3555	Ibid.; Vm7 3555. 18th c. violin ms.
Vm7-4867	Ibid., Vm7 4867. Post 1715, violin ms.
Vm7-6307-1	See Inventory 39.
Vm7-6307-2	See Inventory 42.
Voigtländer	Copenhagen, ibid., Musikafdelingen; Mu 6610.2631. Post 1642, keyboard ms.
Voorn-I	Voorn, H. *De Papiermolens in de Provincie Noord-Holland,* De Geschiedenis der Nederlandse Papierindustrie: 1. Haarlem: Papierwereld, 1960.

Voorn-II	_____. *De Papiermolens in de Provincie Zuid-Holland,* De Geschiedenis der Nederlandse Papierindustrie: 2. Womenveer: Drukkerij Meijer, 1973.
Walther	See Inventory 12.
White	White, John, ed. *François Dandrieu, Music for Harpsichord.* University Park: Pennsylvania State University Press, 1965.
Witzendorff	See Inventory 2.
Wolffheim	Unlocated. 1630-1650?, keyboard ms.

PREFACE

This work began with a love of French harpsichord music. It manifested itself in a thirty-page graduate school paper which evolved into a five-volume dissertation at The University of Michigan under the title, "The Sources of Seventeenth-Century French Harpsichord Music." A task of this magnitude imposes certain limitations: Any of the larger manuscripts would be a logical basis for a more detailed study than can be presented here, but the more general overview provides a frame of reference. The foreign sources must be discussed primarily in terms of the few French pieces they contain, and it is also virtually impossible to follow the network of concordances to all of seventeenth-century music. To present descriptions of the sources without discussing and ultimately playing the music is myopic, yet musical judgments can benefit from the external evidence in the sources. In short, musical sources relate to all other aspects of music, but a source study cannot follow its own implications to their conclusions. It is a foundation and a tool for future use.

The procedures that were followed in writing this study often determined which sorts of information were included. After the study of the secondary literature of the field was completed, a bibliographic approach was chosen. Although a useful microfilm collection of most of the sources was slowly amassed, it became clear that dependable descriptions of the manuscripts could only be based on first-hand examinations. With very few exceptions, all of which are noted in the Commentary, every source was examined in person. After three months of travel to various libraries, I compiled the Catalog in Paris, using the Bibliothèque nationale as the primary reference library.

As the physical descriptions and thematic inventories of the sources were made, a thematic index was compiled. The incipits of all of the compositions which were or might be part of the repertoire were reduced to a numerical code and entered into the file along with numerous related materials. This concordance file of approximately 4,000 incipits was the main tool which produced the network of concordances in the Catalog. The presentation and evaluation of the concordances are among the primary functions of this study.

Such a detailed examination of the sources necessitated the curtailment of other areas of research. The most significant of these is biography; the French archives still hold many of the answers to the troubling biographical questions which plague evaluations of this repertoire, but such research cannot be profitably approached from the narrow standpoint of seeking the identity of specific persons. All of the biographical information in this study, unless otherwise noted, is drawn from the secondary sources specified in the List of Composers. Similarly, primary research on the watermarks which were traced from the sources must be left for specialists in that field.

The present publication is an extensively revised and corrected version of my dissertation. Insertions and deletions have been made on almost every page, two newly "discovered" sources have been added to the Catalog, and others have been added to the Commentary (portions of which are entirely new). The sections of the work have been rearranged for easier use, and a complete Index has been added. Lamentably, the fiscal exigencies of publication forced those footnotes which could not be incorporated into the text to become endnotes. In order to prevent the confusion of conflicting "Gustafson numbers," the original numbering of the Inventories has been preserved, insertions being designated with letter suffixes. Thus, for example, the Inventory inserted between 22 and 23 is called 22a. A bibliographic work of this size inevitably contains errors; the material has been checked and rechecked in an effort to make it accurate in all details, but it is logical to assume that errors of commission as well as omission remain.

Because this work required research in many libraries and other locations, the number of individuals who contributed to the study is correspondingly large. Staff members of all of the institutions which are mentioned in this work are thanked with sincerity for their assistance and hospitality. In this category, special mention must be made of the following librarians: François Lesure, Bibliothèque nationale (Paris); Wallace Bjorke, University of Michigan (Ann Arbor); Vincent Duckles, University of California at Berkeley; Watkins Shaw, honorary librarian, St. Michael's College (Tenbury Wells, Worcestershire); Robert Münster and Renata Wagner, Bayerische Staatsbibliothek (Munich); Inge Henriksen, The Royal Library (Copenhagen); Rolf Dempe, Wissenschaftliche Allgemeinbibliothek des Bezirkes Schwerin; and Susan T. Sommer, New York Public Library. W.J. Oxenbury, on behalf of the trustees of the estate of the late Thurston Dart, allowed a manuscript from that unsettled estate to be examined for this study. Adalbert Meier (Memmingen, Bavaria) was gracious in allowing a manuscript from the Ottobeuren abbey's collection to be studied in his home. Stanley Sadie (London) was extremely kind in permitting the reading of many articles which were awaiting publication in the sixth edition of *Grove's Dictionary of Music and Musicians*. Especially warm thanks are extended to Guy Oldham (London) both for allowing his manuscripts to be included in this study and for his valuable comments and perceptions.

PREFACE

A number of scholars were most generous in making suggestions and providing information from their own research. Alan Curtis (Berkeley), Kenneth Gilbert (Paris), Alexander Silbiger (Madison, Wisconsin), Howard Schott (Oxford), Renate Brunner (Freiburg) and Barry Cooper (Aberdeen) were particularly helpful in the data and ideas which they contributed. R. H. Tollefsen (Utrecht), Hubert Bédard (Maintenon), David Ledbetter (Manchester, England) and Thomas Taylor (Ann Arbor) also deserve thanks.

Glenn Watkins and David Crawford of the University of Michigan provided significant guidance and encouragement in the writing of the first version of this work. Richard Wood (publisher, UMI Research Press) and George Buelow (Bloomington) went beyond the call of duty in arranging for the publication of a manuscript which is in some ways a publisher's nightmare. Special thanks go to Meredith Lays, who spent great time and effort in helping with the assembly of the original catalog.

More than any other individual, it was David Fuller (Buffalo, New York) who was the guiding spirit and constant adviser to this project. Mr. Fuller provided the initial concept of the study and contributed both information and incisive opinions as the work evolved. He has set an example of scholarly cooperation which few can equal.

My greatest debt is to Arthur Lawrence, who was involved with every phase of this work, from the first tentative ideas to the proofreading of the final text. Without his help at every level, from evaluating large concepts to searching for typographical errors, this study would never have appeared.

INTRODUCTION

To those who succumb to the extraordinary beauty and subtlety of French harpsichord music, the questions of the origin and development of the style inevitably occur. The answers have remained obscure largely because a foundation of detailed studies was not laid before the superstructure of conclusions appeared. No study has presented an authoritative statement of what exactly constitutes the repertoire of seventeenth-century French harpsichord music, its quantity or its current location. For almost a century, virtually every scholar of early keyboard music has referred to the "Bauyn" manuscript, for example, but not even a title inventory of its contents has ever been published. Scholars have long recognized the problem of the lack of French sources from 1531 (Attaingnant) to about 1650, but an evaluation of foreign keyboard manuscripts which contain French music has never been offered. Rather, a few isolated foreign manuscripts were seized upon as the missing links in the history of French harpsichord music, without placing them in their proper context. For these reasons, the present study presents descriptions, evaluations, inventories and concordance studies for all of the known sources of seventeenth-century French harpsichord music.

The title, *French Harpsichord Music of the 17th Century: A Thematic Catalog of the Sources, with Commentary,* involves some very specific delimitations. Throughout this work, the following definitions remain in force:

"French" refers to music written by composers who lived primarily in France. While composers from the Spanish Netherlands (modern Belgium) are excluded, Dumont is included because he emigrated to Paris early in his career. No native Frenchmen have been excluded because of expatriation.

"Harpsichord music" is the most difficult of the terms to define. It signifies all the written repertoire which was played by seventeenth-century French harpsichordists, including both music originally written for harpsichord and music transcribed from lute or other instrumental music. It does not include melody-bass vocal scores or organ music. Transcriptions are included if they were arranged for harpsichord by a Frenchman, but such music, even if originally French, is excluded if transcribed by a foreigner. It is the harpsichord music which must be French, not the original models of transcriptions. Reduced scores of operas are excluded if the implied harpsichord accompaniment is to be improvised from a bass line, but fully notated keyboard versions of vocal pieces are included even if the text has been written into the score. In general, French organ music, unlike that from other countries, is very different from harpsichord music. Organ textures were determined by characteristic registrations, and no one could possibly consider a *tierce-en-taille* as harpsichord music, for example, or an unmeasured prelude as organ music. However, some genres, such as measured preludes and certain noëls, are less idiomatic, and were probably played on either instrument; since most such pieces were found in organ sources, they are uniformly considered organ music here.

"Seventeenth century" is used literally here. Using the exact date 1600 to begin the period presents no difficulties because the earliest datable music which could be considered French harpsichord music is from 1629 (Champion), but in defining the end of the seventeenth century, other factors come to bear. For example, Marchand and Le Roux are considered to be eighteenth-century composers here because of the publication dates of their works, 1701 and 1705. Such exclusions, which are made explicit in the List of Composers, are not as arbitrary as they may seem, because the music of these composers did not circulate in seventeenth-century manuscripts, even though some of it was surely composed before the turn of the century. By maintaining a strict cut-off date of 1700, the repertoire actually ends with the music of the generation born before ca. 1640 (Lebègue and Thomelin are the youngest), excluding composers born after 1667 (Dieupart and Marchand are the oldest, with the possible exception of Le Roux, whose birth date is unknown). The last datable music which is included is from 1689 (d'Anglebert) and the earliest which is excluded is from 1701 (Dieupart). In effect, then, "seventeenth-century" French harpsichord music comes from the period ca. 1629 to 1689, and was written by the following identified composers: d'Anglebert, Burette, Chambonnières, Champion, Louis Couperin, Dumont, Geoffroy, Gigault, Hardel, La Barre, Lebègue, Monnard, Montelan, Richard and Thomelin.

A "source" is a musical document, either manuscript or printed, which appeared before 1800. Thus eighteenth-century manuscripts and prints are included if they contain seventeenth-century French harpsichord music. Nineteenth- and twentieth-century prints are referred to as "editions," and manuscripts from that period are ignored altogether. Similarly, "contemporary" means before 1800, and "modern" refers to the period after 1800.

The organization of this work is similar to a scholarly edition of music. The Catalog, like the music of an edition, can be used by itself, but it is clarified and amplified by the Commentary. The work has been written as a reference tool, to be consulted more than read from beginning to end. However, each chapter in the Commentary begins with an introduction and ends with a summary, which together provide a narrative discussion of the subject at hand. The specific source discussions are arranged in approximate chronological order within national groups or subgroups. The important secondary literature associated with the sources is mentioned with corrections and additions to the work of other scholars appended as necessary. The Commentary explains and justifies the conclusions presented in the Catalog and points out at least some of the significant aspects of the sources, suggesting areas for future research. Particularly in the first chapter, brief descriptions of only apparently related sources are given.

CHAPTER I

GERMANIC AND SCANDINAVIAN MANUSCRIPTS

The logic of opening a French source study with discussions of Germanic and Scandinavian manuscripts may not be entirely self-evident. It derives from two factors: the twentieth-century musicological literature has emphasized these sources[1] and, more importantly, only in these manuscripts do we find quantities of pieces with French titles and attributions to French composers before the last forty years of the century. Since no French sources of consequence survive from before 1650, the plethora of *französische Couranten,* etc. is enticing; the pieces actually attributed to French composers seem to be of major significance. This chapter will show that, although there is much French music in these manuscripts, there is very little French harpsichord music until the last two decades of the century. The exceptions do not disprove the generalization, and they will be discussed in detail: *2-Witzendorff, 4-Lynar, 5-Munich-15031, 6-Munich-1511e, 7-Munich-1511f and 8-Hintze.* Following is a list of the sources which will be discussed, arranged in approximate chronological order within two categories:

Household Mss

Eÿsbock	*Thott*	*Darmstadt-1198*
Linz	*Nuremberg*	*9-Ihre-284*
1-Copenhagen-376	*Berlin-40624*	*Stockholm-176*
Wolffheim	*Professional Mss*	*10-Schwerin-617*
Imhoff	*4-Lynar*	*Stoss*
Leningrad	*Voigtländer*	*Ottobeuren*
Drallius	*Uppsala-409*	*Grimm*
2-Witzendorff	*Uppsala-134:22*	*11-Ryge*
Berlin-40147	*Skara*	*Minorite*
Rés-819-2	*5-Munich-15031*	*12-Walther*
Celle	*6-Munich-1511e*	*13-Möllersche*
3-Berlin-40623	*7-Munich-1511f*	*14-Schwerin-619*
Stockholm-2	*8-Hintze*	*Berlin-30363*
Stockholm-228	*Darmstadt-17*	*Berlin-8551*
Lüneburg-1198	*Darmstadt-18*	*15-Berlin-30206*

Household Keyboard Books

Germanic and Scandinavian keyboard manuscripts can be divided roughly into two categories: household and professional. This division is based on the nature of the contents of the sources, not solely on the competence of the scribes or owners.[2]   The household, or amateur, tablatures were anthologies of the pieces which a family enjoyed and from which they learned the rudiments of music.   A typical book (e.g. *1-Copenhagen-376* and *2-Witzendorff,* the first two inventories in the Catalog) almost always contained a haphazard sampling of popular tunes, dances and chorales.   Occasionally a piece by a named composer was entered into the book, and even more rarely a full-textured harpsichord composition (by Scheidemann, for example) found its way into the collection.   Often they were compiled over a period of years, with several hands of varying skill making their contributions.   The books represent the musical taste and practice of middle-class northern (i.e., Protestant) families--those in which music-making was an important part of home life and in which, to judge from the keyboard manuscripts, sacred and secular music were freely intermingled.

There is a predictable core repertoire to be found among these books, with the same melodies set over and over again, from "Courante la vignon" to "Nun komm' der Heiden Heiland."   What one does not find, however, is the frequent recurrence of the same settings of these tunes; when modern scholars of this literature cite "concordances," they are usually reporting the similarity of two melodies, not the full textures of the settings.   This point deserves to be emphasized because French harpsichord music can largely be characterized as two-handed pieces in which the melody is often one of the less-striking features.   Thus the very nature of Germanic household books precludes the likelihood of finding quantities of French harpsichord music within them.   Almost certainly, some of the same tunes were set for harpsichord in France in the early seventeenth century, as there is ample evidence that such tunes were central to much French music in general.   There are, however, no other early French harpsichord sources to prove the point.   *54-Gen-2350/57* could well be early enough to be an exception and it does include at least a few popular tune settings, such as "Courante de la reyne" and "La Vignon."   Such tunes are discussed in *56-Mersenne* ("Traité de la voix et des chants," pp. 170-171), for example, where the author sometimes speaks of the melody titles as dance types rather than as just melodies.   The La Barre setting of "O Beau Soleil" therein suggests that tune-setting was an important concept specifically in keyboard music.   Even if one had the materials available to cite melody concordances with early French harpsichord manuscripts, however, it would not indicate that these Germanic manuscripts contained French harpsichord music, but that both cultures drew upon the same, largely French, melodies.

The derivation and circulation of these popular tunes is far beyond the scope of the present study, but the following list of melody concordances for one of the most popular of the tunes, "La Vignon," illustrates how extensive a network is involved. The list is undoubtedly far from complete. It is derived in part from *Dickinson;* Renate Brunner, who has made an extensive concordance file of such melodies, simply gave up in dismay with this ubiquitous tune.

Keyboard settings:

> *1-Copenhagen-376* #35, Courante Lavignon ... La Duble
> *4-Lynar* #69, Courante La Vigon
> *Drallius l.* 23v, Courant
> *Imhoff l.* 16v, Courante
> *54-Gen-2350/57* #7, Vignonne
> *2-Witzendorff* #33, Curant Lavion
> *Lüneburg-1198* p. 112, Courant Lavion
> *9-Ihre-284* #95, La Viona ... La Double d' Joh Lor
> *Vat-mus-569* p. 96-97, Courante Lauignone ... Variation
> pᵃ della Corrente L'auignone

Lute settings:

> *Basel,* Courante Lavignone
> *Sloane-1021 l.* 54r, Courant La Vignon
> *Sloane-2923 l.* 21v, Courante lavingon
> *Ballard-1614* Courante Septiesme, La Vignonne

Other settings:

> *Brade,* XXXII
> *Starter* p. 26, L'Avignonne
> *Valerius* p. 174, La Vignonne
> *Finspong* p. 22, 24 [the second is a different melody:] Lavione nouvelle
> *Bang,* Med lyst vil jeg begynde
> *Eyck* I *l.* 13v, Lavignone; Tweede Lavignione
> *Oude* #474-VII, l'Avignonne
> *56-Mersenne* Traité de la voix p. 170 [mentions "La Vignonne," but does not present the melody]
> *Rossi-Palazzo* III-7, L'Auignone Corrente

Eÿsbock. *Provenance:* Frankfurt, ca. 1600? *Location:* Stockholm; Kungliga Musikaliska Akademien, Tabulatur 1. *Description:* 64 *l.*, folio format, 31.5 x 20 cm. Watermark #80. Modern 3/4 imitation vellum binding, 32.4 x 21 cm. *Notation:* New German organ tablature, written page by page. *Scribes:* 2-3 unidentified hands. The format and terms used in the bibliographic notes for manuscript citations are explained below, pp. 148-151.

The earliest household book containing music by an identified French composer was written for a young lady from Frankfurt named Elisabeth Eÿsbock (Eijsbock, Eisbock). Thurston Dart published a title inventory of the tablature and listed a number of melody concordances, primarily to English sources.[3] *Eÿsbock* is a splendid example of the extent to which French airs were assumed by the *Bürgerschaft,* as the first page attests:

> Madama
> Elisabett Eÿsbock
> gehordt dis bucgh
> A Madama:
> Madamaselle Elisabetha Eisbock de francofort
> apertient ce p[rese]nt: Liure qui le trouue ou le
> prendt et non le rand e[s]t ung grand Forfant [Forfait].
> Le verd de Mer lunique Colleur.
> Je adore pour mon bonheur.
> Tel qui desire na respos &c-

The manuscript is undated, but both Dart and Brunner consider it to be from about 1600. The following composers can be identified:[4] Conversi, Dowland, Ferretti, Godard, Jacob, Lasso and Philips. Three inscriptions might indicate other composers, rather than merely titles:

> Corante de prinse Parma [#23]
> galyard d'Italÿ Durulÿ [#27]
> Allamande d frederico [#55]

As one can deduce from the list of composers, *Eÿsbock* contains a great many intabulations of vocal compositions, a style which did not remain a part of the Germanic household book repertoire. Otherwise, this book presents all of the elements to be found in the later manuscripts: settings of popular tunes, dance movements and chorales. Here it is a chanson composer, Godard, who represents the French. The piece cannot be considered French harpsichord music any more than the Conversi madrigal intabulation can be considered Italian harpsichord music; they are German harpsichord pieces based on foreign models. An intabulation *by* a French composer is known in another manuscript, but it was written in open score and was probably not intended for keyboard at all, although it has been published in a moden edition as an organ work. It is the "Fantasia A 4o sopra 'Anchor che col partire'" by Nicholas de La Grotte (*Bonfils-29* p. 11). Bonfils argues (p. 3) that the organ could be an alternate performance medium in view of several other open score publications, but the harpsichord is not involved in such considerations. The same Bonfils edition contains an intabulation tentatively attributed to the sixteenth-century composer Clément de Bourges. The following other French titles are in *Eÿsbock*; they are not concordant with known French harpsichord compositions:[5]

> Allamande Damour [#2]
> Alamande fortune helas pourquoy [#3]
> Gallÿarde D'engliterre [#20]
> Corantte de fransie [#22]
> Gailiard d'engleterre [#26]

Linz. *Provenance:* Austria (?), 1611-1613 (dated on spine and *l.* 1). *Location:* Linz; Oberösterreichische Landesmuseum, Musik Hs. 3 (*olim* Inv. IVo 9647). *Description:* i, 185 p., oblong quarto format, 14 x 19.6 cm. (trimmed). Watermark #33. Contemporary parchment binding, 14.8 x 20.3 cm. *Notation:* New German organ tablature. *Scribes:* 2-3 unidentified hands.

Linz is another early household tablature. The binding is stamped, "A.S.P. 1613," and the first page carries the notation, "Angefangen den 6 Septembris 1611." The 108 pieces are a typical mixture of tunes, dances and chorales. The following composers are named: Hauβmann, Peuerl and Strauβ. One title might be construed as a French attribution, however, a "Ballata Mercurÿ" (pp. 110-111), which could refer to one of the lutenists named Mercure. It is unlikely, although possible, that it could be John Mercure (ca. 1580/90-pre 1660) in view of the early date of *Linz*, but it could be Pierre "d'Orléans," who was active by 1611. In either case, the piece in question could not be termed French harpsichord music, since it would be a Germanic transcription of French lute music. The following other French titles are in *Linz*:

> Curanta francesca [pp. 38-39]
> französche Tanz [pp. 74-75]
> Curanta fransequina [pp. 104-105]

None of the pieces has concordances to French harpsichord music and Brunner has found melody concordances to non-French sources. The vogue for French dances and tunes was already established at this early date in Germany, as is illustrated by the collection of dances for instrumental ensembles published by Michael Praetorius in 1612. His *Terpsichore* consisted not only of French dances, but of some of the same melodies ("Courante la reyne," etc.) which are found in the keyboard manuscripts under discussion here.

Copenhagen-376 (Inventory 1)

This manuscript is the most important of the household books. Norlind[6] was the first musicologist to mention this tablature, and Hamburger[7] dealt with it later, emphasizing its importance as a document of the "lost period" in French keyboard suite development. His article includes a number of transcriptions and prompted a reply from Van den Borren, who identified the composer of one Sarabande as Germain Pinel.[8] This pair of articles became the foundation for all later appraisals of seventeenth-century French keyboard music, most notably that in Apel's monumental study of early keyboard music, and they were the basis of Anthony's assessment of *1-Copenhagen-376* as the earliest source of French harpsichord music.[9] Epstein also discussed the manuscript and its relationship to the history of the suite, presenting some transcriptions.[10] Schierning provided a basic inventory and summarized the other scholarly discussions of the source, prior to 1956.[11] In 1962, a master's thesis by Mráček, a student of Apel, dealt extensively with the music of *1-Copenhagen-376* from an analytical point of view, accompanied by many transcriptions.[12] Most recently, the fine study already cited was written by Dickinson. The latter dissertation discussed the manuscript from both bibliographic and musical standpoints, citing numerous melody concordances in the commentary, with a complete transcription of the tablature.

The primary attraction of *1-Copenhagen-376* is that it contains two very early dates, "1626, 3. Jan" (*l.* 2v) and "1639. 3 Januar." (*l.* 7v). This seemed the ideal manuscript to close the gap in the history of French harpsichord music: it provided dated, attributed, French harpsichord music from the third or fourth decade of the century. However, a number of factors contradict this assessment.

All of the scholars before Dickinson failed to take into account the fact that there are leaves lacking from the volume between the two dates, leaving much room for doubt as to the meaning of the first date. The second date (1639) comes very early in the tablature, the second quire, and is probably not an indication of the volume's completion date. Since most of the concordances cited by Dickinson come from mid-century sources, it seems likely that the tablature was not completed until about 1650, and it is possible that some of the pieces were added even later.

That the pieces were not entered in strict chronological order further complicates the issue; blank spaces left by one scribe were later filled in by another. Dickinson corrected Hamburger's assertion that *1-Copenhagen-376* was written by a single hand; the number of scribes is unclear, but at least three hands can be distinguished. Dickinson (1:34) attempted unsuccessfully to be more precise about the number of scribes and presented several facsimiles to illustrate the wide range of hands (1:23-39). Brunner also considered the matter in vain ("Conversations") and I studied the manuscript both on microfilm and in person, but a definitive statement is still elusive. Certain details, such as the formation of final bars, are similar in otherwise quite different hands, and all of the hands are rather sloppy. It would seem that there are as many as eight different writing styles, but many of these are probably by the same hand at different times, with different pens. A resolution of this problem is essential to further precision in evaluating the source.

Following Hamburger's article, scholars have attempted to decipher some obscure marks on what is now the final leaf of the manuscript (*l.* 34), pasted to a modern end paper:

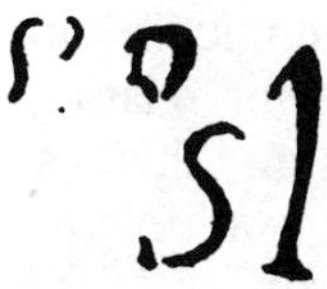

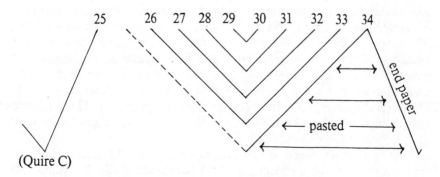

Fig. 1. Letters on *l.* 34r of *1-Copenhagen-376*

Dickinson (1:56-57) refuted Mráček's speculation (p. 89) that they should be read as "S D ST," meaning S[crips] D[elphin] ST[rungk]. They probably have no more meaning than any of the other miscellaneous marks in the manuscript where various scribes tried out their pens before starting to copy music into the book. Furthermore, leaf 34 was not the original end of the manuscript: if it were part of the outer sheet of the fourth quire, there would be a *lacuna* between *l.* 25 and *l.* 26, as can be seen from this diagram of the quire:

Fig. 2. Quire D of *1-Copenhagen-376*

There is no such *lacuna.* Also, *l.* 33v was written as a single page, rather than as half of two facing pages, suggesting that it was the final page of the manuscript. It would seem that *l.* 34 was placed in its current position when the manuscript suffered its twentieth-century rebinding. The leaf might be one of the those missing from the outer sheet(s) of the second quire.

The contents and handwriting show that the compilers of *1-Copenhagen-376* were Germanic, but the exact provenance of the manuscript remains undetermined. There are English pieces in *1-Copenhagen-376*, which is not typical of these books. Dickinson pointed out that there were both French and English musicians at the court of Christian IV of Denmark, and it is probable that *1-Copenhagen-376* was originally Danish. The manuscript must be viewed as an incomplete anonymous household tablature which was gradually compiled by several people, perhaps a family, in the middle third of the seventeenth century.

The most important factor relating to French music is that the French composers named in this source were lutenists, not harpsichordists. There are two pieces attributed to Frenchmen, "Allamande de M: Mechanson" (#50)[13] and "Allemande de: Mr: Pinell." The pieces follow each other in the latter part of the manuscript and may have been entered into the book at midcentury. Lute originals have not been found for either piece, but the composers must be Mesangeau and Pinel, French lutenists whose works are found in many lute and harpsichord manuscripts in Germanic and Scandinavian countries, as well as in France. The evidence that these are lute pieces is found in the nature of all Germanic household keyboard manuscripts, rather than within *1-Copenhagen-376* itself: in tablature after tablature we find the names Du But, Gaultier, Mesangeau, Mouton, Pinel and others--all known to be lutenists, not harpsichordists. Norlind (p. 186) discussed the tablature from this standpoint in 1906 and Apel (*-HKM* p. 506) pointed out that the pieces might be adaptations from lute originals. Although the editors of *Souris-M* did not find a lute version of this Allemande, there is no reason to assume that *1-Copenhagen-376* is the exception to the norm. A lutenist could have written a few harpsichord pieces, with the same low range and *brisé* texture as one finds in the transcriptions, but some evidence would have to be found to prove it. The logical assumption is that the French pieces in German and Scandinavian keyboard manuscripts are Germanic transcriptions of French lute compositions.

One other piece in *1-Copenhagen-376* has been attributed to Pinel on the basis of a concordance, the Sarabande #48. In addition to the keyboard settings listed in the Catalog, *Dickinson* (1:92-94) cited a number of concordances to non-keyboard sources. However, the many melody concordances to the piece, and the fact that it comes between two settings of other popular melodies, raise the question of whether we are dealing with two transcriptions of the Pinel Sarabande, or merely melody concordances to the same tune which Pinel used. Although there are some considerable differences between the *Faille* and *1-Copenhagen-376* settings, especially in the second strain, an attribution to Pinel appears justifiable. The two doubles are totally different and are not involved in the attribution question.

Ex. 1. Sarabande by Pinel (*1-Copenhagen-376* #48 and *Faille l.* 121v)

The pieces by La Barre (#39-40) pose a more difficult problem in determining their relationship to French harpsichord music. While Mesangeau and Pinel are both names which were clearly associated with lute music, La Barre is the name of a family of Parisian musicians which included lutenists, harpsichordists, organists, a singer and a flutist. Throughout the present study, the La Barre problem will recur frequently; none of the keyboard pieces attributed to La Barre can be shown positively to be from lute originals, but circumstantial evidence will be presented to suggest that most of the compositions in non-French sources are transcriptions from lute music (cf. pp. 58-60).

Dickinson (1:88-90) attributed the Allemande (#39) to La Barre on the basis of its similarity to *27-Gresse* #21 and *3-Berlin-40623* #72. The version in *1-Copenhagen-376* is somewhat different from the other two and is a fifth lower. Harpsichord compositions were rarely transposed, and the few examples which are known (e.g., *35-Bauyn-I* #118) are changed by a step only, not a fifth. Lute transcriptions, on the other hand, are commonly found in keys a fourth or a fifth apart, since lute tablature can be transcribed into one key as easily and logically as another (e.g., *45-Dart* #40 and *66-Perrine* #1). It is therefore probable that the La Barre Allemande was a lute composition originally, which would also account for the substantial differences among the three texts.

The Sarabande (#40) which follows this Allemande is more tenuously related to La Barre. The melody is the same as *29-Chigi* #32, a Sarabande in D Minor attributed to La Barre, but it is also found in a nonkeyboard source (*Eyck*), and the *29-Chigi* setting bears no resemblance to the *1-Copenhagen-376* version. La Barre may have composed the melody which circulated without his lute setting of it, or

Ex. 2. Allemande by La Barre (*1-Copenhagen-376* #39, *3-Berlin-40623* #72 and *27-Gresse* #21)

Ex. 2. Allemande by La Barre (*1-Copenhagen-376* #39, *3-Berlin-40623* #72 and *27-Gresse* #21) (continued)

he may have made a setting of an already popular tune. In either case, the Sarabande in *1-Copenhagen-376* is probably not a harpsichord composition by La Barre.

Ex. 3. Sarabande by La Barre (*29-Chigi* #32 and *1-Copenhagen-376* #40)

No concordances to French harpsichord music have been found for the unattributed pieces in *1-Copenhagen-376* which bear French titles, but Dickinson cited many melody concordances to other Germanic sources. Thus one must assume that in *1-Copenhagen-376*, as in the other manuscripts discussed in this chapter, each title represents either the name of a melody or, in the case of "Courãte de Delphin" (#55), an attribution in the French language.

With the possible exception of the La Barre pieces, then, *1-Copenhagen-376* does not contain any dances or other pieces which can be considered French harpsichord music. The significance of the manuscript has been greatly exaggerated because it was discussed in isolation, not as part of a long tradition of Germanic and Scandinavian household books, and because it was assumed that all of the manuscript was written before 1639. Along with other household manuscripts, it does bear an important relationship to the dispersal of French melodies and to the transcription of French lute music. *1-Copenhagen-376* is more advanced than most of the others in the use of *style-brisé* texture, but it is not a source of French harpsichord music.

Wolffheim

Little can be said about this manuscript, formerly owned by Werner Wolffheim, because it is currently unlocated.[14] It seems to have dated from the second quarter of the century and contained music attributed to a French name: a Sarabande by "Du Charreart," who is unidentified. The name could be a corruption of Du Caurroy, in which case the Sarabande was probably a transcription from an instrumental work.

Imhoff. *Provenance:* Vienna, 1649 (dated *l.* 1r). *Location:* Vienna; Österreichische Nationalbibliothek, Musikabteilung, Hs. 18491. *Description:* 46 *l.*, 5 quires (A/14, B/4, C/16, D/2, E/10), folio format, 31 x 19.5 cm. Watermark #77. Modern 1/2 leather binding, 32 x 20.5 cm. *Notation:* New German organ tablature (7 systems per page, written page by page). *Scribes:* primarily hand A to *l.* 41r, with one addition in hand B (*l.* 40r) and several additions in a modern hand; hand C from *l.* 42r to the end.

The remaining "early" Germanic household tablatures date from midcentury. *Imhoff* is well-known through the German literature on seventeenth-century keyboard music; a title inventory with melody incipits has long been available[15] and the manuscript has been discussed by Epstein, Wolf, Schierning and others. Furdell has made the most recent study of *Imhoff.*[16] One point of great confusion has been the date on the first page, variously given in the literature as 1629 or 1649:

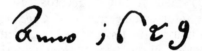

Fig. 3. Date of *Imhoff*

The script is admittedly unclear, but the third digit is a known type of seventeenth-century German four. This reading, which presumably is the date of copying, is supported by the fact that the composer David Schedlich, who was only twenty-two in 1629, is mentioned in three different parts of the manuscript: "Da Sch. Courante," *l.* 17v-18r; "Aufftzug D.S.," *l.* 25v; and "Ballet A: David Schedlich," *l.* 41r. Schierning (p. 111) and Brunner concur with this dating. It is a matter of some importance, since the collection would be of greater significance if it could be shown to be twenty years older.

None of the 117 pieces can be linked directly to France. Furdell (p. 23) attributed a Volte (#13, *l.* 6r) to Robert Ballard II, stating that it is a simplified version of the Volte published in Ballard's second lute book in 1614, *Souris-Ba-II*, p. 41. However, the two versions are very dissimilar, and the relationship is quite tenuous (see Ex. 4).

Imhoff provides the following French-related titles and melodies, none of which has concordances, other than melodies, to French sources. The following list is based on Furdell (pp. 23-26):

> Die Schäfferin [# 18, *l.* 7r][17]
> Couranta [la reyne] [# 34, *l.* 13r]
> Couranta [la vignon] [# 42, *l.* 16v]

Ex. 4. Incipits of Two Voltes in *Imhoff* and *Ballard-1614*.

Leningrad. *Location:* Leningrad; Library of the Academy of Sciences, QN 204. I have not seen this manuscript in person, and I am grateful to Alan Curtis for the use of his microfilm of it.

Leningrad, the first piece of which is dated 1650, was described with a title inventory and selective edition in *Curtis-MNN* (pp. XII-XVII, XXXII-XXXIX, 59-72). One Ballet (*l.* 3v-5r) is attributed to "Jacob Fuckart," probably the Frenchman Jacques Foucart who is represented in *Kabinet* and is mentioned in *56-Mersenne.* It is doubtful that Foucart, a violinist who is not known to have written keyboard music, is responsible for more than the melody of this piece.

The following list of French titles provides a clear example of an important linguistic distinction: the use of the word *französisch* (abbreviated here as "Frantz") to mean French style, rather than French provenance.   Scheidemann, who is typically identified as "H.S.M." in manuscripts, wrote many French dances like the Courante listed here, as did other mid seventeenth-century Germans.

> Curant [# 14, *l.* 8v][18]
> Courant Frantz H.S.M. [# 19, *l.* 15v]
> Serbande [# 22, *l.* 19v][19]
> Droevige Princesse [# 24, *l.* 20v]

Drallius.   *Location:*   Lüneburg; Ratsbücherei, Mus. Ant. Pract. KN. 146. *Description:*   191 *l.* (originally at least 194: 3 *l.* lacking), 17 quires (A/12, B/8, C/8, D-H/12, I/10, J-N/12, O/10, P/12, Q/11), upright quarto format, 21 x 16.5 cm.   Watermark # 48.   Original parchment binding from a Latin ms, 20.2 x 16.2 (*sic*).   *Notation:*   New German organ tablature (4 systems per page, written across facing pages). *Scribe:*   1 unidentifed hand.

The owner of this tablature signed and dated it, "Joachimus Drallius Anno 1650" (*l.* 1r).   The large collection of 250 pieces is particularly rich in courantes (87), but none of them (nor any of the other dance movements) has been found in a French source.   *Drallius* was briefly cited by Schierning (p. 112), and the Lüneburg library's printed catalog provides melody incipits for the anonymous pieces.[20] Melody concordances for many of the pieces can be found in Dickinson's dissertation and Apel also drew from this source (*Apel-HKM,* p. 383). He is probably in error to assume that Drallius wrote the book: household tablatures were more often written by the teacher of the owner when they are in a single hand.   The following French titles appear:

> Correnta frantzö G b mol [# 29, *l.* 19v]
> Chansson Franc: Ex clavi D [# 30, *l.* 20v][21]
> Courant [la vignon] Ex clavi D [# 34, *l.* 23v]
> Ein Fr. gert [?] Dantz [4 meas. fragment, *l.* 31v]
> Saraband [# 94, *l.* 60v][22]
> Saraband [# 128, *l.* 81v][23]
> Courant Matamoselli [# 164, *l.* 118v]
> Male content [# 174, *l.* 128v]
> französiche Allmand. Autor H.S.M. [i.e. Scheidemann;
>   # 194, *l.* 148v]
> Volte du Tambour [# 198, *l.* 152v]

Courante Monsior [#219, *l.* 175v][24]
Eine frantzosiche Saraband [#238, *l.* 189v]

Witzendorff (Inventory 2)

2-Witzendorff is exceptional in several respects. Not only does it carry a date, but the owner, who in this case seems also to have been the scribe, noted specifically that he began on January 7, 1655 and finished the volume on June 7, 1659, in Lüneburg. It is carefully written and is amateurish in its contents only, not its appearance. The tablature contains, in addition to the expected tunes, dances and chorales, the surprise of "Currant Gombonier" (#94). It is the earliest datable piece of indisputably French harpsichord music in a foreign source: Works by La Barre are at least in part earlier, but the identity of the presumed Frenchman, La Barre, is uncertain. The pieces attributed to "Chapel" in *26-Bull* (1629) are definitely the earliest pieces, but the identification of Chapel as the Frenchman Champion is not beyond doubt. *8-Hintze,* containing a piece by Chambonnières, could be earlier, but it cannot be dated with certainty.

Chambonnières' Courante here is in as corrupt a version as the spelling of the composer's name; without the written attribution, it is doubtful that anyone would have suspected that this starved little piece, with its melody-accompaniment texture, was the work of the composer who is normally associated with the origins of *style-brisé* harpsichord writing. A comparison of the incipit with its concordant versions shows that Witzendorff took "Curant" to mean mostly a melody. Chambonnières' published version has a strong tenor line, which is typical of *clavecin* music; in this case it is actually in canon with the soprano. In *2-Witzendorff,* there is no real tenor voice, the rhythm of the melody is simplified and even the bass line is changed, incorporating some notes from the original tenor voice an octave lower.

The other attribution to a named composer in *2-Witzendorff,* the "Curant Messaugea" (#99), was almost certainly intended to read "Courante Mesangeau." As with the Mesangeau pieces in *1-Copenhagen-376,* no lute original for the Courante has been found. No information can be supplied for the other French titles found in *2-Witzendorff.* It is surprising that a manuscript of 103 compositions should contain only one title in the French language, when the only named composers in the manuscript are French and when, more exceptionally, it contains a piece of French harpsichord music. Some French melodies are present, however, e.g. the "La Vignon" melody, Germanized as "Curant Lavion" (#33). *2-Witzendorff* is, however, not a manuscript of a francophile court harpsichordist, but is instead a Germanic household keyboard book.

Berlin-40147

This source is among the many from the Deutsche Staatsbibliothek collection which have not been located since the Second World War.[25] *Berlin-40147* was discussed at length by Epstein and then by Riedel, who relied on Epstein's information.[26] Epstein dated it as ca. 1660-1680, based on internal evidence, and cited the following composers: Besard, Froberger, Krieger, Pesenti, Schedlich, and Valentin Strobel (which one is unclear). Among the many concordances cited by Epstein, was the "La Princesse" melody.[27] The large (170 leaves) manuscript, written in keyboard score of two six-line staves, contained many dance suites in addition to tunes and chorales. Except for citing the French lutenist Besard, Epstein did not identify any music of French provenance.

Rés-819-2. *Provenance:* Germany, post 1661 (date of ballet transcription).
Location: Paris, Bibliothèque nationale, département de la musique (fonds conservatoire), Réserve 819 (2).

The manuscript music appended to a copy of a 1645 printed book deserves brief mention here. The music was discussed in detail, with thematic incipits, by Wallon in an article which is accurate and complete.[28] The music is written in at least four hands, some in new German organ tablature and some in keyboard score. The only identified composers are Frescobaldi, Froberger and Lully. As the century progressed, the ubiquitous lute transcriptions were intermingled with Lully opera transcriptions, as the Italian impressario's dominance of French music spread across Europe. The dating of such manuscripts is thus greatly facilitated: the inclusion of an "Entrée" in G Minor from Lully's *Ballet de l'impatience* (II-1), as "Rolfilis" (i.e. Bel Iris) on *l.* 72r, is certain evidence that the music was not transcribed until sometime after the ballet's premiere in 1661.

Such transcriptions were exceedingly common in professional Germanic manuscripts in the last two decades of the century, but they are less typical of the household books. This particular tune became very popular in Germanic and Scandinavian sources, as well as in the Netherlands. The melody is found in Dutch song books from 1663 and 1722, is referred to in several other song books, and is the basis of other keyboard settings:

CO: cf. *3-Berlin-40623 #*1
       cf. *11-Ryge #*48
       cf. *28-Brussels-926 l.* 3r
       cf. *Terburg*

cf. *Skara* #35
cf. *Van-Eijl* #25
ED: cf. *Noske* #25 (& pp. XXXVI-XXXVII), *Bangert*
p. 78.

In *Rés-819-2* there is no other French music to be found among its dances, chorales and tunes.

Celle. *Provenance:* Celle (West Germany), 1662 (dated). *Location:* Celle; Boman Musik Bibliothek, 730. *Description:* 2 p.l., 314 p., upright quarto format, 20 x 15.5 cm. Watermark #46. Contemporary full leather binding, 20.7 x 16.5 cm. *Notation:* New German organ tablature (4 systems per page, written page by page). *Scribes:* 2 (?) hands; the first wrote at least through p. 292, although the style and ink varies considerably. For a complete inventory of *Celle*, see Jos Harro Schmidt, "Eine unbekannte Quelle zur Klaviermusik des 17. Jahrhunderts: Das Celler Klavierbuch 1662," *Archiv für Musikwissenschaft* 22 (June, 1965): 1-11.

The recent discovery of a large tablature from the 1660's in Celle touched off one of the most acrimonious controversies to be found in the literature of this field. At issue was the attribution of two pieces to Sweelinck on the basis of the manuscript's titles, "Bergamasca M.G.P.S. . . . Nona variatio . . . Anno 1662 den 26 Maÿ in Zell"; and, "Allemande de chapelle [with variations] M. Jean Piterson . . . finis M.J.P.S."[29]

The question from the French standpoint is not whether the pieces should be attributed to Sweelinck, but whether the original Allemande was written by Jacques Champion II "de la Chapelle," Chambonnières' father. The one point of agreement in the Sweelinck controversy is that M. Jean Piterson, whoever he was, wrote the variations on the Allemande. Thurston Dart made a compelling, if conjectural case for interpreting the word "Chapel" as an attribution to Champion,[30] and it is not impossible that an allemande by Champion travelled through Holland, acquiring variations, and then made its way to Celle. It is impossible to confirm the assertion, however, because there is no allemande by Champion with which to compare this one. The only dance works attributed to Champion are a Pavane and Galliarde (*26-Bull* #18-19). The textures of these pieces are not at all similar to that of the *Celle* Allemande. Since both *26-Bull* and *Celle* show no evidence of close connection to French music, the stylistic comparison is not only between dissimilar forms, but between two corrupt sources. There is also no music by any other French harpsichord composer of Champion's generation to assist in the stylistic consideration of the Allemande. Most significantly, the melody of the piece was a common one, appearing in sources from ca. 1607 to 1669 (Schmidt, *Mededeelingblad*, pp. 61-62).

In summary, the "Alemande de chapelle" may be a setting of a melody by Chapel (i.e., Champion), a setting by Chapel of a popular melody, or an anonymous piece which is titled "de chapelle" without reference to Champion. If Champion did write either the melody or the piece, it is probably in a very corrupt version in *Celle*, having been turned into the theme for a set of Dutch variations and now found in a household German tablature from 1662 (see Ex. 5).

In other respects, this large manuscript is fairly typical of its genre. It contains the following other French titles, a few of which are explained in notes:

> Branle de Champagne [p. 15]
> Allimanda fransch [p. 16]
> Courant fransch [p. 17]
> Laure de paris [p. 18][31]
> Arien fransch [p. 25]
> Arien fransch [p. 29][32]
> Courant Fransch [p. 34]
> Courante Frantz fransch [p. 103]
> Lamutard Novelle fransch [p. 140][33]
> Arien fransch [p. 152]
> Sarabanda fransch [p. 153]
> Liedt fransch [in another ink:] NB laboure fransch [p. 156]
> Latesse. Arien fransch [p. 158]
> Aria fransch [p. 162][34]
> Les Tricote fransch [p. 163][35]
> Brandle de paris [p. 164]
> Courant La du Chesse [p. 166][36]
> Arien fransch [p.168]
> Courant frantz ... 6. variatio [p. 170]
> Letriquotes glotere fransch [p. 247][37]
> Aria fransch [p. 277]
> Brandel Fransch [p. 290]

Berlin-40623 (Inventory 3)

3-Berlin-40623, like *Berlin-40147*, is unlocated and the information in the Catalog inventory is entirely derived from Epstein.[38] The list of titles shows nothing surprising for a household book from 1678: tunes (including "Bel Iris," a transcription from a Lully ballet), chorales and dances. One anonymous Allemande, which fortunately was published in Epstein's appendix, is the same as the "Almande LB" of *27-Gresse* (#21). "LB" is to be interpreted as La Barre, since the Allemande in *27-Gresse* is followed by a Courante which is attributed to La Barre in

Ex. 5. "Alemande de chapelle" from *Celle*, p. 94.

three other sources, and then a Sarabande which is elsewhere attributed
to "Beare." However, the Allemande seems to be a transcription of a
lute piece, since it is found in a variant version, transposed by a fifth in
1-Copenhagen-376 (see Ex. 2, above).

Stockholm-2. *Provenance:* Sweden, ca 1680? *Location:* Stockholm; Kungliga Musikaliska Akademien, Tabulatur nr. 2. *Description:* 45 p., 5 quires (A-C/4, D/8, E/2, 1 *l.*), oblong quarto format, 16.3 x 20.5 cm (trimmed). Watermarks #17, 79. Modern (1916) vellum-covered boards, 17.3 x 21.3 cm. *Notation:* New German organ tablature.

Stockholm-228. *Provenance:* Sweden, post 1685 (date of an opera transcription). *Location:* Stockholm; Kungliga Bibliothek, S. 228 (currently [1975] on loan to the Kungl. Musikaliska Akademien). *Description:* 61 *l.* (originally 62 *l.*: 1 *l.* lacking after *l.* 16), 8 quires (A-B/8, C/7, D-G/8, H/6), oblong quarto format (trimmed). Watermark #15. Contemporary 3/4 leather binding, marbled boards. *Notation:* New German organ tablature (3 systems per page, written across facing pages) to *l.* 53r; from *l.* 54v to the end: keyboard score (two 5-line staves, 3 systems per page, written page by page); clefs: F/4, C/1. *Scribe:* 2 (?) amateur hands. *Marginalia:* "Stockholm . . . 7 Decemb 1759 CHI" (?) on the back cover; gift note, "John Ericsson Maj 1866" on the front cover.

Two household books from Sweden contain named French composers. *Stockholm-2* is undated, but probably comes from the last third of the century. It is a rather small collection which includes three transcriptions from the lute works of Gaultier. Which Gaultier is seldom clear (cf. the List of Composers and Work List, Appendices D and C, below). All three pieces here are known in lute originals and are, in fact, among the most popular of the Gaultier pieces, circulating widely in Germanic and Scandinavian countries:

> Courant si Apelle le Bell Hommicide [p. 30][39]
> Courant immorteel de Mons: Gautier [p. 32][40]
> Le Canon Courante de Gautier [p. 34][41]

The only other French title confirms the suspicion that the lute was the source of such pieces:

> Gavotte de Lut de Mademoiselle Konig marque [p. 34]

The second of these Swedish books, *Stockholm-228,* can be dated as after 1685, the date of the premiere of Lully's *Roland*: the "Aria le Françoise galand" (*l.* 9v) is actually a transcription of the Gavotte "C'est l'amour" from the Prologue of *Roland.* Another Lully tune, the popular "Rolfilis" (i.e. Bel Iris from *Ballet de l'Impatience*) is found on *l.* 20v. The entire manuscript is a mixture of tunes, dances and chorales, the first section written in new German organ tablature, the second in keyboard score. The lute origins of many of the pieces are thrice made explicit, with the titles "Air de Luth," (*l.* 4v), Air de Luth a Moll," (*l.* 7v) and "gavote von der Laute" (*l.* 57v). The following composers are named: Du But, Mercure (John),[42] Strobel and Verdier (Pierre III?). All of them, except possibly Verdier, were lutenists, and all except Strobel were French. The following other French titles suggest popular tunes, *airs de cour,* opera transcriptions and French-style dances, but none is French harpsichord music:

> Gavott La Reÿne [*l.* 4v]
> Lä Folie de Hispagne [*l.* 10v]
> Le Galliard [*l.* 16v]
> La Boure [*l.* 17v]
> Le infant [*l.* 17Av]
> Aimez aimable berger [*l.* 19v]

Lüneburg-1198. *Provenance:* Germany, 1687 (dated). *Location:* Lüneburg; Ratsbücherei, Mus. Ant. Pract. 1198. *Description:* 1 p.l., 203 p., oblong quarto format, 15.3 x 19.2 cm. Watermarks #19, 36. Paper powdered and fragile. Original parchment binding (with chant notation), 16.5 x 19.3 cm. *Notation:* Keyboard score (two 5-line staves, 3 systems per page, written page by page); clefs: F/4, G/2; or F/4, C/1. *Scribes:* 2 unidentified hands; hand A: pp. 1-121, 134-161; hand B: pp. 122-133, 162-201.

This large manuscript is dated at the beginning by the first scribe, "Ao 1687 2 Marty." It was briefly described by Welter (passim as "Chorales . . . 1687"), who included incipits for the anonymous dances in his catalog. *Lüneburg-1198* is a good example of the pervasiveness of French style in German keyboard manuscripts towards the end of the century. It would not be surprising to find that some of the anonymous dances were original French harpsichord pieces, although none has been identified as such through concordances.

The first twenty-nine pieces are grouped in seven suites, probably all of German origin, followed by forty-eight dances which are partly in suites and partly miscellaneous transcriptions from Lully's operas. The following have been identified: "Air Rolandi" (p. 64) is "C'est l'amour" from *Roland* (1685) Prologue-2; "Menuet" (p. 69) is "Nostre espoit alloit" from *Persée* (1682) IV-6; "Menuet Les Chours (p. 79) is "Que devant nous" from *Atys* (1676) II-4; "Gavotte de Phaeton" (p. 82) is undoubtedly from *Phaéton* (1683); and "Menuet" (p. 84) is found in *Plusieurs Pièces de symphonie* (1685). The section is a mixture of several genres and includes a version of the "La Vignon" melody with a "Variatio" (pp. 112-115). After twelve arias and similar pieces, there are fourteen chorales in *style-brisé* settings, illustrating the mixture of the continuing household book tradition and the fully developed French-oriented harpsichord style of the end of the century. A later hand added a few chorales in simple chordal settings, then forty-six more dances and arias, occasionally grouped in suites. Except for the Lully transcriptions, all of the 149 pieces in *Lüneburg-1198* remain anonymous. This is a rich and largely untapped source of some fine German dance suites.

Thott.   *Provenance:*   Preetz (south of Kiel, then Denmark), 1699-1702 (dated). *Location:* Copenhagen; Det konelige Bibliotek, Haandscrift afd., Thott 292 8o. *Description:* 81 *l.*, octavo format, 9.6 x 15.8 cm. Original full leather binding. *Notation:* New German organ tablature (3 systems per page, written across facing pages; erroneously called lute tablature in the library's catalog). *Scribe:* 1 (?) unidentified hand.

This late Danish manuscript, which was discussed in *Epstein* (pp. 92-93, "K-3"), is dated on the binding, with the initials of the owner, "1699 C.C.T." On the first pages these initials are explained as "Christiane Charlotte Amalia Trölle," with the additional date, "d. 23 Febrivary anno 1702." The contents include a few German and Danish chorales, many dances--some of which are grouped in suites--and three French titles, "Mars," "La Rigadon," and "La Burgunde." In addition, there are a great many minuets. Nothing indicates French provenance for any of the pieces, but a thorough study and transcription of *Thott*, which is beyond the scope of the present study, would be most interesting.

Nuremberg.   *Provenance:*   Nuremberg, 1699-ca. 1721 (dated). *Location:* Nuremberg; Germanisches Museum, Hs. 31.781. *Description:* 81 *l.*, oblong quarto format, 16 x 20.5 cm. Watermark #81. Modern 3/4 vellum-covered boards; contemporary paper boards bound in, 17 x 21.3 cm. *Notation:* New German organ tablature (erroneously listed in this library's catalog as lute tablature).

The incipits of the two "French" pieces in this early eighteenth-century source are reproduced here to emphasize that in such household books the music frequently represents the level of the owners' keyboard technique more than the prevailing style of harpsichord composers. These pieces are typical of the textures to be found in *Nuremberg,* belying the two late dates found therein: 1699 and 1721.

Nuremberg bears no perceptible relationship to French harpsichord music. It contains chorales, German songs and dances; the only named composer is the German lutenist Johann Gumprecht. Epstein cited a few concordances in his discussion of the source, but none of them was to French sources (pp. 92-93, "N").

Ex. 6. Incipits of "französche bauren dantz. 10" and "La galliarda franze. 55" from *Nuremberg*

Berlin-40624

    The last of the Germanic and Scandinavian household books to be mentioned here contained the date 1715. It has not been located since the Second World War, but again Epstein's study provides some basic information.[43] It was a late example of organ tablature, with old-fashioned German dances and songs. It did include the French dance forms (menuet, sarabande, marche, bourrée and ballet), but Epstein did not find indications of French provenance for any of the pieces in this rather primitive manuscript.

Professional Manuscripts

    The sources herewith termed professional are characterized by the absence of household music--chorales and simple tune settings from which one could learn the rudiments of keyboard technique. The division of household versus professional is admittedly arbitrary in a few cases in which the contents of a manuscript are professional, but the scribe was certainly unskilled. In general, however, all of the sources discussed in this group share a propensity for better, more idiomatic harpsichord music, often by named composers, than is found in the household manuscripts. In twelve cases, music by French harpsichordists is included (Inventories #4-15 in the Catalog, below).

Lynar (Inventory 4)

Of all of the sources under consideration, none has been dealt with so extensively and variously by modern scholars as *4-Lynar*. Since it is a major source for the keyboard music of Sweelinck, it was described as early as 1894 and as recently as 1968; its place of origin has been assigned as far north as Holland and as far south as Austria; it has been dated as early as 1610 and as late as the 1650's; the compiler and scribe has been ingeniously named as both Matthias Weckmann and Jan Reincken.

Werner Breig has given a summary of the past analyses of the pair of Lynar manuscripts, "A-1" (here called *4-Lynar*) and "A-2," in conjunction with a detailed inventory.[44] Little can be added to his well-considered discussion of the manuscripts as a whole; the conclusions which follow are largely based upon his article. The manuscripts are collectively named for the former owner, Count Lynar from Lübbenau. The *sigla* and pagination were established by Seiffert for the thirteen Lynar manuscripts: Lynar A-1, A-2, and B-1 through B-11 (B-11 is sometimes referred to as "C-1"). Only A-1 contains music pertinent to this study, but it was written by the same scribe as A-2.

4-Lynar is roughly organized by composers and national schools, and it is a remarkably broad sampling of seventeenth-century styles and genres. This very heterogeneity contributes to the difficulty in assigning a definite date or place of origin to it.   The international list of composers centers around a single generation, namely that born around 1560, but includes some born as late as 1590. Those represented in the companion volume (A-2) are from the same generation: John Bull (ca. 1563-1628), William Byrd (1543-1623), Christian Erbach (ca. 1570-1635), Giovanni Gabrieli (ca. 1555-1612), Orlando Gibbons (1583-1625) and Tarquino Merula (d. post 1652). All of this music could have been collected ca. 1615; one of the watermarks has been found in a 1614 document, supporting an early dating for *4-Lynar*. However, the closing pieces of the manuscript (#78-81, perhaps in a new hand) probably come from ca. 1650 or later, since they exhibit a mixture of Italian and French styles typical of midcentury German writing.   Also, *Lynar-A2* contains pieces by Tarquino Merula which could date from as late as 1652. Attempts to name the compiler as Weckmann[45] or Reincken[46] have been convincingly disputed and shed no light on the dating of *4-Lynar*.[47] *Apel-HKM* (p. 507) dated it "in the 1630's at the latest," but the author did not cite evidence for his conclusion.   Breig suggested that the manuscripts (A-1 and A-2) were compiled over a period of years or even decades by a single scribe.   He contended that the hand of the music and that of some of the titles were not the same, but that the musical scribe may have been the same throughout the manuscripts.   In summary, one can only say with certainty that *4-Lynar* contains repertoire from as early as ca. 1615, but the compilation of the manuscript may have extended to as late as ca. 1650.

The geographical provenance can be determined only in the vaguest way on the basis of the spellings of the titles and names; the scribe was almost certainly German, with perhaps some sort of Dutch influence. In 1624, in his *Tabulatura Nova*, Scheidt called two six-line staves "Dutch tablature," but this does not indicate Dutch provenance for the manuscript, since the notation was known in Germany at least by midcentury. Breig's contention that the content of the two manuscripts was most typical of the musical life of southern Germany is a reasonable theory, but it cannot be said to prove south German or Austrian provenance beyond doubt.

The group of French courantes which concerns us here contains four by La Barre. Three were attributed by the scribe and the fourth (#63) can be tentatively attributed on the basis of the title of the following piece, "auttre courante de la Barre," although the "auttre" could refer to #62 rather than #63. Two of the French pieces are definitely transcriptions from lute pieces by Gaultier (#66) and Ballard (#68)[48] and one piece (#67) is presumably French, since the scribe included it in the French group. For the same reason, the setting of "La Vignon" (#69) may also be considered French, although it is equally possible that it belongs with the German tune setting which follows the French group.

The extent to which the entire group is French is open to some question. The pieces exhibit several characteristics which are not typical of pieces in French sources: interpolated variations (the form A A^1 B B^1 rather than A B A^1 B^1, cf. #69); the double slash ornament; written-out trills; and most significantly, diminution procedure. Diminution variations were certainly known in France, as is evident from those written by Pierre La Barre III for *56-Mersenne*, but the procedure is most typical of English music, and this group of pieces does directly follow a group of works by the virginalists in *4-Lynar*. It is quite probable that the French pieces came to this manuscript by way of England. The hypothesis is strengthened by the fact that a great number of pieces by La Barre are found in English sources and that the Ballard Courante is known in *Cherbury*, an English lute manuscript.[49] Three of these French pieces (#63, 66 and 69) use the English double slash ornament, which was also known on the continent but not in France, while another three (#62, 64 and 65) use the continental trill sign ($\sim$). It is interesting that these signs are kept discrete in *4-Lynar*; the scribe seems to have reproduced disparate sources at least partially unchanged, rather than transcribing them into a single notational style. If this theory is correct, the La Barre pieces came from two different sources.

The suite which closes the manuscript (#78-81) is the only other music in 4-*Lynar* which might be suspected to be of French provenance. However, the rich *style-brisé* textures infused with imitation and the Italianate Fantasia suggest a German composer writing at midcentury. The pieces share notational peculiarities, including the use of dots ("staccato marks") in conjunction with specific motives in both the Allemande and the Courante, which suggest a new hand or the same hand at a later time. It is most reasonable to assume that the anonymous suite was written by a contemporary and countryman of Froberger.

Voigtländer. *Provenance:* Denmark (?), post 1642 (publication date of printed book). *Location:* Copenhagen; Det konelige Bibliotek, Musikafdelingen, Mu 6307.2131/6. *Description:* 8 *l.*, appended to a copy of Gabriel Voigtländer, *Erster Theil allerhand Oden vnnd Lieder* . . . (Sorø: 1642) [Mu 6610.2631]. *Notation:* New German organ tablature (written across facing pages). [I have seen this source only on microfilm.]

The manuscript music appended to this exemplar of Voigtländer's 1642 book was added at an undetermined time after that date and has been discussed in the German literature as well as by Dickinson.[50] Among the six pieces are two which are by Melchior Schildt ("Gleich Wie dass feuer M.S.," with two variations, *l.* 1v; and "Paduana Lagrima M. Schildt," *l.* 2v), one by Scheidemann ("Englishe Mascarada oder Juden Tantz HSM," with variations, *l.* 4v), and two by "J.R.R.," which probably signifies the Danish organist Johann Rudolf Radeke ("Courant Saraband Ex A J.R.R.," with variations, *l.* 6v; and "Engelischer Mascharada Ex G J.R.R.," *l.* 7v). The melody of the "Frantzösche Liedlein Ex D" (*l.* 8v) was a popular tune in France under the title "Air de Lampons," but the setting and variations are thought to be by Scheidt.[51] There is, then, no French harpsichord music in *Voigtländer.*

Uppsala-409. *Provenance:* Sweden, ca. 1650-1662 (dated). *Location:* Uppsala; Universitetsbibliotek, IMhs 409. *Description:* i, 93 *l.* (irregularly numbered), 31.7 x 20.7 cm. Original vellum-covered boards, 33 x 21 cm. *Notation:* New German organ tablature.

Uppsala-134:22. *Provenance:* Sweden, ca. 1650-1662?,. *Location:* Uppsala; Universitetsbibliotek, IMhs 134-22. *Description:* 1 *l.*, folio format, 21 x 32 cm. Disbound, silked. *Notation:* New German organ tablature (4 systems on recto and verso).

These two Swedish manuscripts contain music by French instrumental composers. The first has several dates in the 1650's and early 1660's, and the second is probably from the same period. *Uppsala-409* is available in a complete modern edition with commentary,[52] and *Uppsala-134:22* contains only one piece, the "Testaments a 5" by Belleville.[53] In both cases, the manuscripts are scorings of ensemble music, not keyboard music. The use of the new German organ tablature for such scores does not imply that the music was intended for keyboard performance, since the texture of the music was not adapted to conform to the reaches of the hand, nor were any other changes made to create idiomatic keyboard textures out of the instrumental lines. (*Darmstadt-1198* is a similar example of an instrumental score notated in new German organ tablature.) The following French names are listed as composers: Belleville, Dumanoir, La Croix and Verdier. No harpsichord music is known to have been written by any of these composers.

Skara. *Provenance:* Sweden, 1659-post 1661 (dated and ballet transcription). *Location:* Skara, Sweden; Stifts- och landsbibliotek (Högre Allmanna Läroverks musiksamling), Skara 493 b (nr 31). Photocopy in Uppsala; Universitetsbibliotek, IMhs 137. *Description:* 70 *l.*, oblong quarto format, 15.5 x 20 cm. Watermark #50. *Notation:* First and third sections in new German organ tablature (3 systems per page); second section (*l.* 39r-41v) in guitar tablature. *Scribe:* Gustaf Düben (1624-1690). [I have examined only the photocopy of this manuscript.]

This manuscript came to light in 1965, when the Skara collections were being inventoried for RISM. Shortly thereafter, Rudén published a thorough description of the manuscript, including an inventory with melody incipits for all of the pieces.[54] The Swedish organist Gustaf Düben twice initialed and dated *Skara,* "G.D. Anno 1659 Den 15 [?] April," after the first piece, and "G.D. Dat: 16 xbr [i.e., December] 1659" on *l.* 19r, about midway through the first section. The manuscript was not completed until at least 1661, since there is a transcription from a ballet of that date (#35, see below). The following composers are represented: Düben, Gaultier, Henrecÿ,[55] Pinel, Sparr and Tresure. Düben, Sparr and perhaps Henrecÿ were Swedish; Tresure was a composer who seems to have worked in England during the reign of Charles I;[56] Gaultier[57] and Pinel were French lutenists whose names were commonplace in Germanic and Scandinavian keyboard manuscripts.

Skara contains dance movements almost exclusively, some organized in three-to-four movement suites or key groups, but mostly assembled in no particular order. The majority of the titles have been frenched, but none of the pieces is original French harpsichord music. The following seventeen pieces, from a total of forty-three, have some French aspect:

Allamanda Joan Tresor [#2]
Courant J.T. [#3][58]
Sarabanda J.T. [#4]
Bransle l'empeureur [#13]
NB. Courant Monsʳ Gautier [#20][59]
Saraband Monsʳ Gautier [#21]
Allamanda Monsʳ Gautier [#22]
Courant Monsʳ Gautier [#23][60]
La Princesse [#26][61]
La Mattelott [#27]
La Grand Boureau [i.e., La grande bourrée, #28]
Gauotte d'angu [#29][62]
Saraband Henrecÿ [#32]
Courant Mʳ Pinell [#33]
Air [#34][63]
Air de Ballet [#35][64]

Munich-1503*l*, Munich-1511e, Munich-1511f (Inventories 5-7)

The group of manuscripts held by the Bavarian State Library is not only intriguing, but is more significant than has been hitherto recognized. They were described by Maier in his catalog of 1879[65] and they were discussed by Epstein in more detail (pp. 65-71, sources "M-2," "M-3," and "M-4").

The manuscripts share similarities of notational style, concordances and even the same paper. However, *5-Munich-1503l* is quite different from the other two in that it consists almost exclusively of original harpsichord music by identifiable composers; the other two books largely contain easy settings of popular tunes. Three pieces from *7-Munich-1511f* (#12, 14 and 17) appear to have been copied directly from *5-Munich-1503l*, raising the suspicion that the more professional of the books is the parent of the other two. *5-Munich-1503l* may well be the book of a teacher, whereas the second two could be those of his students. All three volumes, especially the second two, are so carelessly written that it is impossible to be sure of the exact number of hands involved in each manuscript, but a careful comparison suggests that no hand wrote in more than one of the books. Epstein (p. 69) says that all three manuscripts are apparently in the same hand, citing the similarity of the spelling of "Arthua" (a misreading of "Artus"), but he did not consider the matter of scribes in detail. From the standpoint of the formation of the letters and clefs, there are great differences; but a novice is not apt to have a consistent hand, which casts doubt on the meaning of the differences.

How and when did the manuscripts find their way to the Munich library? All that is known is that they were there long enough before Maier's 1879 catalog that he could give no information on provenance. It is logical to assume that they were from the Munich court, but there is no evidence to support the assertion. The manuscripts are French in all details. While the paper cannot be specifically identified, the watermarks are French: the grapes of #53 are rare outside of France, and the "L" combined with a fleur-de-lis emblem (#24) stands for the king, Louis. L's with other French emblems were common devices of French paper mills. The musical notation also reflects French practice: five-line staves using the F^3 clef in the left hand, in conjunction with either the C^1 or G^2 clefs for the right hand. The letter notation (see Ex. 7) does not use the letter h, as in German practice, but rather "b#" or "B♮," depending on the context. The note f-sharp is sometimes indicated by a tail on the f, as in new German organ tablature, but the same indication is also found in the unquestionably French version of the notation in *32-Oldham*. The terms "becarre" and "1. ton," and the use of the trill sign (〜) as the only ornament sign, all reflect French musical practice. The titles and other writing in the volumes are in French, and all but one of the identified composers are French. The one exception is Froberger, to whom the "allemande tres bonne" (*5-Munich-15031* #5) is attributed in *Stoss*. Since a number of pieces by Froberger circulated in Parisian manuscripts, undoubtedly as a result of his visit there in 1652, this Allemande, if it is really by Froberger, could have entered the Munich collection via France.[66] The most conclusive evidence for the French origins of these manuscripts is an organ manuscript, *Munich-1503k* (cf. Maier, item 265), in the same hand as *5-Munich-15031*, which contains anonymous pieces and registrations in the French organ style. Such music was much less exportable than the *style-brisé* harpsichord style. The unanswerable question is this: how and when did these manuscripts come to Germany? It is very plausible that one of the many French musicians who were imported by German courts brought two keyboard books with him (*5-Munich-15031* and *Munich-1503k*) and two blank books as well. His students, probably children at the court, then used the blank books to copy some pieces from the teacher's music. On the other hand, it is possible that the manuscripts never reached Germany until after their completion, or were compiled entirely at a francophile German court (but by a Frenchman, to judge by the handwriting).

The dating of the books is as problematical as assigning geographical provenance. There are no dates written in them and the paper cannot yet be dated. The youngest of the composers, Froberger, was born in 1616; therefore an anterior date of ca. 1636, when he was twenty, is certain. But two concordances to *Veron*, a ballet manuscript, as well as the above-mentioned Froberger visit to Paris, suggest a later date: the melody of *7-Munich-1511f* #23 appears as a space filler directly after the 1657 ballet *L'Amour malade* in *Veron*. Similarly, #26 is at the end of the ballet *Palais royal* (1660) section; here it is unclear if the piece was taken from the ballet or if it is again a space filler. Because of the lack of any detailed source studies for ballet music, the issue could not be solved here. *Veron* is a consciously chronological collection and the compiler considered these melodies to be "from ca. 1660," whether or not one of them is actually from a ballet of that date. The use of figured bass (*7-Munich-1511f* and *Munich-1503k*) suggests a midcentury date, as *basso continuo* was adopted very late in France; the basse de trompette in *Munich-1503k* (#10) is also consistent with this dating. Pieces with titles such as "Entrée de ballet" and "trompette" are certainly transcriptions from stage music and eventually a concordance may be found to specify the dating of these manuscripts. By negative reasoning one can assume that the group does not come from much later than 1675: sources with such strong French ties and numerous transcriptions would include pieces from Lully operas if they were compiled when all of Paris was singing tunes from *Alceste* (1674) and *Thésée* (1675).

The first volume is significant for its musical content. Not only does it have a copy of Chambonnières' popular "Sarabande jeunes zéphirs,"[67] but it is the only source of two Allemandes by Dumont. However, the carelessness and obvious errors of the notation do not suggest a scribe who was a master or closely associated with the Parisian harpsichord world, since he spelled Chambonnières "Chambonnier." The initial letter is unclear; it could be "Sambonnier," as read by Epstein and others, or "Chambonnier." Several variants of the name were used, but in French sources there is always a final e or es, so that the r is pronounced. "Sambonnier" and "Chamboner" are known in English sources (*18-Ch-Ch-1236* #3 and *60-Playford* #71), and "Gombonier" is in a German manuscript (*2-Witzendorff* #94).

A few of the Catalog entries need specific explanations:

5-Munich-15031 #4: This Gigue, which was also copied as *7-Munich-1511f* #17, is related to a lute Gigue by Pinel; Danckert pointed out the correspondence and presented both versions for comparison.[68] The second strains are quite different and thus the 1656 lute manuscript[69] was not the direct model for the Munich keyboard version. The piece is, however, a version of Pinel's lute Gigue, not merely a melody concordance with it.

5-Munich-15031 #6: The melody concordances which are listed for this Sarabande only share similar beginnings. This suggests that they belong to a melody family, a concept discussed by Devoto.[70]

5-Munich-15031 #10: This Courante, not just the melody, is found in *44-LaPierre,* a French manuscript. Therefore, the composition was probably written originally as a harpsichord piece by a French composer. It is further evidence of the totally French nature of the repertoire in this Munich manuscript.

6-Munich-1511e #11: One of the surprises of the present study was the discovery of numerous concordances for Monnard's Sarabande, which ranks with such pieces as Lebègue's and Hardel's gavottes (*64-Lebègue-I* #43 and *35-Bauyn-III* #50) as one of the most popular pieces of seventeenth-century French harpsichord music. This is even more unexpected since so little of Monnard's music has survived today, and we cannot even be certain which Monnard composed the piece.

7-Munich-1511f #25: This is a setting of an exceedingly popular noël, "À la venue de Noël." In addition to the sources cited in the Catalog, settings can be found by Balbastre, Beauvarlet-Charpentier, Charpentier, Michel Correte, Dandrieu, de Lalande, Lebègue (in the third organ book), Raison and Tapray. The list of composers who used this tune could be trebled if one continued into the nineteenth and twentieth centuries.

Most of the other pieces in the Munich manuscripts are either settings of popular melodies, transcriptions from unidentified stage music, or are from other instrumental music (such titles as "Branle").

Another significant aspect of the second two manuscripts is the use of a curious letter notation, which might be called "French letter score." Epstein (p. 67) commented on the notation, making a case for considering it an expedient for melody-bass versions of instrumental pieces, in contrast with original harpsichord music. However, four pieces (not just the one noted by Epstein) exist in both notations: *5-Munich-15031* #4, 10, 14 and *6-Munich-1511e* #12 (all in keyboard score) are the same as *7-Munich-1511f* #12, 15, 17 and 18 in French letter score. The latter piece, "La Princesse," is not an exact transcription of one from the other. Furthermore, Monnard's Sarabande is a "real" harpsichord composition (see Ex. 7) and many of the anonymous dances in French letter score are not in melody-bass textures. This notation is found in two other sources: *55-Redon* (1661) and *32-Oldham* (ca. 1650-1661). In the former, only a tuning chart uses the letters; in the latter, two pieces by d'Anglebert are written--probably in the composer's hand--in a more sophisticated version of French letter score. The notation must have enjoyed a certain currency in France at midcentury, since it is found in four manuscripts; in its more professional form, rhythm was indicated for the melody in the same manner as lute tablature (see Ex. 10, p. 94), but in the Munich version, rhythmic signs are totally absent. The two Munich examples which use French letter score are from unskilled hands, according to the hypothesis that they are the writings of students;

they cannot be expected to illustrate elaborate notation. But in view of the *32-Oldham* pieces, it is obvious that French letter score was not confined to beginners or sketchy transcriptions: it was a genuine keyboard notational system. A comparison of two versions of Monnard's Sarabande shows that the seemingly incompetent Munich version is really not very different from the professional *24-Babell* text. Both of these are very close to the Parisian *35-Bauyn* and *38-Gen-2348/53* readings of the Sarabande, already published by Bonfils.

Ex. 7. Sarabande by Monnard (*24-Babell* #56 and *6-Munich-1511e* #11)

In short, the Munich manuscripts are an important source for the study of seventeenth-century French harpsichord music. Although their current location is German, they can be considered French in every other way. They transmit a modest amount of unique French harpsichord music, and are rare examples of an almost totally lost notational system.

Hintze (Inventory 8)

8-Hintze, unlike the Munich group, is very much prized for its musical content: it provides an excellent text and programmatic title for the Froberger "Memento mori" (#5). Riedel discussed the manuscript in detail, giving its history from the time of its purchase in the nineteenth century by Louis Hintze to the present, and discussing the question of the identity of the scribe.[71] After comparing a number of hands in Lüneburg sources, he concluded that the scribe of both *8-Hintze* and *Lüneburg-147* was probably Matthias Weckmann, but that it is not certain. *Lüneburg-147* is an undated collection of keyboard suites, miscellaneous dance movements, toccatas, etc. There is no doubt that one of the two hands is the same as that in *8-Hintze*, but it is not absolutely certain that it is the same as *Lüneburg-207:6* which is almost surely in Weckmann's hand. Assuming that *8-Hintze* was written by Weckmann, its date could be no later than 1674, the year of his death. The youngest composer, Kerll, was twenty in 1647, and a toccata was attributed to him as early as 1650 in Rome (Kirchner: *Musurgia universalis*, v. 2). Weckmann is supposed to have met Froberger in Dresden sometime between 1647 and 1655, and watermark #10 is of a type which is found in many Dresden documents.[72] All of these factors point to a dating earlier than was previously thought, even as early as 1647, but more likely ca. 1650-1655. It is possible that Weckmann was using old paper, after 1655 when he moved from Dresden to Hamburg, and it must be remembered that the other watermark (#92) has not been identified. Thus a more cautious dating is adopted here, "ca. 1650-1674."

8-Hintze seems to have been two separate manuscripts originally, since the last page of the first quire (*l.* 5v) is soiled as if it had served as a cover; the first leaf of the second quire is lacking, so that there is neither confirmation nor denial from its state of cleanliness of whether the quire was once a separate manuscript. There is at least one other leaf lacking, which shows that the original manuscripts contained at least twenty (six plus fourteen) leaves. This is best illustrated diagrammatically:

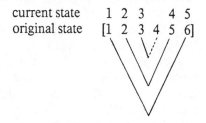

Fig. 4. Quire A of *8-Hintze*

current state   6   7   8   9   10   11   12   13   14   15   16   17   18
original state   [1   2   3   4   5   6   7   8   9   10   11   12   13   14]

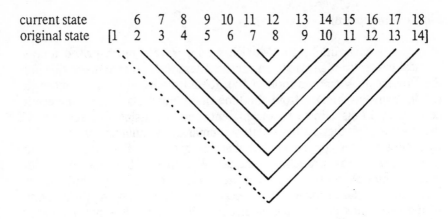

Fig. 4. Quire B of *8-Hintze*

The evidence for this determination is the stains caused by the transfer of acid from the ink of one page onto the facing page. The stains on *l.* 3v do not match the writing on *l.* 4r; and *l.* 4v does not reflect *l.* 5r (or any other page). Since all of the leaves are now loose, other possibilities exist for the original arrangement, but the diagrams in Fig. 4 are the only plausible configuration which does not require additional sheets in the first quire. The lacking leaves do not affect any of the pieces now in *8-Hintze*, since they concluded at the bottoms of pages at the crucial moments, but some additional compositions have been lost. There must also have been additional leaves in the second quire, since the rest of the Froberger Suite which is mentioned (cf. *#5*) is not in the manuscript in its present state.

The use of two different papers (watermarks *#10* and *92*) further supports the claim that the quires were originally two different manuscripts. Finally, based on the shades of ink, it is unlikely that the hand of the titles is different from that of the music (as Riedel suggests). The ink of some of the musical alterations or corrections, however, is quite different and they are labelled "Pohlman." It seems that the later hand made the changes, rather than the same scribe giving alternate readings from several sources before him (Riedel's hypothesis).

The French aspect of *8-Hintze* is explicit from the original title page, "Franzosche Art Instrument Stücklein." It is a fascinating collection merely from the standpoint of what was considered to be French style: the German composers Froberger, Erben and Kerll; the actual Frenchmen Artus (presumably transcribed by a German) and Chambonnières; the pair of composers whose pieces circulated mostly in English manuscripts, La Barre and Tresure; popular tunes, including one which seems to have no French connection at all (#10, usually known as "Ach, Amarillis"); and one *style-brisé* setting of an Italian title ("Ballo di Mantova," #28).

The most significant piece for the study of French harpsichord music is La Barre's Courante (#11). Although La Barre's pieces in *I-Copenhagen-376* are probably lute transcriptions, this Courante is the only known example of a piece by La Barre which exists in both lute and harpsichord settings. Unfortunately, conclusions cannot be readily gleaned from this concordance because of two factors. First, it is not certain which version was the original. Normally one assumes that such pieces were transcribed by German harpsichordists from the widely circulated French lute music. This is probably also true in the case of *8-Hintze*, but the only known lute source for the Courante is *Saizenay-1* (1699),[73] which also contains transcriptions for lute of harpsichord music by François Couperin. The second problem is that there is no other harpsichord concordance for the piece. Is this the same La Barre who is known in English manuscripts? The piece is not attributed in *8-Hintze*, but Tresure, who is often found in the same manuscripts as the "English" La Barre (cf. pp 64-65), is both represented and named in this source. If it is originally a lute Courante and if it is the same La Barre, one would have some certain evidence about his identity; one would know that he was a lutenist and that he worked in France, not England, since *Saizenay-I* is an exclusively French manuscript. Our knowledge of the activities of the members of the La Barre family is sufficiently hazy to prevent specific attributions. Pierre IV (ca. 1634-1710) seems to have been both a lutenist and harpsichordist, and he was born in the appropriate generation for inclusion in *8-Hintze*. Yet he was too young to be the "English" La Barre, whose works are found as early as 1652, when Pierre IV was about nineteen. The La Barre puzzle remains one of the greatest confusions in the study of seventeenth-century French harpsichord music. The Courante in *8-Hintze* provides another link between the lute and harpsichord in the music of La Barre.

Darmstadt-17. *Provenance:* Darmstadt (?), 1672 (dated). *Location:* Darmstadt; Hessische Landes- und Hochschulbibliothek, Mus. ms. 17 (*olim* 2897). *Description:* 28 *l.*, oblong quarto format, 15.7 x 20.5 cm. Watermark #5. Original (?) paper-covered binding, 16.3 x 20.5 cm. *Notation:* New German organ tablature (4 systems per page, written page by page). *Scribe:* 1 unidentified hand, the same as *Darmstadt-18.*

Darmstadt-18. Idem., except: *Provenance:* . . . 1674. *Location:* . . . Mus. ms. 18 (*olim* 2898). *Description:* . . . Watermark #4. *Scribe:* the same as in *Darmstadt-17* with the possible exception of the title page.

The pair of manuscripts, *Darmstadt-17* and *Darmstadt-18*, are the most explicit available examples of the importance of French lute music to German harpsichord repertoire. Both manuscripts were discussed by Epstein (pp. 82-83, "D-1" and "D-2"), who provided title inventories for them. They were also briefly discussed with several other manuscripts from the Darmstadt court, by Noack.[74] Both *Darmstadt-17* and *Darmstadt-18* have ornamental title pages which are unusually precise:

> Allemanden Couranten
> Sarabanden, Giquen, Cavotten auß
> unterschiedlichen Tonen mit sonderbarem fleiß
> von der Lauten und Mandor auff das
> Spinet von einem beedes der Lauten
> Mandor Vnd deß Clavier Verstän-
> digen abgesetzet, Anno 1672.
> den 18. May. p.

and:

> Neue Allemanden, Couranten, Sarabanden,
> Giquen, Cavoten Unnd Canarien mit sonder-
> bahrem Fleiß Von der Angelique und Lau- [*sic*]
> auff das Clavier gesetzt: auff einem Spinet
> zu spielen
> Anno 1674
> den 1. Februarÿ .p.

Many of the forty pieces remain anonymous, but the identified composers were all lutenists, as the title pages lead one to assume: Gaultier,[75] Gumprecht[76] and Strobel;[77] "Dorserÿ" is also named, but he cannot be identified.

Darmstadt-1198.   *Provenance:*   Darmstadt (?), midseventeenth-century. *Location:*   Darmstadt; Hessische Landes- und Hochschulbibliothek Mus. ms. 1198 (*olim* 2898/1). *Description:*   1 p., full sheet, 33 x 44.5 cm. Watermark #97. Unbound. *Notation:*   New German organ tablature (6 systems, written on the recto only). *Scribe:* 1 unidentified hand, not the same as in *Darmstadt-17* or *Darmstadt-18.*

The three pieces called "courante commune" which comprise the total contents of *Darmstadt-1198* also cannot be considered French harpsichord music. They are literal scorings from instrumental works, perhaps French, written strictly in four voices and frequently exceeding the normal reach of the hands at the keyboard.

Ex. 8. "Courante commune," *Darmstadt-1198* #2, Beginning of Second Strain

Ihre-284 (Inventory 9)

The Catalog entry for this rather large manuscript needs little comment. The collection is dated 1678 and 1679, but the later hands may have added music somewhat after these dates. The pieces were not entered in the book in chronological order, as can be seen from the list of scribes. The French contents are almost entirely transcriptions, and much of the non-French music is also borrowed from instrumental ensembles, the stage, lute and viol. In addition, there are some settings of popular tunes of French derivation (e.g., #111, "Courant Madam"). In general, *9-Ihre-284* transmits the art of intabulation as practiced by Johann Lorentz and others.

The greatest significance for French harpsichord studies is the inclusion of music by the pair of composers La Barre and Tresure. The Allemande and Sarabande which surround the La Barre Courante (#48) can be tentatively attributed to La Barre also, since they form a suite. Compiled rather than composed suites were very common (e.g., the organization of *24-Babell* or *36-Parville*),[78] and therefore it is not certain that the two unattributed movements are by the same composer. However, in Germanic and Scandinavian sources especially, the allemande-courante-sarabande group tended, this late in the century, to be circulated as a single entity (see the suite grouping of *10-Schwerin-617*). Tresure is represented by a single Sarabande (#76).

Stockholm-176. *Provenance:* Sweden (?), post 1681 (date of an opera transcription). *Location:* Stockholm; Kungliga Biblioteket, 1 p. *l.*, 62 *l.* (*l.* 22-62 are blank), with 2 *l.* from another manuscript laid between *l.* 21 and 22. Irregular folio format, 10 x 20.3 cm. Watermark #95. Full leather binding with gilt monogram and crown stamped on both covers (tracing #108), marbled end papers, 11 x 21 cm. *Notation:* New German organ tablature (3 systems per

page, written across facing pages); inserted leaves: lute tablature.
Scribe: 1 unidentified hand.   *Marginalia:*   front end paper, recto,
"No 97" in manuscript, then in print, "Gripsholms Bibliothek. Für ej
begagnas ut om denna Kungl. Borgen."   Verso, in manuscript, ". . .
Frau Grijsholms Bibliothek, 12 Juni 1867."

This anonymous tablature of sixteen pieces illustrates the
changing taste of Germanic and Scandinavian harpsichordists in the last
two decades of the century, as transcriptions from Lully operas vied with
French lute music in popularity. The inclusion of the well-known
"Entrée d'Apollon" (*l.* 14v) from *Le Triomphe de l'amour* indicates that
Stockholm-176 was compiled after the opera's premiere in 1681. To
judge on the basis of the general contents of the manuscript, it was
probably written not many years after that date, as French lute music
soon went out of vogue. The following composers, all lutenists except
Lully, are represented: Du But, Ennemond Gaultier,[79] Lully, Mouton
and Strobel.

In addition to the identified Entrée by Lully, there are two
compositions which are obviously transcribed from stage music, although
they have not been specifically identified: "Air pour les trompettes," *l.*
6v; and "Air pour les Espagnols," *l.* 20v. The three pieces in lute
tablature which are laid into the volume do not correspond to any of the
keyboard transcriptions, although they are written by the same hand.
There is no original French harpsichord music in *Stockholm-176.*

Schwerin-617 (Inventory 10)

This source is also dated on the basis of a transcription from a
Lully opera: *Amadis* (1684).   *10-Schwerin-617* is most important as a
source of Froberger's music.   Epstein (p. 94) pointed out that it also
represents the beginning of the end of new German organ tablature; the
notation was known and used well into the eighteenth century, but *10-
Schwerin-617* was presumably written in the late 1680's in north
Germany where the tablature was the normal notation, and it is already
in keyboard score.[80] None of the pieces is attributed by the scribe, but
enough have been identified to perceive the arrangement: the pieces are
grouped in compiled suites, beginning with a prelude, followed by an
allemande-courante-sarabande group by a single composer. Some suites
include a gigue, which comes either in the "Froberger position," after the
allemande, or after the sarabande. The rest of the pieces in the suite, or
key group, are drawn from disparate sources. The pattern is not unlike
d'Anglebert's organization of *33-Rés-89ter* or *68-d'Anglebert.*

The scribe of *10-Schwerin-617* was extraordinarily neat.   His
hand was rather unsteady, but he went to the extreme of adding many

guide lines to align the notes on the large pages. Musically, the manuscript is a source of dubious quality, since it appears to have been written by an organist with more concern for the geometry of the page than the content of the music.

The only French harpsichord music is Lebègue's Gavotte, which is the most circulated piece of the entire repertoire. There are two basic versions of the Gavotte; this one is related to that known in *46-Menetou* (#102), rather than Lebègue's published version, *64-Lebègue-I* #43, which does not use the dotted notation. In view of the performance practice of *notes inégales*, it is not surprising to see these two notations circulating; the two versions would probably have sounded the same when played by a French harpsichordist. The published version, like that in *10-Schwerin-617*, is barred incorrectly for a gavotte, although some versions have the normal gavotte barring (*46-Menetou* #102, for example).[81] The piece was written by 1661, since it acquired a Double by Louis Couperin who died in that year. It circulated in manuscript in Germany and the *10-Schwerin-617* version was not copied from the 1677 print.

Stoss. *Provenance:* Strasbourg region, post 1684 (date of an opera transcription). *Location:* Paris; Bibliothèque nationale, département de la musique, Vm7 1818. *Description:* 55 *l.*, oblong quarto format, 17.7 x 31 cm. Green vellum-covered boards. *Notation:* Keyboard score (two 5-line staves, 3 systems per page, written page by page). Clefs: C/1, F/4, G/2. *Scribes:* 2-3 (?) hands, one perhaps that of Joan Stoos.

Stoss is similar to *10-Schwerin-617* in that it is also an important but problematical Froberger source,[82] and in that it, too, is dated on the basis of a transcription from *Amadis* (1684): The Ouverture is on *l.* 47v; the Ouverture to *Isis* (1677) is on *l.* 24v. Tessier published a discussion and inventory, editing the unique Froberger Allemande in the incomplete *Stoss* version along with the unattributed *5-Munich-15031* reading (#5).[83] The manuscript was described in Brossard's catalog, where the hand was identified in a conjectural manner as that of "Stoos" or "Stoss."[84] However, the manuscript was written by two, or more likely three, different hands and the identity of Stoos (Stoss) is unknown, so that Brossard's statement is of little value. There are original or transcribed pieces by Colensi, Froberger, Kelz, Kerll, Lanciani, Lully, Pasquini and Stoos, including some nonkeyboard airs for voice and bass. The pieces are generally grouped in compiled suites, many of which remain anonymous, but they appear to be of German authorship, not French. The only French music in *Stoss* is transcribed from pieces by Lully.

Ottobeuren. *Provenance:* Ottobeuren, 1695 (dated). *Location:* Ottobeuren, Allgau (Schwaben, Bayern); Benediktiner-Abtei, Musikarchiv und Bibliothek, MO 1037. *Description:* 164 p., 10 quires (A/11, B/6, C/10, D/8, E/5, F-G/8, H/9, I/12, J/5), folio format, 32.7 x 21 cm. Watermark #78. Original paper binding, with title in two later inks, "Autoribus . . . Breiberg." The binding paper is the verso of a manuscript, 33 x 21 cm. *Notation:* Keyboard score (two 5-line staves, 6 systems per page, written page by page). Clefs: C/1, G/1-2, F/4; usually F/4, G/2. *Scribe:* Pater Anton Pad. Estendorffer (1670-1711).

This interesting source of keyboard music has received very little attention from qualified scholars because it has been inaccessible.[85]   A dissertation was written by Tilsen, a student of Sandberger, in 1922 which provided helpful biographical information about the scribe and contributed some background information about music at the Ottobeuren abbey.[86]   However, Tilsen failed to provide even a title inventory for the manuscript which was the basis of her dissertation.

Ottobeuren reflects the musical taste of the twenty-five year old Bavarian organist who compiled it in 1695.   Among the 164 pieces are works by Dufaut, Ebner, Estendorffer (the scribe), Froberger, Gaultier, Kerll, Lobert (i.e., Lambert?), Muffat, Pinel, Poglietti and Ramer.   The manuscript is divided into two large sections, the first of which ends on page 117 and closes with the dated signature of Estendorffer; the second half is written by the same hand, but apparently at a later time, as there are some variations in the handwriting.   The latter section is subdivided into nineteen *partiae,* which are suites or groups of pieces arranged generally by key, but admitting miscellaneous pieces.   All of the compositions in the first section of the manuscript and in the first eight *partiae* of the second section (i.e., pp. 1-141) appear to be of Germanic origin, but the closing *partiae* are exclusively French, including some forty-six compositions, almost all of which have descriptive titles.   A few of these pieces can be specifically identified as transcriptions from lute music and three of the four named composers were lutenists: Dufaut, Gaultier and Pinel.   The fourth composer, represented by a single Allemande, is "Lobert," which could be a corruption of Lambert, another French lutenist.   *Ottobeuren,* then, is one of the largest keyboard sources of French music to be found in Germany, but none of the pieces is likely to be French harpsichord music.   Rather, the manuscript is further evidence of the wide circulation of French lute music in all parts of Germany.   Estendorffer had a large collection of such pieces to draw upon and his sources probably came quite directly from France, in view of the extensive use of French descriptive titles.   Estendorffer is represented earlier in *Ottobeuren* as a composer as well as scribe, and the French pieces may well be his own transcriptions. The titles of the French section are as follows:

>Partia Nona [d]
>La Brave Allemande de Mr. Gautier [p. 141]
>L'Immortelle Courrante de Suitte du mesme [p. 142][87]
>La Courieuse Sarabande de Suitte du Mesme . . . Duble
>[p. 142]
>L'estourdie Guique [p. 143]
>Partia Decima [d]
>All[eman]da Mr. de lobert [i.e., Lambert?] [p. 144]
>La Glorieuse Courr[ante]. [p. 144]
>Sarabande [p. 145]
>Guique [p. 146]
>Partia Vndecima [d]
>La Greable All[eman]da [p. 146]
>L'aymable Courr[ante] [p. 147]
>La Succincte Sarab[ande] . . . Double [p. 147]
>La Gage [Sage?] Guique [p. 147]
>Partia Duodecima [d]
>La Verdure All[eman]da. [p. 148]
>Le printemps Courr[ante]. [p. 148]
>La iodlie de boiare Sarabda . . . Double [p. 149]
>La ieunesse Guique [p. 150]
>Partia Decima Terza [F]
>La Theologie Allemande du Mnsr pinel [p. 150]
>La Philosophie Courrante [p. 151]
>L'Astrologie Sarabande [p. 152]
>La Poesie Guiq' de suitte de Mr du favt [p. 152][88]
>Partia Dec. Quarta [F]
>L'Industrie All[eman]de de Mr Gautier [p. 152]
>La discretion Courrente [p. 153]
>La Charitable Sarabande [p. 153]
>La recoissante Guique [p. 154]
>Partia Decima Quinta [B♭]
>La cloche All[eman]de [p. 154]
>L'Importunes de Svittes Courrent [p. 155]
>La divertissante Sarabande [p. 155]
>La facheuse Guiq. [p. 156]
>Partia Decima sexta [a]
>La Noble Allemand [p. 157]
>La Civile Courrant [p. 157]

La Juste Sarabande [p. 158]
L'inclination Guique de suitte de Mr. du faut [p. 158]
    Partia Decima Septima [G]
la bergere Allemande de Mr. Gautier [p. 158]
L'Incomparable Courrante de suitte du mesme [p. 159][89]
La delicate Sarabande du mesme de suitte [p. 159]
La vive Guique [p. 160]
    Partia Decima Octava [d]
L'Impatience Allemande [p. 160]
La passable Courrante [p. 161]
La posie Sarabande [p. 161]
Sarabande [p. 161]
Courrente [p. 162]
    Partia Dec. Nona [d]
Allemande la Menlancholie [p. 162]
Courrante [p. 163]
Sarabande [p. 163]
Guique [p. 163]
La Charmante Pavane de Mr du faut [p. 164]

Grimm. *Provenance:* Demmin (Germany), 1699 (dated). *Location:* Vienna; Österreichische Nationalbibliothek, Musikabteilung, Cod. 16798. *Description:* 136 *l.*, 35 quires (A/3, B-N/4, O/2, P-HH/4, II/3), oblong quarto format, 21.7 x 28.3 cm. Watermark # 3. Full leather gilt-tooled binding, 22.4 x 30.4 cm. *Notation:* Keyboard score in 3 colors (green lines, red titles and fingerings, black notes). *Scribe:* Christian Grimm.

This Froberger source from the turn of the century is well known. An inventory is available in the Vienna State Library's printed catalog,[90] and it was discussed by Riedel (*Quellen,* p. 123) and was used by Adler (*Adler-II,* source Y). The following composers are represented: "Sign Cob" (Coberg?), Corelli, Froberger, Grimm, Lully, Pachelbel, Pez, Steffani and Telemann. Although there are a number of anonymous dance suites in *Grimm* written in the then international *style-brisé* texture, the only identifiable French music is transcribed from Lully's operas: "Les Songes funestes" from *Atys* (1676) III-4 on *l.* 80v, and the Ouverture from *Ballet de l'amour malade* (1657) on *l.* 88v. Most of the pieces from *l.* 70v to the end of the volume appear to be opera transcriptions; I have not attempted to identify them.

Ryge (Inventory 11)

The music of *11-Ryge* is found at the back of a geneological book for the Ryge family. Since the family history mentions dates from

1607-1810, it is not possible to use the dating of the family book as a certain guide to the dating of the musical section. The music could not have been entered before 1687, the date of the first printing in Paris of *65-Lebègue-II,* from which two suites were copied. However, the earliest copyist date in the family history (recounting earlier times) is 1712 ("Scribebam et Signabarn Hauniae, die 15.tio Julÿ Anni MDXII," p. 5). This strengthens the logic of assuming that the Lebègue pieces reached Germany a dozen-or-so years after their appearance in Paris, that is, about 1700. Since the music was notated entirely in new German organ tablature, it is likely to have been written not too long after the turn of the century.

The relationship of *11-Ryge* to Buxtehude is not yet known, but it was clearly a close one. Since so much of the music is attributed, and misattributed, to him, a strong case can be made for *11-Ryge* being a copy of Buxtehude's autograph manuscripts. The attributions are probably those of the copyist who assumed that the music in Buxtehude's hand had been composed by the famous Lübeck organist. Buxtehude almost certainly studied and therefore probably copied *65-Lebègue-II:* not only are the two misattributed suites exact copies from the print, but a third is similar enough to three consecutive Lebègue pieces that it seems to be a conscious parody. The "Allemand," "Courant" and "Saraband" in C Major (*11-Ryge* #65-67, *Bangert* Suite IV) are attributed to "DBH." They are similar to the "Allemande," "Courante" and "Sarabande" in G Major by Lebègue (*65-Lebègue-II* #35-37, *Dufourcq-L* pp. 79-81). Both strains of the Allemandes open with almost exactly the same themes and textures (see Ex. 9). The pieces then diverge considerably, but make use of the same characteristic motives. The thematic similarity of the Courantes is less striking, and the Sarabandes have little more than surface resemblance to each other. In view of the unmistakable relationship between the Allemandes, however, the entire Buxtehude suite can be considered a parody or an homage to Lebègue.

Whether or not *11-Ryge* is a direct copy of Buxtehude's autograph manuscripts, it is the only known source of most of the harpsichord music which is there attributed to him. Since two of the suites are actually by Lebègue, and a third is modelled on Lebègue's pieces, the authenticity of all of the Buxtehude works in *11-Ryge* is open to question. It is doubtful that there are any unknown suites by Lebègue in the manuscript because the two identified suites are definitely copied from the printed versions, not from manuscript copies. The pieces appear in the same order, with omissions, and the texts of the *11-Ryge* and *65-Lebègue-II* versions have only the slightest differences. Pieces which circulated from composers' manuscript versions show substantial differences, as can be seen by comparing the incipits of the concordances

Ex. 9. Incipits of Allemandes by Buxtehude (after *Bangert*, p. 13) and
Lebègue (after *Dufourcq-L* p. 79)

cited in *62-Chamb-I, 63-Chamb-II* and *68-d'Anglebert.* Lebègue's
harpsichord pieces seem to have circulated very little in manuscript.
None of the pieces attributed to Buxtehude in *11-Ryge* is identifiable as a
known work by another seventeenth-century French harpsichordist. A
detailed stylistic study of Buxtehude's harpsichord music, comparing it
both to Lebègue's books and to contemporary Germanic music, and
carefully differentiating the *11-Ryge* pieces from those found in other
sources, is an intriguing project which awaits attention.

Minorite. *Provenance:* Vienna (?), post 1708 (dated on *l.* 74v: Juni j708).
Location: Vienna; Minoritenkonvent, Ms 743. *Description:* 119 *l.*
(originally 128: first 8 *l.* and last 1 or more *l.* lacking), oblong
quarto format, 23.5 x 28 cm. Watermark #38. Disbound.
Notation: Keyboard score (two 5-line staves). *Scribes:* 3
unidentified hands: A, dated 1708/9; B-C, probably early 18th
century. *Marginalia:* 2 numerations in pencil, with some further
numeration in ink.

A title inventory,[91] facsimile of a page,[92] and microfilm[93] of this
early eighteenth-century manuscript are available for study. The named
composers are Fischer, Froberger, Handel, Lully, Muffat, Pasquini,
Reutter and Richter. There are several unattributed pieces which are
probably transcriptions of pieces of Lully, including one (*l.* 50r) which is
known in *36-Parville* (#116) as "Air des Sorciers." Two of Lully's
compositions are identified: "De Mr Baptiste de Lulli Ouuerture La

Grotte de Versaille" (*l.* 44r) and "Passacaille armide" (*l.* 44v). Otherwise, there is no French music in *Minorite*.

Walther (Inventory 12)

12-Walther is one of a group of three manuscripts which come from the "Krebs legacy." As major Bach sources, they have been the subject of much scholarly scrutiny which culminated recently in an entire book devoted to the three manuscripts.[94] The provenance and dating adopted here are taken from Zietz's detailed study of the handwriting and biographies of the scribes; the French compositions were all copied about 1712 by Walther. The seventeenth-century suites were obviously copied from the published texts, but *12-Walther* is interesting in that it is the only indication of the circulation of d'Anglebert's suites in Germany. In addition, it reflects the continued popularity of Lebègue's music. In 1712, Walther's taste in French music encompassed the early eighteenth-century composers Clérambault, Dandrieu, Dieupart, Le Roux and Marchand, along with the seventeenth-century's d'Anglebert, Lebègue and Nivers, the latter represented by organ music.

Möllersche (Inventory 13)

This source has also received much scholarly attention because of its connection with J.S. Bach. Dürr's discussion supercedes earlier writings,[95] except Wolffheim's.[96] Dürr established that the primary hand is that of J.S. Bach's copyist, Johann Bernhard Bach, and that *13-Möllersche* was written between 1717 and 1719. The Lebègue suites are copied from *64-Lebègue-I* and it is interesting to note what changes were made, other than clefs and minor notational adjustments. All of the preludes are omitted; the first two suites are in reversed order; the Sarabande in F (#50) is placed before the Gigue of that Suite (#59); and the ornament table is after rather than before the suites. It is not surprising that an eighteenth-century German would have ignored the unmeasured preludes, since the style was so foreign,[97] but the changes in order seem capricious in such an extensive and careful copy. The significance of *13-Möllersche* from the French perspective is that it presents Lebègue as the representative of seventeenth-century French harpsichord style in a Bach manuscript.

Schwerin-619 (Inventory 14)

This source reflects the pervasiveness of French music at German courts like that in Schwerin. The dating of the manuscript is very approximate. Some of the music was composed no earlier than

1700, when Dandrieu and Rameau were about eighteen years old. While *14-Schwerin-619* must have been compiled some years later, the dating adopted here, "ca. 1720?," is conjectural. Most of the pieces by Dandrieu and Rameau were printed in editions from 1706-1734, but the *14-Schwerin-619* versions differ considerably and therefore represent manuscript circulation of the music, not copies of the prints. Lebègue's pieces, on the other hand, are selective copies from *65-Lebègue-II*. The first twenty pieces of *14-Schwerin-619* are exactly the same as the second, third and fourth suites in *65-Lebègue-II*, omitting one piece (#18, perhaps an oversight). They are followed by ten miscellaneous pieces from the last two suites of the same print. The popular Gavotte from *64-Lebègue-I* (*14-Schwerin-619* #91) could have been copied from one of the many manuscript sources of the composition; this is particularly likely in view of the fact that its Double (#91a) is unique.

The large number of pieces by Dandrieu, including a unique Bourrée (#93, duplicated as #120) and Gigue (#102), raises the suspicion that some of the unidentified compositions might also be by that composer; but *14-Schwerin-619* is such a miscellaneous collection that one cannot make even tentative attributions on the basis of the groupings of pieces. For example, one might have assumed that #110-113 were all by Dandrieu, since the first and last pieces are found in Dandrieu prints; but #111 is actually a Lully transcription. Nevertheless, the sources from which the scribe worked were obviously close to Dandrieu, and some of the transcriptions may be his. The possibility that #95-96 form an otherwise unknown suite with #94 is too enticing to ignore altogether. A more detailed stylistic consideration of the manuscript is beyond the scope of the present study, since the questions concern eighteenth-century music. The only seventeenth-century French harpsichord music in *14-Schwerin-619* is by Lebègue.

Berlin-30363. *Provenance:* Germany, post 1723 (date of an opera transcription). *Location:* East Berlin; Deutsche Staatsbibliothek, Mus. Ms. 30363. *Description:* 9 *l.*, 36.5 x 26 cm. (trimmed).

Berlin-8551. *Location:* West Berlin; Staatsbibliothek der preussischer Kulturbesitz, Mus. Ms. 8551. *Description:* 9 *l.*, 25.5 x 32.5 cm.

Berlin-30206 (Inventory 15)

These manuscripts are so late that they merit only the most summary mention here. The few pages which comprise *Berlin-30363* contain thirty-nine pieces, all of which appear to be French, but the only seventeenth-century compositions are transcriptions from Lully operas (which held the stage in Paris well into the eighteenth century). The following composers are represented: Campra, Colin de Blamont, François Couperin, Dandrieu, Destouches and Lully.

Berlin-8551 is a copy of a manuscript which was in the hand of J.S. Bach.[98] It includes two suites by Dieupart, one of which is misattributed to de Grigny. There is no known harpsichord music by the latter composer.

It is surprising that *15-Berlin-30206* contains a composition by d'Anglebert, as all of the other composers in the source were mideighteenth-century Germans or Italians. It has no other relationship to seventeenth-century French harpsichord music.

Summary

The forty-four Germanic and Scandinavian manuscripts which have been discussed here are rich in French music. They contain numerous transcriptions of French music for lute, stage and instrumental ensembles. The household books, especially, draw heavily upon a large repertoire of popular tunes of French derivation. Frequently the transcriptions preserve little more than the melodies of the originals, and the distinction between them and settings of popular tunes is not a clear one. The professional manuscripts transmit quantities of overtly French-style dances by German keyboard composers such as Scheidemann and Froberger. The one genre which is substantially absent from the manuscripts is French harpsichord music. Before about 1700, eighteen compositions by French harpsichordists are found in Germanic or Scandinavian keyboard manuscripts: ten by La Barre (some, if not all, of which are actually transcriptions from lute music), three each by Chambonnières and Dumont, and one each by Champion (uncertain attribution), Monnard and Lebègue.

The manuscripts can be divided chronologically into four groups. The only early sources of French harpsichord music in Germanic countries are *1-Copenhagen-376* and *4-Lynar,* and their repertoire is by the elusive La Barre. In both cases, the pieces may have been entered into the manuscripts as late as midcentury. The manuscripts from the middle of the century are the most important, especially *5-Munich-15031,* which contains two unique pieces by Dumont. The late seventeenth-century and early eighteenth-century sources are interesting from an historical perspective, showing the French influence on Germanic keyboard music.

There are only five manuscripts from ca. 1600-1640. With the exception of *4-Lynar,* all of them belong to the household genre and their value as musical sources is therefore compromised. Most of the French music they transmit was written by identifiable lutenists, with the possible exception of La Barre's pieces. In the lists which follow, all of the French composers represented in each source are cited in the third column, both harpsichordists and nonharpsichordists:

Eÿsbock	ca. 1600?	Godard
Linz	1611-1613	Mercure (?)
4-Lynar	ca. 1615-1650	Ballard, Gaultier, La Barre
1-Copenhagen-376	1629-ca. 1650	La Barre, Mesangeau, Pinel
Wolffheim	ca. 1630-1650	Du Caurroy (?)

The eighteen sources from the middle of the century, about 1640-1675, show a continuation of the dominance of lute music as the French aspect of their repertoire. A number of them draw heavily upon French stage and instrumental sources as well, and the popular French melodies continued to be common. Most of the few compositions by French harpsichordists (Chambonnières, Dumont, Monnard, and perhaps Champion and La Barre) which are found in Germanic sources, are from these midcentury manuscripts:

Voigtländer	post 1642	use of French melodies only.
Imhoff	1649	use of French melodies only.
Leningrad	1650	use of French melodies only.
Drallius	1650	use of French melodies only.
8-Hintze	ca. 1650-1674?	Artus, Chambonnières, La Barre
2-Witzendorff	1655-1659	Chambonnières, Mesangeau
Upsala-409	ca. 1655-1662	Belleville, Dumanoir, La Croix, Verdier
Uppsala-134:22	ca. 1655?	Belleville
Skara	1659-post 1661	Gaultier, Pinel
5-Munich-15031	ca. 1660?	Artus, Chambonnières, Dumont, Pinel
6-Munich-1511e	ca. 1660?	Monnard
7-Munich-1511f	ca. 1660?	Artus, Pinel
Berlin-40147	ca. 1660-1680	Besard
Rés-819-2	post 1661	Lully
Celle	1662	Champion (?)
Darmstadt-17	1672	Gaultier, Gumprecht
Darmstadt-18	1674	Gaultier
Darmstadt-1198	16??	Anon. transcriptions

In the last quarter of the seventeenth century, there was a marked change in the nature of the French music which was included in Germanic and Scandinavian keyboard manuscripts. Although lute music still contributed to sources through the 1680's (and somewhat exceptionally to *Ottobeuren*, 1695), transcriptions from Lully operas increasingly dominated the French contents of the eleven manuscripts from about 1675-1700:

3-Berlin-40623	1678	La Barre, Lully
9-Ihre-284	1679	Artus, Brullard, Dumanoir, Gaultier, La Barre, Lully
Stockholm-2	ca. 1680?	Gaultier
Stockholm-176	post 1681	Du But, Gaultier, Lully, Mouton
10-Schwerin-617	post 1684	Lebègue, Lully
Stoss	post 1684	Lully
Stockholm-228	post 1685	Du But, Lully, Mercure, Verdier
Lüneburg-1198	1687	Lully
Ottobeuren	1695	Dufaut, Gaultier, Lambert (?), Pinel
Grimm	1699	Lully
Thott	1699-1702	French titles only.

Only in the ten eighteenth-century sources is there any significant quantity of French harpsichord music. Lebègue is represented in four manuscripts and d'Anglebert in two. In both cases, the presence of the music is the result of the circulation of the printed versions of their compositions. Chambonnières, whose works were also published, is totally absent, and d'Anglebert is only minimally represented. It was Lebègue who was the ambassador for seventeenth-century French harpsichord music in Germany, and the manuscripts which included his music were directly associated with three of the most important German composers of the era: Buxtehude, Walther and J.S. Bach.

Nuremberg	1699-1721	French titles only.
11-Ryge	ca. 1700?	Lebègue, Lully
Minorite	1708-17??	Lully
12-Walther	ca. 1712-post 1731	d'Anglebert, Lebègue
Berlin-40624	post 1715	French dance forms.
13-Möllersche	1717-1719	Lebègue, Lully
14-Schwerin-619	ca. 1720?	Collasse, P. Gaultier, Lebègue, Lully
Berlin-30363	post 1723	Lully
Berlin-8551	ca. 1725?	de Grigny (misattribution)
15-Berlin-30206	ca. 1750-1770	d'Anglebert

CHAPTER II

ENGLISH MANUSCRIPTS

In English harpsichord sources, the French influence is restricted almost exclusively to the works of Jonas Tresure (who was probably not French at all), La Barre and John Mercure. Their representation in manuscripts from about 1650 to the turn of the century is considerable, and the development of *style-brisé* texture in English compositions of the period can be directly related to these composers. It is not until about 1690 that any substantial amount of music by the important clavecinists is found in England. Even then, the works of Chambonnières and others are not common; in fact, they are largely limited to the pieces in Charles Babell's manuscripts (*23-Tenbury* and *24-Babell*).

English keyboard music of this period has not been extensively studied, as scholars have naturally centered their attention on the earlier virginalist school, concerning themselves with the manuscripts discussed here primarly as sources for editions rather than for historical writings. Most of the discussions which have been published are found in the single-paragraph entries in critical reports of various volumes in the *Musica Britannica* series. Caldwell surveyed the history of English keyboard music in a recent book, but the French aspect of the repertoire has been left almost entirely undiscussed.[99] Apel dealt with this era in five pages which are a lucid summary, but of little help to a detailed study (*Apel-HKM*, pp. 748-753). Pereyra discussed English sources in the Paris Conservatory collection (now in the Bibliothèque nationale) in a series of articles in the 1920's and '30's.[100] Barry Cooper recently completed a thesis on keyboard music of the middle and late baroque period and his future published writings will undoubtedly be the most authoritative in the field.[101]

The following manuscripts will be discussed:

16-Cosyn	*19-Heardson*	*22a-Roper*
Oxford-IB	*20-Ch-Ch-378*	*23-Tenbury*
17-Rogers	*Bod-576*	*24-Babell*
18-Ch-Ch-1236	*21-Rés-1186bis*	*Bod-425*
	22-Ch-Ch-1177	*25-Bod-426*

Cosyn (Inventory 16)

Thurston Dart summarized the history of *16-Cosyn* in his commentary to the *Musica Britannica* edition of John Bull's works.[102] The manuscript was acquired by Benjamin Cosyn, who made the index in 1652, adding fifty pieces to those already there. Cosyn's hand is known from a holograph collection[103] and Dart's assertion that the hands are the same has not been disputed. Nearly all of the pieces which were already in the manuscript are by John Bull and may be in Bull's hand. Here, however, it is exclusively the pieces which Cosyn added in or before 1652 which are of concern. *16-Cosyn* contains eight pieces by La Barre and three (including the misattributed #101) which can be ascribed to Tresure.

La Barre is named twice, both times as "Monsier ([or] Mr) Bare." "Bare" and "La Beare" can be considered English corruptions of "La Barre" on the basis of two sets of relationships. First, *16-Cosyn* #100 is found in *18-Ch-Ch-1236*; there it is titled "Corant Mr Bare," but in the same manuscript "La bar" is used as an attribution to another piece (#8). Second, the "Saraband Beare," *17-Rogers* #22, is found in the same suite as the "Almande LB" of *27-Gresse* (#21).

It has already been pointed out that the identity of La Barre is a vexing problem. The known works can be divided into two groups: those which circulated in foreign sources and those found in French sources. With only two exceptions, the groups are discrete.[104] For convenience, the composer of the pieces in French sources is here called the "Bauyn La Barre," and the composer of the others, the "English La Barre." Only two of the works can be attributed to any of the known members of the La Barre family and it is possible that the "English" and "Bauyn" La Barre designations represent more than two composers. Until further biographical information is uncovered in French and perhaps English archives, it is futile to attempt to assign the forty-two pieces to one or another of those members of the family who are sketchily identified in the List of Composers (p. 325). The exceptions are the Variations on "Tu crois ô beau soleil" in *56-Mersenne* (by Pierre III) and the Allemande/Gigue in *35-Bauyn III* (by Joseph). Since *16-Cosyn* is dated and shows no sign of having been compiled gradually, it can be considered the earliest datable source of the music of the English La Barre.[105] The presence of the pieces in a highly professional source in the hand of a known composer proves the importance of the works to the English repertoire. It comes as little surprise, then, to see La Barre's pieces recur in English manuscripts.

The pieces of the English La Barre circulated almost entirely in English sources. Of the eighteen sources which contain his pieces, all but five have definite English connections. Nine sources are of English provenance (*16-Cosyn, 17-Rogers, 18-Ch-Ch-1236, 19-Heardson, 20-Ch-Ch-378, 22-Ch-Ch-1177, 59a-Handmaide, Oxford-IB* and *Drexel-5609*). Three sources (*1-Copenhagen-376, 4-Lynar* and *27-Gresse*) contain English pieces, suggesting that the La Barre pieces could have come from England. The remaining harpsichord manuscripts show no English connection (*3-Berlin-40623, 8-Hintze, 9-Ihre-284, 29-Chigi* and *31-Madrid-1360*). The only French source is *Saizenay-I*, a lute manuscript. La Barre is one of the very few French names to be found in English manuscripts. It does not seem logical that a Parisian harpsichordist from the La Barre family would be represented with twenty-nine pieces in English sources, while Chambonnières, the famous court harpsichordist, is found only twice before 1690 (*18-Ch-Ch-1236* #3 and *60-Playford* #71). The other clavecinists, d'Anglebert, Louis Couperin, Hardel, Monnard and Richard, are totally absent, and Lebègue's ubiquitous Gavotte (*21-Rés-1186bis* #12) is the only piece by that composer in a seventeenth-century English source.[106]

One possible explanation for La Barre's presence in English sources is that he was in fact active in England. Many musicians are known to have emigrated as a result of the marriage of the daughter of Henri IV to Charles I, in 1625.[107] It is possible that a La Barre, too, emigrated, and that some of his pieces would have already entered circulation in French manuscripts (and thence to other continental sources), while the majority would have entered English and English-derived sources. The lutenist John (Jean) Mercure is known to have moved across the Channel by 1641, and his works are found in some of the same sources as those of the English La Barre. In some cases, Mercure's works are quite obviously transcriptions from lute pieces, and it must be assumed that none of them was originally written for the harpsichord, although no lute sources of his music are known.[108]

The English La Barre may also have been a lutenist. One work is known in a French lute manuscript (cf. *8-Hintze* #11), and one other piece by a La Barre is found uniquely in *Besard*, a 1617 lute publication. It has already been pointed out that two other keyboard pieces by La Barre are almost certainly transcriptions from lute works (cf. *1-Copenhagen-376* #39-40). Although none of these lute works or transcriptions occurs in English sources, a pattern of concordances suggests that they may be works of the English La Barre (cf. p. 296): *1-Copenhagen-376* #39 occurs as *27-Gresse* #21; *27-Gresse* #22 occurs in four English sources, and also as *29-Chigi* #30; *29-Chigi* #32 is related to *1-Copenhagen-376* #40. Secondly, although *8-Hintze* #11 is not found in any other keyboard manuscripts, *8-Hintze* does contain a piece by Tresure, who is known largely in English sources. On the basis of this reasoning, it is likely that most, if not all, of the works in non-French sources are by the English La Barre, and that they were originally written for lute, transcribed for harpsichord by Englishmen. A significant exception to the pattern is found in *20-Ch-Ch-378* (#3, q.v.).

A second hypothesis is that the La Barre pieces all entered the English repertoire as harpsichord pieces about 1625, and continued to circulate thereafter, but that no later French harpsichord music was imported. This theory is implied in the acceptance of the English La Barre works as otherwise lost examples of French harpsichord music, but it ignores the lute connection of some of the pieces and the documented parallel career of John Mercure. Until biographical and stylistic studies of French and English keyboard music shed more light on the problem, the first hypothesis is the more logical explanation for the plethora of La Barre works in England in view of the absence of other known French harpsichord compositions.

A few of the entries in the Inventory of *16-Cosyn* require further explanations:

#44: This Courante, the most circulated of the La Barre and Tresure works, is here considered to be by La Barre because three sources attribute it to that composer, while only two manuscripts name Tresure. It is impossible to separate the works of the English La Barre and Tresure definitively, and almost any of the works attributed to either composer could actually be by the other (cf. *#*101). The confusion is greatest in *19-Heardson* (cf. pp. 64-65).

#48: Cosyn apparently started to attribute the piece to La Barre, or intended to copy another work on the page, but corrected his error. It is on one of the several pages which Cosyn pasted over an existing page in the manuscript when he acquired it.

#63, 77: As in the Germanic and Scandinavian countries, the use of the word "French" in a title usually implies Gallic style rather than provenance.

#66: Cosyn pasted the Masque over another piece, the title of which can be read through the paper as "Almaine." Cosyn's index lists "Mr Bares Almaine," which presumably applied to the Allemande which is now covered. The music cannot be read through the page, but the hand appears to be Cosyn's.

#101: The concordances, except for *18-Ch-Ch-1236* *#*6, are to settings of the same melody, which was a popular tune.

Oxford-IB

This manuscript is currently unlocated and has never been described in detail. Hendrie met the owner of the source by chance ca. 1960, while he was working on his Gibbons edition. She declined to allow it to be examined, but did send Hendrie a photocopy of one page, which contained a Courante by La Barre (also attributed to Tresure and Gibbons).[109] Prof. Hendrie has not had further contact with Mrs. I.B., and has no record of his dealings with her.[110] Barry Cooper conjecturally, but plausibly, linked *Oxford-IB* to a manuscript which had been described in 1904:

Lowe:

> One, or possibly two, MSS in private hands, compiled by Edward Lowe. One is listed as "IB" in Hendrie ed./ *Gibbons*, which states that the owner lives in Oxford; . . . This MS is presumably the same as one also compiled by Edward Lowe and also in private hands, formerly in the library at Rydal Hall, Westmorland (the chances of there being two MSS in private hands both known to have been compiled by the same person seem remote). This one, dating from 1652, is mentioned in Scholes/*Puritans* and is described briefly in *The Flemings at Oxford*, ed. J.R. Magrath (Oxford Historical Society, xliv), Oxford, 1904, p 541. Magrath gives the titles of six pieces in the MS ("Sacke and Sugar," "Duke of Richmonds gigg," "The Water Man," "Psalm tunes," "Sarabande" and "A Voluntarye") but no composers.[111]

Since the only known piece of concern to the French repertoire is found in *16-Cosyn*, also from 1652, *Oxford-IB* contributes nothing to this study, although it is possible that other La Barre pieces are in the unlocated manuscript.

Rogers (Inventory 17)

This English household manuscript has long been studied as a resource for the history of keyboard music. Sir John Hawkins copied almost all of *17-Rogers* for his own use (in *Drexel-5609*, which has no independent value as a source), and it has been a well-known manuscript to all more recent scholars of English music. Two recent editions of *17-Rogers* have made this source readily available. The first (*Sargent*) is complete except for the vocal pieces and Byrd's *Battle* (#28). The second (*Cofone*) is a curious quasi-facsimile edition which presents the complete manuscript, although it ignores the fact that the book was written in two sections, one from each end. *Cofone* presents the pieces in a single order from front to back, so that those in the latter section appear in reverse order from that in which they were actually written. Both editors misconstrued the French attributions of "Beare" (La Barre) and "Mercure" (John Mercure, also indicated with the astrological sign for Mercury, ☿ , with #69).

The date "1656" over the index at the beginning of the volume indicates that all of the pieces at that end of the book (#1-72), which includes all of the French compositions, had been entered by that date (#95 was present in the first group as #23). The use of the title, "When the King enjoyes his owne againe" (#10), is further confirmation of the pre-Restoration date of *17-Rogers*. The manuscript is a household collection which is exceedingly miscellaneous in its arrangement, with very few pieces grouped by key or composer.

The pieces by Mercure (#66 and 69) are presumably transcriptions from lute works. Five of the six La Barre compositions are found together, with two pieces intervening, as #21-27. They were probably copied from a single source which was closely related to La Barre, since the scribe of *17-Rogers* seems to have made no attempt to create groups within the keyboard pieces. The sixth piece (#95) was added independently, as it is a variant of the version of the Courante found as #23. The concordances cited for #22 and 23 are all to substantially different versions of the pieces, with the exception of *18-Ch-Ch-1236* #34, which is very similar to *17-Rogers* #23.

Ch-Ch-1236 (Inventory 18)

Caldwell (pp. 152, 248) briefly mentioned *18-Ch-Ch-1236*, which was compiled by William Ellis (cf. #68-75). Caldwell confirmed the authenticity of Ellis' hand, but doubts that he wrote another Oxford manuscript, *Ch-Ch-1113*, which contains no French music other than a "Courante Francise" on p. 4.[112] Since Ellis was born in 1620 and Bryne ca. 1621, *18-Ch-Ch-1236* was probably not compiled until at least ca. 1650, but there is no certain indication of when it was compiled before Ellis' death in 1674. Dufaut is not known to have been in England before ca. 1670, and it is therefore likely that the manuscript was compiled towards the end of Ellis' life. Barry Cooper dealt with the manuscript in some detail and has suggested that the pieces by Fer(r)abosco are in that composer's hand.[113]

The order of *18-Ch-Ch-1236* is somewhat confusing when viewed in microfilm. Like many keyboard books, it was written from both ends. The end which has been supplied with modern numeration by leaves was considered the back originally; the other end, listed first in the Catalog Inventory, has original pagination as well as an index from earlier in this century. Further complicating the numeration of the volume is the intermixing of leaf and page numbers (see "Marginalia" in the Catalog entry).

Four French composers are represented in *18-Ch-Ch-1236*: Chambonnières, Dufaut, La Barre and Mercure. Dufaut and Mercure were both lutenists and both emigrated to England. As has already been hypothesized, this is probably true of La Barre as well. It is curious that one Courante was attributed to both La Barre and Tresure only seven pages apart (#1 and 8). They are variant versions of the same piece and Ellis apparently did not realize that he had already copied the same piece from a different source. Ellis shows himself again in #47 to be a careless and mechanical scribe, as the last five measures of the Courante are notated with the lower staff misplaced by three beats before the upper. Although manuscripts are frequently misaligned, this discrepancy is so great and the alignment of the wrong notes is so precise, that it is obvious that this copy was never read or played.

Chambonnières' Courante (#3) is the most unexpected piece in the collection; it is the only composition by that composer in an English harpsichord source from before 1690. The concordance to *24-Babell* does not indicate further English circulation of the Courante, as the French pieces in *24-Babell* were derived from a plentiful supply of French keyboard manuscripts from well after 1674. Similarly, the other exceptional English Chambonnières manuscript, *22a-Roper*, drew directly on French sources.

Heardson (Inventory 19)

The identification of the principal scribe of *19-Heardson* as Thomas Heardson (with additions by Albertus Bryne) was proposed in *Hendrie* (p. 92). Cooper, on the basis of a comparison to a known example of Bryne's hand and the spelling of the name as "Bryan" in *19-Heardson*, rejected the Bryne autograph theory.[114] The authenticity of hand A as Heardson's has not been disproven, but the evidence is circumstantial, based essentially on the large number of Heardson's works found in the manuscript. All of the French works in *19-Heardson* were written in the main hand.

The dating of *19-Heardson* which is adopted here ("ca. 1664?") is taken from the engraved portrait which is tipped into the volume. This date is no reliable indication of exactly when the manuscript was compiled, but there is no other specific evidence for dating it, and the date is at least plausible. It can be no earlier than about 1641, when Bryne was twenty; there is no evidence, however, of whether it was compiled before or after the Restoration. From the French standpoint, the specific dating is not of great significance, since works by the French composers in the manuscript are already known in English sources from 1652 and 1656 (*16-Cosyn* and *17-Rogers*) and the continued circulation of the pieces during the rest of the century is proven by the inclusion of a piece by Tresure in a manuscript from 1702, *24-Babell* (#161).

It should be noted that the microfilm which has been reproduced for many years, and upon which past analyses and editions have been based, skips pages 118-119, thus omitting two compositions (#72-73).

19-Heardson has been a problematical source for scholars of English keyboard music because of its unreliable attributions. The discrepencies include #46, "Mr. Gibbons," which is known elsewhere to be by La Barre (or Tresure); and #66-67, attributed to Bull, but known to be by Gibbons. Scholars have been justifiably unwilling to trust any of *19-Heardson*'s attributions if they could not be confirmed in other sources. Thus Hendrie felt free to suggest that the three Courantes #46-

48 might really be by La Barre or Tresure, since they are stylistically atypical of Gibbons and the other Gibbons misattribution (#46) was actually by La Barre. Similarly, he suggested that #40 could be by La Barre, since it appears in *17-Rogers* before two pieces by La Barre (*Hendrie*, pp. 90, 92, 103). The possibilities cannot be disproven, but there is no compelling evidence, stylistic or otherwise, to make such specific attributions of the pieces.

19-*Heardson* is the largest source of the music of Jonas Tresure. In the case of La Barre, part of the identification problem stems from the fact thay many musicians have been identified with that name. With Tresure, the opposite situation obtains: absolutely nothing is known biographically. The scribe of *19-Heardson* clearly considered him to be French, listing him as "Monsier Tresor" in the index, not "Mr," as he did for the English names. On the basis of the name alone, however, one can be reasonably certain that he was not a Frenchman. The following variants of the name are found: Jonas Tresure (adopted here as the primary spelling in order to agree with Barry Cooper's article in *Grove-6*), Tresor, Treser and Tresoor. Jonas is not only an unlikely French name, but French composers were almost never known by their given names. A search through the Catalog will yield almost no examples of attributions to French composers in either French or foreign manuscripts with even a first initial, quite unlike the names of composers of other nationalities. The French reticence in this regard, which still persists today, causes great problems in distinguishing members of a family from one another; but it also suggests that a composer identified by both names is not French. "Trésor" is a French word, but not a French name; however, "Tresoor" can be found as a Dutch name (it appears in the Amsterdam telephone directory), and one can easily see how it could be corrupted from Tresoor to Tresor to Treser and then to Tresure, which looks deceptively French. Thus it is very unlikely that Tresure was a French composer. Since he was considered French and was linked in manuscripts with the Frenchmen La Barre and Mercure, it is probable that he was foreign to England, most probably a French-speaking emigrant from the Spanish Netherlands.

As with the English La Barre, most, if not all, of the Tresure sources are either English or English-derived (cf. p. 311). The connection between the two composers is so great that it is impossible to separate them entirely. Of twenty-one sources, eighteen contain pieces by La Barre and fifteen contain Tresure; thus twelve of the sources have music of both composers, including several conflicting attributions. Aside from the attributions in *19-Heardson*, one must contend with such contradictions as *18-Ch-Ch-1236* #1 and 8, attributed to both composers in the same manuscript; or *16-Cosyn* #101, which follows a Courante by La Barre there, but a different Courante by Tresure in *18-Ch-Ch-1236*

(#6). *19-Heardson* attributes #65 to Tresure, but it is found in *20-Ch-Ch-378* (#2) as "Corant (la) Barr." *19-Heardson* is also contradictory within itself, as #69 is attributed to La Barre at the end of the music, but to Tresure in the index. Thus it is impossible to unravel a definitive work list for either composer from the tangle of attributions. The lists in Appendix C present all of the works which can be assigned to either composer, citing the conflicts. The works ascribed to La Barre have been included as full entries (i.e., with incipits) in the Inventories, as possible genuine French harpsichord compositions. The works attributed to Tresure alone have been given abbreviated entries (i.e., without incipits) as non-French music.

Ch-Ch-378 (Inventory 20)

The authenticity of *20-Ch-Ch-378* as the autograph of Henry Aldrich, Dean of Christ Church College in Oxford, is not beyond doubt. *Hendrie* (p. 91) treated the matter gingerly, stating that the script was "possibly that of Dean Aldrich, but not in his most elegant hand." The dating adopted here represents the maturity of Aldrich and assumes that he was indeed the scribe. The manuscript gives little help from internal evidence since it consists almost entirely of short anonymous pieces in fantasy or prelude style. The watermark evidence is inconclusive, but the genre of the mark is found in sources from 1672 to 1719, which supports the assertion that *20-Ch-Ch-378* comes from the end of the seventeenth century.

The date of the manuscript is of some concern to French studies because this source provides the only link between the English La Barre and the Bauyn La Barre. The Courante #2 is clearly related to the English La Barre group of concordances (even if the Tresure attribution in *19-Heardson* is correct), but the Allemande #3 is found in *35-Bauyn.* Except for this one piece, the two groups of La Barre pieces are totally distinct. The concordance is a direct contradiction of the La Barre hypothesis thus far promulgated here.

One explanation is that the Bauyn La Barre was the same composer as the English La Barre. This thesis is untenable, however, because it ignores the lute aspect of some of the concordances. It is not likely that a Gigue-allemande[115] such as #3 would have been composed for lute, and in any case the two harpsichord settings are substantially the same, proving that it was on both sides of the Channel as a harpsichord piece. A second, more likely possibility is that *20-Ch-Ch-378* #3 is an unusual example of the circulation of actual French harpsichord music in England. Particularly since the manuscript is so late, it is quite possible that the Allemande was transmitted more-or-less directly from Paris, while the Courante #2 came from the continued circulation of the

English La Barre's pieces. The two pieces are stylistically quite different from each other, but there is no Gigue-allemande by the English La Barre with which to compare #3. "English La Barre" and "Bauyn La Barre," it must be remembered, are code names adopted here which may well stand for more than one composer each. The circulation pattern of the compositions could be more complicated than has been deduced to date.

Bod-576. *Provenance:* (England, post 1679) (transcription from *Bellérophon*). *Location:* Oxford; Bodleian Library, Ms. Mus. Sch. F 576. *Description:* 100 *l.* (numbered as 1-59 *l.* from one end, and 1-75 p. from the other; originally 104 *l.*: 4 *l.* torn out); oblong quarto format, 15.3 x 19.5 cm. Watermark (not illustrated): variant of #79. Full leather gilt-tooled binding, green cloth ties, 16.3 x 20.5 cm. *Notation:* Mixed. New French lute tablature and keyboard score (two 6-line staves); clefs: F/4, G/3, duplicated with C clefs. *Scribes:* 4 unidentified hands. A: *l.* 1-59r (lute tablature); B: p. 1-71 (keyboard score); C: p. 74-75 (lute); D: texts in English on *l.* 66v-67r, 70v.

This mixed book of lute and harpsichord pieces contains compositions by Ennemond Gaultier, Du But, Pinel and Mouton in lute tablature, along with many anonymous pieces. There are also a number of lute songs with French texts and one "Gigue de Mouton" with an English text on the same page (but seemingly unrelated): "From grave lessons . . ." (*l.* 66v-67r). The twenty-five keyboard pieces are entirely unattributed, but one Allemande (p. 36) is known to be by Tresure in *Van-Eijl* (#4). Therefore, the following Courante and Sarabande could also be by Tresure, although the Praeludium which opens the suite is probably German or English, to judge by the texture. The book is almost entirely French-texted and could have been compiled by Frenchmen or francophile Englishmen. The hand which wrote the keyboard pieces is more German in appearance than either French or English, but the English text cited above and the watermark suggest that *Bod-576* was compiled in England. In any case, the only relationship to French harpsichord music is a transcription of the Ouverture to *Bellérophon* by Lully (p. 54-59) and the piece(s) by Tresure.

Rés-1186bis (Inventory 21)

The Catalog entry for this late-century English manuscript needs little explanation. The only identified French harpsichord music is Lebègue's Gavotte (#12). The "French Lesson: Chacone" (#11) might be of French provenance, perhaps originally an instrumental or opera chaconne. Farinel's Ground (#16) is a transcription of the French violinist's *Folies d'Espagne* variations, which circulated in England as a result of his stay at the English court from 1675-1679.

Ch-Ch-1177 (Inventory 22)

The dating of *22-Ch-Ch-1177* is based on the birth date of the youngest composer, Henry Purcell, who was twenty in 1680. It is likely that the manuscript was not compiled until at least a decade later, perhaps after 1696, the date of the posthumous publication of Purcell's harpsichord suites. The date 173(3?) on the original cover is no indication of the date of the compilation as it seems to be a memo scribbled by an owner of the book regarding the loan of another book (see "Marginalia" in the Catalog entry). There is no French music in the manuscript other than the unique Sarabande by La Barre (#2), which presumably belongs to the English La Barre group.

Roper (Inventory 22a)

This English book has escaped attention in spite of its ready availability since 1950, when the Newberry Library purchased it from a book dealer in Connecticut. Its previous history cannot be traced, but the organization, marginalia and handwriting of *22a-Roper* clearly place it in the "household manuscript" category. At one end it is signed with "Mary Rooper her Booke," and at the other, "Elizabeth Roper ÷ her Booke 1691." The contents, written in a variety of hands, some skilled and some not, reflect a somewhat haphazard collection of pieces from which one learned to play the harpsichord, rather than the systematic or unified compilation of a professional musician. In all probability, Mary and Elizabeth Roper (Rooper) were recusant sisters who studied the harpsichord, one passing the book on to the other. They seem to have had first a Francophile teacher and then a typical Englishman, as the first pieces at both ends of the book are French. The volume is remarkable and rare evidence of the presence of French harpsichord music in Great Britain before the turn of the century, and is all the more striking for being in the hands of amateurs.

If any French music is to be found in such a manuscript, it is not suprising that the composers turn out to be Lebègue, Chambonnières and Lully. As is to be expected, Lebègue's pieces parallel the printed texts of *64-Lebègue-I* and *65-Lebègue-II* almost exactly and can be presumed to be at least indirect copies of the prints. In the case of Chambonnières, however, it is interesting that although the pieces (#58-59) have enough variants from the texts in *62-Chamb-I* (including unique Doubles, #58a and 59a) to suggest that they are not copies from the print, the ornamentation and the pairing of the two Courantes do reflect the print. A few other pieces deserve comment:

#13: The spelling of the title, "Double de le gige," is quite clear and suggests that Hand A, which entered most of the French music, was not that of a native Frenchman.

#29-29A: The settings, not just the melodies, of this Menuet and Double are the same (with minor differences) here and in *48-LaBarre-6.* This must, then, have circulated as a genuine harpsichord piece, not a transcription.

#30: Scribe C was obviously thinking in the wrong clef, as the right hand is a third too high in the first strain. The texture is almost exactly the same as in *48-LaBarre-6,* but in both cases it is little more than a melody and bass. The piece is clearly a transcription in view of its existence in both D Minor and G Minor among the concordant versions.

#32-34: This group is almost certaintly by a single composer. The ornamentation symbols are those first used by d'Anglebert and then by Le Roux, and are not found in the table on *l.* 49v-50r of *22a-Roper.* The incipit for #33a is omitted because it would be a duplicate of #33.

Tenbury (Inventory 23), Babell (Inventory 24)

The name Babel, or Babell, will probably never be spoken in modern times without at least passing reference to one of Burney's more memorable diatribes:

> This author acquired great celebrity of wire-drawing the favourite songs of the opera of *Rinaldo,* and others of the same period, into *showy* and brilliant lessons, which by mere rapidity of finger in playing single sounds, without the assistance of taste, expression, harmony, or modulation, enabled the performer to astonish ignorance, and acquire the reputation of a great player at small expence.[116]

It was William Babell who was guilty of these excesses. Although other critics such as Hawkins dealt with him more kindly, the volumes of flamboyant harpsichord transcriptions which Babell published beginning in 1709 give some justification for Burney's unflattering commentary. There are, however, no fewer than seven volumes of music--two printed and five in manuscript--from around 1700 which are quite different in style, but which are also generally attributed to William Babell. The most important of these earlier books is the enormous *24-Babell.* The dichotomy of the styles between the early and later works is not the only problem associated with the blanket attribution to William Babell: the earliest of the books in the *oeuvre* was published in

Amsterdam in 1697 when he was an English boy of about seven. Clearly there is something askew in Babell's biography.

William Babell's precise birth date is not known. He died in Islington (near London) on September 23, 1723, and he was buried at All Hallows Church, Bread Street in London, where he had been the organist since 1719.[117] His age at death was not noted in the church records, but Hawkins somehow determined after the publication of his *General History of the Science and Practice of Music* in 1776 that he had been "about the Age of thirty-three."[118] He had married in 1718, when he would have been about 28, but the earliest references to his career are from 1707-8 when he was playing second violin at the Queen's Theatre in the Haymarket.[119] Such a position is not unreasonable for a promising musician at age seventeen, and only two years later he published the first book of the infamous harpsichord transcriptions. Others followed beginning in 1716, but in 1711 came the first newspaper notice of his performing career as a harpsichordist:

> Hume's Dancing School, Frith Street, 24 April: a consort for the benefit of Signora Lody, with 'a new Cantata with a Solo on the Harpsichord perform'd by Mr Babell Junior, with a Variety of Concertos, and other Pieces Compos'd and perform'd by Mr Corbett and others of the best Masters.' [*The Spectator*, April 21, 1711][120]

From this time until his death twelve years later (due to excessive drinking according to Burney and Hawkins) he was frequently cited as a public performer. The significant factor in the early concert notice is that he is spoken of as "Mr Babell Junior." The elder Mr. Babel(l) has slipped almost entirely from the history books, but it was he who was responsible for the early works attributed to the family name, and a sketchy biography can be pieced together.

Hawkins stated merely that William Babell's father was a bassoonist at Drury Lane until he was eighty. No records of such activity can be found, but the father, whose name was Charles, did play bassoon, bass and violin at the Queen's Theatre in the Haymarket for 15 sols per day at the same time as his son was there (in 1707-8, William for 8 s).[121] He was resident in London by 1700, when he dated and signed *Bod-393*, "achevé a Londres 1700, Charles Babel," although in 1697-98 he had been employed as a bassoonist in "la troupe de Sa Majesté Britannique" at the Hague. By 1713 he was retired and received a pension as one of the musicians of the "late Prince of Denmark's Musick" until 1716. He probably died then, as he is not mentioned in William's will, written in 1720.[122] The only published clue that he was more prominent than most bassoonists is a newspaper notice from 1707.

Since the notice does not stipulate "Mr Babell *Junior*," there is little doubt that this is Charles, not William:

> At the Desire of several Persons of quality. During the time of the Horse-Races the beginning of August next. In Nottingham there will be perform'd a Consort of Vocal and Instrumental Musick: The Vocal Part to be performed by Mr Hughs, which will be a Collection of Songs taken out of the operas of Camilla, Thomyris, and Arsinae; with the Accompanyments as they are Originally done in said Operas by Mr Corbett, Mr Babell, and others . . . [*The Daily Courant*, July 23, 1707][123]

The real importance of Charles Babell, however, lies in the music he left, not his performing career. He was a talented and prolific arranger of instrumental and vocal music who also had an especially close connection to the Parisian school of harpsichordists. There are at least about 1,000 pieces which were arranged or copied by the elder Babell, and many of them have survived only in his books. The seven located volumes are as follows:

> 1. **Trios-1.** *Provenance:* Amsterdam, 1697 (advertised). *Location* (only complete ex.): Durham; Cathedral Library, C 53i. *Description:* 3 printed part-books, 61 pieces, "Trios /de Differents Autheurs /Choisis & Mis en Ordre par M[R] BABEL . . . Livre Premier /a Amsterdam ches /Estienne Roger Marchand Libraire."

> 2. **Trios-2.** *Provenance:* Amsterdam, 1700 (advertised). *Location* (only complete ex.): Durham; Cathedral Library, C 53ii (bound with *Trios-1*). *Description:* 3 printed part-books, 68 pieces, "TRIOS /de Differents Autheurs /choisis et mis en ordre par M[r] BABEL /LIVRE SECOND /a Amsterdam chez Estienne Roger /Marchand Libraire."

> 3. **Newberry.** *Provenance:* London, ca. 1700? *Location:* Chicago; Newberry Library, Special Collections, Case MS Vm 350 B113t. *Description:* 2 part-books in ms (*basse-continue* lacking), (index title:) ". . . Trois Cents Cinquante Trio, /Preludes de Basse: Recits;- /a Londres par Ch. Babel."

> 4. **Cummings.** *Provenance:* London?, ca. 1700? *Location:* South Bend; private collection of the author; previously owned by William H. Cummings[124] and Alfred Cortot. *Description;* 3 part-books in ms, ". . . quatre vingt et quelques Preludes; Recits; et acompagnemts . . ."

> 5. **Bod-393.** *Provenance:* London, 1700. *Location:* Oxford; Bodleian Library, Ms. Mus. Sch. E 393. *Description:* ms score, pieces for one or two voices with lightly figured bass, "Airs /Italian a chanter /C.B. . . . acheve a Londres 1700 /Charles Babel."

6. **23-Tenbury.** "Ce liure arpartient /a g^m [Guillaume, i.e. William] Babel 1701, London."

7. **24-Babell.** "RECUEIL DE PIECES CHOISIES /POUR LE CLAUESSIN /1702 /WILLIAM BABEL" (cover stamping).

Most of these volumes have been misattributed to William Babell, at least by implication: *Trios-1* and *Trios-2* are given an erroneous date, "ca. 1720," in the Durham Cathedral Library's printed catalog.[125] A manuscript note by Arthur S. Hill in the front of *Newberry* states that both it and *Cummings* are in the hand of William, according to a letter from Ellis, causing Hill to conclude that the music was written by Charles and copied by William; Ellis probably took the hand to be William's because his name is stamped on the cover of *24-Babell.* This stamping led others to attribute *24-Babell* to the son, although Gloria Rose (in a note inserted in the front of *24-Babell)* called attention to the fact that it was probably written by Charles Babel, known to her through *Bod-393.* 23-Tenbury, which has escaped scholarly attention almost completely, was owned by William and probably was compiled especially for the budding harpsichordist, since the ownership note is in the scribe's (i.e. Charles') hand. The handwriting of the manuscripts (*Newberry, Cummings,*[126] *Bod-393, 23-Tenbury* and *24-Babell*) is unquestionably the same. It is neat and consistent, using the same formations of clefs, notes and letters; even the layout of the pages is the same in most of the sources, using a red margin line. That the hand is that of Charles, not William, is made explicit by the signature in *Bod-393.*

Most of the contents of *23-Tenbury* were recopied into *24-Babell,* including all of the pieces in the repertoire which is of concern to the present study. The order of the pieces in *24-Babell* is unrelated to that of *23-Tenbury,* and it would appear that Charles re-used the same sources, augmented with many more, rather than copying his own manuscript. *24-Babell* is an extraordinary collection whose value, particularly to French music, has been unrecognized. It is not surprising that the manuscript has received so little attention,[127] because it is a formidable task to identify the 296 largely unattributed pieces. Undoubtedly more of the compositions will be identified, but the Inventory in the Catalog assigns composers to sixty percent of the compositions, laying some basis for an evaluation of the source.

24-Babell can be considered an important and excellent source of French harpsichord music. Babell was obviously a francophile in the extreme, frenching even the titles of the English pieces.[128] The list of composers includes d'Anglebert, Chambonnières, Louis Couperin, Dieupart, Hardel, La Barre, Lebègue and Monnard. In addition, there are many transcriptions from French composers: Charpentier, Gaultier,

Gillier, Lully, Marais and perhaps Valois. Froberger's Gigue (#107) and Rossi's Passacaille (#166) also probably came from Paris, where they are known to have circulated. Twenty-three of the forty-two pieces in Dieupart's harpsichord book are scattered in *24-Babell* (Brunold-D #1-11, 14, 22-25, 31, 36-40, 42). The works had been published by 1701.[129] While Babell may have copied the pieces from the print, it is noteworthy that he attributed a piece not found in the print (*24-Babell* #105) to Dieupart and that another piece is transposed from F Major in the print to E Major in *24-Babell* (#172). A second example of such a transposition is found in an English print, *Harpsichord-3*, also from 1702. The "Minuett Madam Subilgny" (#21 in *Caldwell*, p. 212) is in G Minor there, but is actually a Menuet in F Minor by Dieupart (*Brunold-D* #41). An immigrant to England by ca. 1707, Dieupart may have already established English connections by 1702, supplying Babell with manuscripts which contained more pieces than those which were published. Dieupart may have been the source of all the French music, either in England or while Babell was on the continent. Clearly the French connection was to the inner circles of the Parisian harpsichord world, since the works of Louis Couperin are found in few manuscripts in France and in no foreign sources other than *24-Babell*. Excluding Couperin's Doubles, which circulated with Lebègue's and Hardel's Gavottes, and a Chaconne that is probably by another Couperin, the works are found in only eight sources, all of which are French except for *24-Babell*. This is in contrast to twenty-one for Chambonnières and eleven for d'Anglebert (cf. the work lists in Appendix C.) The works of Hardel, except for his Gavotte, are even more rare.

In addition to the importance of a new source for four pieces by Louis Couperin (#222 and 252-254), *24-Babell* is especially significant in providing two unknown Doubles to works by Chambonnières (#184a and 200a). Whether or not the Doubles are by Chambonnières, they are almost certainly French, as Babell did not add Doubles to other pieces in his manuscripts. Undoubtedly there are some unique works by seventeenth-century French harpsichord composers in *24-Babell*, but Babell's almost total lack of attributions and his rampant intermingling of pieces from disparate sources make modern speculative attributions very difficult. However, the large number of pieces in the very carefully notated volume, the majority of which are now identified, makes it an excellent subject for rigorous stylistic comparisons in an effort to assign some of the anonymous works to known composers. With or without composer attributions, *24-Babell* contains many unknown excellent harpsichord pieces.

The following compositions require specific comments:

#8-9: These pieces are sufficiently different from the versions in *65-Lebègue-II* to suggest that they were not copied from the print, and

24-Babell is an exception to the pattern of circulation of Lebègue's works. The other compositions by Lebègue (#60 and 85-86) parallel the printed texts more closely, but presumably all of the works came from a common manuscript source. It is also interesting to note that the title to #8 stipulates that the two Menuets are to be played in alternation, that is in A-B-A form. While this may be strictly a foreign intrusion into seventeenth-century performance practice, it may be that Mr. Babell is reflecting an option which is not made explicit in French sources.

#12-15: The entire Suite is almost certainly by King, since it occurs as a group, anonymously, in another English manuscript, *Clark-M678*, and the Allemande (#12) is attributed to King in *Egerton-2959*.

#31: This is one of many examples of the inclusion of an extraneous work in a Suite. The Menuet is not in the Dieupart print (cf. *Brunold-D*), although it may be by Dieupart if the Suite was copied from a Dieupart manuscript, rather than the print.

#34-42: The heading of the Suite, "Pieces de Mr Baptiste," must refer to Draghi; the textures of the pieces exclude the possibility of transcriptions from Lully's operas and Loeillet was only fourteen when *24-Babell* was compiled. Perhaps #38-40 should not be included in the group attribution because they do not occur in the anonymous B Minor Suite in *Clark-D173*. None of the pieces are in Draghi's six printed suites from 1707.

#161, 187, 223-224: Tresure's Courante (#161) probably shows the continued English circulation of his pieces, whereas the pieces by the Bauyn La Barre (#187 and 223-224) are intermingled with pieces which definitely came from Paris. There are no compositions by the English La Barre in *24-Babell*.

#204: d'Anglebert's Chaconne is very close to the autograph text (*33-Rés-89ter* #7), but the variations are presented in a different order.

#209: This setting is very close to that in *36-Parville*.

#222, 224: The similarity of the incipits of Louis Couperin's and the Bauyn La Barre's Courantes is too great to be coincidence. It probably reflects an homage of one composer for the other. The pieces are not the same after the opening of each strain, which excludes the possibility that they were both settings of a popular melody.

Bod-425. *Location:* Oxford; Bodleian Library, Ms. Mus. Sch. E 425. *Description:* same paper as *25-Bod-426* (watermark #13) and matching binding.

Bod-426 (Inventory 25)

Both of these manuscripts are in the same anonymous principal hand, and they both mention "Master Colin" in marginalia or attributions. *Bod-425* includes a transcription from *Le Someil d'Ysse* (1697) by Destouches and a second hand entered the date "December 1732" in the manuscript.

The only seventeenth-century French harpsichord music in either volume is Hardel's popular Gavotte (*25-Bod-426* #20), but the French influence throughout both books is apparent from the use of the French language.

Summary

Of the fourteen English manuscripts surveyed in this chapter, one (*Bod-425*) can be dismissed as of only peripheral interest. The other thirteen fall into two categories: those which contain the music of the English La Barre or Tresure, and those which contain music by known French harpsichordists. Three sources are in both groups: *18-Ch-Ch-1236*, *20-Ch-Ch-378*, and *24-Babell*.

Because of the uncertainties of dating, the first five La Barre - Tresure sources can all be considered "midcentury" manuscripts. The order of precedence is relatively unimportant to French studies, since at least two are definitely dated in the 1650's. The remaining four manuscripts can similarly all be considered "late-century" or "ca. 1700" sources. The nine manuscripts as a group show the importance of the La Barre and Tresure works to the English harpsichord repertoire, in spite of the likelihood that they were originally composed for lute:

16-Cosyn	1652	La Barre, Tresure
Oxford-IB	1652 (?)	La Barre
17-Rogers	1656	La Barre, Mercure
18-Ch-Ch-1236	ca. 1650-1674	Chambonnières, Dufaut, La Barre, Mercure, Tresure
19-Heardson	ca. 1664?	La Barre, Mercure, Tresure
20-Ch-Ch-378	ca. 1675-1710?	La Barre, Tresure
Bod-576	post 1679	Lully, Tresure
22-Ch-Ch-1177	post 1680	La Barre
24-Babell	1702	d'Anglebert, Chambonnières, Charpentier, Louis Couperin, Dieupart, Gaultier, Gillier, Hardel, Bauyn La Barre, Lebègue, Lully, Marais, Monnard, Tresure, Valois

With the singular exception of *18-Ch-Ch-1236*, the seven manuscripts which actually contain French harpsichord music all come from turn-of-the-century sources. French harpsichord music was simply not a significant part of the English repertoire until this late date:

18-Ch-Ch-1236	ca. 1650-1674	Chambonnières, Dufaut, La Barre, Mercure, Tresure
20-Ch-Ch-378	ca. 1675-1710?	La Barre, Tresure
22a-Roper	ca. 1691	Chambonnières, Lebègue, Lully
21-Rés-1186bis	post ca. 1680	Farinel, Lebègue
23-Tenbury	1701	Chambonnières, Collasse, Louis Couperin, Dieupart, Hardel, Lebègue, Lully, Monnard, Valois
24-Babell	1702	d'Anglebert, Chambonnières, Charpentier, Louis Couperin, Dieupart, Gaultier, Gillier, Hardel, Bauyn La Barre, Lebègue, Lully, Marais, Monnard, Tresure, Valois
25-Bod-426	post 1708	Godeau, Hardel, Lully
Bod-425	post 1708	French language.

CHAPTER III

DUTCH AND BELGIAN MANUSCRIPTS

The great Dutch statesman and musician, Constantin Huygens (1596-1687), left a corpus of musical correspondence which is collectively one of the most useful sources of information about seventeenth-century music, particularly harpsichord and lute music.[130] Huygens was an intimate of the Parisian harpsichord world, leaving documentation in the form of letters or references to Chambonnières, Dumont, La Barre (Pierre III and Pierre IV, in addition to the singer, Anne), and Richard. Huygens acknowledged receipt of a forty-one measure Allemande by Dumont,[131] he stated that one of the printed Dumont Allemandes was well-known to him,[132] and he thanked Chambonnières for sending him compositions.[133]

The apparent richness of Huygens' library of Parisian music might lead one to expect significant sources of seventeenth-century French harpsichord music in the regions north of Paris, but such is not the case. The Huygens manuscripts are lost, and the few harpsichord sources which will be discussed in this chapter contain no significant amounts of French harpsichord music. In general, they parallel the Germanic and Scandinavian household tablatures, their French contents being limited to settings of French tunes, stage music and transcriptions of lute music. *26-Bull*, containing works attributed to Chapel, is the most important exception to the pattern. The following manuscripts will be discussed:

Faille	*Terburg*	*27-Gresse*
26-Bull	*Brussels-27.220*	*28-Brussels-926*
Beatrix	*Brussels-24.106*	*Van-Eijl*

Faille. *Provenance:* Flanders (?), ca. 1625? *Description:* 131 *l.* (unnumbered, with many blank); oblong quarto format. *Notation:* keyboard score (some 5-line, some 6-line staves). *Scribes:* 3-5 unidentified hands.

This household keyboard book belonged to Écorcheville and is listed in the 1920 catalog of his library,[134] but it has not been located since. Van de Borren made a complete copy of *Faille* which is still extant[135] and published an inventory with a discussion of the manuscript.[136] He also referred to *Faille* in his pioneer study of English keyboard music.[137]

There is no French harpsichord music in *Faille*, but there is a transcription from Guédron's *Ballet de madame* of 1615 ("C'est trop Courir les eaux," *l.* 1), a setting of a Sarabande by the lutenist Pinel (cf. pp. 12-14) and settings of popular tunes ([Amarillis], *l.* 7; "Cecilia," *l.* 10; "Une jeune fillette" [with variations], *l.* 67; and "Courante la Roÿne," *l.* 123). The only other identified composers in *Faille* are Bull and Ferrabosco.

Bull (Inventory 26)

26-Bull was compiled in Antwerp where John Bull lived after leaving England. Its importance lies chiefly in its value as a source of English music. Thurston Dart studied the manuscript in detail during the preparation of his Bull edition (*Dart-BI* and *Dart-BII*) and considered the matter of the Bull attributions in the light of other Bull sources. Since some of the attributions in *26-Bull* proved incorrect (cf. #5, 49 and 50), Dart assumed that the scribe, Bull's overly faithful friend, Messaus, freely attributed all of the pieces to Bull which he had before him. Dart proposed alternate ascriptions on the basis of style for a number of the works (cf. #1, 4, 46a, 59 and 72), in spite of the attributions to Bull in the manuscript. In the process of this speculative analysis of the music and the source, Dart produced one of the most ingenious theories in this field.[138] He noted that the word Chapel (Chappel, La Chappelle, etc.) was associated with four works in *26-Bull* as well as several others in a lost Bull source.[139] The Champion family is known to have carried the designation "de la Chapelle" (including the younger Champion, Chambonnières; cf. *35-Bauyn-I* #28, "Chaconne de Mr Dela Chappelle dit Chambonnières"). Dart concluded that Bull probably became acquainted with the contemporary member of the family, Jacques II (father of Chambonnières), acquired some of Champion's pieces and dedicated one of his own to the Parisian organist. Thus Dart discounted the attributions in the body of *26-Bull* #17-19 in favor of the Chapel titles in the index, interpreting them as Champion attributions. Similarly, he conjectured that #20, "het Joweel voor cappelle 162i" (index title), was by Bull, but dedicated to Champion.

From the standpoint of French-related sources, nothing can be added to Dart's clever hypothesis. It cannot be supported by stylistic evidence, as there is no other harpsichord music by Champion or any French contemporary with which to compare the pieces. Certainly they display no evidence of the textures which characterize French harpsichord music of the following generation, and *chapelle* is a common word, designating a place often associated with music. The theory remains an intriguing, but currently untestable one. Only one other piece has been discovered with a Chapel title (cf. pp. 23-25), and it sheds no light on the question.

Beatrix. *Provenance:* Brussels?, ca. 1660? *Location:* Brussels, Bibliothèque royale Albert Ier, département de manuscrits, MS III 900. *Description:* 368 p. (irregular numeration); oblong quarto format, 15.6 x 20.1 cm. Watermark #74. Original full leather, gilt-tooled binding, gilted edges, metal clasps, 16.4 x 20.5 cm. *Notation:* keyboard score (two 6-line staves, 2 systems per page, written page by page). Clefs: F/4, G/3. *Marginalia:* Inside cover, "ex libris Julü Peeters Bruxellensis." Original pagination to p. 169.

Not until 1968, when it was purchased in Brussels, did this household manuscript come to light. It has not been studied in detail, but a brief discussion appeared in the library's acquisition bulletin, which proposed the approximate date of 1660.[140] The volume is entirely French-texted, but appears to contain no Parisian harpsichord music. There are numerous chansons and transcriptions from ballets, but no composers are named, and none has been identified. The front cover and end paper have miscellaneous doodles, including the note, "Dame Beatrix," with a monogram. The household nature of the book is confirmed by the rules of music at the beginning and the childish poetical notations throughout the volume, much like a young girl's multi-purpose notebook (e.g., "penser a Moÿ /Come Je pense A Vous" after a Sarabande, pp. 56-57). The scribe wrote a rather extensive note which seems too naïve to have been intended for a serious musician:

> Lors que vous Jouls anterex [?] de versifier vne/Ballet; vous poudre prendre celuÿ / que iay mis au page 40, il est fort /propre, pour cela; Jaÿ aussÿ changé les cloches, cela me sembloit /trop simple, comme je [?] le faisiet. [p. 112]

Beatrix is a promising source for future study, but it is not directly related to French harpsichord music.

Terburg

One other amateur book was said to date from mid-century and to contain similar repertoire. A book belonging to Gesina Terburg (1633-1690), the daughter of a Dutch artist, was first discussed by Pirro,[141] who had obviously seen it. He gave no citation, however, and it cannot now be located or traced. According to Pirro, it contained these French titles:

La Boisvinette
Belle Iris[142]
La Mostarde Nouvelle[143]

Pirro was correct in saying that they were fashionable French airs, that is, melodies from the popular repertoire and from the stage.

Brussels-27.220. *Location:* Brussels; Conservatoire royale de musique bibliothèque, cf. XY 27.220.

Brussels-24.106. Idem, cf. XY 24.106.

The first of these sources is listed in the library's hand-written card catalog under the entry for Chambonnières, with the identification, "Pièces de clavecin. ms XVIIe siècle." It cannot be located within the library, and it has never been mentioned in the secondary literature.[144]

The second Chambonnières source, seemingly from the early eighteenth century, is also missing from the same collection. It is listed as a "Recueil copié par Philidor." The library also holds a nineteenth-century manuscript copy of *62-Chamb-I* and *63-Chamb-II* (shelf #26.651) which should not be confused with the missing sources.

Gresse (Inventory 27)

Curtis discussed *27-Gresse* in the preface to his selective edition (*Curtis-MMN*, pp. XIX-XXIII) when the manuscript was still in private hands. The presentation there needs only minor revisions and amplifications. When *27-Gresse* was recently acquired by the Utrecht Institute for Musicology, it was studied by R.H. Tollefsen, who wrote an unpublished paper describing the manuscript and contradicting several of Curtis' statements.[145]

Curtis was mistaken in stating that two hands wrote *27-Gresse*; three hands can definitely be distinguished. Also, Curtis' conjecture that the "LB" of #21 might be the German organist Leonhard Beer can now be discarded in favor of La Barre, since the Courante and Sarabande which follow are attributed elsewhere to La Barre. Tollefsen attempted to read the "L" of "LB" as an uncompleted "A" of the title Allemande. In view of the La Barre concordances, there is no doubt that the letters are "LB." La Barre's suite precedes a suite by Sandley (#24-27) which is known from *Musick's Handmaide* and the two suites are surrounded by two other suites which are at least in part by Tresure (#16-19 and 30-34).[146] It is therefore possible that all of these pieces came from England, not France, although transcriptions from Lully are interspersed between the dance suites (#20, 29 and 37-38). Tresure probably composed at least the allemande-courante-sarabande tryptich of the two suites attributed in part to him, since four other suites in the manuscript are composed rather than compiled suites: #21-23 by La Barre; 24-27 by Sandley; and 41-43, 46-48 by Gresse.

The French aspect of *27-Gresse* is considerable. There are melodies of French derivation, transcriptions from Lully works and pieces by the English La Barre. With the possible exception of La Barre's suite, however, there is no French harpsichord music in *27-Gresse.*

Brussels-926 (Inventory 28)

This well-worn volume became available to the scholarly world in Antwerp in 1968. It was briefly described in the Brussels Royal Library acquisitions bulletin (*Quinze Années,* p. 504, item 458), but it has not yet received detailed attention. The two primary hands (B and C) were organists, probably from Antwerp or Brussels, and the chief importance of *28-Brussels-926* is as an organ manuscript. It provides organ works by the Frenchmen Boyvin, Lebègue, Nivers and Thomelin. The latter composer is represented by a "Duo ré du Mr Thomelin" (*l.* 69v) which brings the total of known Thomelin works to two (cf. *41-Thomelin*).

One of the Allemandes in *28-Brussels-926* (*l.* 39r) is a five-measure modulation from G Major to A Major. The name "allemande" is appropriate only in that the piece is in $\frac{4}{4}$ meter, but the term was the loosest of the dance designations in the seventeenth century. The allemande was the most stylized of the keyboard forms, maintaining no predictable rhythmic pattern other than quadruple meter. Tombeaux and gigues are called "allemande" in manuscripts, and Gigault wrote an "Allemande par fugue" (*67-Gigault* v. 2, p. 16). Therefore it is not too surprising to see the brief passage at hand labelled "allemande."

The next three Allemandes in *28-Brussels-926,* however, are *style-brisé* pieces, at least one of which came from Paris. The third (*l.* 66r) is by Lebègue, and the first two (*l.* 64v and 65r) are somewhat similar stylistically. It is possible that all three are by Lebègue, and the third shows enough minor changes from the printed version to suggest that it might have been copied from a manuscript source. In all of the pieces, the scribe indicated no ornaments. This is one of only two manuscripts in which there are anonymous works which have any likelihood of being by Lebègue (the other is *48-LaBarre-6*).

Most of the other harpsichord pieces in this manuscript are transcriptions of stage music. This is true for some of the dances which have not been specifically identified here, such as *l.* 16r, "Gauotte" which is known as "Goutons bien les Plaisirs" in a volume of instrumental trios (*Newberry*, also mostly transcriptions) in the hand of Charles Babell.

Van-Eijl. *Provenance:* Arnhem, The Netherlands, 1671 (dated on cover, "ANNA MARIA [back:] VAN EYL. /ANNO i67i"). *Location:* Amsterdam; Toonkunst-Bibliotheek, 208 A 4. *Description:* 3 p.*l.*, 97 *l.*; folio format, 31 x 20 cm. Watermarks #14, 49. Original parchment binding, gilted edges. *Notation:* Keyboard score (two 6-line staves, 5 systems per page, written page by page). Clefs: G/3, F/4. *Scribe:* Gisbert van Steenwick, teacher of Anna Maria van Eijl.

The "Klavierbuch Anna Maria van Eÿl" is well known and is available in two modern editions, *Röntgen* and *Noske*. Although no French harpsichord music appears in the household collection, several compositions have French connections through popular melodies, an opera transcription and one Allemande by Jonas Tresure (#4, *l.* 5r), the presumed Netherlander associated with the English La Barre. The following composers are represented among the thirty-three pieces: Berff, Broeckhuisen, Froberger, Kerll, Lully, Scheidemann, Schop,[147] Steenwick and Tresure. The French-related titles are:

> Serband |FINIS /à G Steenwick org [#5, *l.* 5v-7r][148]
> La Princesse . . . [#12 and #20, *l.* 14v-16v, 32v-33v][149]
> Serband |FINIS /à Gisb. Steenwick [#13, *l.* 17v-20r][150]
> Saraband |Broeckhuisen |à Georg Berf, organist [#16, *l.* 24v-28v][151]
> Bel Iris [#25, *l.* 36r][152]

Summary

The nine manuscripts from The Netherlands and Belgium can logically be divided into household and professional categories, not unlike the Germanic and Scandinavian manuscripts. With the exception of *28-Brussels-926* and possibly both *26-Bull* and *27-Gresse,* none of these northwestern sources contains French harpsichord music.

Of the five household collections, two are lost (*Faille* and *Terburg*), and one (*27-Gresse*) is considerably more professional in its latter sections. Among the pieces with French associations, only the pieces by the English La Barre in *27-Gresse* could be considered French harpsichord music. The manuscripts and their French aspects are as follows:

Faille	ca. 1625?	Guédron, Pinel
Beatrix	ca. 1660?	ballet transcriptions
Terburg	post 1661	Lully
27-Gresse	post 1669	Artus, La Barre, Lully, Tresure
Van-Eijl	1671	Lully, Tresure

Two of the four professional manuscripts are currently missing (*Brussels-27.220* and *Brussels-24.106*) and their contents are unknown, except that both are Chambonnières sources. *26-Bull* is an exceptional manuscript, containing music which would be the earliest datable seventeenth-century French harpsichord music, if the Chapel titles represent attributions to Champion. The last manuscript in the list is of more importance to French organ music than harpsichord music:

26-Bull	ca. 1629	Champion (?)
Brussels-27.220	16--	Chambonnières
28-Brussels-926	post 1670	Boyvin, Dumanoir, Lebègue, Lully, Nivers, Thomelin
Brussels-24.106	ca. 1700?	Chambonnières

CHAPTER IV

ITALIAN AND SPANISH MANUSCRIPTS

It was an Italian, Giovanni Battista Lulli, who came to dominate music in France in the last third of the seventeenth century, but the musical borrowing was not reciprocal. There is almost no French music of any sort in Italian harpsichord manuscripts, and as far as one knows the same is true of the little studied Spanish sources.

Six manuscripts have been located which are exceptions to the pattern. They are not significant in showing the dissemination of French music to the Latin countries, but are an indication of the great popularity of certain pieces. The fact that pieces by La Barre, Monnard and Hardel, as well as the inevitable transcriptions from Lully operas, appear even in Italy and Spain attests to their fame. The six manuscripts are the following:

Bologna-360	*30-Cecilia*
29-Chigi	*Madrid-1357*
Vat-mus-569	*31-Madrid-1360*

Bologna-360. *Provenance:* Northern Italy, ca. 1640-1680. *Location:* Bologna; Civico Museo bibliografico musicale, Mss AA 360. *Description:* 192 *l.*, 16 x 24 cm. *Notation:* Mixed (keyboard score, violin, 2 violins with organ bass, guitar number and letter tablature, lute, tromba marina, vocal).

This manuscript, as well as the other Italian sources discussed here, has been studied in some detail in an excellent dissertation by Alexander Silbiger.[153] Although there are three dates mentioned in *Bologna-360*, 1661, 1671 and 1681, Silbiger feels that the great variation of handwriting of the principal scribe suggests an even longer period of compilation. Only two composers are named in this strange mixture of pieces, Frescobaldi and La Barre, and no others have been identified. La Barre appears not to be the "English La Barre" who is found in another Italian keyboard manuscript of the period *(29-Chigi).* The "Minuet di Monsu Labarra" on *l.* 67v is for violin and is not concordant with any known keyboard work. This Italian household manuscript seems to have no other tie to French music.

Chigi (Inventory 29)

The Chigi group of manuscripts at the Vatican Library was also studied in detail by Silbiger, and an inventory of their contents had already been published by Lincoln, who studied them in preparation for a selective and rearranged edition of their contents.[154]   Apel-HKM also drew from the manuscripts, relying on Lincoln's article and edition. Of the five manuscripts in the group, only 29-Chigi ("Chigi Q IV 24") contains French harpsichord music. The manuscript has not been dated with exactness, but Silbiger (p. 201) points out its connection to pieces published by Frescobaldi in 1637 and suggests that it may have been written as early as the decade before midcentury.

The first of the French dances (#30) is attributed to La Barre and the others are ascribed to "the same." The concordances for #30 place the pieces in the group belonging to the English La Barre, but there is no discernable indication that any other pieces came from England.   On the other hand, there is also no indication beyond the corrupted French name, "Monsū della Bara," to suggest that the pieces came directly from France.   29-Chigi, then, neither contradicts nor confirms the English La Barre hypothesis discussed in connection with 16-Cosyn.

Vat-mus-569.   *Provenance:*   Rome, ca. 1660-1665.   *Location:*   Rome;
    Biblioteca Apostolica Vaticana, Ms. Vat. mus. 569.   *Description:*   1
    p.l., i, 118 p., 16 x 22 cm.   *Notation:*   Keyboard score (1 six-line
    and 1 seven-line staff).

Silbiger was the first scholar to call attention to this Roman manuscript.[155] It is dated on p. 88, "Del Sig⁰ Pietro Arnò dall 19 gbῖa [November] 1663."   Four composers are represented in Vat-mus-569: Pietro Arnò, G. B. Ferrini, Fabritio Fontana and Bernardo (Pasquini?). Virginio Mutii and Bonaventura Mini are also named in the manuscript. Silbiger has suggested that the name "Arnò," with its illogical accent mark, might be a corruption of a French name, "Arnauld," and that the pieces in that section of the manuscript (pp. 88-113) might be of French origin.

No musician named "Arnauld" has yet been identified, but there are indeed several French aspects to this section of the manuscript. In addition to the use of French generic titles, "Courante," "Branle," and "Variation" in place of the usual Italian equivalents, there is the use of the French trill sign ($\wedge\wedge$).   Three popular French tunes are found: "Courante Lauginnone" (La Vignon) on p. 96, "Courante La Duchesse" on p. 103 (also found in the very Italian section of the manuscript as "Corrente," pp. 27-28) and the tune known as "La Coquille," here given as "Branle" on p. 112. In addition, the "Sarabanda" on pp. 98-99 is the same tune as the "Sarabande Simple" on *l*. 4r of *28-Brussels-926* and the Sarabande on *l*. 8v of *Stockholm-176* (where it is surely a transcription from a lute tablature). No more specific links to France have been established for *Vat-mus-569*, and it seems to reflect French style in the same way that many Germanic manuscripts of the period did, rather than transmitting original French harpsichord music. It is possible that continued research into Roman keyboard music will establish a connection to the French community there.

Cecilia (Inventory 30)

This late manuscript is also a completely Italian source which has one French section. Here, however, there is no doubt that the keyboard music is of French provenance. *Apel-HKM* (p. 747) called attention to *30-Cecilia* and its French aspect, and Silbiger (pp. 235-237) studied it more closely. Most recently, a fine master's thesis by Anderson has provided a thematic index of the manuscript.[156]

The contents of the source remain largely anonymous, and the dating is based primarily on the French pieces which have been attributed here. Since François Couperin is represented by a Canarie (*l*. 54r-v), the manuscript, or at least that section of it, cannot have been written very much before the turn of the century. Couperin's harpsichord music did not circulate extensively even in France in the seventeenth century, even though some of it was undoubtedly written before 1700, when he was thirty-two. The Canarie here is in quite a different version from the 1713 published text, and it was probably derived from one of the many manuscript copies which Couperin mentioned and deplored in his preface to that first book.

Lebègue's Gavotte (*l*. 47r) and Monnard's Sarabande (*l*. 48r) are the most popular works of those composers. It is likely that the other dance movements in the section came from France also, either as turn-of-the-century harpsichord pieces or as transcriptions. The anonymous organ pieces are of more interest to French studies than the few harpsichord dances. It is curious that an Italian would have brought back pieces which were so extremely unidiomatic for Italian organs. The collection may represent the musical souvenirs of an Italian's trip to Paris.

Madrid-1357
Madrid-1360 (Inventory 31)

The four large volumes which were collected for or by Martin y Coll from 1706 to 1709, were inventoried in 1946 by Anglès and

Subirá.[157]   Anglès had previously inventoried and discussed the manuscripts in his edition of the Cabanilles works (*Anglès* pp. LVII-LXII). The volumes consist, as one would expect, almost exclusively of Spanish music, but two of them contain a few French pieces. In *Madrid-1357*, the only identifiable French piece is a "Minué francés" (pp. 51-52), which is actually a transcription of "Que n'aimez vous" from Lully's *Persée* (1682) IV-6. A "Zarabanda francesa despario . . . [Gigue] . . . Aire de Chacona . . . Canzion al misme aire" group (pp. 88-92) remains anonymous, but may also be French in origin, as is certainly a "Minué franqueza" (p. 232).

31-*Madrid-1360* is a richer source of French music. Not only are the popular Sarabande by Monnard and Gavotte by Hardel present (the latter with Louis Couperin's Double, which frequently accompanied it), but there is an entire group of transcriptions from French music. They draw upon Lully, Gaultier (Pierre "de Marseilles"?) and French popular tunes, including "La Princesse" (#24/10). The scribe carelessly labelled the latter piece as the last of a series of minuets, but the tune is set in its usual duple meter. Of greater interest is La Barre's Sarabande (#23/1). Although the piece belongs to the English La Barre group, it appears to have come directly from France along with the other pieces in this section, not England. Presumably most, if not all, of the pieces from at least #23 to 41 are in some sense French, but it is not likely that significant unique pieces of seventeenth-century French harpsichord music are among them.

One other relationship between Spain (or Portugal) and French harpsichord music should be mentioned here, the ubiquitous *folia* variations, which usually went under the title "Les Folies d'Espagne." The following sets of variations for harpsichord all use the same tune and figure in the present study. With diligence, this list of *folias* could be extended *ad nauseam*:

> 3-*Berlin-40623*
> 10-*Schwerin-617* #2
> 21-*Rés-1186bis* #14
> 21-*Rés-1186bis* #16
> 31-*Madrid-1360* #26
> 33-*Rés-89ter* #21, 68-*d'Anglebert* #49, 15-*Berlin-30206*
>   p. 40
> 34-*Gen-2357 [A]* #1
> 34-*Gen-2357 [A]* #2
> 44-*LaPierre* p. 4, 2A
> 44-*LaPierre* p. 58
> 45-*Dart* #59
> 45-*Dart* #63

46-Menetou #88
RCM
Stockholm-228 l. 10v
Grimm l. 47r
Nuremberg #8
Berlin-30363 l. 3v
Bod-576 p. 16

Summary

The six Italian and Spanish manuscripts listed here contain copies of the most popular French music in the seventeenth-century harpsichord repertoire. In addition, the music of the English La Barre is shown to have been so famous that it was included as a substantial proportion of the French pieces which were carried south. The following is a list of the manuscripts and the French composers found in them:

Bologna-360	ca. 1640-1680	La Barre (violin)
29-Chigi	ca. 1650?	La Barre
Vat-mus-569	ca. 1660-1665	Arnauld?
30-Cecilia	ca. 1700?	François Couperin, Lebègue, Lully, Monnard
Madrid-1357	1706	Lully
31-Madrid-1360	1709	Louis Couperin, Gaultier, Hardel, La Barre, Lully, Monnard

CHAPTER V

FRENCH MANUSCRIPTS

With very few exceptions, "French" is synonymous with "Parisian" in the context of seventeenth-century harpsichord manuscripts. *55-Redon* and probably *37-Geoffroy* come from what are still called "the provinces" (anywhere in France outside the Paris city limits), but all of the other sources are presumed with varying degrees of certainty to be from the capital. Little is known of manuscripts in provincial locations, but France is one of the few countries in modern Europe where treasures are being uncovered regularly, particularly in private hands. Only a few years ago, for example, it was thought that the total of surviving seventeenth-century French harpsichords was about a half a dozen, but more than twice that number are now known.[158] One can realistically hope that in some of the *chateaux* which silently hold these instruments, a few of the manuscripts which were once used with them are still on the book shelves. It is also still possible that the provincial municipal archives hold such sources, as many such libraries have not received cataloging attention since the *Catalogue géneral* was compiled at the turn of the present century.[159] However, the centrality of Paris was real, not illusory. The musical life of the country revolved around that city and its opera king Lully, just as all political eyes turned toward King Louis.

With only one possible exception (*54-Gen-2350/57*) all of the known seventeenth-century harpsichord manuscripts date from the second half of the century. Almost all of them, in fact, date from after 1677; the only unqualified exceptions are *32-Oldham* (ca. 1650-1661) and *55-Redon* (1661). The most important of all French harpsichord manuscripts, *35-Bauyn*, probably comes from as early as 1658, but it, like *38-Gen-2348/53*, could also be logically dated as late as the 1690's.

The sources defy neat categorization. For the purposes of this discussion, they have been divided into four groups: autographs, large collections, smaller collections and household manuscripts. Several of the sources could be placed in more than one of these classifications, and the distinction of "household" versus "professional" is not as sharply drawn as in the Germanic and Scandinavian manuscripts.

Most of these French manuscripts have never been discussed in scholarly publications. Many have been used as the bases of editions of the works of the major composers, but few have received detailed entries in the editors' critical reports. It is an unfortunate fact that *Le Pupitre*, the series which has presented new editions of much of this music, provides minimal editorial notes.

The following manuscripts will be discussed:

Autograph Mss	*41-Thomelin*	*48-LaBarre-6*
32-Oldham	*42-Vm7-6307-2*	*49-RésF-933*
33-Rés-89ter	*43-Gen-2354*	*50-Paignon*
34-Gen-2357[A]	*44-LaPierre*	*LeBret*
Large Collections	*45-Dart*	*51-LaBarre-11*
35-Bauyn	*46-Menetou*	*St-Georges*
36-Parville	*47-Gen-2356*	*52-Rés-2671*
37-Geoffroy	*Burette-407*	*53-Oldham-2*
38-Gen-2348/53	*Burette-408*	**Household Mss**
Smaller Collections	*Burette-409*	*54-Gen-2350/57*
39-Vm7-6307-1	*Burette-410*	*55-Redon*
40-Rés-476	*Arsenal-410/24*	

Autograph Manuscripts

Three manuscripts are now known to have been written by seventeenth-century clavecinists. Two of them, *32-Oldham* and *33-Rés-89ter*, are among the half dozen or so most important sources of the repertoire. The third, *34-Gen-2357[A]* is relatively inconsequential. Several other manuscripts may have been written by the composers themselves, but it cannot be proven. *40-Rés-476* and *Thiéry* were written by a single scribe who must have been closely associated with Nivers. *36-Parville*, *46-Menetou*, *48-LaBarre-6* and *51-LaBarre-11* were all at least partially written by the Berkeley La Barre, who could be the unidentified composer or arranger of some of the pieces in those manuscripts. Finally, although *37-Geoffroy* is not an autograph manuscript, it is a large source which contains the music of a single composer exclusively and is therefore related to this category.

Oldham (Inventory 32)

David Fuller characterized *32-Oldham* as "one of the most important discoveries for the history of keyboard music made in this century. . . ."[160] The only published discussion of the source is the useful and accurate article by the manuscript's owner, Guy Oldham,[161] and most of the music remains unpublished. Louis Couperin's Suite (*32-Oldham* #106-109) is available on an out-of-print recording (DGG ARC-3261), along with a selection of the organ works. The Allemande and Sarabande from the same Suite in *Curtis-Co* (#14 and 5) were based on the *32-Oldham* versions of the pieces; the Allemande is found uniquely in *32-Oldham*. Several facsimiles of pages in *32-Oldham* have appeared in the owner's articles and in Dufourcq's multi-volume series devoted to the French classic organ.[162]

A few comments, in addition to the information found in the Catalog entry, can be added to Oldham's discussion of the manuscript. There can be little question that the primary hand (F) is that of Louis Couperin, on the basis of the many signed pieces in the book. Thus it can be dated with certainty as before 1661, the year of his death. *32-Oldham* probably contains the hands of both Chambonnières and d'Anglebert as well. The d'Anglebert hand (B) is now known from *33-Rés-89ter*. The signature which is above #4 and 12 in *32-Oldham*, as well as the formation of the G clefs, are basically the same as in *33-Rés-89ter*.[163] Furthermore, the use of little curves to indicate appoggiaturas and mordents, which only d'Anglebert employed in the seventeenth century, is found in all four pieces in hand B, not just in the two pieces composed by d'Anglebert. Chambonnières' hand (D) is more problematic, since it is known only from one letter,[164] but the writing is sufficiently similar to support the strong circumstantial evidence that the scribe is the composer himself. Chambonnières' pieces in hand D, unlike those in hand C, are unattributed in the manuscript, and #16 and 18 were both left almost finished with evidence of corrections in the same hand, as if they had been composed directly into the volume. It seems incredible that one manuscript could contain the hands of the three most important composers of the seventeenth-century French harpsichord school, but that appears to be the case. Since Louis Couperin and d'Anglebert were both students of Chambonnières, it is plausible that this book passed among them, finally becoming the property of Couperin. The indentity of the other three hands (A, C and E) remains an especially intriguing mystery.

One factor, which was mentioned in passing by Oldham, is the use of French letter score for two pieces. Both pieces are by d'Anglebert and both are in hand B, the presumed autograph of the composer. Although the notational system here is more elaborate than that found in *6-Munich-1511e* and *7-Munich-1511f*, it is fundamentally the same. In the *32-Oldham* version, the rhythm of the melody is indicated above the staves, as in lute tablature, whereas the Munich version has no rhythmic indications. If the notation was used by d'Anglebert, a major composer, it must have been of some consequence. Its visual similarity to lute tablature may reflect the subservience of the clavecin to the lute at midcentury. A comparison of the incipit of *32-Oldham* #12 in the original notation and the 1689 published version of the same piece illustrates the notation (see also Ex. 7, p. 38):

Ex. 10. Incipits of the Gaillarde (Sarabande) by d'Anglebert (*32-Oldham* #12 and *68-d'Anglebert* #26)

32-Oldham is most important as the only source of the organ works of Louis Couperin, but from the standpoint of the harpsichord, it is most significant for its Chambonnières pieces, five of which are unique. The themes of these pieces are made available for the first time in the Catalog incipits (#16, 18, 20-21 and 26).

Rés-89ter (Inventory 33)

Kenneth Gilbert was not the first to associate *33-Rés-89ter* with d'Anglebert, as he pointed out in the preface to his edition of the d'Anglebert works (*Gilbert*, pp. VII-VIII), but he was the first to compare the hand of the titles to the many known examples of d'Anglebert's signature. A detailed article putting forth the evidence showing that *33-Rés-89ter* was written by d'Anglebert himself is forthcoming, and only the conclusions will be given here. The most conclusive d'Anglebert document is one which is dated 6 May 1691 and shows the signatures of the entire family, facilitating the comparison of the formations of the name.[165] There is little doubt that the name as it appears in *33-Rés-89ter* is the same as the signature of Jean-Henri d'Anglebert. There are many examples of the name in *33-Rés-89ter* and other documents with his signature which support this conclusion. It can be assumed, then, that all of the transcriptions in this keyboard manuscript were arranged by d'Anglebert, an attribution confirmed by the stylistic evidence of texture and the use of distinctive ornaments.

The dating of the manuscript can logically be narrowed to a period of three years. It cannot have been compiled before 1677, the date of the premiere of Lully's *Isis*, from which #42c was transcribed.

A posterior date of 1689 is certain, since the composer would have had no reason to recopy fourteen of the pieces which appeared in his own published volume of that year. D'Anglebert drew regularly from the works of Lully and since there is no transcription from *Prosperine* (1680) in *33-Rés-89ter*, and there is one in the print (*68-d'Anglebert* #48), it is probable that the manuscript was completed before 1680. The volume shows no signs of having been compiled over a long period, except for the irrelevant eighteenth-century additions. Thus the likely date of *33-Rés-89ter* is 1677-1680.

Gen-2357[A] (Inventory 34)

This fragment from a manuscript is technically an autograph because of the title of #2, "Couplett des folies d'espagnes de ma fasson." The conjectural date, 1690, is based on the fact that the paper is the same as that found in another manuscript from the same collection, *47-Gen-2356*, which is probably from about 1690. Musically, *34-Gen-2357[A]* is of little significance. It should not be confused with the other manuscript with which it is now bound, *54-Gen-2350/57*. The keyboard manuscripts at the Bibliothèque Sainte Geneviève must have been in considerable disarray when they were put into their rude modern bindings, as a number of them are misbound, necessitating the cumbersome number codes adopted here to distinguish unrelated manuscripts and to bring together separated fragments.[166]

Large Collections

Four manuscripts provide a total of 674 compositions, 557 of which are different pieces of seventeenth-century French harpsichord music (including transcriptions from nonharpsichord works, but excluding doubles). From the standpoint of size and quality, they are among the most important sources of the repertoire. *46-Menetou*, for example, is excluded from this category in spite of its size because it consists almost exclusively of opera transcriptions. Each of these manuscripts is a different type of collection. Together they reflect the entire spectrum of harpsichord music, its origins and styles in the second half of the seventeenth century. They present the most popular works of the repertoire (Chambonnières' works and certain pieces by Monnard and Lebègue) and the most obscure (the works of Geoffroy). Each manuscript is organized differently. There is a large anthology organized by composer, but not in suites (*35-Bauyn*); one source consists of compiled attributed suites (*36-Parville*); another has unattributed suites (*38-Gen-2348/53*); and a fourth has composed suites (*37-Geoffroy*).

Bauyn (Inventory 35)

The single most important source of seventeenth-century French harpsichord music is *35-Bauyn*. It is the largest source of the music of both Chambonnières (*35-Bauyn-I*) and Louis Couperin (*35-Bauyn-II*), while also presenting a wide sampling of other music which was prized by a discriminating Parisian harpsichordist (*35-Bauyn-III*). Although it is a familiar manuscript to virtually all scholars of early keyboard music, this *sine qua non* of clavecin music has never been discussed in detail. The incipits of the works appeared in various locations in Écorcheville's catalog of the Bibliothèque nationale,[167] but an inventory of the manuscript has never been published. The only discussions have been an entry to *MGG* (s.v. "Bauyn") by Reimann, and François Lesure's preface to *Minkoff*, a new facsimile edition of *35-Bauyn*. Their biographical information concerning the Bauyn d'Angervilliers and Mathefelon families, whose coat of arms appears on the covers of the volumes, cannot be improved here. No marriage between these two families has been discovered, and therefore the owner, who may or may not have been responsible for the compilation, cannot be specifically identified. Reimann and Lesure both point out the possibility that he was one Prosper Bauyn (d. 1700), a Parisian who was "maître de la Chambre aux deniers du roi."

Reimann's summary discussion of the contents and dating are superceded by the information in the present Catalog. It should be noted that the Index to *Minkoff* attributed great numbers of anonymous pieces to the last named composer in *35-Bauyn-III* without any justification whatever. There is also no proof that the Hardel of *35-Bauyn* was Gilles as stated in the Preface, or Guillaume as listed in the Index (cf. p. 323 below). Mechanical errors in the Index of *Minkoff* are corrected in the present Catalog Inventory.

It is a great frustration that such an important source is anonymous and undatable. The dating adopted here, "post 1658," is based on the fact that 1658 is mentioned with one piece (*35-Bauyn-II* #122), but there is no indication of how long after 1658 the manuscript was compiled. The repertoire could have been collected as early as 1658, but the close parallels with *36-Parville* (after 1686) in both the selection and readings of the pieces, suggest that the contents of *35-Bauyn* could still have been fashionable in the last decade of the century. Reimann dated it on the basis of the date of Couperin's arrival in Paris and the publication date of *62-Chamb-I*. However, she assumed that any piece copied after the publication date of a print would necessarily be copied from that print. A comparison of the incipits of the post-1670 Chambonnières manuscripts makes it abundantly clear that the pieces continued to circulate in manuscripts without any regard for the printed readings. To cite a specific example, *24-Babell* (1702) includes three pieces which were also in *62-Chamb-I*, two from *63-Chamb-II* and two which were not in the prints. The readings of the works are not at all the same in the eighteenth-century manuscript (*24-Babell*) and the prints. The strongest suggestion that *35-Bauyn* was compiled in the third rather than the final quarter of the century is the absence of any transcriptions from Lully's works. There are, however, no transcriptions from earlier stage works either, and it is possible--even probable, in view of certain peculiarities to be discussed below--that the compiler consciously eschewed such transcriptions.

In an anonymous and undated source, one is drawn to the slightest unusual features which might help to identify it. The only two marginal notations in this very professionally notated manuscript appear to have no meaning other than proving to the scribe that his pen was in order (see "Marginalia" in the Catalog entry; "qui" has been suppressed in *Minkoff*). The greatest inexplicable feature of *35-Bauyn* is the extensive crossing-out of titles and even of one entire piece. The words which were obliterated were carefully covered over, seemingly by the original hand, in neat .d's, thus:

Fig. 5. Title of *35-Bauyn-I* #122, "Gigue la Coquette de Mr de Chambonnieres."

The deletions seem to follow a pattern, but one which is not strictly maintained, and whose significance has not yet been divined. It was the nongeneric titles and three dance names (gaillarde, gavotte and menuet) which were removed from the titles. Is this some sort of moral purging of overly profane or modern elements from a purely secular manuscript? The crossed-out words and those words which seemingly should have been deleted, but were left untouched, are listed below:

Words actually crossed out:

I	#44:	la mignonne
I	#56:	La Madelainette
I	#107:	dit l'Entrien des Dieux
I	#111:	La Drollerie du même Auteur
I	#122:	la Coquette
I	#123:	Gaillarde
I	#127:	Gaillarde

I	# 127a:	Gaillarde
II	# 29:	Menuet de Mr
II	# 54:	Pastourelle
II	# 61:	Gaillarde
II	# 73:	branle de basque
II	# 77:	Gaillarde
II	# 81:	Tombeau de Mr de Blancrocher
II	# 112:	Menuet
III	# 50:	Gauotte
III	# 50a:	de la gauotte
III	# 62:	Gauotte
III	# 63:	de gaillarde
III	# 78:	Menuet

Words of a similar type not crossed out:

I	# 1:	Le Moutier
I	# 3:	La Dunquerque
I	# 30:	la Loureuse
I	# 31:	La toute belle
I	# 57:	Bruscanbille
I	# 98:	La villageoise
I	# 102:	l'afflégée
II	# 103:	La Piémontoise

In addition, one entire composition is crossed out. It is impossible to read in a microfilm or *Minkoff*, but it can be deciphered by reference to the manuscript itself.[168] Stylistically it appears to be exactly what the title implies: an Italian melody transcribed by a Frenchman for harpsichord. The entire piece is as follows:[169]

Ex. 11. Air Italien (*35-Bauyn-III* #17)

The relationship of *35-Bauyn* to *36-Parville* is a close one. The great number of concordances between the two manuscripts and the similarity of the musical texts of specific pieces suggest that they may have been derived in part from the same original manuscripts. Particularly in Louis Couperin's works, the correspondence is striking.

In the 1732 edition of *Le Parnasse*, Titon du Tillet remarked on the rarity of Louis Couperin's works:

Nous n'avons de ce Musicien que trois suites de Pièces de Clavecin d'un travail et d'un goût admirable: Elles n'ont point été imprimées, mais plusieurs bons connoisseurs en Musique les ont manuscrites et les conservent précieusement.[170]

The comment indicates not only that Titon du Tillet knew a manuscript, now lost, which contained three suites by Louis Couperin, but that he was unaware of any manuscript with a large number of pieces, such as either *35-Bauyn* or *36-Parville.*

The high degree of correspondance between the order of Couperin's pieces in *35-Bauyn-II* and *36-Parville* is not proof of their having been derived from a common source, however.   The scribe of *36-Parville* drew suites of pieces which usually contained only one example of each dance type in a key.   Because of the standard practice of presenting pieces in the order of allemande-courante-sarabande-other, the pieces inevitably fall into almost the same order as is found in *35-Bauyn-II.*   There are many omissions, however, because there are fewer pieces in *36-Parville.*   The following list shows the relationship of Couperin's pieces in the two manuscripts:

Abbreviations:

A	Allemande	G	Gigue
C	Courante	Ga	Gaillarde
Ca	Canarie	M	Menuet
Ch	Chaconne	P	Prélude
D	Descriptive title		

Keys are listed in parentheses.   Discrepancies which cannot be explained by key organization are marked with an asterisk.

35-Bauyn-II #	*36-Parville #*	Title,	key
1	2	P	(d)
2	25	P	(D)
3	35	P	(g)
6	45	P	(a)
7	46	P	(a)
10	58	P	(C)
11	59	P	(C)
12	75	P	(F)
13	76	P	(F)
14	101	P	(e)
30	70	A	(c)
31	71	C	(c)
32	72	S	(c)
33	73	G	(c)
34	74	Ch	(c)
36	4	A	(d)

35-Bauyn-II #	36-Parville #	Title, key	
39	*10	C	(d)
41	5	C	(d)
49	6	S	(d)
52	8	Ca	(d)
54	9	D	(d)
55	12	Ch	(d)
57	13	Ch	(d)
58	26	A	(D)
60	28	S	(D)
62	*27	Ch	(D)
63	30	A	(e)
64	31	C	(e)
65	32	S	(e)
67	77	A	(F)
68	78	C	(F)
72	85	S	(F)
77	*84	Ga	(F)
82	88	A	(G)
84	89	C	(G)
87	*98	S	(G)
88	100	Ga	(G)
89	99	Ch	(G)
92	36	A	(g)
93	37	C	(g)
95	*39	Ch	(g)
96	38	S	(g)
102	47	A	(a)
106	48	C	(a)
110	50	S	(a)
112	53	M	(a)
116	102	A	(b)
117	103	C	(b)
118	104	S	(b)
123	*7	G	(d)

Key organization:

35-Bauyn-II	36-Parville
(Préludes)	
C	
c	
d	d
D	D
e	e
F	
G	
g	g
a	a
b	

35-Bauyn-II   *36-Parville*

C
C
F
G
e
b

The compositions by La Barre in *35-Bauyn-III* (#32, 34, 55, 61, 66 and 69) are part of a group of pieces which are by the "Bauyn La Barre." With the exception of #32, they are unrelated to English sources,[171] and the pieces by the English La Barre discussed above. Two of the three pieces here were copied twice: #32 is a variant of #66, and #34 of 61. In both cases, the scribe copied them once with the name Allemande and once called Gigue (cf. a similar procedure in *66-Perrine*). One (#61) is attributed to Joseph La Barre (1633-pre 1678), but the others cannot be specifically attributed. It is probable that all of the works by the Bauyn La Barre are by Joseph, but it is at least possible that the one piece was ascribed to him to distinguish it from the others. The following pieces require further comments:

I #6, 94: The readings are not exactly the same, suggesting that this Courante was copied from two different sources.

I #7: Although the piece is included here in the group of courantes, it is not a courante in style. The courante title is only implied here ("Autre du même Auteur") and the nongeneric title in *24-Babell* is preferable: La Sotise.

I #18, II #28: This is the only proven case of a mistaken attribution in *35-Bauyn*. To judge on the basis of style, the simple Sarabande could have been written by either Chambonnières or Louis Couperin, which is undoubtedly the reason that the conflicting attribution has escaped notice until now.

I #20: The similarity of d'Anglebert's Gaillarde, cited in the concordances, to this Sarabande probably represents an homage to his teacher, Chambonnières.

I #36: Although "Les Barricades" is called a courante here, it is in the style of a gigue. The nongeneric title from *62-Chamb-I* is preferable. The similarity to an Allemande by La Barre (III #32) shows the closeness of the gigue form to certain allemandes (here called "gigue-allemandes") and may also represent an homage of La Barre for Chambonnières. The Allemande by Dumont (*59-Dumont-1657 l.* 31v) is even more similar to that of Chambonnières.

I #64: This Courante is actually a duplicate of #63 except that the scribe omitted the tenor voice in the first measure. It was copied a second time apparently in order to present it with a G^2 clef in place of the C^1 clef of #63. The reason for this practice is not clear, since both clefs were used often enough in contemporary sources that one can assume that they were easily read by seventeenth-century harpsichordists. The same phenomenon occurs in *32-Oldham*, #15 and 15a, another piece by Chambonnières.

I #70-71: These are exact duplicates except for the one slight variant shown in the incipit. Presumably the scribe stopped copying after #70 and began again with the same piece by mistake.

I #73: This is exactly the same as #63.

I #86: Curtis included this Chaconne in his edition of Louis Couperin's works on the basis of the "overwhelming evidence of style," rejecting the ascription in *35-Bauyn*. The attributions in this manuscript are generally very accurate, although one mistake has been identified (cf. I #18).

I #91: This Courante provides an example of the seventeenth-century use of the double dot (meas. 1); double dots are also found in *32-Oldham* (see also *35-Bauyn-II* #35). It is also further proof of the closeness of *35-Bauyn* to *36-Parville*. Of the five concordant versions, the one in *36-Parville* is the closest to this one. There are a few exceptions to this pattern (e.g., I #79), but many of Chambonnières' pieces here must have come from the same sources as were used for *36-Parville*.

I #118: This Sarabande is a rare example of a transposed harpsichord piece. Aside from the peculiar pieces in *37-Geoffroy*, original harpsichord music was almost always copied in its original key, unlike transcriptions (cf. *33-Rés-89ter* #9-9a). It is noteworthy that the transposition here is only by one step (cf. *24-Babell* #172 for another example).

II #6: *Brunold-Co* omitted the third section of this Prélude by mistake, but *Brunold/Dart-Co* confused the issue further by adding the lacking section as a separate piece in Appendix III. The correct version is found in *Curtis-Co*.[172]

II #86: The similarity of the theme of this Courante to that of *68-d'Anglebert* #3 presumably constitutes another homage.

II #90-90a: The pieces were garbled in the *Brunold-Co* but were corrected in *Brunold/Dart-Co*.

II #97: The notation at the end of the piece, "Paris au mois de Decembre 1656," undoubtedly stems from Couperin himself. There are many such notations in the holograph of the organ works, *32-Oldham*.

II #112-112a: The original Menuet is probably not by Couperin, since only the Double is attributed to him in both *35-Bauyn-III* and *36-Parville*.

III #5: This Toccata might have been played or copied in Brussels in 1650, but it could not have been composed then. It appears in an autograph manuscript by Froberger which is dated 1649 in Vienna ("B" in *Adler-I*; cf. Schott, I:33). It is surprising that a Frenchman would make the agreement error found in the title, "Toccat*a* . . . fatt*o*. . . ."

III #11-14, 73:   These pieces by Froberger are known exclusively from Parisian manuscripts.

III #16: This Fantaisie is unique, but Adler included it in his Froberger edition, presumably on the basis of unstated stylistic grounds and because it follows other Froberger works in this manuscript. *35-Bauyn-III* is exceedingly miscellaneous and the juxtaposition of pieces is little help in attributing them. In any case, Fantaisies are generally organ works, not harpsichord pieces.

III #21-22, 39: Measured preludes are generally found in organ manuscripts, not as harpsichord pieces. They are, however, frequently unidiomatic for either instrument.

III #35-38:   The voice leading of the first three pavanes is unusually strict for harpsichord music; the fourth is more free. They are probably transcriptions from instrumental works.

III #42:   This Pavane is probably a transcription from an English lute piece. The use of the C^2 clef is common in transcriptions from lute works, because of the low, close voicing which typifies the music (cf. #52, 64, 65 and 90, which are all known to be by lutenists and use C^2 clefs in the harpsichord versions).

III #44-49:   Hardel's suite must have circulated as a complete unit, although it has not survived in any other manuscript intact. The title in *44-LaPierre* (p. 45) specifies "Première Courante," suggesting that it was copied from the entire suite. The second Courante was not copied.

III #51: This may be based on d'Anglebert's transcription of the piece. Except for ornamentation, the texts are almost identical.

III #58, 87: The slight variants between the two versions are noted in *Bonfils-13.*

III #59: This is almost a duplicate of #53. The variants are noted in *Bonfils-18.*

III #63:   It is curious that while Chambonnières, Louis Couperin and even Hardel are well represented in *35-Bauyn*, d'Anglebert is absent except for this piece. It is consistent with the compiler's avoidance of stage transcriptions, however, since d'Anglebert was both musically and personally associated with the little Italian impresario.

III #68: Adler attributed this Sarabande to Froberger without comment. There is no justification for considering it Froberger's work.

III #71-72: Oldham made a case for doubting that these pieces are by different composers because they are associated in *32-Oldham*, but the conjecture is fruitless. They could have come together in *32-Oldham* and then circulated together without having been written by a single composer. Without other supporting evidence, there is no reason to reject the attributions in *35-Bauyn.*

III #79: This, like #42, is probably a transcription of an English lute piece, to judge by the texture and clefs.

III #87: The slight variants between this and #58 are cited in *Bonfils-13.*

III #91: Rossi's Passacaille might be a transcription from an instrumental or vocal work by that composer. He is not known to have written harpsichord music, but he was a connoisseur.[173] No original for the Passacaille has been found in *Orfeo* (which was composed and premiered during his Paris stay) or in Caluoris' catalog.[174] In view of the texture of the piece, it must be considered an original harpsichord work until definite evidence proves otherwise.

III #92: This Gigue by Richard uses the same theme or at least opening motive as a Gigue by Froberger which was known in Paris. Froberger's piece can be dated September, 1649,[175] before his Parisian visit (1652). Thus it was probably Richard who imitated Froberger, rather than Froberger honoring the Parisian.

Parville (Inventory 36)

36-Parville, like *32-Oldham,* is a major seventeenth-century harpsichord manuscript which has come to light only recently. Alan Curtis described the circumstances of its appearance in the Berkeley collection with a large group of related manuscripts in 1968. He promptly published a title inventory and description of the entire collection and subsequently used *36-Parville* as the main source for his Louis Couperin edition.[176]

The most important pieces are those in the main hand (A), but the last hand of the volume (I) is of great significance historically because it is the same as the hand which is found in several other Berkeley manuscripts, and it is therefore almost certainly that of the Berkeley La Barre (see pp. 116-117 for a discussion of this La Barre and the subsequent history of the Berkeley collection). The manuscript must have been acquired by that La Barre in the early eighteenth century, and it is possible that it had been compiled (hand A or hands A-H) by an earlier La Barre, or someone close to the family. This is particularly likely in view of the fact that there are nine pieces by the Bauyn La Barre in *36-Parville* (all in hand A), more than are found in any other single source (cf. p. 296). Hand A cannot be that of Joseph La Barre, the most likely identification of the Bauyn La Barre, since he died before 1678 and hand A of *36-Parville* wrote in the book after 1686. Pierre IV (1634-pre 1710) is the most logical choice among the family members who have been identified. The binding was added after the compilation was complete and therefore the "M. de Parville" of the cover stamping is probably a later owner.

The cross marks which are found at the tops of most of the pieces in *36-Parville*, like a number of other French manuscripts, probably are the marks of a copyist, indicating that he had copied (or intended to copy) the pieces into another manuscript. They are clues which could lead to tracing one manuscript to another, but no such relationships have yet been deduced among the known French sources.

The organization of *36-Parville* (hand A only) is the clearest example of compiled suites in a French source. Each key group follows a similar pattern in the order of the movements: prélude-allemande-courante-sarabande-other. The "other" category usually consists of a gigue, canarie or chaconne, followed by gavottes, gaillardes and opera transcriptions. There is frequently more than one dance of a given genre, and the order of dances after the sarabande(s) is no more standardized than the length of the entire group. Whether or not these groups should be taken specifically as suites--that is performing orders, as opposed to anthologies from which to derive suites--is a separate and difficult issue. The similarity of the organization here to other French sources--especially *33-Rès-89ter* and the printed collections, Inventories 62-65 and 68--indicates that the pattern of the *36--Parville* groups was universal, and therefore was surely also the correct performing order. The extreme variation in the length of such groups and their lack of circulation as single entities prove that no specific large group should be considered an inviolate suite.[177]

A few pieces require specific comments:

#1: Although this Prélude is not attributed in the manuscript, no such piece, with a fugal, fully notated middle section, is known by any composer other than Louis Couperin.

#24: *Curtis-Berkeley* (p. 161) was in error in citing a concordance to *Egerton-814*, which contains an unrelated chanson with the same title. The piece in *36-Parville* is a Lully transcription.

#44: The tune in the chanson manuscript, *Egerton-2514*, is a somewhat different version.

#52a: This Double circulated widely with Hardel's Gavotte. It was even copied into a 1717 violin manuscript (*Vm7-4867*), which also contains versions of pieces by François Couperin and Lully among the violin works.

#54-57: The copyist obviously entered the titles separately from the pieces, perhaps in small groups. With *#54*, he entered the title for *#55* and so forth, realizing his errors at *#57* and then going back to correct them.

#79, 82: This Courante appears twice in both *35-Bauyn* and *36-Parville*, but in *35-Bauyn* the same version was copied twice in succession, an obvious error. Here the second copy (*#82*) is quite a different text, copied from a different source.

#97: The first strain of this unique Courante in G Major is remarkably similar to a Courante in F Major by Lebègue (*64-Lebègue-I* *#39*).

#110-111: In view of the fact that these transcriptions follow one known to have been made by d'Anglebert and that they also use ornament signs which were part of his vocabulary, there is good reason to suspect that he may have been the arranger of all three pieces.

#116: This Chaconne is very unusual in that it appears in three different keys and with three quite different titles in the concordant keyboard versions. It is known to be in Lully's *Ballet des muses*, but its placement in *46-Menetou*, as well as its title there ("Pleurs d'atis"), suggest that it was also used in a production of *Atys*.

#143: There are several melodies which add the title "Menuet de Poitou" (cf. *36-Parville* *#53*, as well as Écorcheville, *Catalogue*, 4:210, 212, 213, 216, 217).

#144: This Prélude is not known elsewhere, but its opening is identical to *35-Bauyn-II* *#6*, lending great support to Curtis' attribution of the piece to Louis Couperin on stylistic grounds.

Geoffroy (Inventory 37)

This manuscript is a strange and self-contained chapter in the history of French harpsichord music. It was discussed in some detail by Roche, who provided sufficient biographical information to prove that the Geoffroy of the manuscript was certainly the organist Jean-Nicolas Geoffroy who died in 1694.[178] In the same year that Roche wrote her study, a master's thesis *(Campbell)* on *37-Geoffroy* appeared; it includes transcriptions of some of the pieces. Apel's comment on *37-Geoffroy* is clever and apt from the standpoint of the style of the music, but it is wrong in its dating:

> Its very interesting contents, however, point to a later time, about 1730-40. Various pieces give the impression that an 18th-century Satie is involved. [*Apel-HKM,* p. 815, n. 45]

Apel made his judgments on the basis of the harmonic characteristics of the pieces, no doubt, but the biographical evidence cannot be ignored. The dance titles and the lack of pictorial titles are also in keeping with seventeenth, not eighteenth-century practice.

37-Geoffroy is the largest source of the music of a single composer in this repertoire. Some of the dances are in relatively full *style-brisé* texture, similar to that used by Lebègue, but many are brief two-voiced pieces which are little more than sketches. The scribe who made the anthology gives the impression of having been an overly earnest, very myopic clerk. The 255 pieces are squeezed into 180 pages, with every available space used. Some pieces continue in three to five miscellaneous locations. A piece such as #220 is "entered" in the manuscript, but it could never be played without being recopied, since one must turn from p. 138 to the bottom of p. 30 and then to the bottom of p. 61 to complete it. The scribe gave elaborate, redundant directions and cross references to the pieces. The result is a "scholarly edition" in the pejorative sense.

Also singular in *37-Geoffroy* is the use of transpositions for many of the pieces. The reason for the laboriously copied versions is not clear, but it must be related to the occasionally strange chromatic writing and the temperament(s) assumed by the composer. Although the pieces sometimes wander a great distance harmonically, the principal keys which were used, as well as the nomenclature and signatures for them reflect a conservative concept of tonality which was still tied to the church modes.

Not a single piece by Geoffroy has been found in another manuscript. They seem not to have circulated at all, but the scribe frequently refers to pieces copied from the composer's "opera de clauecin," including some which apparently appeared there in another key. The references give the impression that the "opera" was a published volume, or at least a fair copy, of an organized collection. The following pieces in *37-Geoffroy* were drawn from it:

1	Allemande la confidente (c)
35	Allemande de la plaisante gaye (D)
46	Danse villageoise (D)
80	Allemande la resueuse (F)
95	Gavotte serenade (G)
96	Menuet Serenade (G)
102	Rondeau (G)
103	Rondeau (G)
105	Danse paysanne (G)
106	Air de bergère (G)
107	Air de bergère (G)
108	Air de bergère (G)
109	La Muzette (G)
125	Basque (a)
163?	Menuet (F; in E in the "opera")
216	Rondeau petite niaizerie (g)

220   Allemande la sans pareille (G)
222   Menuet (G)
224   Rondeau fantaisie (G)
225   Danse paysanne (G)
234?   Chaconne (G; in A in the "opera")
251   Dialogue pour le clavecin et des violes (E)
252   Dialogue pour le clavecin et des violes (G; in A
       in the "opera")
253,
254   Grande pièce de joye (g)

255?   Symphonie pour 3 violes (G; in A in the "opera")

In addition, the following pieces were marked with a circle, seemingly a copyist's mark, and may have been taken from or copied into another source:

118-121
124-125
226-227

A careful examination of the music of Geoffroy and a discussion of its relationship to the history of harpsichord music would be a valuable project. As in the music of Gesualdo in the sixteenth century, the pieces are a peculiar combination of a traditional idiom with a harmonic vocabulary which is sometimes so mannered as to seem bizarre.

Gen-2348/53 (Inventory 38)

There is no external basis on which this source can be even approximately dated. It is here given the same date as *35-Bauyn* because it contains similar repertoire, with the addition of a group of anonymous French organ pieces.

Only one piece is attributed in *38-Gen-2348/53* itself (#38, "Gigue La Villageoise De Mr Chambonnieres"). Most of the works are known elsewhere, and the majority are by Chambonnières. The readings of the known pieces are very good and this manuscript is therefore an important source even though it is considerably smaller than the other manuscripts discussed in this group. The seven pieces which remain anonymous (#7, 8, 11, 15, 19, 30 and 35) have been ignored by scholars, but they are certainly works of one of the major composers of the Parisian school, like all of the other harpsichord pieces in the manuscript. Some, if not all of of them are probably by Chambonnières.

Smaller Collections

The manuscripts which are discussed in this group are of slightly less significance than those in the preceding categories. Most of them, however, have at least one or two features which are unique and make them important sources of seventeenth-century French harpsichord music.

Vm7-6307-1 (Inventory 39)

This manuscript could also logically be categorized as a household manuscript. The mixture of viol and harpsichord music draws attention to the fact that the viol was considered to be essentially a chordal instrument like the lute and harpsichord, not a melody instrument like the violin. As in the household books, the harpsichord section opens with an unmeasured prelude, a student's first piece. The manuscript is otherwise of little importance and is unrelated to the source which has been bound with it, *42-Vm7-6307-2.*

Rés-476 (Inventory 40)

It is greatly to be lamented that the new edition of this manuscript (*Bonfils-LP*) has perpetuated the erroneous association of Geoffroy with it by listing that name on the cover in large letters. As the preface to that edition explains (p. VIII), *40-Rés-476* has absolutely nothing to do with Geoffroy except that it was numbered with, and presumably acquired with another manuscript in the Conservatory collection which does contain the music of Geoffroy, "Rés-475," here called *37-Geoffroy.* Bonfils suggested that the manuscript might have been compiled about 1690 because #30 is a continuo part for a motet by Nivers which was published in 1689. However, *40-Rés-476*--like the exclusively organ manuscript, *Thiéry* (cf. *Bonfils-25*), in the same hand--is closely related to Nivers in style and content. There is no reason to assume that the continuo part could not have been written for a pre-publication manuscript copy of the motet. Therefore the dating adopted here is slightly earlier, "post 1679," based on the presence of a transcription from *Bellérophon.* *Bonfils-LP* is otherwise both accurate and useful, containing well-chosen facsimiles.

40-Rés-476 is primarily important as a source of organ music. The hand is uniform until #27, where it changes. It is also different, but not enough to suggest a different scribe, in #35. It would seem that the pieces at the end of the manuscript were added later, thus explaining the sudden appearance of harpsichord pieces in a manuscript which contained organ music up to that point. *Howell* presents the Lully transcriptions as organ music, but his argument cannot be given credence because it ignores the many other examples of the presence of harpsichord and organ music in the same manuscripts (e.g. *38-Gen-2348/53*). The Lully transcriptions have a texture which is very different from the organ music in the volume, and they are much more highly ornamented. *Howell* is also flawed by the fact that *Thiéry* is cited as the source of the pieces ("rés 2094" in place of "Rés 475"), and a series of typographical errors establishes Lully as an eighteenth-century composer!

Thomelin (Inventory 41)

This single sheet was found in a printed volume of music in 1939. There are no marginalia in that volume or in *41-Thomelin* to show that they ever had any relationship to each other. The date ("ca. 1680-1700") is a conjecture based on the composer's life span: ca. 1640-1693. No other harpsichord music is known by Thomelin, although an organ piece has recently been discovered (*28-Brussels-926 l.* 69v).

Vm7-6307-2 (Inventory 42)

Although three of the pieces in this manuscript remain anonymous, they are undoubtedly transcriptions from operatic music, like the identified pieces. The melody of #2, "La Furstenburg," was exceedingly popular over a long period in France.[179] *42-Vm7-6307-2* is one of many examples of the importance of Lully operas to the French harpsichord repertoire.

Most of the compositions in the Catalog Inventories which are known to be by Lully have been located in one or another of the stage works or in one of the volumes of miscellaneous trios. However, a few pieces such as *42-Vm7-6302* #11 cannot be located (cf. p. 308). One assumes that they, too, are transcribed from such instrumental originals, but there is a possibility that Lully composed some music for harpsichord. He is known to have studied the instrument in Paris, and he could have written a few keyboard dances.

Gen-2354 (Inventory 43)

This brief manuscript from the end of the century is also of minor importance. The last three pieces have not been identified, but they appear consecutively in *47-Gen-2356*, establishing a link between the two manuscripts from the Sainte Geneviève collection. The title of #3, "Ballet du Basque" and the tunefulness of all three melodies are typical of music transcribed from stage scores. If these are transcriptions, both manuscripts present not only the same tunes but the same harpsichord arrangements.

LaPierre (Inventory 44)

Geneviève Thibault (Mme de Chambure) was one of the most important forces in the Parisian harpsichord world in this century. Her collection of instruments and manuscripts and her control as curator of the Conservatory collection made her a major resource for harpsichordists and scholars. At least one manuscript which was in her collection is relevant to this study, but the complicated legal proceedings which followed her sudden death have made it completely unavailable at the time of this writing.[180] David Fuller studied *44-LaPierre* in 1966 and kindly allowed his notes to be used as the source of information for the Catalog Inventory presented here. He had copied incipits for most of the pieces, which allowed the identification of them here. The incipits were taken as rough notes for his personal use, and because of their fragmentary nature it was decided not to include them in the Catalog below.

The compilation of the manuscript probably began in 1687 when "Mlle de La Pierre began to play the harpsichord" (*l.* i). The date and name at the other end of the volume (Mad^e Le Noble, 1730) are probably irrelevant, since almost all of the pieces at that end were copied from the 1687 end. It is possible that *44-LaPierre* was originally two manuscripts, one copied from the other, which were subsequently bound together. If it was always a single volume, the pieces at the Le Noble end were obviously copied from the same sources as those at the La Pierre end. The collection is quite miscellaneous, with pieces frequently grouped by key, but without any perceivable "suite" ordering.

A few works are of particular interest:

p. 1, 34, 56, 1A, 43A: 44-LaPierre contains an unusual number of unmeasured preludes. All but the last are notated in mixed note values similar to the style of Lebègue.

p. 12: This Courante was hitherto known only in the Munich sources. Its presence here in a French source is further evidence of the French origins of the Munich manuscripts. The concordance to an English source, *22a-Roper*, suggests that this Courante was unusually popular.

p. 14-15: The first Rigaudon, which acquired a Double by Louis Couperin (*36-Parville* #67a), can now be paired with a second one. It is not clear whether they are related to the following Rigaudon, but only the first two were copied into the other end of *44-LaPierre*, the second probably also coming from *Acis et Galathée.*

p. 16: The reading of the name "Favier" is not certain. Two French violinists by that name were active at Versailles (cf. p. 321).

p. 20: It is not yet clear whether this is the same Double as is found in *32-Oldham,* or another one on the same Courante.

p. 59A, 61A: The models for these pieces have not been identified, but the keyboard textures are not the same in the various concordances, proving that they are transcriptions, presumably from stage music.

Dart (Inventory 45)

45-Dart has never been studied or discussed by a scholar other than its late owner, Thurston Dart. He cited his manuscript twice in editions, but he never described it.[181] The most important piece is the Chaconne #31 which Dart included in his Louis Couperin edition in an appendix. He pointed out that it could have been written by any member of the Couperin family. Attributions on the basis of style are very unreliable when one is dealing with short pieces written in a common idiom, but if there is one style which stands out as singularly recognizable, it is that of the chaconnes by Louis Couperin. They share a propensity for low-voiced textures with extravagantly beautiful harmony derived from the use of dissonance and nonchord tones. Nothing could be less like the simple Chaconne in *45-Dart.* A second clue to the real origin of the piece is a concordance to *46-Menetou* where the same theme and two of the same variations are found along with two quite different variations. Since almost all of the pieces in *46-Menetou* are opera transcriptions, as are many in *45-Dart,* it is probable that this Chaconne is also a transcription. The Chaconne is surrounded by known Lully transcriptions in *46-Menetou,* but one cannot make definite assumptions on the basis of the juxtaposition of pieces in manuscript collections: *46-Menetou* #102 is also in a section of transcriptions, but it is an original harpsichord piece by Lebègue. If this Chaconne is a transcription, the substantial differences between the two versions would be understandable. Whether or not a Couperin made the arrangement in *45-Dart,* or was actually responsible for the original, it is almost certainly not a harpsichord work by Louis Couperin.

The second important aspect of *45-Dart* is the inclusion of two unique works attributed to Chambonnières (#61 and 62). The pieces are in the inelegant hand of the earliest scribe (A), and the Courante #62 in particular is inaccurately notated, as one can see by looking at the rhythm of the second measure of the incipit. Such rhythmic imprecision is not found in other pieces in the manuscript and may not be simple carelessness on the part of the scribe. It is possible that the pieces were originally in French letter score and were here transcribed by someone with an imperfect understanding of how to effect the transition from one notation to the other (cf. Examples 7 and 10, pp. 38 and 94, above).

The first scribe of *45-Dart* had intended to copy large segments of *64-Lebègue-I*. He chose the pieces to be copied and numbered the pages in his manuscript, with many omissions, to agree with the numeration of the print from one to seventy-four (*l.* 1-17v in the modern numeration of *45-Dart*). The plan was not carried out, and only the first few pieces coincide correctly with the pages in *64-Lebègue-I*. All of Lebègue's compositions, however, are exact copies from *64-Lebègue-I* or *65-Lebègue-II*. The spaces left by the first scribe were later filled in by two or three other hands, and some pieces begun by one hand were completed by a later hand, resulting in the complicated list of scribes presented in the Catalog. For convenience, the scribe is identified with each piece in the Inventory, as well as in the summary at the beginning of the manuscript entry.

#1:   Marchand's Gavotte is unique. It is not clear which Marchand is the composer. The likely member of the family is Louis, who is excluded from the Catalog because his pieces were published after 1700.

#42: The Chaconne appears in *Musick's Hand-maid*, part two, in a "corrupt" version. Dart substituted this reading in the revision of his edition of *Dart-HII*. The name in *45-Dart* is difficult to read with certainty; it could be Verdre or Vendre. It is probably a corruption of Verdier, a family of French musicians whose works were transcribed for keyboard in other manuscripts (cf. *Stockholm-228* and *Uppsala-409*).

#67:   Although the model for this Rigaudon has not been identified, the discrepancies among the keyboard concordances strongly suggest that it is a transcription.

Menetou (Inventory 46)

Like *36-Parville*, this manuscript has additions in the presumed hand of the Berkeley La Barre (hand B) and it, too, seems to have become a part of his library. It was named in *Curtis-Berkeley* (pp. 129-133) after Françoise-Charlotte de Senneterre de Menetou, who sang a number of airs for Louis XIV which she supposedly composed herself at the age of nine in 1689. The airs are found in *46-Menetou* as *#77-82*.

Almost all of the pieces in *46-Menetou* are transcriptions from Lully's operas. At the beginning of the manuscript they are grouped by opera, with a few exceptions; at the end, the collection becomes miscellaneous. Some of the music is really not keyboard music at all, but voice with continuo or "melody-bass" texture (#63-82). Most of the pieces, however, have fully notated harpsichord textures, even when they have been underlaid with text (e.g., #28).

Gen-2356 (Inventory 47)

This manuscript can be dated, but not with certainty. One piece, #10, is attributed to "Mr. Bura L aisné." If "Bura" is a variant of Burette (also spelled Buret), the elder Burette would probably be Claude (d. ca. 1700), who was a celebrated harpist and composer. His son, Pierre Jean, was a medical doctor and musical theorist. There would have been no need to specify "the elder" in a musical manuscript until Pierre Jean was old enough to have achieved some prominence, perhaps not until he was about twenty-five, in 1690. Discounting the Burette attribution, *47-Gen-2356* cannot have been compiled before 1676, because it contains a transcription from *Atys* (#17), which was premiered in that year.

47-Gen-2356 is an important source of seventeenth-century harpsichord music, in spite of its modest size. It contains a unique Courante and Double by Richard (#9 and 9a) and four harpsichord pieces by Louis Couperin. Furthermore, there is a unique, but incomplete, piece (#1) attributed to Couperin in the style of the known Carillons. The work was left out of *Brunold-Co*, apparently because it was incomplete, and it has not been noted by other scholars. The presence of Couperin's works is less valuable from the standpoint of establishing musical texts, since other good sources are known for the dance pieces, than as a sort of credential for the manuscript itself. Louis Couperin's pieces circulated only in select circles, and any manuscript which contains some of them was necessarily derived from sources close to the true connoisseurs of Parisian harpsichord music. For that reason, the anonymous works in such manuscripts should be seriously considered from a stylistic point of view in an attempt to relate them to known composers. An example in this manuscript is #7 and 7a. The Thematic Index provided a concordance which identified #7 as a Sarabande by Froberger which is known to have circulated in Paris, and #7a is a unique Double to it. On the basis of style, there is reason to suspect that the Double, too, is by Froberger.

The Sarabande #13 is one of many of Pinel's works that were presumably transcribed from lute originals. The texts of the *35-Bauyn*, *36-Parville* and *47-Gen-2356* versions of this piece are almost identical, however, and it would appear that it circulated as a harpsichord piece, perhaps transcribed by a prominent harpsichordist whose own pieces are found in the same manuscripts.

Burette-407 · Burette-410
Arsenal-410/24

In 1748 a catalog was made of the library which had been amassed by Pierre Jean Burette, who had died the previous year. It included a number of books on music, printed scores and musical manuscripts. Among the manuscripts are four which contained seventeenth-century French harpsichord music.[182] All are now unlocated, although *Fétis* (s.v. "Burette") cited *Burette-409* as if it were then extant. The entries are:

> [*Burette-407*:]   Piéces de Clavecin composées par J. de la Chapelle, Sieur de Chabmonniéres, Ordinaire de la Musique de Roi; & par Louis & Claude [i.e., Charles?] Couperain, Organistes de Saint Gervais, recueillies & notées par P[ierre] J[ean] Burete, D.M., MS, 1695, obl. v.m.

> [*Burette-408*:]   Piéces de Clavecin, composées par divers Auteurs, recueillies & notées par P[ierre] J[ean] Burette, D.M.P., MS, 1695, obl. vm.

> [*Burette-409*:]   Piéces de clavecin et de harpe composées par Cl[aude] Burette, musicien du Roi, natif de Nuys-en-Bourgogne, recueillies et notées par P[ierre] J[ean] Burette son fils, D.M.P., MS, 1695, obl., v.m.

> [*Burette-410*:]   Symphonies de tous les Opera de Jean-B. Lully, Surintendant de la Musique du Roi; mises sur le Clavecin, avec toutes les parties qui peut comporter le jeu de cet instrument; par Pierre-Jean Burette, D.M., Par MS obl. 2 vol. v.m. [n.d.]

Another unlocated manuscript is listed in the catalog for the library of the Arsenal in Paris. It was a "méthode de clavecin" and it cannot be found or further identified.[183]   It was probably from the eighteenth century as are all of the other harpsichord manuscripts in this library, but there is no way to be certain.

LaBarre-6 (Inventory 48)

Eleven manuscripts were named "La Barre 1" through "La Barre 11" in *Curtis-Berkeley* in conjunction with title inventories of the collection. Curtis numbered them in roughly chronological order and they are a unified set in a single principal hand. The hand is assumed to be that of "Monsieur De La Barre Organiste," as he signed himself inside the covers of two of the volumes (*La Barre-5* and *LaBarre-7*). None of the identified members of the La Barre family can logically be linked to an organist who lived until at least 1724, the anterior date of the last volume. Here he is called the "Berkeley La Barre" to distinguish him from the "English La Barre" and the "Bauyn La Barre."

The La Barre volumes also include *36-Parville* and *46-Menetou*, both of which have La Barre's hand as later additions to previously compiled manuscripts. The entire set of volumes was purchased at a book shop in Paris, seemingly in the 1950's, by an American expatriot collector who sold them to the University of California at Berkeley in 1968. Efforts to trace their previous history have been fruitless, but there is reason to suspect that at least two more volumes of the set exist. Each book has, in addition to the normal library markings, a red crayon number. These numbers were probably applied by the book dealer or a collector. They are consecutive with two exceptions:

Red numbers:	Manuscript:
1194	*51-LaBarre-11*
1195	*LaBarre-1*
1196	*LaBarre-5*
1197	*48-LaBarre-6*
1198	*LaBarre-10*
1199	*LaBarre-2*
1200	*LaBarre-8*
[1201]	?
1202	*LaBarre-4*
1203	*36-Parville*
[1204]	?
1205	*LaBarre-9*
1206	*46-Menetou*
1207	*LaBarre-7*
1288 [i.e., 1208?]	*LaBarre-3*

One can only wonder what and where 1201 and 1204 are.

48-LaBarre-6, like all of the La Barre series, is primarily an opera score. The few harpsichord pieces which are clustered in one section of the manuscript are of particular interest, however. Along with five pieces known to be by Lebègue (#26, 36, 37, 39 and 40), are several which are very similar to Lebègue's in style and one (#24) which has an identical opening to that of a Lebègue piece. Especially the Prélude #24, the Allemande #25 and the Prélude #29 might well be his works. Some of the pieces in the section have been identified as transcriptions, but it is always possible that the transcriber was Lebègue and that the entire section is by one composer. All of the manuscript works with contemporary attributions to Lebègue are found in his published works, *64-Lebègue-I* and *65-Lebègue-II*, and most of the manuscript copies of the pieces are very close to the printed versions, as are those in the manuscript at hand. If *48-LaBarre-6* represents manuscript circulation of the pieces and does indeed include unique pieces, it would be exceedingly unusual and would suggest a link between the Berkeley La Barre and Lebègue. The two musicians could not have been of the same generation, however, because Lebègue was born about 1631 and the Berkeley La Barre could not have been born much before 1650 (he was alive after 1724).

RésF-933 (Inventory 49)

This is the first of the eighteenth-century manuscripts to be mentioned here which contain some seventeenth-century harpsichord music. It is dated on the basis of the age of the composers represented. The youngest is William Babell, who was supposedly born about 1690, and he probably was at least twenty-five before his pieces surfaced in France. There are transcriptions from Campra's *Les Festes venitiennes* (1710), #18-19, in the manuscript, which place it definitely in the early eighteenth century. The date of the melody "Oh gué Lanla" (#22), 1712, is taken from a volume of airs (*Rès-Vma-ms-7/2*), but it is probably only approximate.

Hardel's Gavotte and its Double by Louis Couperin (#13-13a) are the only representatives of the seventeenth century. *49-RèsF-933* also demonstrates the long-lasting popularity of Lully's works, both on the stage and in transcription.

Paignon (Inventory 50)

50-Paignon is also not significant for a quantity of seventeenth-century harpsichord music. Lebègue's Gavotte (#11) is the only piece from this repertoire which appears in the manuscript. More interesting is the Clérambault treatise, which is otherwise unknown. The name at the end of the "Regles D'Accompangnement" is in the same hand as the rules themselves and may well be that of Clérambault. The manuscript warrants further investigation from this standpoint. No attempt has been made to search out a sample of Clérambault's hand, as the matter is beyond the scope of the present study.

LeBret.   *Provenance:*   France (Paris?), early eighteenth century.   *Location:* Bibliothèque Sainte Geneviève, MS 2382 (*olim* VF 40 754/32). *Description:* 58 p. (30 written).

Another manuscript in the Sainte Geneviève library is titled "Oeuvre De M.r Le Bret." It consists of ten harpsichord pieces, nine of which are unattributed and therefore presumably are works of Le Bret. One piece is titled "L'embarrassante" on p. 7 and has the note that it is "parmi les pieces de M. Couperin &c [?] à la page 28 & Suit." The Rondeau cannot be located in the harpsichord works of François Couperin, and it is not clear to what work the "page 28" refers. In view of its style, the piece is not likely to be by one of the earlier members of the Couperin family.

LaBarre-11 (Inventory 51)

This is the last of the La Barre manuscripts in the collection (cf. pp. 116-117, above). Some of the pieces were copied in the Berkeley collection from Dandrieu's publication of 1724 (*Dandrieu-4*) which provides the anterior date for this manuscript. Although there is very little seventeenth-century music in the volume, *51-LaBarre-11* does contain a unique group of pieces by Montelan, which appear to be original harpsichord music. Only one other piece is attributed to Montelan in a keyboard manuscript, a Rigaudon (*44-LaPierre*, p. 58A).

St-Georges. *Provenance:* France, post 1724? *Location:* Paris; Bibliothèque nationale, département de la musique, Vm8 1139. *Description:* 57 l.

This manuscript is tentatively dated here on the basis of the inclusion of Dandrieu's "La Fête de village," which was published in 1724 in *Dandrieu-4*.[184] The incipits of the pieces in this manuscript, which has on the cover: "Mr. de ST. GEORGES," are given in Écorcheville's catalog (4:105-110). The only music which can be identified as coming from the seventeenth century is Hardel's popular Gavotte, entered without attribution on *l.* 52. The only other identified composers are François Couperin (pieces from Book I), Dandrieu and one "M. de Duë" (Bertin de la Doué?).

Res-2671 (Inventory 52)
Oldham-2 (Inventory 53)

52-Rés-2671 is dated by its watermark, which contains the date 1742. Because of a peculiar sense of bureaucratic literal-mindedness which is unsurpassed outside France, French papermakers put "1742" in their marks for some years after a law had been phrased in such a way that it included the then-current year. The paper makers complied with the law exactly. Therefore, "1742" is only an anterior date for the paper. *53-Oldham-2* dates from at least a decade later, as it contains a transcription from Rousseau's *Le Devin du village*.[185]   It is interesting to see isolated pieces by Chambonnières still appearing in manuscripts a century after they were composed.

Household Manuscripts

Two manuscripts have been grouped separately here because they are particularly clear examples of books used by amateurs to learn to play the harpsichord. The distinction of household and professional is not as significant in French sources as in Germanic and Scandinavian manuscripts, and several of the manuscripts already discussed (e.g., *50-Paignon* and *44-LaPierre*) could have been included here. They were not because in one case, *50-Paignon*, the manuscript is an example of an eighteenth, not seventeenth-century household book; and in the other, the amount of important harpsichord music elevated it to the previous category.   Both of the household manuscripts cited below have particularly interesting aspects.

Gen-2350/57 (Inventory 54)

This manuscript, like many sources which were written by musicians of questionable competence, is difficult to date. Because of the uneven character of all of the writing, it is difficult to determine the number of hands. It may be the work of one hand at different times. The inexperience of the musicians is made evident not only in the minimal technical demands of the pieces, but in the use of letters written below the notes to help identify them (cf. #1-7). Therefore, style cannot be considered as a means of dating *54-Gen-2350/57*, and conversely one cannot take the textures of these pieces as evidence of the prevailing harpsichord style for the date which will be tentatively put forth here. The style reflects the possibilities of unskilled fingers.   This point has been emphasized here because *54-Gen-2350/57* is the only known French harpsichord manuscript which could date from before 1650. All of the identified repertoire could have been collected very early in the century, and the watermark genre is found in sources from 1611 to 1630. The type of repertoire, largely airs with or without text, is not typical of later harpsichord manuscripts and the lack of Lully pieces in a book of transcriptions from vocal music is not likely to have been compiled after about 1670. On the other hand, this manuscript does use figured bass (*l.* 8v, 9r), which was uncommon in France before midcentury.

There is no music in *54-Gen-2350/57* which can be identified as original harpsichord music. Some of the pieces are from airs by Guédron, some are from instrumental branles by Chancy and Cordier (the latter known as "Boccan")[186] and some are settings of popular tunes such as La Vignon (#7) and Courante la reyne (#14). If the pieces titled Ballet, especially the "Ballet nouveau" (#28), were identified, a sure dating could be established. "Ballet du Soleil" might refer to "Ballet du Soleil pour la Reine," which was performed in 1621.[187]

Redon (Inventory 55)

55-Redon was discussed in an obscure French periodical by Fournier, who was intrigued by the manuscript from the standpoint of local cultural history.[188] The owner of the book, Mlle Claude Redon (*l.* 5v) has been identified as a member of a Clermont family. She must have been born around 1650, since she married in 1668 and died between 1718 and 1720.[189] She would, then, have been a child or young teenager when she studied harpsichord from this book.

55-Redon is not significant as a source of important music, but the fact that it is specifically dated is of help in studying other manuscripts. The date applied most strictly to the tuning chart on *l.* 5v-6r, but one can logically apply it as an approximate date for the entire book. Courante Iris (#23) was clearly not derived from the 1670 printed version (*62-Chamb-I*), although this fact does not prove that the manuscript pre-dated the print. Two of the pieces, #21-23, are in the assured hand of a teacher. The rest are simple dances, chansons and untitled, unidentified pieces. Most of them are certainly transcriptions from other mediums. The Gigue #4 is presumably from a lute piece by Gaultier, although no original has been located. The pieces with long descriptive titles (#2 and 15) are obviously from vocal models, and the Ballet titles (#18 and 20) are presumably from stage music. Three exceptions to this generality are the Prélude #16, the Courante de madame #21 and Chambonnières' Courante Iris #23, all of which are idiomatic harpsichord music.

The notations used in *55-Redon* should be pointed out. This is the only French harpsichord source which uses six line staves. Furthermore, the tuning chart is presented in French letter score. Since it is only a chart, the notation is not striking, but it provides a fourth example of the otherwise-lost system (cf. *6-Munich-1511e, 7-Munich-1511f* and *32-Oldham*).

Ex. 12. Riecle generalle pour bien apprendre accorder Lespinette
pour /Madmoiselle Claude Redon ce cinquiesme septembre 1661
[55-Redon, l. 5v-6v]

Summary

The thirty-one harpsichord manuscripts discussed in this chapter can be divided into three chronological groups. No manuscripts of significance survive from before 1650, and for most of the manuscripts discussed in this chapter which do not contain Lully transcriptions, the dating is exceedingly problematical.

Five manuscripts can be considered to be from before about 1675. One, *54-Gen-2350/57*, could be from as early as about 1630, but its household nature diminishes its value as a representative source from any period. The most important manuscript from the standpoint of size, *35-Bauyn*, could conceivably date from as late as the final quarter of the century. None of these manuscripts contains transcriptions from Lully operas, but arrangements from other vocal and instrumental mediums are common to all but *32-Oldham*. In the lists which follow, all of the seventeenth-century French composers who are represented in each manuscript are listed in the third column.

54-Gen-2350/57	ca. 1630-1670	Chancy, Cordier, Guédron
32-Oldham	ca. 1650-1661	d'Anglebert, Chambonnières, Louis Couperin, Hardel, Monnard, Richard
35-Bauyn	post 1658	d'Anglebert, Chambonnières, Louis Couperin, Dumont, Gaultier, Hardel, La Barre, Lebègue, Lorency, Mesangeau, Monnard, Pinel, Richard, Vincent
38-Gen-2348/53	post 1658?	Chambonnières, Louis Couperin, Monnard
55-Redon	1661	Chambonnières, Esty (?), Gaultier, La Pierre

Only in the last quarter of the century, probably the last two decades, do we find numerous manuscripts of French harpsichord music. Almost all of the seventeen manuscripts contain transcriptions from Lully operas, which usually provide the only specific anterior dating for the sources. Three of them (*Burette-407, -408* and *-409*) are unlocated, and at least three could be from after 1700 (*45-Dart, 37-Geoffroy* and *48-LaBarre-6*).

33-Rés-89ter	post 1677	d'Anglebert, Chambonnières, Louis Couperin, Gaultier, Lambert, Lully, Marais, Mesangeau, Pinel, Richard
39-Vm7-6307-1	post 1678	Lully
40-Rés-476	post 1679	Louis Couperin, Lully, Nivers
41-Thomelin	ca. 1680-1700?	Thomelin
42-Vm7-6307-2	post 1684	Lully
43-Gen-2354	post 1685	Lully
36-Parville	post 1686	d'Anglebert, Chambonnières, Louis Couperin, Gaultier, Hardel, La Barre, Lebègue, Lully, Richard
44-LaPierre	post 1687	Chambonnières, Favier, Hardel, Lully, Monnard, Montelan
45-Dart	post 1687	d'Anglebert, Campra, Chambonnières, Couperin,

		Farinel, Gaultier, Hardel, Lebègue, Lully, Verdier
46-Menetou	post 1689	d'Anglebert, Lambert, Lebègue, Lully, Menetou
47-Gen-2356	ca. 1690?	Burette, Chambonnières, Louis Couperin, Lully, Pinel, Richard
34-Gen-2357 [A]	ca. 1690?	anonymous
37-Geoffroy	post 1694	Geoffroy
Burette-407	1695	Chambonnières, Couperin
Burette-408	1695	unknown
Burette-409	1695	Claude Burette
48-LaBarre-6	post 1697	Berthet, Campra, Collasse, Lebègue, Lully

The nine eighteenth-century French manuscripts show the occasional circulation of works by some of the seventeenth-century clavecinists, especially Chambonnières. *51-LaBarre-11* provides unique pieces by Montelan, but otherwise all of the music of concern to this repertoire is known from earlier sources.

49-RésF-933	post ca. 1715	Campra, Louis Couperin, Hardel, Lully
50-Paignon	1716	Lebègue, Lully
LeBret	17--	(Couperin, Le Bret)
51-LaBarre-11	post 1724	d'Anglebert, Lully, Montelan
St-Georges	post 1724?	Hardel
52-Rés-2671	post 1742	Chambonnières
Burette-410	pre 1747	Lully
53-Oldham-2	post 1752	Chambonnières
Arsenal-410/24	17??	unknown

CHAPTER VI

PRINTED SOURCES

After Attaingnant's collection of 1531,[190] no collection of harpsichord music appeared in Paris until 1670. The five harpsichord books by seventeenth-century clavecinists all appeared between 1670 and 1689: two each by Chambonnières and Lebègue and one by d'Anglebert. A sixth book, by Elizabeth Jacquet (de la Guerre), also came out during this period, but no exemplar can be located. Works of their colleagues (Louis Couperin, Dumont, Geoffroy, Hardel, La Barre, Monnard, Thomelin, et al.) were never published in collected editions.

A number of French harpsichord pieces did appear in print before 1670, but in each case the pieces were isolated in publications which were essentially concerned with nonharpsichord music. In some cases, the harpsichord pieces are musical illustrations in didactic works, and in others they are addenda to a composer's vocal and instrumental works. One print, *60-Playford*, is not a harpsichord source at all, but it contains a piece by Chambonnières which was presumably transcribed from a harpsichord work. A second print, *66-Perrine*, is only nominally intended for harpsichord performance. The following printed sources will be discussed:

56-Mersenne	*63-Chamb-II*
57-Denis	*64-Lebègue-I*
58-Dumont-1652	*65-Lebègue-II*
59-Dumont-1657	*66-Perrine*
59a-Handmaide	*67-Gigault*
60-Playford	*Jacquet*
61-Dumont-1668	*68-d'Anglebert*
62-Chamb-1	

Mersenne (Inventory 56)

Père Mersenne, in his famous music encyclopedia of 1636, included an example of keyboard score which antedates any other datable piece of seventeenth-century French harpsichord music. Although these diminutions appear in the organ section of *Harmonie universelle*, they were intended as an illustration of harpsichord music. Mersenne's personal exemplar of the encyclopedia includes a manuscript Fantaisie by Racquet which was to have illustrated organ style (*Lesure*, Traité des instruments 6:392[a] et seq.). The text preceding the diminutions casually refers to them as organ music, but in the harpsichord section Mersenne specifies them as harpsichord style, which is similar to that of the harp, in contrast to the organistic writing of Racquet's Fantaisie. A marginal note in Mersenne's hand makes it clear that it is the diminutions which are being discussed. The notes reads, "page 394 du /6. Liure de orgue," which is the location of the diminutions; he then says:

> . . . & parceque le clauier de l'Orgue n'est pas different de celuy du Claucin, il n'y a nul doute que les Organistes la [i.e., La Barre's "O beau soleil"] peuuent toucher, quoy qu'il y ayt de certaines particularitez au toucher de l'Orgue qui ne sont pas à celuy de l'Epinette, comme ie diray dans vn liure particulier, dans lequel ie donneray vn autre exemple pour monstrer ce que peut faire l'Orgue, & ce qui luy est propre [i.e., Racquet's Fantaisie]. [*Lesure*, Traité des instruments, 3:164].

The diminutions constitute one of the few pieces by a La Barre which can be attributed to a specific member of the family. It was Pierre III who held the court appointment of "Organiste du Roy & de la Reyne," as Mersenne identified him in the heading to the piece. The exact role of Louis XIII in the composition is not clear. He undoubtedly wrote the text of the chanson and probably the melody. La Barre could have harmonized the set the tune as part of "putting it in tablature." The chanson circulated later in various publications, including *Musurgia universalis* of Athanatius Kirchner (Rome: 1650; p. 690), but without the diminutions.

Only the simple first setting of the chanson was published completely in *56-Mersenne.* Thereafter, the incipit of each variation is given. This abbreviated printing emphasizes the didactic purpose of the variations. If one could realize the entire variation by seeing the procedure used in the first measure, the piece can be considered little more than a mechanical exercise. La Barre's diminutions are evidence that the procedure was known in France in the early decades of the seventeenth century, but a dictionary illustration of a compositional technique is a poor example of stylistic harpsichord music.

Denis (Inventory 57)

No significant French harpsichord music survives from before 1650, and yet this book appeared before mid-century, dealing with tuning and other aspects of harpsichords. Like the many contemporary references to the ownership of harpsichords and spinets, it is evidence of a flourishing Parisian harpsichord school whose repertoire is now lost. Inventories of estates left by amateur and professional musicians and similar legal documents provide a record of many musical instruments.

For the first half of the century, references have been found to 140 *épinettes*, 24 *clavecins*, 14 clavichords and 7 claviorgana. The distinction between *épinette* and *clavecin* is hazy, as the former was often used as a generic term, but was also used specifically for a spinet. Twice as many lutes are mentioned, but instruments of the harpsichord family were clearly of great importance.[191]

The first edition of *57-Denis* (1643) did not contain musical illustrations,[192] but the second edition (1650) presented a modulating Prélude which was to serve as a test of a harpsichord's temperament. The Prélude is presumably a composition by the author. Even more than La Barre's diminutions in *56-Mersenne*, this piece is functional and basically unmusical. *57-Denis* is an extremely important document for the study of the history of French harpsichord music and its performance practice, but it is only nominally a source of actual music.

Dumont-1652, -1657 and -1668 (Inventories 58, 59 and 61)

Dumont's *Cantica sacra (58-Dumont-1652)* is frequently misdated by ten years. An edition appeared in 1662, but Ballard published the first edition in 1652. The confusion arises because Bonfils cited the date 1662 without specifying that it was the second edition (*Bonfils-13*, p. 4). There is no exemplar of the *basse-continue* part book of the earlier edition in the Bibliothèque nationale, and Bonfils accurately listed the edition he had at hand. By 1655, the publication was already known to Constantin Huygens (p. 24), who commented on the "Allemande grave" therein.

All three of Dumont's publications which contained harpsichord music were essentially vocal collections. The harpsichord pieces were included as extra added attractions, if not filler. It is to be lamented that Dumont never published a separate volume of his harpsichord works, only thirteen of which have survived. Four were printed in the vocal collections; the rest are found in manuscript sources (cf. Appendix C, p. 292). In addition, there are a number of Préludes in two parts which Dumont sanctioned for organ as well as instrumental performance (cf. *59-Dumont-1657*, "Au Lecteur"). A selection of the latter pieces appears in *Bonfils-13*.

The printed works all exist in two versions: keyboard and instrumental. The keyboard versions were the original concepts of the pieces, according to Dumont's statement in the preface ("Au Lecteur") to *59-Dumont-1657*:

> . . . Ceux qui joüent de l'orgue ou de Clavecin, y trouveront aussi plusieurs [i.e., 2] Allemandes en Tablature d'Orgue, lesquelles j'ay mises à troi Parties pour les Violles, qu'on pourra joüer separément ou accompagner l'Organiste. . . .

Examples 13-15 show the relationships of the readings of one piece from each print:

Ex. 13. Incipit and Close of the First Strain of an Allemande by Dumont
(*58-Dumont-1652 I.* 24v)

Ex. 14. Incipit and Close of the First Strain of an Allemande by Dumont
(*59-Dumont-1657, l. 31v*)

        The prominent mention of the organ as the keyboard medium
for these secular pieces is largely explained by the fact that the volumes
were expressly prepared for the "Dames Religieuses" (*59-Dumont-1657,*
Au Lecteur). In texture and form, they are suited primarily to the
harpsichord, and they were considered harpsichord pieces in their own
time. Huygens (pp. 23-24) wrote to Dumont regarding the Allemande in
58-Dumont-1652 as well as a manuscript Allemande, both in the context
of harpsichord music, with no mention of the organ.

Ex. 15. Incipit and Close of the First Strain of an Allemande by Dumont
(*61-Dumont-1668, l. 36v*)

Handmaide (Inventory 59a)

That La Barre's Courante (#43 in *59a-Handmaide*) should be
included in John Playford's harpsichord miscellany of 1663 is not
surprising. It is found in three other English sources from midcentury,
two of them dated in the 1650's. It does provide another example of
overly-free hands in modern attributions, in that it was assigned to
Benjamin Rogers in both *Dart-HI* and *Rastall* because it follows an Ayre
by Rogers. There is an important distinction between that misattribution
and the suggestion that #13 and 15 might be by La Barre or Tresure, as
listed in the Catalog entry below. In the case of #13-15 we are dealing
with an Allemande-Courante-Sarabande group, and such a suite was
usually treated as an inviolable unit; such was not as often the case with
pairs of movements. The other conjectural attributions in *Dart-HI* have
been included with a cautionary question mark in the Inventory here.

Other French associations in *59a-Handmaide* include the melody
of #22 which seems to have originated with Artus, and that of #27, the
popular "La Chabotte" tune. In the additions which are found in the
1678 edition of *59a-Handmaide* are two other French melodies, one from
the Ballet royal of 1654 (*Dart-HI* #73) and the other from Lully's *Atys,*
which premiered just two years earlier ("Que devant vous" II-4, suitably
titled here "The New Minuet," Dart-HI #74).[193]

Playford (Inventory 60)[194]

In 1666, John Playford brought out a volume of music for the popular cittern, a member of the guitar family. The collection was consciously directed towards musical amateurs, with a delightfully chauvinistic preface, which includes the comment, ". . . Nor is any Musick rendered acceptable, or esteemed by many, but what is presented by Foreigners; Not a City Dame though a Tap-wife, but is ambitious to have her Daughters Taught by a Monsieur La Novo Kickshawibus on the Gittar. . . ." Playford (p.i) emphasized that his was an easy method of playing, not using "all those difficult full Stops with which former Lessons were stuft with."

Most of the airs in 60-Playford are anonymous, but there is a "Sarabande La Chamboner" which is of interest here. The piece is not a known work by Chambonnières,[195] but "Chamboner" is too close to the French name to be logically interpreted otherwise. The form of the attribution might suggest that the Sarabande had been written in honor of Chambonnières, rather than by him. However, the piece occurs in a group of seventeen pieces by named composers, not in the larger group of pieces with descriptive titles. It is probably a transcription of a lost harpsichord work by the famous court harpsichordist. The entire Sarabande is shown in Ex. 16, below.

Chamb-I, Chamb-II (Inventories 62-63)

Not until the last two years of his life did the recognized leader, and, seemingly, the founder, of the Parisian harpsichord school publish some of his pieces. Although the second book is not dated, it appears to have been issued simultaneously with the first. The first volume has a florid title page by Jollain, but no comparably elaborate page was engraved for 64-Chamb-II. Thurston Dart (Dart-Ch, p. I) speculated that Jollain broke a single volume in two, lest the one large tome prove too expensive to sell. The sixty pieces of the prints appeared long after they had begun circulation in manuscript copies, and the variants among the concordances are substantial, as Chambonnières pointed out in his Preface with more than a touch of irritation. Not all of the discrepancies should be attributed to copyists' license or carelessness. In the published works, there is a profuse use of ornamentation which is not found in any of the manuscript sources, including those pieces in the presumed autograph of the composer.[196] These ornaments seem to have been added at the time of the publication of the works, probably in conjunction with more substantial changes to the texts.

The printing of engraved music was not only expensive, but tedious and damaging to the plates.[197] It is not surprising, then, that

Ex. 16. Sarabande La Chamboner (60-*Playford* #71)

most surviving exemplars of the prints have at least slight variations and
that many of them are from worn plates. Two states of Chambonnières'
first book and three of the second can be distinguished. Each exemplar
of the second book is slightly different, and it is difficult to determine an
exact chronology of the issues.

Although Chambonnières' works were widely circulated in manuscript both before and after the appearance of the prints, no subsequent editions appeared.[198] Lebègue's and d'Anglebert's prints were pirated in Amsterdam at the turn of the century, but Chambonnières' pieces were not. The explanation may lie less with any lack of popularity of the works than with the ready availability of Chambonnières' music. Printed music was expensive and Chambonnières' pieces were widely circulated in cheaper manuscripts, unlike those of Lebègue and d'Anglebert.

Perhaps because of the value of the prints, they are usually in better condition than manuscripts today. There is seldom marginalia in them and rarely are they heavily thumbed. It would seem that they were collected and copied more than they were used as performance scores. One exemplar of *63-Chamb-II*, however, contains an interesting manuscript addition. On p. 48, which was printed with blank staves,[199] a melody was written in the exemplar held by the Bibliothèque Sainte Geneviève. The piece was not continued, but it may be the upper voice of a Courante by Chambonnières which the owner intended to add to the collection. It is not known elsewhere.

Ex. 17. Courante Melody (*63-Chamb-II*, ex. 4, p. 48)

Lebègue-I and Lebègue-II (Inventories 64-65)

The bibliographic description of Lebègue's prints is more complicated than that of Chambonnières'. Four issues of the Paris edition of *64-Lebègue-I* can be distinguished among the known exemplars, and a fifth was reported, although it is now unlocated.[200] The second through fourth issues were printed before the privilege expired in 1685, but the fifth suppressed the privilege notice and so must have been printed after 1685. The second edition can be dated as 1697 on the basis of advertisements in the catalogues of the Roger firm in Amsterdam.[201] Only three exemplars of *65-Lebègue-II* are known, and each is different. In the Bibliotheque nationale's exemplar, p. 59 of *64-Lebègue-I* was printed in place of p. 59 of *65-Lebègue-II*. Dufourcq did not consult another exemplar for his edition of the works, and he stated simply that the beginning of the affected piece was lacking. The complete piece is found in the other two exemplars.

Ex. 18. Gigue by Lebègue (*65-Lebègue-II*, ex. 2, #30)

The title page of the second edition of *64-Lebègue-I* contains an interesting sentence which demonstrates that the style of the pieces was not familiar to the Amsterdam musical public. Although the comment does not cite the préludes specifically, they must have been the reason for the statement, since dance movements in Lebègue's relatively uncomplicated style were known to harpsichordists of all nationalities in the first decade of the eighteenth century. The comment is as follows:

Comme Plusieurs Personnes ignorent la Maniere de joüer ces Pieces
et Par Consequent /n'en Connoissent Pas la Bemué on Avertie ceux
qui seront Curieux de les Entendre de /S'Adresser a Monsieur
Marquis Maistre de Clavessin a Amsterdam

An extensive exception to the typical lack of marginalia in harpsichord prints is found in the fourth exemplar of *64-Lebègue-I*. On the front end paper is a dated copy of a letter from Lebègue with an English translation, both in the translator's hand. The letter is obviously a reply to a query from Mr. William Dundass, regarding the performance of unmeasured preludes. The translation is dated July 3, 1684, providing rare evidence of the presence of Lebègue's music in England only seven years after its publication, as well as the only known instructions on performance practice of unmeasured preludes from a composer.[202]

One of the most popular pieces in the repertoire was published in *64-Lebègue-I*, the Gavotte #43. It was the only piece by Lebègue which circulated widely in manuscripts without reference to the prints. It was an early work, written before 1661, since one of the doubles it acquired was written by Louis Couperin, who died in that year. In all, five different doubles for the Gavotte have survived:

1. By Lebègue:		*13-Möllersche*
		23-Tenbury #6a
		24-Babell #60a
		64-Lebègue-I #43a
2. By Louis Couperin		*35-Bauyn-III #54a*
		36-Parville #146
3. Anonymous #1		*36-Parville #68a*
4. Anonymous #2		*50-Paignon #11a*
5. Anonymous #3		*14-Schwerin-619 #91a*

Perrine (Inventory 66)

Perrine was a lute teacher who published two works in 1680. The first was a method introducing a staff notation for lute music, replacing lute tablature.[203] The second, *66-Perrine*, amounts to an anthology of pieces for the use of those who had learned to play from the new notation. Beside the normal noteheads in the score nearly microscopic letters indicate the lute fingering. One of the arguments which Perrine used in order to encourage the use of score notation was that it was essentially the same as nonlute notation. His title page reflects that argument: ". . . auec des Regles pour les [i.e., les pièces] toucher parfaitemt sur le Luth et sur le Clauessin."

The book is, then, technically a harpsichord publication as well. However, the textures of the pieces were designed for the lute, as can be seen in the incipit for #3, second strain, where the compass of the hands at the keyboard is exceeded. *66-Perrine* is lute music in a new notation, not harpsichord transcriptions of lute music.

An interesting phenomenon occurs in *66-Perrine.* Two pieces (#3 and 7) are printed twice in their entirety with only a change of meter signature. What was first an "Allemande" was repeated as a "Gigue." The use of ¢ for a gigue and C for an allemande relates to tempo, giving the faster pace to the gigue. This specific distinction does not occur elsewhere in harpsichord music, although allemandes and gigues are often closely related (cf. *35-Bauyn-III* for several examples of another sort of intermingling of the terms).

Gigault (Inventory 67)

Gigault published two keyboard works in the 1680's. The first, *67-Gigault,* was divided into two volumes; the second was a single book which is exclusively comprised of organ music.[204] Almost all of the pieces in *67-Gigault* are noël variations. They are not particularly idiomatic for any instrument, but are here considered organ music because noëls were generally published in organ sources, not harpsichord books.

One Allemande was included in the collection. It is quite out of place and appears to have been included as an afterthought. Like the harpsichord pieces in *56-Mersenne* and *57-Denis,* it is a didactic work, here illustrating how to add passing tones ("ports de voix") to a melody as ornamentation. The title, "Allemande par fugue," is unique; it is the only piece called a fugue in the seventeenth-century French harpsichord repertoire. In form, the piece is a Gigue-allemande, a piece in dotted rhythm, in either quadruple or triple (i.e., duple-compound) meter, which begins imitatively. Those in quadruple meter are frequently called allemande or gigue indiscriminately. The use of "fugue" in the title emphasizes that one of the few elements which allemandes have in common is a contrapuntal texture.

67-Gigault is a carelessly engraved print of limited significance. The first volume has two fragments on its last page, where at least one page was not copied onto the plates. The pagination of the second volume, from pp. 3-5, is confused, with evidence of sloppy corrections to the pagination elsewhere.

Jacquet

One book of harpsichord pieces is known to have been published in Paris by Élisabeth Jacquet (de la Guerre) in 1687, but no exemplar can be located. According to a notice in *Mercure galant,* the book contained pieces which were calculated for performance on either harpsichord or viol with bass. One suite was specifically mentioned as being written in imitation of the lute, and it would certainly be interesting to be able to examine the textures of those pieces. The account is as follows:

> Cette mesme Demoiselle, qui n'a encore que vingt [i.e., 28] ans, vient de donner au Public un Livre de Pieces de Clavessin qu'elle a dedié au Roy. . . . Ce Livre gravé au burin contient plusieurs suites de differens tons, et plusieurs Preludes, Fantaisies, Toccades, Allemandes, Courantes, Sarabandes, Gigues, Canaries, Menuets, Gavotes, et Chaconne. La pluspart de ces Pieces sont propres à estre joüées sur un dessus de Violon ou de Viole avec une Basse, et toute la seconde suite est faite à l'imitation de Luth.[205]

d'Anglebert (Inventory 68)

The distinction of issues and editions becomes blurred among the exemplars of *68-d'Anglebert.* Four states exist: two issues of the first edition bear the date 1689; a second "edition" is really the second issue of the first edition, with a new title page dated 1703; the third edition appeared in Amsterdam in 1704/5. The 1703 Paris edition has a type-set title page which Ballard added to the remaining stock of the previous issue. That Ballard did not run a new issue from the old plates is confirmed by the fact that the 1703 edition has the same watermark as the first edition, second issue.[206]

The large number of surviving exemplars of *68-d'Anglebert* and the pirated Amsterdam edition attest to the popularity of the pieces, but the lack of wide circulation of the pieces in manuscript sources must qualify this conclusion. It was the last harpsichord publication in France before the end of the century, and it provides the last datable music of the seventeenth-century French harpsichord repertoire, for although it is labelled "Livre Premier" on the title page, no second volume ever appeared.

Summary

The fifteen printed sources discussed here are of two types: those which contain a few miscellaneous French harpsichord pieces and those which are the "pièces de clavecin" of a composer. All of the large collections come from 1670-1689, but a number of significant isolated pieces date from as early as the 1650's (Dumont).

Three didactic harpsichord works are found in seventeenth-century French publications (*56-Mersenne, 57-Denis* and *67-Gigault*). Three sources provide isolated pieces by Dumont (*58-Dumont-1652, 59-Dumont-1657* and *61-Dumont-1668*), and three prints (*59a-Handmaide, 60-Playford* and *66-Perrine*) are only secondarily related to French harpsichord music. One source, *Jacquet,* is lost. The following is a list of the publications of secondary interest, with the dates of their first issues and the clavecinists represented in each:

56-Mersenne	1636	La Barre (Pierre III)
57-Denis	1643, 1650	Denis
58-Dumont-1652	1652	Dumont
59-Dumont-1657	1652	Dumont
59a-Handmaide	1663	La Barre
60-Playford	1666	Chambonnières
61-Dumont-1668	1668	Dumont
66-Perrine	1680	Gaultier (D. and E.)
67-Gigault	1682	Gigault

The six books of "pièces de clavecin" are the most important sources of seventeenth-century French harpsichord music, except of course for the unlocated *Jacquet.* All of them were engraved in the composers' lifetimes and with their cooperation and control. It does not go without saying that the prints made in a composer's city reflect his direct involvement, but there is other evidence to support the assertion here. In the case of Chambonnières' books, the preface indicates that his motivation was to provide an authoritative text in view of the many unfaithful manuscript copies of his pieces that were circulating--a sentiment which François Couperin repeated in the preface to his first book of harpsichord pieces. Lebègue's books suggest less concern for the printed text, but like those of Chambonnières, they show that corrections were made between issues. D'Anglebert's book has a more explicit suggestion of the composer's role in the form of a note at the end of the second issue: "Reveu et corrigé."

These books have been correctly viewed as the most authoritative sources for the pieces which they transmit. The most prominent clavecinists who are absent from this list of editions are Louis Couperin, Dumont, Hardel, La Barre and Thomelin. It was a minority of the Parisian harpsichordists who published their works in the seventeenth-century, and no one was honored with an edition after 1704/5 until the twentieth century.

62-Chamb-I	1670	Chambonnières
63-Chamb-II	1670	Chambonnières
64-Lebègue-I	1677	Lebègue
65-Lebègue-II	1687	Lebègue
Jacquet	1687	La Guerre
68-d'Anglebert	1689	d'Anglebert

CHAPTER VII

SUMMARY

French harpsichord music of the seventeenth century survives in a diverse group of sources. A few date from the early part of the century, while the majority are late seventeenth-century sources; some are carefully notated scores and others are carelessly written household books; a number can be traced directly to specific composers, while most are both anonymous and difficult to date. The sources which are most important in establishing musical texts for the major composers are well known, including the printed harpsichord books (*62-Chamb-I, 63-Chamb-II, 64-Lebègue-I, 65-Lebègue-II, 68-d'Anglebert*), and the major French manuscripts (*32-Oldham, 33-Rés-89ter, 35-Bauyn, 36-Parville, 37-Geoffroy*). There are many other sources which provide unique or preferable readings of isolated pieces. These sources, too numerous to list here, can be identified through the concordances given in the Catalog and the lists of works in Appendix C. The entire group represents the raw material for an historical analysis of French harpsichord music.

All of the numerical totals in this section must be regarded as approximate because of the many unsure attributions, overlapping categories and unidentified compositions in the repertoire. No attempt has been made to formulate a grand total of how many "pieces" constitute the seventeenth-century French harpsichord repertoire, because such a number would have to be burdened with so many qualifications and definitions that it would be of little value. The number of incipits in the Catalog is 1,564. A total of 762 pieces can be attributed to fourteen seventeenth-century clavecinists:

d'Anglebert (93)
Burette (1)
Chambonnières (148)

Louis Couperin (134)
Dumont (13)
Geoffroy (207)
Gigault (1)
Hardel (7)

La Barre (42: Pierre III [1], Joseph [1], English [29], Bauyn [11])
Lebègue (95)
Monnard (3)
Montelan (5)
Richard (12)
Thomelin (1)

The sources contain 291 transcriptions from Lully works, representing 189 different Lully pieces. It is amazing to see the nonharpsichordist Lully responsible for more harpsichord pieces than any of the clavecinists except Geoffroy. Transcriptions from the works of the lutenists, especially Denis and Ennemond Gaultier, also account for a considerable portion of the French or French-derived harpsichord repertoire of the seventeenth century.

This Commentary has discussed 119 sources. They can be divided into four chronological groups:

> 1600-1650 (13)
> 1650-1675 (40)
> 1675-1700 (40)
> 1700-1800 (26)

Of these sources, 70 actually contain music which could be considered seventeenth-century French harpsichord music and are therefore inventoried in the Catalog:

> 1600-1650 (6)
> 1650-1675 (23)
> 1675-1700 (26)
> 1700-1800 (15)

The value of virtually all of the early sources is compromised in one way or another, and no major sources for the repertoire survive from before 1650. The most significant midcentury sources are *32-Oldham* and *35-Bauyn*. The printed sources are of great importance in establishing musical texts, but because the few large ones are all from after 1670, the manuscripts are of greater significance both for the music they contain and for an historical discussion of the style.

The thirteen sources from the first half of the seventeenth century share lute music and popular melodies as their French touchstones more than original French harpsichord music. The English La Barre is represented in two sources (*1-Copenhagen-376* and *4-Lynar*), probably by transcriptions from his lute pieces, and Pierre La Barre III is the composer of a harpsichord illustration in *56-Mersenne*. The piece in *57-Denis* is purely didactic and the attributions to Jacques Champion II in *26-Bull* are not certain. The one French manuscript of this group, *54-Gen-2350/57*, is not only difficult to date, but is clearly of a household nature. In the lists which follow, all of the French composers represented in each source are listed. Jonas Tresure is also included because of his close relationship to the English La Barre. In the later lists, eighteenth-century French composers are excluded. Only the names of the harpsichordists listed at the beginning of this chapter denote the presence of original French harpsichord music.

Eÿsbock	ca. 1600?	Godard
Linz	1611-1613	Mercure (?)
4-Lynar	ca. 1615-1650	Ballard, Gaultier, La Barre
Faille	ca. 1625?	Guédron, Pinel
26-Bull	ca. 1629	Champion (?)
1-Copenhagen-376	1629-ca. 1650	La Barre, Mesangeau, Pinel
54-Gen-2350/57	ca. 1630-1670	Chancy, Cordier, Guédron
Wolffheim	ca. 1630-1650	Du Caurroy (?)
56-Mersenne	1636	La Barre
Bologna-360	ca. 1640-1680	La Barre (violin)
Voigtländer	post 1642	French melodies only
57-Denis	1643, 1650	Denis
Imhoff	1649	French melodies only

We are relatively rich in French-related sources from the third quarter of the century. The forty sources listed below include the most important sources for the repertoire, *32-Oldham* and *35-Bauyn*, as well as the first published *livres de clavecin* (*62-Chamb-I* and *63-Chamb-II*). The lutenists are still represented in great numbers, and beginning as early as the 1660's, the name of Lully is to be expected in harpsichord sources. The three Munich manuscripts (Inventories 5-7) are French in every sense but location, but the other foreign sources are almost totally devoid of original French harpsichord music, especially if the pieces by the English La Barre were originally composed as lute works.

Leningrad	1650	French melodies only
Drallius	1650	French melodies only
18-Ch-Ch-1236	1650-1674	Chambonnières, Dufaut, La Barre, Mercure, Tresure
29-Chigi	ca. 1650?	La Barre
32-Oldham	ca. 1650-1661	d'Anglebert, Chambonnières, Louis Couperin, Hardel, Monnard, Richard
8-Hintze	ca. 1650-1674?	Artus, Chambonnières, La Barre
16-Cosyn	1652	La Barre, Tresure
58-Dumont-1652	1652	Dumont
Oxford-1B	1652 (?)	La Barre
2-Witzendorff	1655-1659	Chambonnières, Mesangeau
Uppsala-409	ca. 1655-1662	Belleville, Dumanoir, La Croix, Verdier
Uppsala-134:22	ca. 1655?	Belleville
17-Rogers	1656	La Barre, Mercure
59-Dumont-1657	1657	Dumont
35-Bauyn	post 1658	d'Anglebert, Chambonnières, L. Couperin, Dumont, Gaultier, Hardel, La Barre, Lebègue, Lorency, Mesangeau, Monnard, Pinel, Richard, Vincent

38-Gen-2348/53	post 1658?	Chambonnières, L. Couperin, Monnard
Skara	1659-post 1661	Gaultier, Pinel, Tresure
60-Playford	1666	Chambonnières
Beatrix	ca. 1660?	ballet transcriptions
5-Munich-15031	ca. 1660?	Artus, Chambonnières, Dumont, Pinel
6-Munich-1511e	ca. 1660?	Monnard
7-Munich-1511f	ca. 1660?	Artus, Pinel
Vat-mus-569	ca. 1660-1665	Arnauld?
Berlin-40147	ca. 1660-1680	Besard
55-Redon	1661	Chambonnières, Esty (?), Gaultier, La Pierre (?)
Rés-819-2	post 1661	Lully
Terburg	post 1661	Lully
Celle	1662	Champion (?)
59a-Handmaide	1663	Artus, La Barre, Tresure
19-Heardson	ca. 1664?	La Barre, Mercure, Tresure
61-Dumont-1668	1668	Dumont
27-Gresse	post 1669	Artus, La Barre, Lully, Tresure
62-Chamb-I	1670	Chambonnières
63-Chamb-II	1670	Chambonnières
Brussels-27.220	16--	Chambonnières
28-Brussels-926	post 1670	Boyvin, Dumanoir, Lebègue, Lully, Nivers, Thomelin
Van-Eijl	1671	Lully, Tresure
Darmstadt-17	1672	Gaultier, Gumprecht
Darmstadt-18	1674	Gaultier
Darmstadt-1198	16--	anon. transcriptions

The forty sources from the last quarter of the century include the important d'Anglebert sources (*33-Rés-89ter* and *68-d'Anglebert*) as well as the complete works of Lebègue, which are contained in *64-Lebègue-I* and *65-Lebègue-II*. *36-Parville* is a major source for both Louis Couperin and the Bauyn La Barre, and all of the surviving works of Geoffroy are in *37-Geoffroy*. Most of the works of Burette have been lost, as have been sources for Louis Couperin and Chambonnières (*Burette-407*, *-408* and *-409*). Both the French and foreign sources are frequently dominated by Lully tunes, and transcriptions from lute music continue to form a part of the repertoire.

20-Ch-Ch-378	ca. 1675-1710?	La Barre, Tresure
64-Lebègue-I	1677	Lebègue
33-Rés-89ter	post 1677	d'Anglebert, Chambonnières, Louis Couperin, Gaultier, Lambert, Lully, Marais, Mesangeau, Pinel, Richard
3-Berlin-40623	1678	La Barre, Lully
39-Vm7-6307-1	post 1678	Lully

9-Ihre-284	1679	Artus, Brullard, Dumanoir, Gaultier, La Barre, Lully, Tresure
40-Rés-476	post 1679	L. Couperin, Lully
Bod-576	post 1679	Lully, Tresure
66-Perrine	1680	Gaultier
Stockholm-2	ca. 1680?	Gaultier
41-Thomelin	ca. 1680-1700?	Thomelin
21-Rés-1186bis	post ca. 1680	Farinel, Lebègue
22-Ch-Ch-1177	post ca. 1680	La Barre
Stockholm-176	post 1681	Du But, Gaultier, Lully, Mouton
67-Gigault	1682	Gigault
10-Schwerin-617	post 1684	Lebègue, Lully
Stoss	post 1684	Lully
42-Vm7-6307-2	post 1684	Lully
Stockholm-228	post 1685	Du But, Lully, Mercure, Verdier
43-Gen-2354	post 1685	Lully
36-Parville	post 1686	d'Anglebert, Chambonnières, L. Couperin, Gaultier, Hardel, La Barre, Lebègue, Lully, Richard
Lüneburg-1198	1687	Lully
44-LaPierre	post 1687	Chambonnières, Favier, Hardel, Lully, Monnard, Montelan
65-Lebègue-II	1687	Lebègue
Jacquet	1687	La Guerre
45-Dart	post 1687	d'Anglebert, Campra, Chambonnières, Couperin, Farinel, Gaultier, Hardel, Lebègue, Lully, Verdier.
68-d'Anglebert	1689	d'Anglebert, Lully
46-Menetou	post 1689	d'Anglebert, Lambert, Lully, Lebègue, Menetou
34-Gen-2357[A]	ca. 1690?	anon.
47-Gen-2356	ca. 1690?	Burette, Chambonnières, L. Couperin, Lully, Pinel, Richard
22a-Roper	ca. 1691	Chambonnières, Lebègue, Lully
37-Geoffroy	post 1694	Geoffroy
Ottobeuren	1695	Dufaut, Gaultier, Lambert (?), Pinel
Burette-407	1695	Chambonnières, Couperin
Burette-408	1695	unknown
Burette-409	1695	Cl. Burette
48-LaBarre-6	post 1697	Berthet, Campra, Collasse, Lebègue, Lully
Grimm	1699	Lully

Thott	1699-1702	French titles only
Nuremberg	1699-1721	French titles only

The twenty-six eighteenth-century sources include an important English manuscript, *24-Babell,* which contains unique French pieces. *51-LaBarre-11* also transmits a small number of unique works, but the other manuscripts are more interesting as demonstrations of what pieces from the repertoire remained popular. Chambonnières is encountered a full century after many of the pieces were written (*53-Oldham-2*), and Lebègue is often found in Germanic and Scandinavian manuscripts. Lully's pieces are still ubiquitous, and while d'Anglebert's works circulated occasionally, those of Louis Couperin were true rarities already cherished in the early eighteenth century.

11-Ryge	ca. 1700?	Lebègue, Lully
Brussels-24.106	ca. 1700?	Chambonnières
30-Cecilia	ca. 1700?	Lebègue, Lully, Monnard
23-Tenbury	1701	Chambonnières, Collasse, L. Couperin, Dieupart, Hardel, Lebègue, Lully Monnard, Valois
24-Babell	1702	d'Anglebert, Chambonnières, Charpentier, L. Couperin, Dieupart, Gaultier, Gillier, Hardel, Bauyn La Barre, Lebègue, Lully, Marais, Monnard, Tresure, Valois
Madrid-1357	1706	Lully
Minorite	1708-17??	Lully
25-Bod-426	post 1708	Godeau, Hardel, Lully
Bod-425	post 1708	French language
31-Madrid-1360	1709	L. Couperin, Gaultier, Hardel, La Barre, Lully, Monnard
12-Walther	ca. 1712-post 1731	d'Anglebert, Lebègue
Berlin-40624	post 1715	French dance forms only
49-RésF-933	post 1715	Campra, L. Couperin, Destouches, Hardel, Lully, Marais
50-Paignon	1716	Lebègue, Lully
13-Möllersche	1717-1719	Lebègue, Lully
14-Schwerin-619	ca. 1720?	Collasse, P. Gaultier, Lebègue, Lully
Berlin-30363	post 1723	Lully
51-LaBarre-11	post 1724	d'Anglebert, Lully, Montelan
St-Georges	post 1724?	Hardel
Berlin-8551	ca. 1725?	de Grigny (misattribution)
LeBret	17--	(Le Bret, Fr. Couperin)
52-Rés-2671	post 1742	Chambonnières
Burette-410	pre 1747	Lully
15-Berlin-30206	ca. 1750-1770	d'Anglebert

53-Oldham-2	post 1752	Chambonnières
Arsenal-410/24	17??	unknown

This study was conceived as a tool for future research. Its primary function is to provide precise information about the sources of seventeenth-century French harpsichord music, defining and identifying the repertoire. However, because there is a large quantity of raw material in the Catalog, it can be put to use in several ways, some of which were not foreseen at the outset of the project.

Stylistic comparisons of the art of transcription, for example, can be carried out with the pieces specified in the work lists for Gaultier and Lully (Appendix C). The intervalic patterns of the melodies of this repertoire are already codified in the Thematic Index; even a perusal of the numerical lists shows recurring patterns which could be the basis for further investigation. Many thematic and textural similarities of specific pieces are cited in the Commentary and Catalog as borrowings or "homages," and these relationships seem to reflect a major aspect of seventeenth-century compositional practice which bears further study. All of the ornament signs which are found in the pieces are set forth at the left-hand edges of the incipits, providing data for the student of that aspect of performance practice, and the "Marginalia" sections of the Catalog entries cite the addition of fingerings or other such markings in the sources.

The possibilities for future work in this field are many, and only a few have been cited here or in the individual entries in the Commentary. This source study is a beginning, not an ending.

CHAPTER VIII

EXPLANATION OF THE CATALOG

General Organization

The purpose of the Catalog is to provide a detailed description in tabular form of the sources of seventeenth-century French harpsichord music. All of the known sources appear in the Catalog, and all of the sources which are entered contain at least one composition by a seventeenth-century French harpsichordist. The format of each description is standardized as much as possible, but the diversity of the sources necessitates occasional inconsistencies: Some large manuscripts which have been inventoried by other scholars and which have only a few pieces pertinent to this study are given summary treatment here (e.g., *4-Lynar*). Existing numbering schemes of pages, leaves or compositions are retained whenever possible, rather than changing them all into one arbitrary system.

The physical descriptions of printed sources differ somewhat from manuscript citations. Manuscripts which are privately or semi-privately held sometimes receive less full descriptions, due to the limitations of time which politeness dictated when they were studied. Unless otherwise noted in the Commentary, every source has been examined personally, but two sources (*3-Berlin-40623* and *44-LaPierre*) were unavailable even in microfilm, and only the information from secondary sources could be included in the Catalog.

The Catalog entries present data and conclusions. The data are contained in the inventories, which include complete literal transcriptions of the titles and incipits of the compositions in the sources, as well as concordance and edition citations. The conclusions are listed at the beginning of each entry: provenance and date, as nearly as can be determined on the basis of all types of evidence; current location; physical description; notations(s) used; number and identity of the scribes; significant marginalia; and a summary of the composers represented and the general organization of the contents of the source. The justifications or qualifications of the conclusions and the interpretation of some aspects of the data are found in the Commentary. Access to the data by melodic themes, library shelf numbers, composers and watermarks is provided by the indices, appendices and bibliographies.

The seventy sources are inventoried in the order in which they are discussed in the Commentary, which is roughly chronological within national groups or subgroups:

1-4	Germanic and Scandinavian household mss
5-15	Germanic and Scandinavian professional mss
16-22a-28	English mss
26-28	Dutch and Belgian mss
29-31	Italian and Spanish mss
32-34	French autograph mss
35-37	French large professional mss
38-53	French small professional mss
54-55	French household mss
56-59a-68	Printed sources

Bibliographic Terminology

The richness of the international bibliographic vocabulary gives the appearance of considerable specificity, but the opposite situation actually obtains. In order to avoid confusion, all of the terms adopted here will be defined.

The term "leaf," abbreviated with an italic letter (*ℓ*.) to avoid confusion with the numeral one (1), is used to denote the single piece of paper which is comprised of two pages. "Recto" (r) and "verso" (v) designate the front and back of a leaf. Sources which have already been supplied with pagination, whether contemporary or modern, will be discussed in terms of pages (p.).

In the descriptions of the sources given at the beginning of each inventory, the format is listed. "Folio format" has the following definition: A volume written on sheets of paper folded once, each sheet making two leaves or four pages. In practice, a double-size sheet could have been used and folded twice or a quad-size sheet folded three times to give the same format.

"Quarto" has the corresponding meaning for volumes in which each leaf is (or was) part of a quartet of leaves. Most keyboard manuscripts are in "oblong quarto format," that is, the width is greater than the height; the opposite shape is here called "upright quarto format." The diagrams in Figure 6 illustrate the derivation of the most common formats from the original sheet. They also show the typical shapes of these formats and the locations of the watermarks in each, which are the most helpful identifying factor in determining format. The exact size of the leaves and the binding are not implied by the format terms. In the Inventories, they are always given in centimeters, using the formula of height followed by width (e.g., 15 x 22 cm. for a typical oblong quarto volume).

Any numeration of pages, leaves or musical compositions which already exists in a source is retained, adjusted as necessary. This policy results in the numbering of some pieces, for example, as "2" and "2a,"

complete unfolded sheet

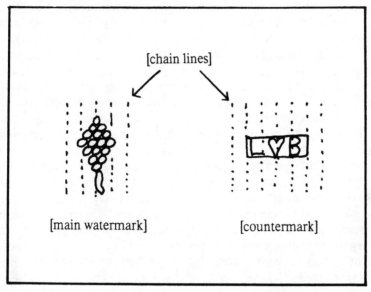

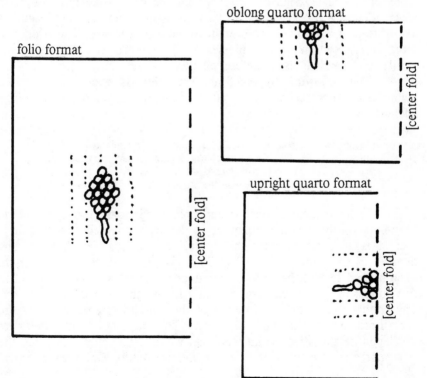

Fig. 6: Format Illustrations

even if they are not musically related, if piece "2a" had been omitted in the original numeration. An entirely new numeration, although more correct, would be unnecessarily confusing because of the conflict between the numbers in the source and those in this Catalog. Similarly, if a numeration has been established by another scholar, it is retained and adjusted here. Only in a few instances was a numeration so hopelessly incorrect that a new system has been introduced, but the old numbers are also listed in the Inventories of the sources for reference.

Many manuscripts were written from both ends; that is, using both covers as the front by turning the book upside down. In such cases, the inventory from one direction is given only as far as the music continues in that direction; then a second inventory from the other end is listed, with "-A" appended to each number (e.g., a book of 100 leaves might be inventoried as *l.* 1-70 and then *l.* 1A-30A).

The terms "fascicle," "gathering," "quire," "section," "signature" and "stave" are all listed in glossaries as terms for the group of leaves resulting from the placement of several sheets upon one another which are then folded to form leaves. The term "quire" is used here for the following reasons: "Stave" duplicates a musical term; "section" is even more ambiguous. "Signature" refers more strictly to the printer's mark which identifies the group of leaves in question, and "fascicle" signifies any section of a volume, or an entire volume of a series. The American Library Association has expressed a preference for "quire" over "gathering," and it is therefore adopted here.[207]

The following hypothetical description is explained in prose below as a summary and illustration of the bibliographic terminology adopted here:

> *Description*: 1 p.*l.*, 34 (i.e., 33: 5 omitted in numeration), 1 *l.*; 5 quires (A^4, B^8, C^{12}, D^8, E^2); oblong quarto format, trimmed, gilt edges, 17.7 x 23.2 cm. Watermark #150. Contemporary gilt-tooled full leather binding, marbled pastedowns and end papers, 18.5 x 24 cm.

That is, there is one unnumbered preliminary leaf (p.*l.*) at the beginning of the volume, followed by leaves numbered one to thirty-four; this amounts to only thirty-three leaves, however, because one number was skipped ("*l.* 6" follows "*l.* 4"); there is one more unnumbered leaf at the end of the volume. The leaves are grouped in five quires; the first is comprised of four leaves, the second has eight, etc. The format, based on the location of the watermarks, direction of the chain lines and the shape of the leaves, is "oblong quarto"; the leaves are smaller in height (17.7 centimeters) than width (23.3 centimeters) and the watermarks are cut off at the tops or bottoms of the leaves, with vertical chain lines. The leaves were originally larger than their current size, as there is evidence that they were trimmed to form even edges; these edges were then gilded for decoration and to prevent dust from penetrating the volume. A tracing of the watermark is reproduced as number 150 in Appendix A, where it is identified as closely as possible through secondary literature; if the information is significant to the dating or provenance of the source, it is mentioned in the Commentary. The binding appears to be from the seventeenth or eighteenth centuries. Throughout this study, "contemporary" denotes "before ca. 1800" and "modern" signifies "after ca. 1800." The boards (covers) and spine of this hypothetical source are entirely covered with leather, which is decorated with gilt pressed into the leather. "Half leather" bindings have leather only around the spine and "three-quarter leather" bindings have leather on the spine and corners of the boards. The binder of this volume pasted a half sheet of marbled decorative paper to the inside of the covers, thus providing one paste-down and one unnumbered end paper at each end of the source. The outer measurements of the book are 18.5 centimeters high by 24 centimeters wide.

Notational Terminology

Most of the musical terms used here follow current American musicological practice as defined in the *Harvard Dictionary of Music*, but a few terms dealing with notation are not entirely standardized. The least satisfactory of these is "new German organ tablature," which is a marvel of inaccuracy: In the seventeenth century, it was not new, it was not necessarily German, and it was not used exclusively for organ music; it was, at least, always a tablature. It was used in Germanic and Scandinavian countries, most commonly in the northern regions, after ca. 1550. Harpsichord music and even ensemble music were also scored in "organ" tablature. The term will be used here, however, because changing the accepted phrase would probably cause as much confusion as clarification. The terms "French tablature," "Dutch tablature," "Italian tablature," and "English tablature" are sometimes encountered in modern writings, but these historical names all refer to staff notations which are very similar to modern piano score. They have been discarded here, preserving the commonly accepted distinction between "tablature" and "score" (or "staff notation"). One new term is coined here, "French letter score," which denotes the use of letters written in place of notes on five-line staves (see *6-Munich-1511f*).

Clefs are not given descriptive names such as "baritone" or "violin," but are defined by the line on which they are positioned, e.g., F^3, G^2 (an F clef on the third line from the bottom, a G clef on the next-to-lowest line).

Inventory Entries

Each complete entry in an Inventory presents the information necessary to identify the piece, to locate it within the source, and to compare it with concordant readings, as well as with modern editions. Incomplete entries, given for pieces which are not seventeenth-century French harpsichord music as defined in the Introduction, are adumbrations of the complete entry form. They consist of the location in the source, title as given in the source and additional information as appropriate: key, modern edition, etc. It should be noted that the amount and kind of information in incomplete entries varies from source to source. The reader should not assume in such entries that all words subsequent to the title or all known concordances are listed.

While algebraic appearances cannot be altogether avoided, an attempt has been made to use symbols which are self-explanatory as well as concise. The following fictitious complete entry is explained in prose below:

---

29 | [GAULTIER, arr d'ANGLEBERT: *Gigue la verdinguette* (C)]
Gigue /Gautier |fin
I 64v^1-65r^3 ^{3}|11|15| [$^3_4$|12|16|]

CO: 62-d'Anglebert #100, Gigue la verdinguette
cf Stockholm-228 *I* 21v, gigue
ED: Gilbert p 300; cf Souris-G #199, Tessier-G #299.

Fig. 7: Sample Catalog Entry

First line: number, composer, arranger, title, key. The twenty-ninth composition in this source was composed by Gaultier, a lutenist. The keyboard version is by d'Anglebert. The full names and dates of the composers are listed with further biographical information in the List of Composers (Appendix D), and a list of works for both composers is in Appendix C. The standardized title of the piece is "Gigue la verdinguette," and the key is C Major. All compositions are listed as either major (upper case letter) or minor (lower case letter) for practical reasons of thematic indexing; modal aspects of the tonalities have been ignored, and when there is ambiguity, the final chord of the piece is taken to be tonic, using the characteristic inflection of the third scale degree to determine major or minor quality.

Second line: original title. A complete transcription of all of the words appearing in the source is given; the slanted slash (/) indicates a new line in the original, and the vertical stroke (|) denotes that the word "fin" appears at a later point in the composition.

Third line: location and length. The Gigue begins on the verso of the sixty-fourth leaf, on the first system (brace), and ends on the recto of the sixty-fifth leaf, on the third system. It is divided into two strains of eleven and fifteen measures each, with a meter sign of "3." Because of irregular barring, this would amount to twelve and sixteen measures if it were divided evenly into $\frac{3}{4}$ measures. The latter indication is strictly a bibliographic description, showing the length of the piece for identification purposes; it does not suggest that such a barring or meter sign is implied by the musical content of the piece.

Incipit. The thematic incipit serves two functions: It identifies the piece and it provides a visual description of the manuscript. The incipits in the Catalog do not comprise an edition of the music and the editorial policy is not the same as is currently accepted in published music. An edition normally presents what, in the editor's view, the composer intended; these incipits attempt to show what the scribe actually wrote down. The music must be easily read by the modern musician, but it must also show the idiosyncrasies of the source. The most accurate reflection of a manuscript would be an exact facsimile of the opening of each piece, but this procedure would require that the reader be equally comfortable reading new German organ tablature, French letter score, cittern tablature and staves of five to seven lines with movable C, G and F clefs. At the other extreme, a transcription into a purified modern text would make each source appear equally accurate and free of notational peculiarities. The care and style with which a source was written is very significant in determining its importance and reliability, and a heavy editorial hand would be a disservice to other scholars. The compromise solution adopted here is a "quasi-facsimile."

At the extreme left of the incipit are all of the ornament signs which appear in the piece, since they might not all occur in the incipit. Directly to the left of the first double bar is an unchanged copy of the original notation through the first note of the movement. The general style and appearance of the source have been preserved. After the double bar, the beginnings of both strains appear in modern keyboard score. "Strain" is used here to denote one section of the normal binary structure of dance movements. In forms of three or more sections (e.g., pavanes), only the first two are given, as they suffice for identification purposes. Only the themes of variation forms are given, and only the first strains of doubles, since the original pieces have already been identified. Modern rest signs are substituted for the old signs and the use of dots has been modernized, placing them adjacent to the notes to which they apply, and replacing them with tied notes when the value crosses a bar line. The notes are aligned vertically to agree with the rhythmic values and original clef changes are not indicated. The wavy bar lines indicate that the piece continues beyond the transcribed portion. The second double bar denotes the beginning of the second strain. Repetition signs have been omitted altogether, as the symbols are too complicated to have meaning in a mere incipit. The double bar is simply an editorial mark for the beginning of the second strain and it is placed before the musical beginning of the strain, even if it is originally found before a second ending of the first strain. If the strains were not separated by a double bar, a bracketed measure number indicates the location of the beginning of the rationalized second strain.

In all other respects the transcription is a copy of the original notation, including voice leading, beaming, time signature, bar lines, key signature and placement of accidentals (the sharps in the last two measures of the example are not editorial). Obvious mistakes have been left *un*corrected, but mistakes which the scribe himself corrected are presented in the corrected version. The omission of rhythmic values in some notations has been indicated with stemless black note heads. Almost every incipit contains some errors (e.g., the rhythm of the second measure of the tenor voice in the example) and therefore *sic* is not used, since it would serve more to clutter the page than to reassure the reader.

Concordances (CO). In the hypothetical example, the Gigue is found as number 100 in the sixty-second inventory in this Catalog, where it has the title "Gigue la verdinguette." However, the second source is not prefixed with a number, signalling that the source is not inventoried in this Catalog. The List of Abbreviations (pp. xviii-xlii, above) gives a brief identification of *"Stockholm-228"*; the List of Commentaries (pp. xi-xiv) or the Index directs the reader to the discussion of this manuscript in the Commentary. The "cf" before the citation denotes that the piece is related, but not the same; in the case of transcriptions, it usually indicates that the citation is to a different transcription of the same original composition.

Modern editions (ED). The first edition of this Gigue is by Gilbert; a full citation is found in the List of Abbreviations. Since there is no "cf" before the citation, the reader knows that Gilbert consulted this specific source for his edition. The version in "Souris-G" and "Tessier-G," however, are not based on this source, but are editions of the same composition from other sources.

NOTES

[1] The most important single study is Ernesto Epstein, *Der französische Einfluss auf die deutsche Klaviersuite im 17. Jahrhundert* (Würtzburg: K. Triltsch, 1940). This book is still both useful and essentially valid; unfortunately, it has become a rarity. The discussions of French harpsichord music in more standard works also begin with Germanic and Scandinavian sources. The most influential of these reference books are Willi Apel, *The History of Keyboard Music to 1700*, trans. & rev. Hans Tischler (Bloomington: Indiana University Press, 1972; hereafter cited as Apel HKM); and James Anthony, *French Baroque Music from Beaujoyeulx to Rameau* (New York: Norton, 1973).

[2] Renate Brunner is currently completing a dissertation on this subject, "Die deutsche Liebhaber-Klavierbücher des 17. Jahrhunderts" (Ph.D. dissertation, Universität Freiburg, forthcoming). The general perspective of this chapter was influenced by discussions with her held in Freiburg in June, 1975 (hereafter cited as Brunner, "Conversations"). Her dissertation will present a more detailed investigation of most of the Germanic and Scandinavian household keyboard manuscripts which are mentioned here.

[3] Thurston Dart, "Elisabeth Eysbock's Keyboard Book," *Hans Albrecht In Memoriam*, ed. Wilfried Brennecke and Hans Hasse (Kassel: Bärenreiter, 1962), pp. 84-87.

[4] Full identifications for all composers cited in the text or Catalog are given below in Appendix D, pp. 313-334.

[5] This statement, whenever made, indicates that all of the pieces cited, along with many of the other dance movements in the source, were entered into the thematic index file which was the chief finding aid for the present concordance study; cf. the introductory paragraphs to Appendix B, p. 225.

[6] Tobias Norlind, "Zur Geschichte der Suite," *Sammelbände der internationalen Musikgesellschaft* 7 (1905-06): 186.

[7] Povl Hamburger, "Ein handschriftliches Klavierbuch aus der ersten Hälfte des 17. Jahrhunderts," *Zeitschrift für Musikwissenschaft* 13 (1930-31): 133-140.

[8] Charles van den Borren, "Einige Bermerkungen über das handschriftliche Klavierbuch (Nr. 376) der Königlichen Bibliothek zu Kopenhagen," *Zeitschrift für Musikwissenschaft* 13 (1930-31): 556-558.

[9] *Apel-HKM*, p. 505; Anthony, p. 239.

[10] *Epstein*, p. 58, and passim as source "K-1"; Anhang nos. 16-19.

[11] Lydia Schierning, *Die Überlieferung der deutschen Orgel und Klaviermusik aus der ersten Hälfte des 17. Jahrhunderts, eine quellenkundliche Studie* (Kassel: Bärenreiter, 1961; [Ph.D. dissertation, 1956]), pp. 88-90.

[12] Jaroslav Mráček, "Keyboard Dance Music of French Origin or Derivation in the First Half of the Seventeenth Century" (M.A. thesis, Indiana University, 1962).

[13]The editors of *Souris-M* were unaware of *1-Copenhagen-376* and included the Allemande as a copy of Pirro's edition; Pirro had not listed his source, which was clearly *1-Copenhagen-376,* since the texts are identical.

[14]The manuscript is listed in *Versteigerung der Musikbibliothek des Herrn Dr. Werner Wolffheim,* 2 vols., (Berlin: Breslauer & Liepmannssohn, 1928-29), 2: 31, item 48: "Deutsche Orgeltabulatur (1630-1650). Kl.-40. Grüner defekter Einband. 78 beschriebene Blätter. Kosbare handschrift des 17. Jahrhunderts. Auf dem letzten Blatt befindet sich die Angabe: 1630. Auf S. 112 ist die Jahreszahl 1649." The catalog description includes a listing of titles. It was mentioned in Johannes Wolf, *Handbuch der Notationskunde* (Leipzig: Breitkopf & Härtel, 1913-19), 2:31. It was purchased by the Deutsche Staatsbibliothek (Berlin) in 1929, but is among the many manuscripts from that collection which have not been located since the Second World War. I am grateful for information supplied in letters from A. Rosenthal of the Otto Haas firm, London, successor to Leo Liepmannssohn (19 August, 1974) and Dr. Karl-Heinz Köhler, Abteilungsdirektor, Deutsche Staatsbibliothek, East Berlin (27 November, 1974).

[15]*Tabulae codicum manuscriptorum,* 10 vols., (Vienna: 1864; reprint ed., Vienna: Akademischer Verlag, 1965), 10: 143-146, item 18491.

[16]*Epstein,* p. 61 and passim as source "W"; Wolf, 2: 33; Schierning, pp. 111-112. James Furdell, "The Klavierbuch of Regina Clara Imhoff," paper presented at the New York State Chapter of the American Musicological Society at Hamilton College, April, 1969.

[17]The melody is titled "Ein französisch Schäffer Liedlein" in *Berlin-40147.*

[18]The melody was known as "Courante de monsieur" or "Courante la chabotte." This setting was transcribed by Dickinson (1:95), who listed other melody concordances.

[19]The same melody was set by Pinel; cf. *1-Copenhagen-376* #48, *Faille l.* 121v, *11-Ryge* #15, *18-Ch-Ch-1236* #38, *Van-Eijl* #13 and #16, *Drallius* #128. Cf. Ex. 1, above.

[20]Friedrich Welter, ed., *Katalog der Musikalien der Ratsbücherei Lüneburg,* 2nd ed., (Lippstadt: Kistner & Siegel, 1955), passim. Welter gave minimal incipits and did not state the keys of the pieces, although he seems to have arranged them by key within each genre. Often the key of a movement is by no means obvious from a few notes of the melody.

[21]This is probably an intabulation of a chanson, the original being by either a French or non-French composer.

[22]The same melody was set by La Barre; cf. *1-Copenhagen-376* #6, *18-Ch-Ch-1236* #6, *16-Cosyn* #101, *2-Witzendorff* #54, *Eyck-I l.* 36v, *Oude* 731 x 8, *Kabinet* I l. 9v.

[23]The melody is tenuously related to the sarabande melody set by Pinel (cf. Ex. 1, above). This version was transcribed by Dickinson (1:94) for comparison to the *1-Copenhagen-376* setting (*Dickinson,* 2:74). Cf. n. 19, above.

[24]Several concordances of the melody, also known as "La Chabotte," are given by *Dickinson* (1:95-96).

[25]During the war, the library was hastily dispersed to several other cities for safety. Some 400 items which were sent to locations later occupied by the Russians were never returned after the war, and it is unknown which ones still exist and where they are. Some of them had been seen in Poland some years ago by Carleton Smith (Carleton Smith, "Tracking Down Original Scores Missing in the War," *Smithsonian* 6:9 [December, 1975], pp. 87-94). Although Smith's assertion that a political settlement might make the sources available again has been doubted (P.J.P. Whitehead, "The Lost Berlin Manuscripts," *Notes* 33:1 [September, 1976], pp. 7-15), such a restitution was announced recently ("Poland Plans to Give Music Manuscripts to East Germany," *New York Times,* 1 May 1977, p. 70). Officials at the library still have no knowledge of whether *Berlin-40147* or any of the other sources listed here as "unlocated" are among the recently located manuscripts (letter from Jutta Theurich, Wiss. Bibliothekarin, Deutsche Staatsbibliothek, 20 March 1978). Those sources which were evacuated to locations now in the West were moved temporarily to the West deutsche Bibliothek in Marburg and the Universitätsbibliothek in Tübingen; they are now in the Staatsbibliothek der stiftung preussischer Kulturbesitz (West Berlin--Dahlem), but the only more-or-less complete catalog for the manuscripts remains in the Deutsche Staatsbibliothek (East Berlin). An incomplete and inaccurate file of what manuscripts were sent to which locations is in that catalog. *Berlin-41047* is listed as having been sent to Fürstenstein.

[26]*Epstein,* pp. 74-84 and *passim* as source "B-1." Friedrich Wilhelm Riedel, *Quellenkundliche Beiträge zur Geschichte der Musik für Tasteninstrumenten* (Kassel: Bärenreiter, 1960; hereafter cited as Riedel, *Quellen*), p. 93.

[27]CO: cf. *6-Munich-1511e* #12, *7-Munich-1511f* #18, *Skara* #26, *9-Ihre-284* #51, *31-Madrid-1360* #24/10, *Van-Eijl* #12, 20, and *Cassel* "A."

[28]Simone Wallon, "Un Recueil de pièces de clavecin de la seconde moitié du XVIIe siècle," *Revue de musicologie* 38 (Dec., 1956): 105-114.

[29]The debate raged between Jost Harro Schmidt and Frits Noske; the articles, in chronological order, are: Schmidt, ed., *J.P. Sweelinck* [works], Exempla Musica Neerlandica no. 2 (Amsterdam: Vereniging Neerlandse Muziekgeschiedenis, 1965). Noske, "Een apocrief en een dubieus Werk van Sweelinck," *Mededeelingenblad* 20 (Sept., 1966): 27 ff. Schmidt, "Sweelincks Bergamasca und seine Allemande De Chapelle," *Mededeelingenblad* 25 (April, 1968): 58-64 (hereafter cited as Schmidt, *Mededeelingenblad*). Noske, [Review of Schmidt's Sweelinck edition, cited above], *Notes* 24:1 (Sept., 1967), pp. 134-135. Schmidt had the final word: s.v. "Celler Klavierbuch 1662." *MGG-S* (1973).

[30]Thurston Dart, "John Bull's 'Chapel'," *Music and Letters* 40 (1959): 279-282; cf. pp. 78-79, below.

[31]ARTUS, arr: *Bourrée.* CO: cf. *7-Munich-1511f* #24, *8-Hintze* #24, *27-Gresse* #4, *59a-Handmaide* #22. ED: cf. *Dart-HI* #22.

[32]A popular melody. CO: cf. *7-Munich-1511f* #8 and *Veron l.* 21v.

[33]CO (melody): *27-Gresse* #7, *39-Vm7-6307-1* #14, *Terburg.*

[34]CO (melody): *6-Munich-1511e* #15.

[35]Cf. *7-Munich-1511f* #2 and #27; *8-Hintze* #8 & 9; and *27-Gresse* #3 for other pieces called "tricotet"; this melody is not the same as the others.

[36]CO (melody): cf. *7-Munich-1511f* #6, *8-Hintze* #17, *Vat-mus-569,* p. 103, *Veron l.* 22r, *Cassel* Suite VII. ED: cf. *Écorcheville* 2:97.

[37]"Les tricottes d'Angleterre," cf. n. 35, above.

[38]*Epstein,* pp. 84-85, passim as source #B-4" and Anhang #20-24.

[39]CO: cf. *24-Babell* #162, *Stockholm-176 l.* 10v.

[40]CO: cf. *66-Perrine* #1, *33-Rés-89ter* #29, *45-Dart* #40, *24-Babell* #226, *Stockholm-176 l.* 4v, *Ottobeuren* p. 142, *Skara* #20.

[41]CO: cf. *66-Perrine* #18, *Stockholm-176 l.* 5v.

[42]Cf. *Rollin* p. 105, 113, 116.

[43]*Epstein,* p. 97 and passim as source "B-5." It is listed in the Deutsche Staatsbibliothek as having been sent to Fürstenstein (cf. n. 25, above).

[44]Werner Breig, "Die Lübbenauer Tabulaturen Lynar A 1 und A 2," *Archiv für Musikwissenschaft* 25 (1968): 96-117, 223-236.

[45]Max Seiffert, as inscribed in *4-Lynar,* "Jugendautograph des Hamburger Organisten Matthias Weckmann (1620-1674), begonnen 1637 in Hamburg. . . ."

[46]Alan Curtis, "Jan Reinken and a Dutch Source for Sweelinck's Keyboard Works," *Tijdschrift der Vereeniging voor Nederlandse Muziekgeschiedenis* 20:1-2 (1964-65), pp. 45-56. Mr. Curtis has since discarded the hypothesis that Reincken was the scribe (discussion in Berkeley, March, 1975).

[47]Schierning, p. 78; Curtis, p. 45; Breig, p. 232.

[48]Ballard's Courante is not exactly the same as any of the published lute versions, but it is similar enough to be considered a variant of the same piece.

[49]*Provenance:* England, compiled ca. 1608-1640. *Location:* Cambridge; Fitzwilliam Museum, ms 3-1956. *Scribe:* Edward Lord Herbert of Cherbury. Edward Herbert was a traveller and then an ambassador in France from 1608-1619, when he undoubtedly collected the Ballard Courante. Cf. Thurston Dart, "Lord Herbert of Cherbury's Lute Book," *Music and Letters* 38 (1957): 136-148.

[50]Cf. Schierning, p. 91; *Dickinson,* 1:108-113.

[51]*Dickinson* (1:131-132) cites numerous concordances for the melody and concurs with the tentative Scheidt attribution of Werner Breig, "Zu den handschriftlich überlieferten Liedvariationen von Samuel Scheidt," *Die Musikforschung* 22 (1969): 318-328.

[52]Jaroslav John Stephen Mráček, "Seventeenth-Century Instrumental Dances in Uppsala University Library IMhs 409; A Transcription and Study" (Ph.D. dissertation, Indiana University, 1965).

[53]At the bottom of the verso is the title, "Courante a 5." This is probably the title of the piece which followed on the next page, which is now lost.

[54]Jan Olof Rudén, "Ett nyfunnet Komplement till Dübensamlingen," *Svensk Tidskrift för Musikforskning* 47 (1965), pp. 51-58.

[55]Perhaps the same as the lutenist named in *Saizenay-I*, p. 150: Mr. Henry.

[56]Tresure becomes confused with La Barre in English manuscripts; cf. pp. 63-65.

[57]Some of the pieces are by Ennemond Gaultier, and some cannot be attributed to a specific Gaultier; cf. Appendix C.

[58]A variant of *18-Ch-Ch-1236 #5*.

[59]The popular "Courante l'imortelle" by Ennemond Gaultier. CO: cf. *66-Perrine #1, 33-Rés-89ter #29, 45-Dart #40, 24-Babell #226, Stockholm-2* p. 32, *Stockholm-176* l. 4v, *Ottobeuren* p. 142.

[60]CO: cf. *Darmstadt-17* l. 15v.

[61]A popular melody. CO: cf. *7-Munich-1511f #18, 6-Munich-1511e #12, 9-Ihre-284 #51, Van-Eijl #12, 20, Berlin-40147, 31-Madrid-1360 #24/10, Cassel* "A."

[62]CO (melody): cf. *9-Ihre-284 #72*.

[63]CO (melody): cf. *27-Gresse #13*, La coquille [G]; *Vat-mus-569* p. 112, Branle.

[64]LULLY, arr.: "Bel Iris" from *Ballet de l'impatience* (1661). CO: cf. *28-Brussels-926* l. 3r, *3-Berlin-40623 #1, Van-Eijl #25, Terburg, 11-Ryge #48, Stockholm-228* l. 20v; ED: cf. *Noske #25, Bangert* p. 78.

[65]Julius Joseph Maier, *Die Musikalischen Handschriften der Kgl. Hof- und Staatsbibl. in München*, Catalogus codicum manuscriptorum bibliotheccaieregia monacensis 7:1, (Munich: Palmschen Hofbuchhandlung, 1879), items 266 [1503f], 267 [1511e] and 268 [1511f].

[66]See the Froberger pieces in *35-Bauyn-III* and *47*-Gen-2356, for example, some of which are known exclusively from these French manuscripts. Howard Schott considers this Allemande to be a spurious work (cf. p. 45).

[67]It is sufficiently different from the published version of 1670 (*63-Chamb-II #29*) that one can be quite positive that it was copied from a manuscript source.

[68]Werner Danckert, *Geschichte der Gigue* (Leipzig: Kistner & Siegel, 1924), pp. 160-161.

[69]"Lautenbuch Wolckenstein et Rodenegg in Collegio Parmensi 1656." *Location:* West Berlin; Staatsbibliothek der Stiftung preuβischer Kulturbsitz, Mus. Ms. 40068. *Notation:* Italian lute tablature.

[70]Daniel Devoto, "De la zarabanda à la sarabande," *Recherches* 6 (1966): 27-72.

[71]Riedel, *Quellen,* pp. 93-98.

[72]I am indebted to Joshua Rifkin for sharing his research on Dresden watermarks with me. See also p. 174.

[73]A two-volume collection of lute music, dated and signed at the beginning of the second book, "J'ay commenceé ce livre le 4e auoust 1699 De Saizenay." *Location:* Besançon, France; Bibliothèque municipale, ms 279152, 279153.

[74]Fritz Noack, "Die Tabulaturen der hessischen Landesbibliothek zu Darmstadt," *Bericht über den musikwissenschaftlichen Kongress, Basel, 1924* (reprint ed., Wiesbaden: M. Sandy, 1969), pp. 280-281.

[75]The "Courante" in *Darmstadt-17 l.* 15v is the same piece as the "Courant Monsr Gautier" of *Skara* #23; the "Allemande Von der Lauten abgesetzt . . . Allemande Gautier" of *Darmstadt-18 l.* 8v is the "Tombeau de l'enclos" of *66-Perrine* #24. It is not clear in either case which Gaultier was the composer.

[76]Technically a Frenchman, as he was from Strasbourg.

[77]Father and son, both named Valentin, were active at the Darmstadt court. Although Germans, they wrote in the French style and had close Strasbourg connections.

[78]The best history of the suite, summarizing the earlier bibliography and adding considerable new perspectives, is David Fuller, s.v. "Suite," *Grove-6.*

[79]The popular "Courante l'imortelle" on *l.* 4v (cf. n. 59, above), and "Courante la belle homicide" on *l.* 10v (cf. n. 39, above).

[80]Telemann wrote an entertaining anecdote regarding the currency and old-fashionedness of the notation when he was a young student in Magdeburg in the 1690's: "Bevor ich zu solchem Vermögen gelanget war, ließ ich mich auf dem Clavier unterrichten; gerieth aber zum Unglück an einen Organisten, der mich mit der deutschen Tabulatur erschreckte, die er eben so steiff spielte, wie vielleicht sein Grosvater gethan, von dem er sie geerbet hatte. . . . Aber schied ich, nach einer vierzehntägigen Marter, von ihm . . . (Georg Philipp Telemann, *Selbstbiographie* [Hamburg, 1740], facsimile reprint in Willie Kahal, ed., *Selbstbiographien deutscher Musiker des XVIII Jahrhunderts mit Einleitungen und Anmerkungen.* Cologne: Stauffen, 1948; reprint ed., Netherlands: Frits Knuf, 1972.

[81]A gavotte usually starts on the third beat of the measure, rather than the first. The choreography of the dance demands a two-note upbeat. A comparison of the incipits of the many gavottes in the French manuscripts of the Catalog confirms this rule.

[82]There are seven suites known elsewhere to be by Froberger, but with variants here. In addition, one Allemande is attributed to Froberger in *Stoss* only, although Howard

Schott doubts the authenticity of the attribution (Howard M. Schott, "A Critical Edition of the Works of J.J. Froberger with Commentary," Ph.D. thesis, University of Oxford, Wadham College, 1977, 1:35-36). Gustav Leonhardt doubts that any of the anonymous pieces are by Froberger; cf. his "Johann Jakob Froberger and His Music," *L'Organo* 6:1 (Jan.-June, 1968), p. 28.

[83]André Tessier, "Une Pièce inédite de Froberger," *Festschrift für Guido Adler zum 75. Geburtstag*, Studien zur Musikgeschichte (Vienna: Universal, 1930), pp. 147-152. A thematic inventory is also provided in Écorcheville, *Catalogue du fonds de musique ancienne de la Bibliothèque nationale* (Paris: Terquem, 1912) 4:87-96.

[84]". . . Relié en Veau noir," that is, different from the current binding," . . . une pièce du Sr Stoos et plusieurs autres . . . Selon toutes les apparences c'est aussi led. Stoos, ou Stoss, qui a fait et ecrit ce recueil." ("Catalogue des liures de musique théorique et pratique, vocalle et instrumentale . . . qui sont dans le cabinet de Sr. Sebastien de Brossard . . ." autograph manuscript dated 1724. *Location:* Paris; Bibliothèque nationale, département de la musique, Réserve Vm8 20, p. 377. In the fair copy [ibid., Réserve Vm8 21] the citation is on p. 534).

[85]Although the manuscript is officially in the library of the Ottobeuren Abbey, in actuality it has been held privately by a school teacher in Memmingen, and efforts by several scholars to obtain a microfilm of it met with no success until 1976. I am grateful to Dr. Renata Wagner at the Bavarian State Library in Munich for her cooperation during almost a year of correspondence. The film is now obtainable from that library.

[86]Herta Tilsen, "Ein Musikhandschrift des Benediktinerklosters Ottobeuren aus dem Jahre 1695" (typescript dissertation, Munich, 1922).

[87]Ennemond Gaultier; cf. *Souris-G* #66; cf. #1 in Appendix C.

[88]cf. *Souris-D* #77.

[89]Denis Gaultier; cf. *Tessier-G* #59.

[90]*Tabulae codicum manuscriptorum* (Vienna: Akademische Verlag, 1864; reprint ed., 1965), cod. 16798 (not "16789," as misprinted in Riedel, *Quellen*, passim).

[91]Friedrich Wilhelm Riedel, *Das Musikarchiv im Minoritenkonvent zu Wien; Katalog des älteren Bestandes vor 1784*, Catalogus musicus 1 (Kassel: Internationale Vereinigung der Musikbibliotheken, 1963), pp. 95-103.

[92]Facsimile of *l.* 25v, s.v., "Richter, Ferdinand," *MGG.*

[93]From the Deutsches Musikgeschichtliches Archiv in Kassel, or from The Monastic Manuscript Microfilm Library, St. John's University, Collegeville, Minnesota.

[94]Hermann Zietz, *Quellenkritische Untersuchungen an den Bach-Handschriften P 801, P 802 und P 803 aus dem "Krebs'schen Nachlass" unter besonderer Berücksichtigung der Choralbearbeitungen des jungen J.S. Bach*, Hamburger Beiträge zur Musikwissenschaft no. 1 (Hamburg: Verlag der Musikalienhandlung Karl Dieter Wagner, 1969).

[95]Alfred Dürr, "Neues über die Möllersche Handschrift," *Bach Jahrbuch 1954,* pp. 75-79.

[96]Werner Wolffheim, "Die Möllersche Handschrift," *Bach Jahrbuch 1912,* pp. 42-60 and Anhang [1]. See also *Epstein,* passim, as source "B-8."

[97]Lebègue himself commented on the obscurity of the style at the beginning of *64-Lebègue-I,* and the preludes are not known in a single manuscript copy. *65-Lebègue-II* has no preludes at all. Cf. my article, "A Letter from Mr. Lebègue Concerning His Preludes," *Recherches* 17 (1977): 7-14. In *13-Möllersche,* two of the omitted preludes are even mentioned by the scribe in his supplied titles, "Suite avec prelude" (*l.* 86r, 94v).

[98]Cf. *Epstein,* passim as source "B-6."

[99]John Caldwell, *English Keyboard Music Before the Nineteenth Century* (New York: Praeger, 1973).

[100]Marie-Louise Pereyra, "Les Livres de virginal de la Bibliothèque du Conservatoire de Paris," *Revue de musicologie* 20 (1926):204-209; 21 (1927):36-39; 24 (1927):205-213; 28 (1928):235-242; 29 (1929):32-39; 37 (1931):22-24; 42 (1932):86-90; 45 (1933):24-27.

[101]Barry A.R. Cooper, "English Solo Keyboard Music of the Middle and Late Baroque," D. Phil. Thesis, Oxford University, 1974; hereafter cited as Cooper, "Thesis." I did not learn of the existence of Dr. Cooper's dissertation in time to make use of it for this study, with the exception of a passage concerning *Oxford-IB,* which was sent to me after John Caldwell kindly pointed it out.

[102]*Dart-BI,* p. 159 (source "Ba" in *Dart-BI, Dart-BII* and *Hendrie*).

[103]*Location:* London; British Library, R.V. 24 *l* 4. I have not examined this manuscript.

[104]See the work list in Appendix C, p. 296. The Courante #27 in *8-Hintze* is also found in a French lute manuscript, and the Allemande #38 is in both *20-Ch-Ch-378* and *35-Bauyn.*

[105]*4-Lynar* is probably earlier, and *8-Hintze, 18-Ch-Ch-1236, 19-Heardson* and *29-Chigi* could be, but the dating of all five sources is problematical. *56-Mersenne* is dated 1636, but La Barre's diminutions are probably not by the English La Barre.

[106]It should be noted, however, that an exemplar of *64-Lebègue-I* (ex. 4) is known to have been in England in 1684 (cf. p. 135).

[107]A list of musicians "who came over with her" is quoted from a 1625 document in Henry Cart De La Fontaine, *The King's Musick, A Transcript of Records Relating to Music and Musicians (1460-1700),* (London: Novello, 1909; reprint ed., New York: Da Capo, 1973), p. 59. There are no known French harpsichordists cited in that list or elsewhere in the book.

[108]Cf. *19-Heardson* #21 and 43-45. B.A.R. Cooper (s.v. "Mercure," *Grove-6*) arrived independently at the same conclusion that the fragmented texture of some of the pieces suggests their lute origins. See also *Rollin,* preface.

[109]CO: *4-Lynar* #65, Courante de La Barre
           16-Cosyn #44, Coranto:-Mr. Tresure
           18-Ch-Ch-1236 #1, ... Jonas Tresure
           18-Ch-Ch-1236 #8, Corant La bar
           19-Heardson #46, (coranto) Mr Gibbons
           27-Gresse #22, Courante
           29-Chigi #30, Corante de Monsu della Bara

ED: cf. *Bonfils-58* #4, *Maas* #91, *Curtis-MMN* #69, *Lincoln-II* p. 38, *Bonfils-18* #23.

[110]I am grateful to Mr. Hendrie for information supplied in a letter dated 10 January 1976. I attempted to trace the owner in Oxford, but was unsuccessful.

[111]Quoted by the author's permission from Cooper, "Thesis," pp. 477-478. I am grateful to Howard Schott for sending me a copy of the passage on very short notice, and to Mr. Cooper for further correspondence. The deleted portion of the passage contains information which is superceded by my discussion in the preceding paragraph, based on a letter from Mr. Hendrie.

[112]*Location:* Oxford; Christ Church College Library, MS 1113. *Description:* 253 p. *Notation:* Keyboard score (two 6-line staves). I am grateful to Arthur Lawrence for examining the manuscript for me. The issue of whether the scribe is actually Ellis remains open.

[113]B.A.R. Cooper, "The Keyboard Suite in England Before the Restoration," *Music and Letters* 53:3 (1972), p. 317.

[114]Cooper, "Albertus Bryne's Keyboard Music," *The Musical Times,* 113 (1972), p. 143. He is probably mistaken, however, in stating that the last thirteen pieces are in hand C; eleven pieces are by Bryne (#81-90), but #81-87 are written by hand A. It is true, however, that the last thirteen pieces (#78-90) were omitted from the original index, with #78-79 appearing as later additions to the index.

[115]This term is used here to denote allemandes which have imitative dotted openings. Some of them, such as the one under consideration, are titled in sources with either dance name. Examples with very similar themes to *20-Ch-Ch-378* #3 are *62-Chamb-I* #16 and *59-Dumont-1657 l.* 31v. For another type of mixing of the terms Gigue and Allemande, see *66-Perrine.*

[116]Charles Burney, *A General History of Music,* 4 vols. (London: 1776-1789), 4:648-649.

[117]London, Guildhouse Library, MS 5039/1 [All Hallows Church vestry minutes], *l.* 150r-164r; ibid., MS 5038/3 [All Hallows Church financial records], s.v. "1723."

[118]London, British Library, L.R. 39a.6 (Sir John Hawkins, *A General History of the Science and Practice of Music,* 5 vols. [London: Payne and Son, 1776], author's annotated ex.), marginalia s.v. "Babell."

[119]Philip H. Highfill, et al., *A Biographical Dictionary of Actors, Actresses, Musicians, Dancers, Managers & Other Stage Personnel in London, 1660-1800,* 8 vols. projected (Carbondale: Southern Illinois University Press, 1973-   ), s.v. "Babel, William."

[120]Michael Tilmouth, ed., "A Calendar of References to Music in Newspapers Published in London and the Provinces (1660-1719)," *RMA Research Chronicle* 1 (1961): 78.

[121]Highfill, s.v. "Babel, Charles."

[122]Ibid.; William's salary for the organist position at All Hallows was also paid to his wife, Alice, without mention of Charles (London, Guildhouse Library, MS 5038/3, s.v. "1723").

[123]Quoted in Tilmouth, p. 69.

[124]Sotheby and Co. [Auction catalog, 17-24 May, 1917], *Catalogue of the Famous Musical Library of Books, Manuscripts, Autograph Letters, Musical Scores, etc. The Property of the Late W.H. Cummings, Mus. Doc.,* item 201.

[125]R. Alec Harman, *A Catalogue of the Printed Music and Books on Music in Durham Cathedral Library* (London: Oxford University Press, 1968), items 598-599. The correct dating of *Trios-1* (1697) and *Trios-2* (1700) is based on information in François Lesure, *Bibliographie des éditions musicales publiées par Estienne Roger et Michel-Charles le Cève* (Paris: Société française de musicologie; Heugel, 1969), pp. 38, 40.

[126]I recently acquired this source, and can confirm the word of Arthur S. Hill in the ms note inserted in the front of *Newberry.*

[127]Gloria Rose discussed it briefly in her "Purcell, Michelangelo Rossi and J.S. Bach: Problems of Authorship," *Acta Musicologica* 4:40 (1968), pp. 203-219. She sought to prove that a Prelude (*24-Babell* #11) was by J.S. Bach, but cavalierly dismissed the cover date of *24-Babell,* 1702. In view of the other two carefully dated Babell autographs, there can be little doubt that the date should be taken at face value, and that the Prelude cannot possibly be by J.S. Bach. *24-Babell* is listed, but not discussed, in *Caldwell* (p. 240), as well as in Pamela J. Willets, *Handlist of Music Manuscripts Acquired 1908-67* (London: British Museum, 1970), p. 8.

[128]Cf. *24-Babell* #63, "Prelude en Maniere de Chaconne Mr. Purcel" (Not located in Zimmerman's catalog); or #141, "Menuet Anglois Rondeau" (by Clarke).

[129]The Amsterdam print is undated, but was advertised in *The Post Man,* 1701 (Lesure, "Roger," p. 40).

[130]Constantin Huygens, *Musique et musiciens au XVIIe siècle; correspondence et oeuvres musicales,* ed. W.J.A. Jonckbloet and J.P.N. Land (Leyden: E.J. Brill, 1882).

[131]Ibid., p. 23. The Allemande is apparently lost; there is no known Allemande by Dumont which has twenty-four plus seventeen measures.

[132]Ibid., p. 24. Since the letter is dated 1655, the Allemande in question must be the one in *58-Dumont-1652.*

[133]Ibid., p. 25. The letter is dated 1655, fifteen years before the publication of Chambonnières' works.

[134]*Catalogue des livres rares et précieux composant la collection musicale de feu M. Jules Écorcheville* (Paris: Emile Paul, 1920), item 304. The complete entry is as follows: "Orgue. Manuscrit de tablature d'orgue. Danses et chansons (vers 1625). Une trentaine de pages seulement ont été écrites. La plus grosse partie du volume se compose de pages blanches rayées pour la musique. In-4, obl., reliue en veau."

[135]*Location:* Brussels; Conservatoire royale de musique, bibliothèque [Papers of Charles van den Borren, MS Vincent de la Faille, s.s.]

[136]Charles van den Borren, "Le Livre de clavier de Vincentus de la Faille (1625)," *Mélanges de musicologie offerts à Lionel de la Laurencie* (Paris: Droz, 1933) pp. 85-96.

[137]Idem, *The Sources of Keyboard Music in England,* trans. James E. Matthew (New York: Novello, 1914), p. 41, n. 16.

[138]Thurston Dart, "John Bull's 'Chapel'," *Music and Letters* 40 (1959): 279-282.

[139]The manuscript, like *26-Bull,* was part of the Pepusch collection and was inventoried as part of his library in John Ward, *Professors of Gresham College* (London: n.p., 1740), pp. 205-206, item 18, the first of eleven volumes; the second was *26-Bull.* One "Courante de chapelle primi toni" is dated 1619.

[140]*Quinze Années d'acquisitions* [1954-1968], *de la pose de la première pierre à l'inauguration officielle de la Bibliothèque royale Albert Ier* (Brussels: Bibliothèque royale Albert Ier, 1969); cited hereafter as *"Quinze Années:"* p. 506, item 459.

[141]André Pirro, *Les Clavecinistes* (Paris: H. Laurens, 1924), p. 44.

[142]Presumably the air of that name by Lully, arr. from *Ballet de l'impatience* (1661). CO: cf. *3-Berlin-40623* #1, *28-Brussels-926* l. 3r, *Skara* #35, *Van-Eijl* #25, *11-Ryge* #48, *Stockholm-228* l. 20v; ED: cf. *Noske* #25, *Bangert* p. 78.

[143]Presumably the same melody as the following CO: cf. *27-Gresse* #7, *39-Vm7-6307-1* #14, *Celle* p. 140.

[144]It was discovered that the manuscript was missing when I requested it in December, 1975. After a more thorough search of the collection, Prof. A. Vander Linden reported that it could not be found, but that he believed that it still might be in the library (letter, dated 18 February, 1976).

[145]R.H. Tollefsen, "A Fresh Look at the 'Gresse Manuscript'," Utrecht [1975]. (Typewritten).

[146]The letters "JT" with #17 surely stand for Jonas Tresure, who is definitely represented in *27-Gresse* later (#33). Tollefsen read the letters as "JS" or "JF," Curtis as "JS."

[147]The "Courante Schopp" (#18, p. 30) may be a setting of a melody which was also set by Schopp, not actually a composition by him (cf. *Noske* p. XXXV).

[148]Apparently a setting of a popular tune; cf. *31-Madrid-1360* #18.

[149]CO: cf. *6-Munich-1511e* #12, *7-Munich-1511f* #18, *9-Ihre-284* #51, *31-Madrid-1360* #24/10, *Skara* #26, *Berlin-40147*, *Cassel* "A."

[150]CO: cf. *1-Copenhagen-376* #48a, *11-Ryge* #15, *18-Ch-Ch-1236* #38, *Drallius* #128, *Leningrad* #22, *Faille l.* 121v. ED: *Noske* #13, cf. #16; cf. Ex. 1 above, *Hamburger*, p. 139, *Dickinson* #48a, *Bangert* p. 84.

[151]The same melody as #13 (cf. n. 150 above).

[152]Lully, arr. from *Ballet de l'impatience* (1661). CO: cf. *3-Berlin-40623* #1, *28-Brussels-926 l.* 3r, *Skara* #35, *Terburg, 11-Ryge* #48, *Stockholm-228 l.* 20v. ED: *Noske* #25, cf. *Bangert* p. 78.

[153]Alexander Silbiger, "Italian Manuscript Sources of Seventeenth-Century Keyboard Music," Ph.D. dissertation, Brandeis University, 1976, passim. I have seen *Bologna-360* only in microfilm.

[154]Harry B. Lincoln, "I Manoscritti Chigiani di musica organo-cembalistica della Biblioteca Apoltolica Vaticana," *L'Organo* 5 (1967): 63-82; ED: *Lincoln-I-III*.

[155]Silbiger, pp. 224-232. I have not seen *Vat-mus-569* in person and am grateful to Mr. Silbiger for the use of his microfilm.

[156]Lyle John Anderson, "Cecilia A/400: Commentary, Thematic Index and Partial Edition," M.M. thesis, University of Wisconsin--Madison, 1977.

[157]Higini Anglès and José Subirá, *Catálogo musical de la Biblioteca nacional de Madrid,* 2 vols., (Barcelona: Consejo superior de investigaciones cientificas, Instituto Español de musicología, 1946), 1:295-309. I have seen the sources only in microfilm.

[158]None of the published books dealing with harpsichords is accurate for seventeenth-century French instruments because so many have been discovered recently. The inner circle of builders and collectors in Paris have been largely responsible for locating them, but most remain in private hands where even the most prestigious scholars, builders and players are not welcomed.

[159]France, Ministère de l'éducation nationale, *Catalogue général des manuscrits des bibliothèques publiques de France,* 48 vols., (Paris: Plon, Nourit, 1885-1933). All the volumes were searched for seventeenth-century harpsichord manuscripts, but none was discovered other than those which appear below in the Catalog.

[160]David Fuller, review of *French Baroque Music from Beaujoyeulx to Rameau* by James R. Anthony, *Journal of the American Musicological Society* 28:2 (Summer, 1975), p. 383.

[161]Guy Oldham, "Louis Couperin; A New Source of French Keyboard Music of the Mid 17th Century," *Recherches* 1 (1960): 51-60; hereafter cited as Oldham, "Source." I am grateful to Mr. Oldham for allowing me to examine this extraordinary manuscript in detail and for two long and fruitful discussions with him concerning it.

[162]In addition to the illustrations in Oldham "Source," there are facsimiles of #97-100 (Oldham #62-64) as plates 97-99 with his "Two pieces for 5-Part Shawm Band by Louis Couperin," *Music, Libraries and Instruments* (Hinrichsen's Eleventh Music Book)

(London: Hinrichsen, 1961): 233-238. Two facsimiles from *32-Oldham* (#48-49; Oldham #15-16) are identified only as "Cl X" in Norbert Dufourcq, *Le Livre d'orgue français, 1589-1789*, 5 vols.; vol. 4, *La Musique* (Paris: Picard, 1972), plate IV.

[163]These observations were necessarily based on my memory of *33-Rés-89ter*, since it was impossible to place the manuscripts side by side for comparison. The hypothesis demands further confirmation before it can be accepted an absolutely certain.

[164]Facsim. in *Brunold-Tesier*, p. XV (p. XX in the Broude Bros. reprint ed.).

[165]*Location:* Paris; Minutier central, LIII, 104.

[166]*34-Gen-2357[A], 38-Gen-2348/53, 54-Gen-2350/57.* All of the manuscripts from this library are listed with title inventories in Madelaine Garros and Simone Wallon, *Catalogue du fonds musical de la Bibliothèque Sainte-Geneviève de Paris* (Kassel: Internationale Vereinigung der Musikbibliotheken; Internationaler Gesellschaft für Musikwissenschaft, 1967), hereafter cited as Garros, *Catalogue.*

[167]Jules Écorcheville, ed., *Catalogue du fonds de musique ancienne de la Bibliothèque nationale,* 8 vols., (Paris: Terquem, 1910-1914).

[168]Users of the microfilm should also be warned that the film supplied for many years by the library omits two pages (*35-Bauyn-I, l.* 59v-60r), repeats another (*35-Bauyn-II, l.* 71v) and presents the sections of the manuscript in a hopelessly jumbled order.

[169]I am grateful to Alan Curtis, who gave me a copy of his reading of the piece for comparison with my own.

[170]Évrard Titon du Tillet, *Déscription du Parnasse* (Paris: J.B. Caignard fils, 1732), p. 403.

[171]*24-Babell* is a French source in the sense that the French pieces were copied from very late seventeenth-century French manuscripts, not English sources.

[172]For a conversion table of the numberings in the three editions, see my article, "A Performer's Guide to the Music of Louis Couperin," *The Diapason* 66:7 (June, 1975): 7-8, hereafter cited as Gustafson, "Couperin."

[173]Cf. Additional MS 30491, *l.* 23-206, in the British Library (London), containing Neapolitan harpsichord music which is in the hand of Rossi (*Apel-HKM,* p. 424).

[174]Eleanor Caluori, *Luigi Rossi,* Cantata Music Index (Wellesley: Wellesley College, 1965).

[175]Howard Schott (letter, 25 August 1976). Cf. *Adler-I,* source "D."

[176]Alan Curtis, "Musique classique française à Berkeley; pièces inédites de Louis Couperin, Lebègue, La Barre, etc.," *Revue de musicologie* 56:2 (1970), pp. 123-164; hereafter cited as *Curtis-Berkeley.* See also *Curtis-Co.*

[177]Margarete Reimann wrote what has become a standard, but essentially useless study of suite organization; her labored analysis of François Couperin's *ordres* does not produce a form resembling the more Germanic notion of a suite (Margarete Reimann, *Untersuchungen zur Formgeschichte der französischen Klavier-Suite, mit besonderer Berücksichtigung von Couperins 'Ordres'* [Regensburg: G. Bosse, 1940]). *Gilbert*

removed the transcriptions from d'Anglebert's ordering of pieces in *68-d'Anglebert* in order to create "normal" suites, but the original groupings are more typical of French sources. See David Fuller, s.v. "Suite," *Grove-6,* for a discussion of the suite in general, and Gustafson, "Couperin," for the practical application of the principles discussed above in relationship to the music of Louis Couperin.

[178]Martine Roche, "Un Livre de clavecin français de la fin du XVIIe siècle," *Recherches* 7 (1967): 39-73. Ms. Roche has not worked with the manuscript since the time of that article and the areas for investigation which she indicated still await attention. She still intends to publish an edition of the manuscript.

[179]Norbert Dufourcq, "À Travers l'inédit: Nicholas Lebègue; Guillaume-Gabriel Nivers; La Furstenbert et Benaut," *Recherches* I (1960): 205-213.

[180]Mme de Chambure died in August, 1975, shortly after I arrived in Paris to examine the Parisian sources. In April, 1978, the collection was still unavailable. François Lesure is actively involved with the disposition of the manuscripts, and I am grateful to him for information about it.

[181]*Dart-Co,* p. [v], "Un appendice comprend . . . une Chaconne de 'M. Couperin' (manuscrit de la collection personnelle de l'auteur de la nouvelle édition." *Dart-HII,* commentary #27, "Also in a late 17th-century manuscript collection of French harpsichord music now in my possession, here it [the 'Chacone' #27] is called 'Chaconne de Mr. Verdre.' . . . The manuscript clarifies the formal structure of the piece, which has been muddled in *Musick's Hand-maid.* "

[182]*Catalogue de la bibliothèque de feu M. Burette,* 3 vols. (Paris: G. Martin, 1748), 1:44, items 407-410.

[183]Lionel de La Laurencie and L.A. Gastoué, *Catalogue des livres de musique (manuscrits et imprimés) de la Bibliothèque de l'Arsenal à Paris* (Paris: Droz, 1936), p. 74, M 410/24. In the library's exemplar, new shelf numbers have been added to each entry. In place of a new number is the notation "non identifié" for this manuscript.

[184]This manuscript came to my attention too late to allow a detailed study; these comments are based entirely on Écorcheville's catalog entry.

[185]I am grateful to Mr. Oldham for his permission to examine this manuscript, after he had pointed out the presence of Chambonnières' piece in it. I have not studied the manuscript in detail.

[186]These identifications are from Garros, *Catalogue,* pp. 25-26.

[187]Louis-César Lavallière, *Ballets, opéra et autres ouvrages lyriques* (Paris: Bauche, 1760), p. 54.

[188]P.F. Fournier, "Le Piédestal de croix de Nébouzat et les bourrés d'Auvergne," *Auvergne et Méditeranée* 121 (1947): 5-30. I have studied this manuscript only from a microfilm.

[189]Ibid., p. 20, n. 29.

[190]Daniel Heartz, *Pierre Attaingnant Royal Printer of Music* (Berkeley and Los Angeles: University of California Press, 1969), p. 241.

[191]Cf. Madeleine Jurgens, ed., *Documents du Minutier central concernant l'histoire de la musique (1600-1650)*, 2 vols. (Paris: SEVPEN, La Documentation française, 1967-1974); Colombe Samoyault-Verlet, *Les Facteurs de clavecins parisiens, notices biographiques et documents (1550-1793)* (Paris: Heugel, 1966); Donald H. Boalch, *Makers of the Harpsichord and Clavichord 1440-1840*, 2nd ed. (Oxford: The Clarendon Press, 1974); Frank Hubbard, *Three Centuries of Harpsichord Making* (Cambridge: Harvard University Press, 1965). I am grateful to Arthur Lawrence for untangling the conflicting and redundant references among the secondary sources.

[192]Cf. *Curtis-D*, passim. See also Edgar Hunt, "Tuning and Temperament," *The English Harpsichord Magazine* 1:7 (October, 1976), pp. 201-204. I have not examined any exemplar of this book.

[193]I have based this study on a microfilm of the exemplar in the British Library and on the 1678 edition in The Newberry Library. It is beyond the province of French studies to search out other exemplars for bibliographic comparisons.

[194]An exemplar can be found in the Music Room of the British Library. No effort has been made to search for other exemplars of the publication, since it is not a harpsichord source.

[195]Devoto attributed a comment to Robert Stevenson (without specific citation) that this Sarabande was Chambonnières' "Sarabande o beau jardin" (*35-Bauyn-I* #80), but the pieces are not at all the same. Cf. Daniel Devoto, "De la zarabande à la sarabande," *Recherches* 6 (1966): 42.

[196]Cf. *32-Oldham* hand D, especially #10-11, 13, 19 and 23, which also occur in the prints. The variants in *35-Bauyn-I* are shown in *Dart-Ch.*

[197]Cf. Ralph Kirkpatrick, "On Re-reading Couperin's 'L'Art de toucher le clavecin,'" *Early Music* 4:1 (January, 1976), pp. 5-6. François Lesure has conjectured in conversations that no more than 250 or 300 exemplars could be made before a plate was ruined and often a very few exemplars were run at a time.

[198]"Edition" is used here in contrast with "issue." A new issue is printed from the same plates, with or without some changes. A new edition is printed from partially or entirely new plates, with a change in the imprint (publisher and date). The distinction between the two can become hazy at times.

[199]Blank pages and other peculiarities of layout are common in early keyboard editions. Publishers had not yet lost their concern for bringing out editions which could be played without the constant assistance of a page turner.

[200]It belonged to Henri Prunières and was known to Tessier in 1923. It has since dropped from sight. (André Tessier, "L'Oeuvre de clavecin de Nicolas Le Bègue, notes bibliographiques," *Revue de musicologie* 7:7 [August, 1923], pp. 106-112.

[201]Cf. Lesure, *Bibliographie*, s.v. 1697, 313.

[202]I have presented the complete text of the letter in "A Letter from Mr. Lebègue Concerning His Preludes," *Recherches* 17 (1977): 7-14.

[203]Perrine, *Livre de musique pour le lut* (Paris: author, 1680). It contains one complete piece which duplicates *66-Perrine* #18.

[204]Nicolas Gigault, *Livre de musique pour l'orgue* (Paris: author, 1685).

[205]*Mercure galant [Mercure de France]*, March 1687, pp. 178-179.

[206]I am grateful to H. Ross Wood, who generously provided a detailed description of the unique 1703 edition at the Sibley Library. I have not examined it personally.

[207]Elizabeth H. Thompson, *A.L.A. Glossary of Library Terms* (Chicago: American Library Association, 1943), p. 63.

APPENDIX A

WATERMARKS AND OTHER TRACINGS

All of the watermarks which are illustrated here are actual tracings, unless otherwise specified. The notation "eye copy" denotes that the figure is a free-hand sketch of a mark which could not be traced, usually because of library regulations. The rate of photographic reduction can be ascertained by referring to the scale on the first page of the illustrations.

The marks are arranged according to the subject content of the watermarks themselves, following Heawood's classification system, to facilitate comparison with his catalog (see the List of Abbreviations at the beginning of this volume). A few miscellaneous tracings and rubbings are included after the 104 watermarks.

In the first column of the List of Watermarks, arbitrary identification numbers are assigned, with variants and countermarks denoted by letter suffixes (1a, 1b, etc.). The source of each tracing appears in the second column, using the source abbreviations listed at the beginning of this volume. The third column cites reproductions of similar marks. Very rarely are they close enough to cause one to suspect that they are from the same paper mold. The sources of the similar marks are given in parentheses. It must be emphasized that the provenance and dates thus listed refer to the origins of the printed books or documents in which the watermarks were found by the scholars cited; the information cannot be transferred indiscriminately to the marks illustrated in this Appendix.

Mark #11 provides a good example of what can and cannot be concluded from watermark evidence. It is found in two manuscripts in the Bibliothèque Sainte Geneviève, and is similar to two marks in Heawood's catalog (#340 and 341); he traced them from a book or books which were printed in Paris in 1696. One can assume that the paper of these books was made in or shortly before 1696 and that it was probably made in France, since France, unlike England, did not import paper in great quantities. One cannot state, however, that mark #11 in the present Appendix is from Parisian paper made in 1696. The state of research in seventeenth-century paper making is not yet sufficiently advanced to permit such facile identifications. In this case, the identity and activity period of the maker "I C" in the countermark are not known, nor is it certain that the clock genre was limited geographically or chronologically. A more cautious statement is in order: Mark #11 is from paper similar to paper used in the last decade of the century in

Paris, but in any case the two Ste. Geneviève manuscripts are closely related, since they are written on the same paper.

Watermarks, then, provide supporting evidence about various aspects of the manuscripts and printed works from which they were traced, but rarely do they provide certain dating. They are reproduced here, rather than being merely mentioned, because it is probable that some of them will eventually be specifically identified, as paper research progresses.

Index of Letters, Legends and Names

Note: I and J are often interchangeable.

AJ	3, 73	I CONARD	82
AM (MA?)	68	IG	57
AR	65	IGD	72
AS (AJ?)	103	IH (HI?)	92
B	76, 98	IHS	75
BC	75	I J C[USSON]	28, (64?)
[B COLO]MBIER	35, 66	IS (SI?)	40
BONONIA	82x	JB	17
BR	9	[JT?]	14
CB	5	L	18, 24
CGB (CCB?, GGB?)	82x	MA (AM?)	68
CK	77	MARCHA ...	17
...D	102	MC	47
DC (DG?)	59	MF	78
DITERSBACH	10	MG	16
E	96	MIS (SIW?)	94
F ... (?)	4	MOYEN ...	83
FDC	95	MS (SW?)	30
FN (NF?)	80	MSD	85
FP	9	MV	15
GB	60	N	4, 97
GG	100	NF (FN?)	80
HB	6	OR	87
HC (IJC?)	64, 62x	...P	74
HCB (HBC?)	81	PB	15
HI (IH?)	92	PC	(56?), [28]
HONI SOIT ...	21	PD (PL?)	89
...I (I...?)	61	P DANG	83
IC	11, (56?)	PG	55
ICO	48	PRO PATRIA	95

Index of Letters, Legends and Names (Cont.)

R	41, 81	SW (MS?)	30
RG	84	V	42
S ... (?)	12	W	43, 44, 73
SI (IS?)	40	WR	40, 41
SIW (MIS?)	94		

List of Watermarks and Other Tracings

Animal

1   *30-Cecilia*   Cf. *Heawood* #18, 19 (Naples, 1752, 1763); #2795-2798 (Naples, 1751-52).

Bend   Originally the arms of Strasbourg, the mark of W. Riehl, but widely copied elsewhere (cf. *Heawood-I* p. 269).

2   *65-Lebègue-II*   Cf. *Heawood* #63-118 (early 18th century).
     Ex. 3

3   *Grimm*   AJ may represent Abraham Janssen, Dutch maker who worked in Angoulême (cf. *Heawood-II* p. 269).

4   *Darmstadt-18*   No information.

5   *Darmstadt-17*   Cf. *Heawood* #135-140.

Bird

6   *4-Lynar*   Cf. *Heawood* #186-190 (England, 18th century).

Chaplet

7   *62-Chamb-I*   Cf. *Heawood* #227 ff. (Paris, late 17th
     63-Chamb-II   century).

8   *68-d'Anglebert*   Cf. *Heawood* #224 (Paris, 1679).
     Ex. 6

9   *32-Oldham*   No information.

Circle

| 10 | *8-Hintze,* quire A | An almost identical mark with CH is in Dresden (Staatsarchiv, Loc 8687, Nr. 1: Kantorey-ordnung, so Kurfürst Moritz . . ., *l.* 225), dated 1648. Cf. *Briquet* #1398 (Hamburg, 1561; also 1610/19); cf. *Nostitz* #717-719 (none with MH). There were several towns named Dittersbach, but this one is almost surely the one near Dresden (cf. p. 39, above). |

Clock

| 11 | *47-Gen-2356* *34-Gen-2357[A]* | Cf. *Heawood* #340-341 (Paris, 1696). |

Column

| | | Two intertwined columns, the emblem of Charles IX, were much used in France after 1560 and especially by Colombier in Auvergne in the 17th century (cf. *Briquet* pp. 269-270). |

| 12 | *54-Gen-2350/57* | Cf. *Heawood-III* #155-158 (ca. 1611-1620); cf. *Geraklitov* #1501-1504 (1627-1628). |

Coat of Arms

| | | The Amsterdam coat of arms (#13-20) was one of the most common marks from about 1650 and was widely used outside the Netherlands (cf. *Heawood-II*, p. 468). |

| 13 | *25-Bod-426* *Bod-425* | Cf. *Voorn-I* #58 (1706), *Heawood* #356 (Andover, England, 1703). |

| 14 | *Van-Eijl* | Cf. *Heawood* #367 (Holland?, 1683). |

| 15 | *Stockholm-228* | Cf. *Heawood* #430 (variant of *Churchill* #7: 1662). |

| 16 | *27-Gresse* | No information. |

17	*Stockholm-2* (also smaller variant not illustrated)	Cf. *Churchill* #53 (1736), *Churchill* #3 (1654-1685), *Heawood* #395 (n.p., 1663).
18	*9-Ihre-284*	No information.
19	*Lüneburg-1198*	Cf. *Heawood* #352 (Holland, 1697).
20	*22-Ch-Ch-1177*	Cf. *Heawood* #343 (n.p., 1671).
21	*25-Bod-426*, back end papers	Cf. *Heawood* #443 (Essex, 1735), 445. The arms of the English king were common marks throughout the 18th century (cf. *Heawood-II* p. 470).
22	*4-Lynar*	*Heawood* #601 (almost an exact duplicate; Holland, 1614). The origins of the mark are as early as the 15th century (cf. *Briquet* #987).
23	*64-Lebègue-I* Ex. 2, end paper	No information.
24	*6-Munich-1511e*	Cf. *Heawood* #658 (n.p., n.d.). The L probably stands for Louis, since it is combined with the French arms.
25	*6-Munich-1511e*, end papers	No information.
26	*48-LaBarre-6*	Cf. *Heawood* #701-704 (Paris, 1677-1696).
27	*67-Gigault* Ex. 1	Cf. *Heawood* #673 (Paris, ca. 1669).
28	*49-RésF-933*	*Heawood* #715 (very similar; Paris, 1728). The initials probably stand for I. J. Cusson.
29	*41-Thomelin*	Cf. *Heawood* #716 (France, 1718-1722).

Cross

| 30 | *26-Bull* | No information. |

Crown

31	*29-Chigi*	Cf. *Heawood* # 1120 (Rome, 1618).
32	*29-Chigi,* end paper	Cf. *Heawood* # 1129-1133 (Venice, 1565-1610).

Eagle

33	*Linz*	Cf. *Briquet* # 256 (and variants cited there; Germany, 1560-1580), *Heawood* # 1280 (Strasbourg, 1594).
34	*16-Cosyn*: Rés-1184	Cf. *Heawood* # 1248 (Holland, 1618).
35	*66-Perrine*	*Heawood* # 1323 (almost exact; Paris, 1693, 1680). The initials represent the paper maker B. Colombier.
36	*Lüneburg-1198*	No information.

Fleur-de-lis

37	*62-Chamb-I* Ex. 3, end paper	No information.
38	*Minorite*	Cf. *Heawood* # 1566-1644 (Italian).
39	*20-Ch-Ch-378*	Cf. *Heawood* # 1679 (England/Holland, 1695), *Heawood* # 1719 (same, 1699), *Nicolai* XIV/9 (France, 1672).
40	*24-Babell*	This and the following marks (# 40-44) represent a type which was so common as to make specific identifications impossible. It was used especially in Holland, with or without the IHS, from ca. 1640 to the 20th century (cf. *Heawood-I* pp. 275-276).
41	*14-Schwerin-619* 1st section	See # 40.

42	*14-Schwerin-619* 2nd section	See #40.
43	*27-Gresse,* pastedown	See #40.
44	*25-Bod-426,* front end paper	See #40.
45	*65-Lebègue-II* Ex. 1	No information.

Flower

46	*Celle*	No information.

Foolscap

47	*9-Ihre-284*	Cf. *Heawood* #2051 (n.p., n.d.)
48	*Drallius*	Cf. *Heawood* #1918 (London, 1681), *Geraklitov* #1211 (1681). This sort of foolscap, with ICO (I, Conard?), is found ca. 1681-1686 (cf. *Heawood-III*, p. 123).
49	*Van-Eijl*	No information.
50	*Skara* (copied after Rudén in Uppsala photocopy)	Cf. *Geraklitov* #1240-1243 (1653).
51	*19-Heardson*	No information.

Grapes

Bunches of grapes are so ubiquitous in French watermarks that they are useless in identifying paper unless the initials of a countermark can be identified (cf. *Heawood*, s.v. grapes).

52	*50-Paignon*	No information.
53	*7-Munich-1511f* quire C	No information.

54	*49-RésF-933*	No information.
55	*68-d'Anglebert* Ex. 1, end papers	*Heawood* #2198 (very similar; Paris, 1680).
56	*52-Rés-2671*	Cf. *Heawood* #2323 (n.p., 1735), *Heawood* #2232 (Paris, 1643), *Heawood* #2217 (Paris, ca. 1668?).
57	*68-d'Anglebert* Ex. 8, end papers	No information.
58	*35-Bauyn*	No precise information. The countermark appears to have a beehive (or a bell?) between the two illegible initials, similar to *Heawood* #2988 (Paris, 1694).
59	*35-Bauyn* end papers	No information.
60	*38-Gen-2348/53*	No information.
61	*45-Dart*	No information.
62	*36-Parville*	No information.
62x	*22a-Roper*	Cf. *Heawood* #2969 (Paris, 1694).
63	*28-Brussels-926*	No information.
64	*37-Geoffroy*	Cf. *Heawood* #3294 (Paris, ca. 1743). The initials (IC or IJC) could refer to the Cusson firm.
65	*51-LaBarre-11*	No information.
66	*64-Lebègue-I* Ex. 1 and 5	Cf. *Heawood* #2426-2432 (Paris, ca. 1655-1689). The band around the grapes reads in its entirety: B COLOMBIER.
67	*64-Lebègue-I* Ex. 2	No information.

68	*40-Rés-476*	Cf. *Heawood* #2266 (Paris, 1664), *Heawood* #2308 (Brussels, 1704), *Heawood* #2318A (Paris, 1723).
69	*42-Vm7-6307-2*	No information.
Hat		The cardinal's had was a mark of French paper which was imported to England in great quantities (cf. *Heawood-I* p. 283).
70	*17-Rogers,* part 2	Cf. *Heawood* #2582 (London, ca. 1649).
71	*19-Heardson*	No information.
Horn		
72	*19-Heardson*	Cf. *Heawood* #2776 and *Heawood-I* #62 (1639-1659). This mark, with IGD (Girond or I Guesdon?), was used for a relatively short period (1639-1659) (cf. *Heawood-I* pp. 285-286).
73	*10-Schwerin-617*	Cf. *Heawood* #2718 (England [Dutch paper?]), 1683-1686).
Lamb		
74	*Beatrix*	Cf. *Heawood* #2842. This type of mark was used in Dutch papers ca. 1645-1672 (cf. *Heawood-II*, p. 481).
Letter		
75	*68-d'Anglebert* Ex. 2, 3, 6, 8	Cf. *Heawood* #2987 (Paris, 1677), *Heawood* #684 (Paris, 1674).
76	*5-Munich-15031; 7-Munich-1511f,* quires A-B	No information.
77	*Imhoff*	No information.
78	*Ottobeuren*	No information.

Lion

79	*Stockholm-2*, variant in *Bod-576*	Cf. *Heawood* #3141-3142 (London, ca. 1685-1689). This type of mark was made for or by the Dutch from ca. 1650-1700 (cf. *Heawood-II*, p. 484).

Monogram Cipher

80	*Eÿsbock*	No information.
81	*Nuremberg*	Cf. *Voorn-I* #18 (probably from Röthenbach bei Lanf, near Nuremburg).

Name

82	*68-d'Anglebert* Ex. 3, end papers	Cf. *Heawood* #663, 670, 2258, 2306 (London and Paris, last quarter of the seventeenth century).
82x	*62-Chamb-I*, Ex. 6, end papers	No information.
83	*52-Rés-2671* end papers	No precise information. The date 1742 is an anterior date only, as the date was used in papers made for many subsequent years (cf. *Heawood*, p. 31).
	Post or Pillar	Posts are found in London ca. 1615-1670 (cf. *Heawood* #3485-3535). The small columns were typical until the 1640's; some might be of English manufacture, but the origins were probably French (cf. *Heawood-I* p. 287).
84	*16-Cosyn*	No information.
85	*16-Cosyn*	No information.
86	*19-Heardson*	This type could be of German origin (cf. *Heawood-III*, pp. 119-120).

Pot

Most pots were marks of northern and western French makers who supplied England with paper. The size increased ca. 1645 and the mark was no longer extensively used by ca. 1675 (cf. *Heawood-I*, passim).

87 *19-Heardson*   No information.

88 *19-Heardson*   No information.

89 *17-Rogers*   Cf. *Heawood* # 3636 (London, 1655).

90 *16-Cosyn*,   Cf. *Geraklitov* # 579 (very similar; 1631).
    section 1

91 *16-Cosyn*,   No information.
    section 2

92 *8-Hintze*,   No information.
    quire B, after
    reconstructed copy
    in the Yale Library.

93 *10-Schwerin-617*   No information.
    end papers

94 *11-Ryge*   No information.

Pro Patria

95 *Stockholm-176*   No information.

Tower

96 *1-Copenhagen-376*   *Piccard* illustrates many Ravensberg tower marks with the letter E, dated from 1566-1633.

97 *Darmstadt-1198*   *Piccard* illustrates two with the letter N, dated 1615 and 1625.

98 *2-Witzendorff*   No information.

Wreath

| 99 | *68-d'Anglebert*
Ex. 6, title page | No information. |

Uncertain

100	*33-Rés-89ter*	No information.
101	*18-Ch-Ch-1236*	No information.
102	*16-Cosyn*	No information.
103	*9-Ihre-284*	No information.
104	*39-Vm7-6307-1*	No information.

Nonwatermark Tracings and Rubbings

105	*35-Bauyn*, arms stamped on covers	Cf. *MGG*, s.v. Bauyn, for a photograph.
106	*36-Parville*, cover stamping	No information.
107	*19-Heardson*, cover decoration	No information.
108	*Stockholm-176*, cover stamping, owner's monogram: SWE or EWE?	No information.
109	*11-Ryge*, cover stamping	Family monogram.
110	*68-d'Anglebert* Ex. 6, owner's signature: Coroitous [?], 1705	No information.

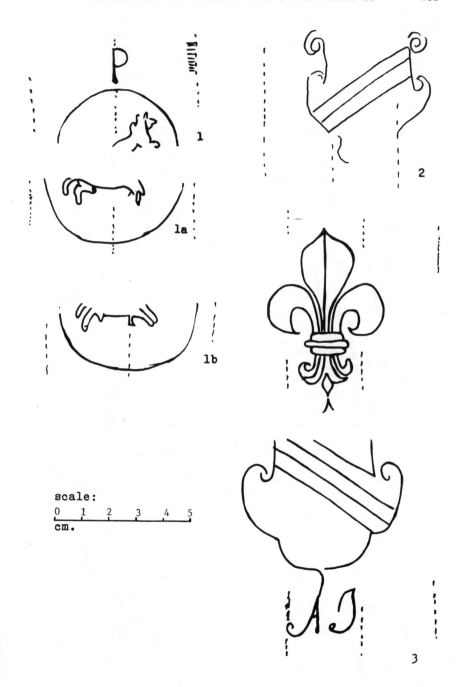

scale:

0   1   2   3   4   5
cm.

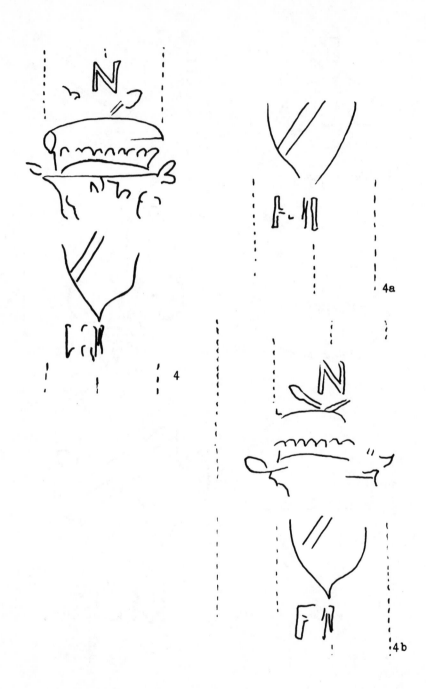

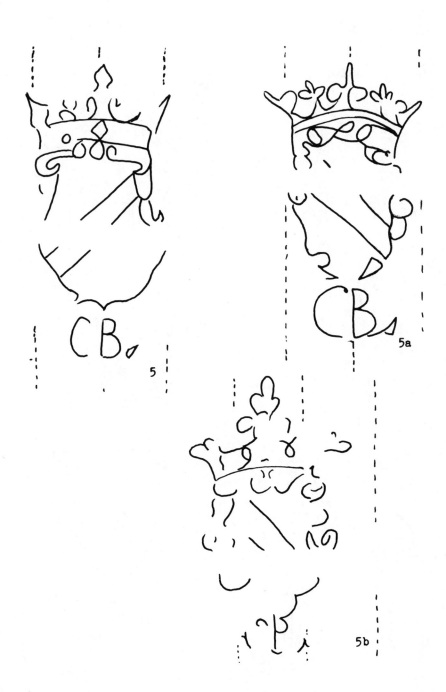

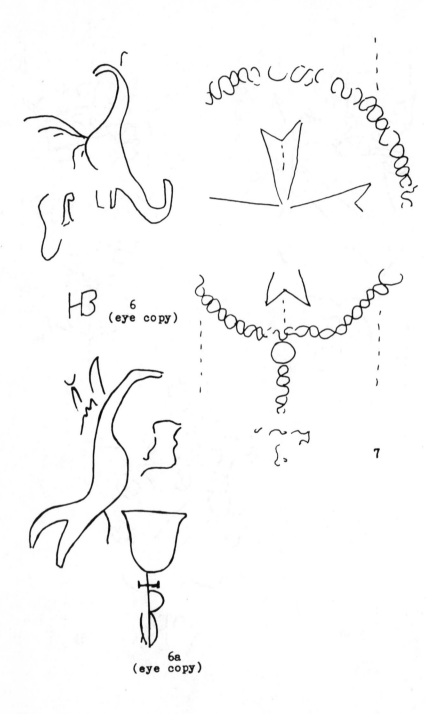

6
(eye copy)

7

6a
(eye copy)

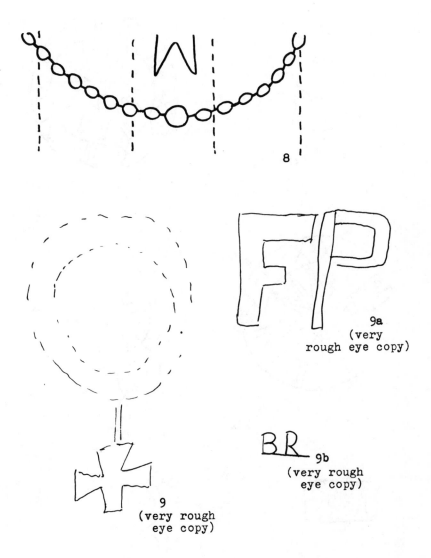

8

9a
(very
rough eye copy)

BR 9b
(very rough
eye copy)

9
(very rough
eye copy)

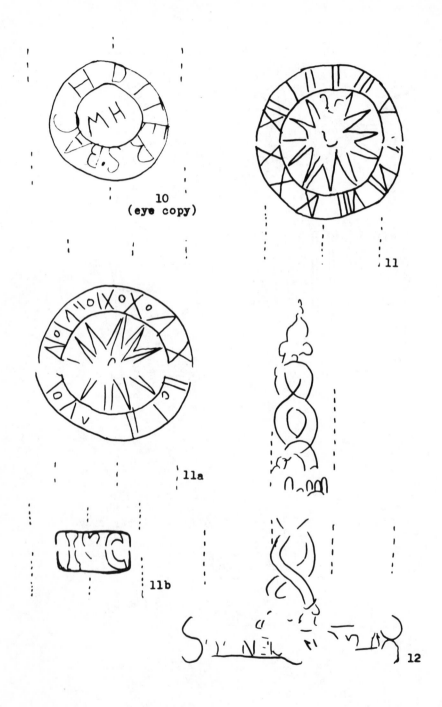

10
(eye copy)

11

11a

11b

12

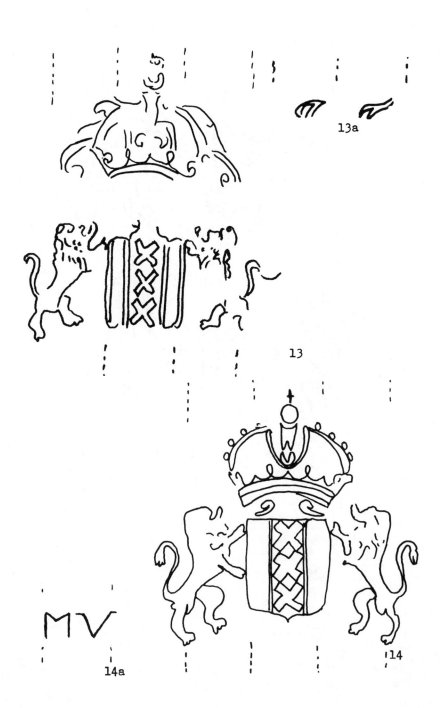

13a

13

14a

14

15

15a

16

17

17a

18

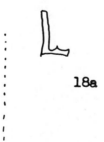

18a

19

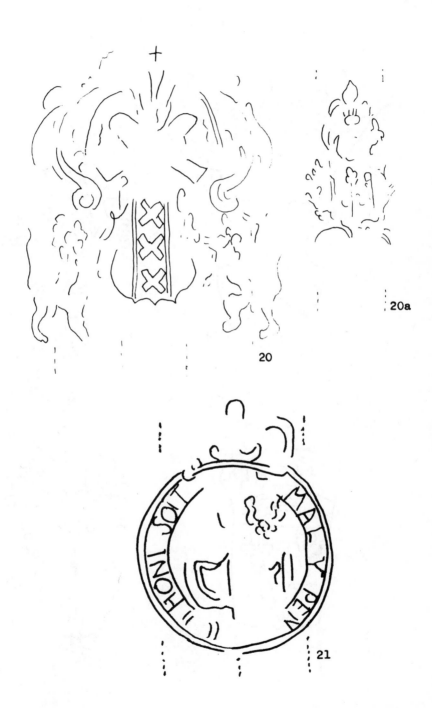

20a

20

21

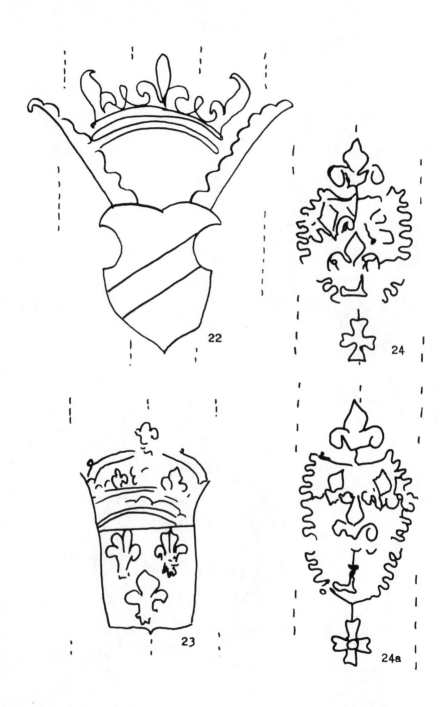

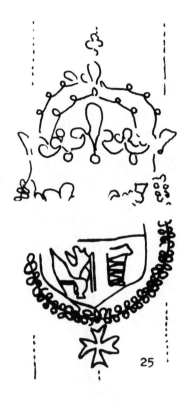

25

26

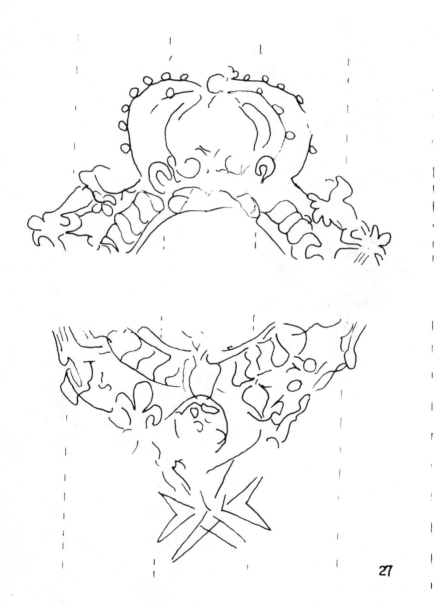

27

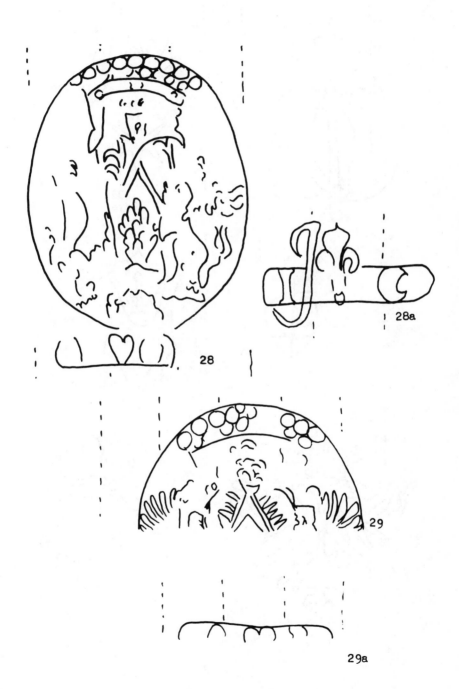

28

28a

29

29a

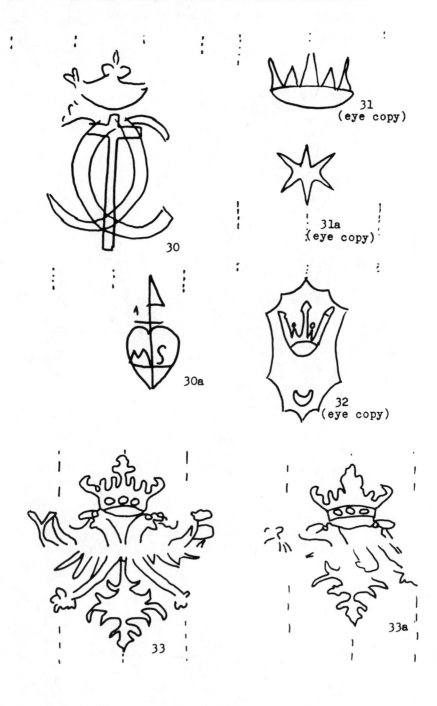

30

31
(eye copy)

31a
(eye copy)

30a

32
(eye copy)

33

33a

34

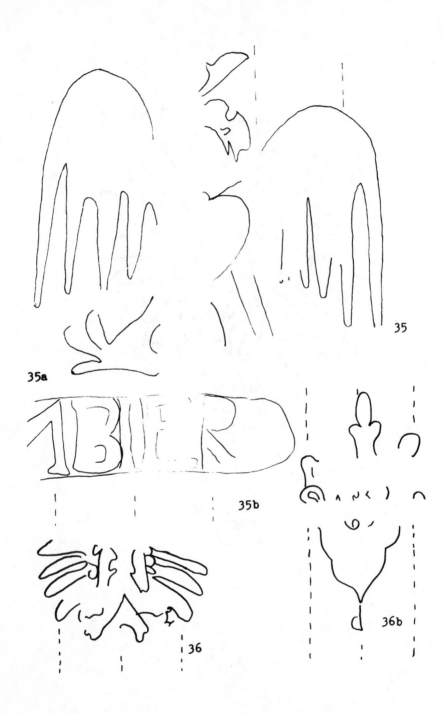

35a

35

35b

36

36b

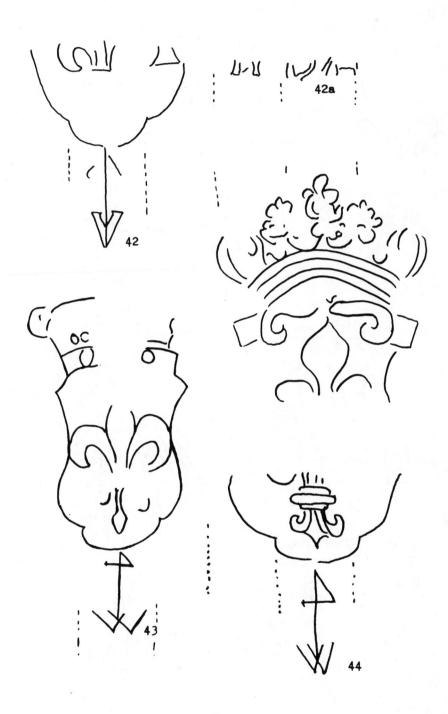

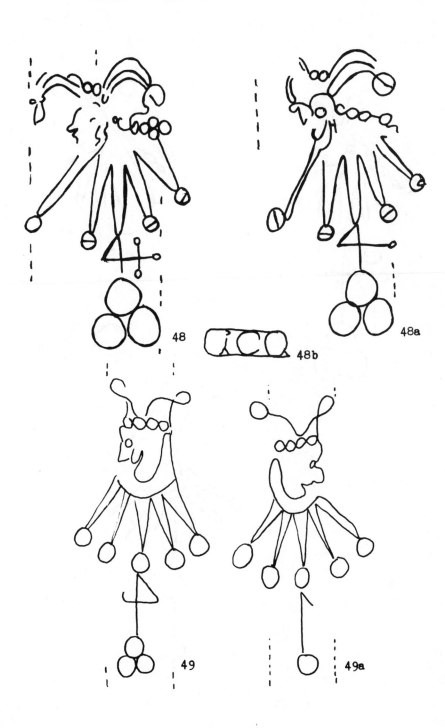

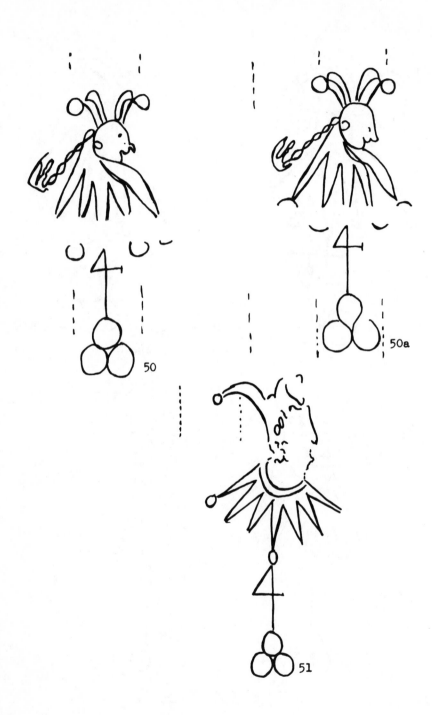

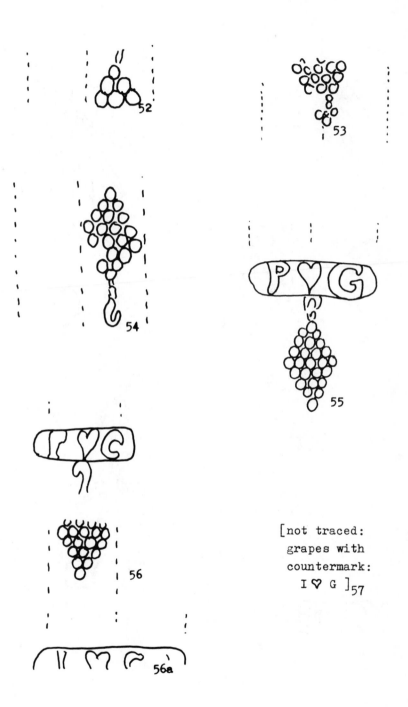

[not traced:
grapes with
countermark:
I ♡ G]$_{57}$

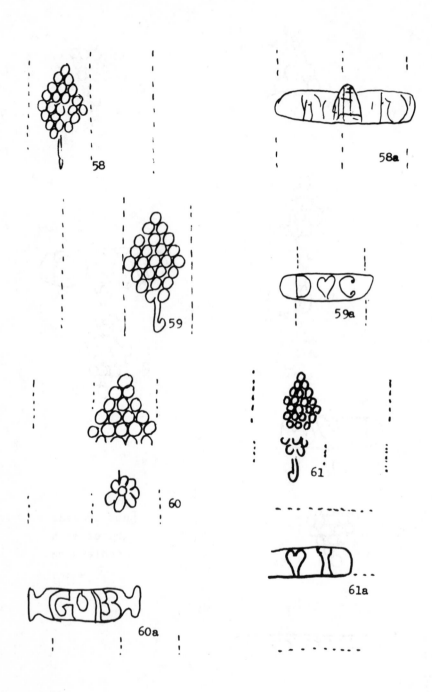

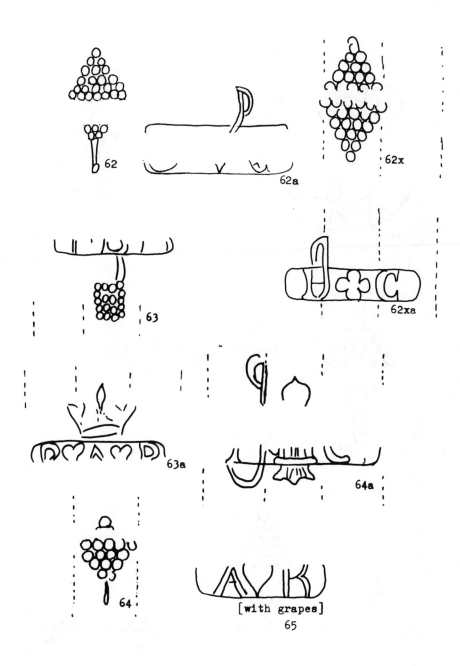

62

62a

62x

62xa

63

63a

64a

64

65

[with grapes]

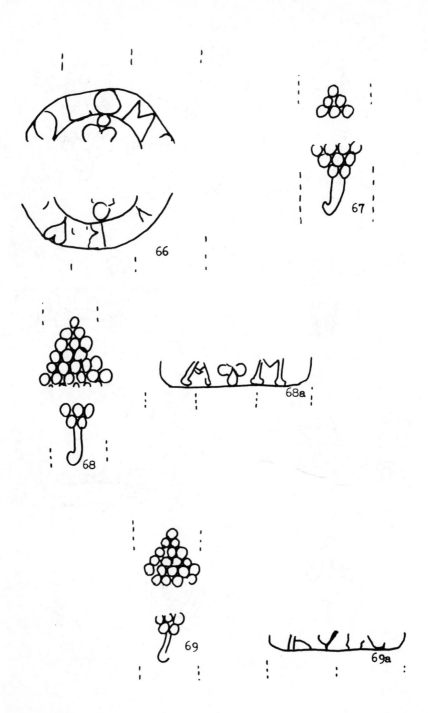

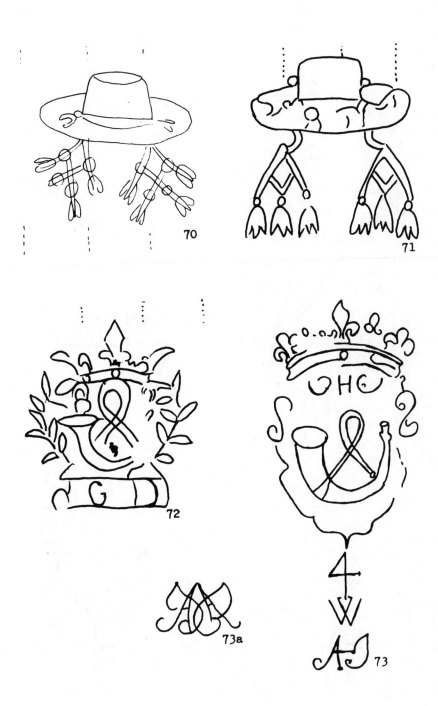

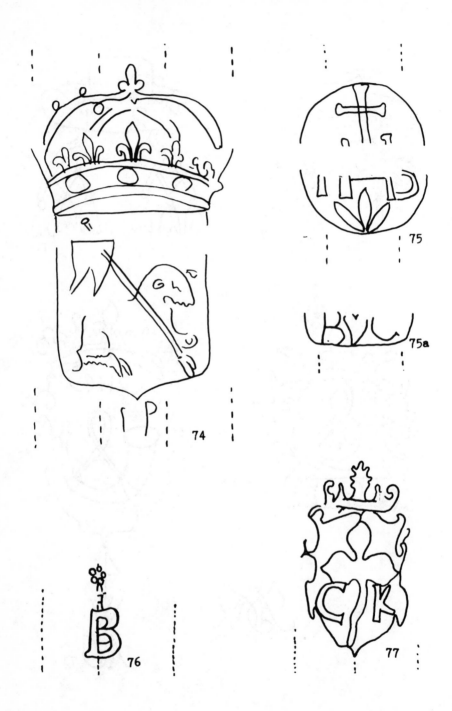

78

78a

79

81

80

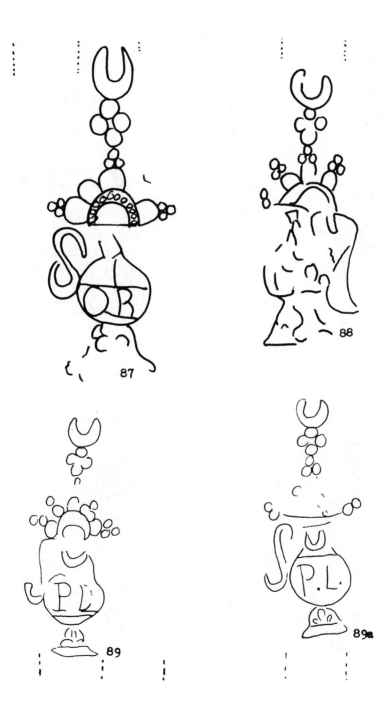

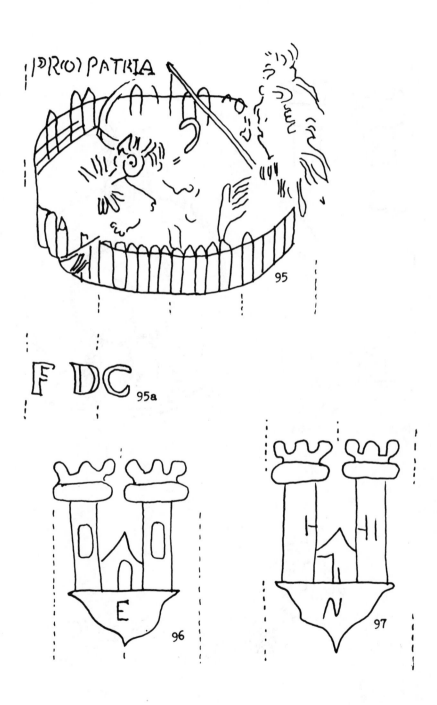

95

95a

96

97

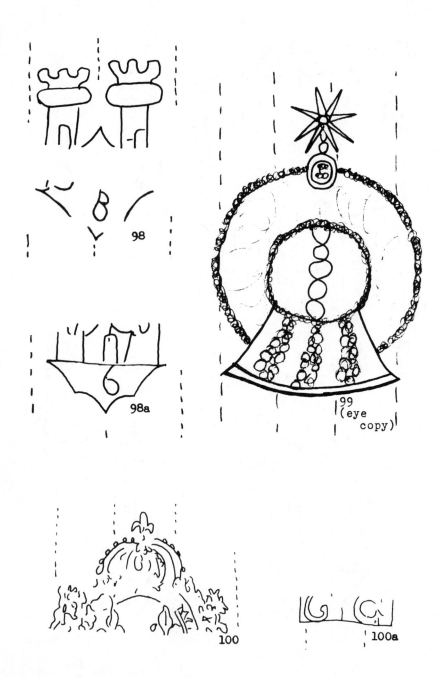

98

98a

99
(eye
copy)

100

100a

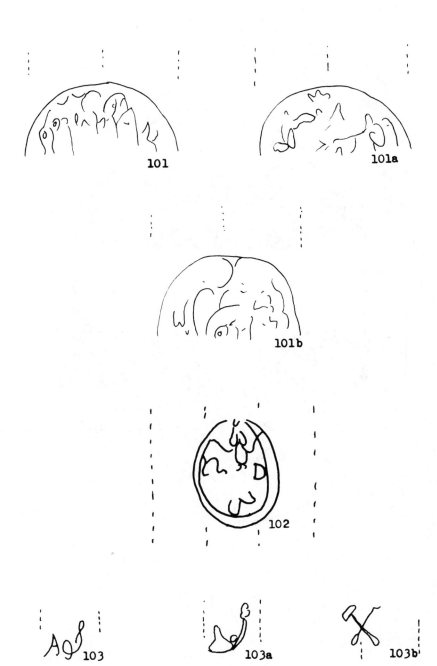

101

101a

101b

102

103

103a

103b

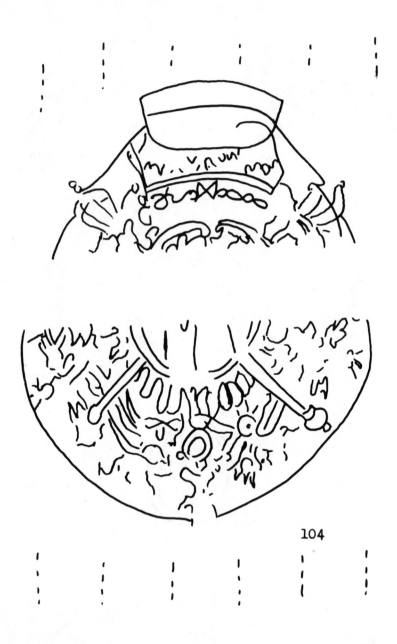

104

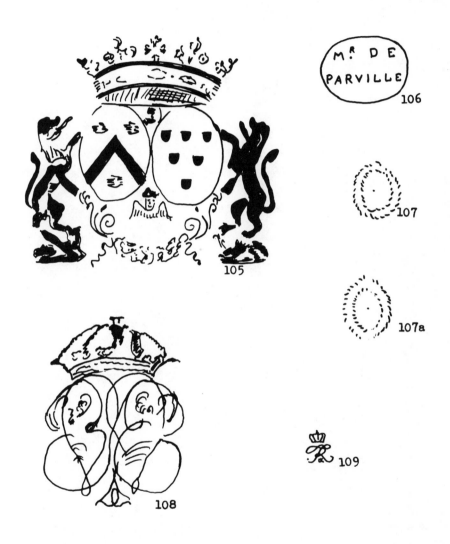

105

106

107

107a

109

108

110

APPENDIX B

THEMATIC INDEX

The Index which follows includes numerical encodings of all of the incipits which are reproduced in this Catalog. The themes are presented in four lists: major, first strain; major, second strain; minor, first strain; and minor, second strain. These themes comprise the most important element of a much larger thematic file which was used to assist in the identification of anonymous pieces in harpsichord sources. The card file from which the present lists were taken includes selected themes from all of the sources and editions which are in any way mentioned in this study.

The encoded themes have been laboriously reproduced here to assist other scholars in the identification of pieces in manuscripts which were not examined for this study. The encoding system is very simple and is the result of two years of experimentation with various approaches to thematic indexing. The following rules apply to the system:

1. The melody notes of a piece are translated into numbers, with "1" as tonic, through "7" as the leading tone. Tied notes and ornamental notes are ignored. Rhythm is not indicated, but bar lines are denoted by a vertical stroke between the appropriate numbers.

2. Deviations from the major scale or the natural minor scale are shown with the appropriate accidentals placed before the affected number (e.g., the melodic minor scale is "1 2 3 4 5 #6 #7 1 7 6 5 4 3 2 1"). Because major and minor themes are not interfiled, there is no need to indicate the inflection of the mediant.

3. The key of the piece is indicated separately, using upper case letters for major keys and lower case for minor keys. If there is ambiguity regarding the key of the work, the final chord is taken to be tonic, and the characteristic inflection of the mediant determines the mode of the encoded incipit.

4. The meter of the incipit is indicated before the key, as either duple ("2") or triple ("3"). Any meter which subdivides by three is considered triple here. Thus $\frac{6}{4}$ is "triple," not "duple compound." This rule allows courantes to be correctly indicated as pieces in triple meter, whether the time signature was 3, $\frac{6}{4}$, or $\frac{3}{2}$.

5. Both strains are indexed because a slight variation in the first few notes of a melody can prevent two versions of a piece from filing next to each other. It is less likely that both strains of a piece would have such variants.

The following examples illustrate the system:

First strain: 1 2|3 3 4 5 5|6 7 1 7 6 5| 3D
Second strain: 5 6|7 7 1 2 1 7|3 2 1 2 7 1| 3D

First strain: 5|5 3 4 5 6 6 5 4|5 4 5 3 2| 2g
Second strain: 3 2 1|#7 #6 5 4 5 4 5 3   2g

Figure 8. Thematic Index Examples

When trying to identify a piece, the reader should take into consideration the possibility of common mistakes or variants, such as missing ties or upbeats, and should encode more than one version of the melody. When the encoded theme is compared to the lists in this Index, the key, meter and placement of the bar lines should be noted before time is taken to compare the melody with the musical incipit of a number sequence which is suspiciously similar. For example, these two melodies begin with almost exactly the same intervals, but they could not possibly be variants of the same piece in view of the meter and bar lines:

2 3 4|5 5 6 5 4 3 4   2G
2 3 4|5 5 6 5 4|3 5   3C

Major, First Strain

|1 1 1 1 1 1 1|1 5 1 5 1 5| 3C   36-Parville #131
|1 1 1|1 2 1 7|6 5 4| 3D   68-d'Anglebert #53
|1 1 1|1| 2 2 2|3|4 4 4 4|#4|5 #4|5   3C   35-Bauyn-III #52
|1 1 1|1|5 6 5 4 3 2|1|1 3 1 7 6   3D   42-Vm7-6307-2 #12
|1 1 1 1 7 6 4|5 4 3 2 1 2 3 3 3   2C   33-Rés-89ter #16
|1 1 1|2 2 2 3 3 3| 3C   35-Bauyn-I #19

|1 1 1 5 1 5 1 2|3 1 3 4 5 4 3 4	2C 32-Oldham #22
1 1 1|5 5 4 3 2 1|	2F 55-Redon #20
1|1 1 7 6 5 5 6|5 3 4|	2G 33-Rés-89ter #33
1 1|1 7 6|6 5|	3C 33-Rés-89ter #6
1 1|1 ♭7 6 5 6 6|6 5 5|	3C 63-Chamb-II #4
1 1|1 ♭7 6|♭7 6 5|	3B♭ 37-Geoffroy #152
|1 1 2|1 1 2|1 7 1 2 1 7 6|5 #4 5	2G 42-Vm7-6307-2 #4
|1|1|2|1 7|1|	3G 35-Bauyn-I #101
1|1 2 2 1|1 5 5 6 4|3 3 4 5|	3G 35-Bauyn-II #90
1 1|2 2 2|3 3 3|3|	3C 62-Chamb-I #10
1|1 2 2|3 3 1 2 3 4|	3G 63-Chamb-II #27
1 1 2|2 4|5 5 6|	3D 35-Bauyn-I #52
1|1 2 3 1 3 4|5	2G 37-Geoffroy #91
|1 1 2 3 1 5 1|7 6 5 3 6 5 4 3|	3B♭ 46-Menetou #115
1|1 2 3 1 5 5|5 6 6 7|1 7 6 5 5	3F 35-Bauyn-II #69
1|1 2 3 1 5 5|6 6 7	3F 55-Redon #21
|1 1 2 3|2 1 2 3 4|3 2 1|	3C 46-Menetou #16
1|1 2 3 2 1 5 5|5|	2G 63-Chamb-II #24
1|1 2 3 2 2 1|7 5 6 7|1	3B♭ 35-Bauyn-II #120
|1|1 2 3|2 7|	2E♭ 57-Denis
1|1 2 3 4|3 2 2 3|1 7 1	3C 35-Bauyn-I #8
1|1 2 3 4 3 4 4|5 3 1 5	3C 32-Oldham #4
|1 1 2 3 4 5|3 2|	3D 35-Bauyn-I #57
|1 1 2|7 1|6 6 5|	3D 35-Bauyn-I #53
|1 1 2|7|5 5 5|	3G 32-Oldham #20
|1 1 2 7|6 6 6 5 6 5 4|	3D 63-Chamb-II #15
1|1 3 2 1|4 3 2 5 5|	2G 68-d'Anglebert #12
1|1 3 2 1 4 4|4 2 5 5 5 3 4 5|	3A 35-Bauyn-II #113
1|1 3 2 1 5 5 6 7|1 2 1 2 3 2 1	2D 37-Geoffroy #34
1|1 3 2 1 7 6|5 5 6 ♭7 5 4|3	3G 37-Geoffroy #92
1|1 3 4 5|5|	3D 35-Bauyn-I #58
1|1 3 4 5|6 2 2 3 2 1|	3D 63-Chamb-II #12
1|1 3 4 6|5 6 5 4|	3G 19-Heardson #69
|1 1 5|1 1 2 3|2 2 3 4|3 1 3|2 3	3C 33-Rés-89ter #9a
1|1 5 1 7 6 5 4 3|4 2 3 4 5 6 5	2C 33-Rés-89ter #9
1 1|5 2 3 4|2 2 3 7|	2B♭ 36-Parville #136
|1 1 5|3 2|1 1 2|	3G 32-Oldham #21
1|1 5 3 1 2 7|1 1 7 6 5 6 4 3|	2D 64-Lebègue-I #13
1|1 5 4 3 2|1 5 6 7 1 2|7 1 2 3|	3F 37-Geoffroy #71
1|1 5 4 3|3 4 5 1 2 3|4 3 2 1 1	3C 35-Bauyn-II #17
1|1 5 4 3|3 5 6 7|	3C 35-Bauyn-I #27
|1 1 5|5 5 2 3 2 1|	3F 35-Bauyn-II #72

Incipit	Source
|1 1 5 5 5 6|5 5 4	3F 38-Gen-2348/53 #11
1|1 5 5 5|6 6 5 5 4|	3G 32-Oldham #19
1|1 5|5 6 5|4 3 #4 5 2 5 5|	3D 35-Bauyn-I #46
1|1 5 5 6 5 4 5|3|	2D 35-Bauyn-II #58
1|1 5 5|6 6 5 5 4|	3G 63-Chamb-II #26
1|1 5 5 6|7 7 1 2 2|	3C 62-Chamb-I #8
1|1 5 6 4|3 3 2|	3G 35-Bauyn-I #100
1|1 5 6 4|3 3 4 5 6 5|	3C 35-Bauyn-I #26
1|1 5 6 5|3 3 3 2|	3G 35-Bauyn-I #100
1|1 5 6 5 4 3|3 2 2 1|	3F 36-Parville #83
1|1 5 6 7 1 3|4 5 6 5	2C 55-Redon #18
1|1 5 6 ♭7 5 4|3 3 5 4 3|	3F 65-Lebègue-II #29
|1 1 5|6 ♭7 6 5 4|3 3|4 5 4 3 4|	3F 37-Geoffroy #212
|1 1 6 ♭7|1 4 4|4 5 6 4	2G 54-Gen-2350/57 #2
|1 1 7 1|2 1 7 6 5|4 4 3 4|	2C 55-Redon #10
1|1 7 1 2|3 2 3|	3C 63-Chamb-II #2
1|1 7 1 2 3 3 4|5 5 1 7 6|	3F 64-Lebègue-I #47
1|1|7 1 2|5 4 3 2|	3C 54-Gen-2350/57 #6
1|1 7 1 5|6 1 7 2 1 3 2 1 3 2 4|	2A 37-Geoffroy #130
1|1 7 1 5 6|5 4 3 4 4 3 4|	3D 68-d'Anglebert #51
1|1 7 1 5 6 6 5 4|3 4 5 3|	2D 68-d'Anglebert #50
|1 1 7 6 5 5 6|5 4|	2G 35-Bauyn-II #82
1 1|7 7 3 3|6 2 2|	2C 46-Menetou #60
|1 1 ♭7|6|5 5 4|	3C 35-Bauyn-I #17
1|1 ♭7 6 5|6 6	3F 35-Bauyn-I #67
1|1 ♭7 6|♭7 6 5 6 5 4|5 4 3|	3D 37-Geoffroy #41
|1 2 1|3 3|2 3 2|	3G 22a-Roper #31
|1 2 1|4 3 2 3|4 3 4 5 1|	3G 36-Parville #129
|1 2 1 5 1 5 1 2|3 1 3 4	2C 35-Bauyn-I #1
|1 2 1 5 6 5|2 1 5 5 6|	3C 64-Lebègue-I #42
|1 2 3|1 2 3|4 3|2 1	3G 54-Gen-2350/57 #4
1 2 3 1 2 3 4 5	0G 7-Munich-1511f #21
|1 2 3 1 3 4|5	2C 35-Bauyn-I #4
1 2|3 2 1|5 2 3|4 3 4|2	3B♭ 36-Parville #130
1 2|3 2 1 5|5 4 3 2 1|	2C 54-Gen-2350/57 #12
|1 2 3 2 2|1 1 1 7 6|	3C 35-Bauyn-I #11
|1 2|3 2 3 1|	3C 45-Dart #41
1 2 3|2 3|1 2|1 1 7|	3F 65-Lebègue-II #34
1 2|3 2 3|1 2 3 4|5 5 5|	3G 38-Gen-2348/53 #35
1 2 3 2 3 1 5|5 4 3 2|	2G 54-Gen-2350/57 #3
|1 2|3 2 3 1|5 6 4 5 3|	3G 37-Geoffroy #96
|1 2 3 2 3 1|5|6 7 1|	3F 65-Lebègue-II #33

1 2|3 2 3 4 3|2 1 2 2|	2F 46-Menetou #110
|1 2 3|2 3 4|3 2 1|2|1 2 3	3G 37-Geoffroy #98
|1 2 3 2 3 4|3 2 1 2 1 7|1 2 3 2	3A 37-Geoffroy #141
1 2|3 2 3 4 4|5 4 3 6 5 4|	2C 33-Rés-89ter #10
1 2 3 3 2 1 5 1	0C 6-Munich-1511e #4
1 2|3 3|2 1|5 4 3 2	2G 54-Gen-2350/57 #8
1 2 3 3 2 1 5 1 7 6 5	0C 6-Munich-1511e #4
|1 2 3|3 2 1|5 6 5 4 3|2 2|1 2 3	3C 46-Menetou #90
|1 2 3|3 2 1|5 6 5|4 3|5 4 3|	3C 39-Vm7-6307-1 #3
1 2 3 3 2 2 5 5 #4 5 5	0C 7-Munich-1511f #22
1 2|3 3 3 2|3 1	2C 54-Gen-2350/57 #11
1 2 3 3 3 4 5 3 3 3 1 2 3 3 3 4	0C 6-Munich-1511e #1
|1 2 3 3 4 5|3 4 2 2 1|	3D 35-Bauyn-II #59
1 2|3 3 4 5 5 6|5 4 3|	2A 65-Lebègue-II #26
1 2|3 4 1 3 4|5 5 7 1|	2C 5-Munich-1503*l* #15
1 2 3 4|2 5 1 2|7 5 1 2 3 4|	2C 37-Geoffroy #16
|1 2 3|4 3|2 2 3 2|	3C 46-Menetou #47
|1 2|3 4|3|4 5 6|	2C 35-Bauyn-III #86
1 2 3 4 5 3 2 3	0C 7-Munich-1511f #19
1 2|3 4 5 4 3|2 4 3|2 1 7 1|2 5	2C 37-Geoffroy #194
1 2 3 4 5 5 1 5 5	0G 6-Munich-1511e #5
1 2|3 4 5 6|4 5 3|	3G 64-Lebègue-I #24
|1 2 3 4 5 6|5 2 4|3 1 3|2 5 6 1	3G 37-Geoffroy #224
|1 2 3 4 5 6|5 3|2 3 1|	3B♭ 65-Lebègue-II #16
|1 2 3 4 5 6|5 4 3 4 5	2C 22a-Roper #1
|1 2 3 4|5 6 5|6 7 1|	3C 5-Munich-1503*l* #7
|1 2 3 4|5 6 ♭7 1 ♭7 6|	3D 26-Bull #19
1 2|3 4|5 ♭6|5|	2D 26-Bull #18
|1 2 3 #4|5 2 2 1 7 6 5 5|	2D 63-Chamb-II #11
1 2|3 5 1 3 4|5 5 7 1|	2C 55-Redon #11
1 3 2 1|5 4 6 5 6|	2G 35-Bauyn-III #92
1 3 4|5 4 5 3|4 3 2 1	2B♭ 35-Bauyn-I #124
|1 3 4 5|5 1 7|6 2 1 7 6 5	3G 62-Chamb-I #29
1 3 4|5|5|2 5|#4 3 #4 5 #4|	2C 35-Bauyn-III #85
1 3 4|5 5 6 6 6 5 4|	2C 36-Parville #67
|1 3 4|5 5|6 7 1 7 6 2|7 6 5|	3B♭ 37-Geoffroy #147
|1 3 4 5|5|7 1 2 3|2|	3D 62-Chamb-I #18
|1 3 4|5|6 2 3 2|	3D 64-Lebègue-I #10
1 3 5|1 3 5|2 5	0C 55-Redon #16
1 3 5 3 2 3 4	0F 35-Bauyn-II #12
1 4 2 3 4 5 6 5 5	0G 7-Munich-1511f #20
|1 5 1 2 3 1 3 4|5 2 5 4 3 1 3|	2C 55-Redon #4

1 5|1 2 3 4|2 2 5 4|3 2 3 1 7 1|	2C 37-Geoffroy #15
|1 5|1 2|3 4 2|3 2 3 4 3|	3C 22a-Roper #7
|1 5 1|2 3 4 5|	3C 46-Menetou #89
1|5 1 2|7 1|2 3 4 3|2 1 2 3 2 1|	2G 42-Vm7-6307-2 #3
|1 5 1|7 1|2 3|4 5	3F 46-Menetou #36
|1 5 3|1 2|3 3 1|	3C 36-Parville #124
|1 5|3 2 1|5 5|7 6 5|1 7 6|1 7 6|	3D 37-Geoffroy #45
|1 5 3 3 2|1 5 3 5 4|	3C 33-Rés-89ter #20a
|1 5 3 4|2 5 3 2 1|	2F 64-Lebègue-I #51
|1 5|3 4|5 6 5 4 3|	3G 68-d'Anglebert #14
|1 5 3|4 5 6|5 5 1|	3D 64-Lebègue-I #11
1|5 3 6 4 4 5|3 3 5|	3G 68-d'Anglebert #16
1|5 4 3|4 2 5|3 4 3 2|	3G 63-Chamb-II #30
|1 5 4 3 4 5|6 5|#4|	3A 35-Bauyn-II #115
1|5 4 3 4 5|6 5 6 7|1 5 5 6 4 3|	3G 35-Bauyn-II #85
|1 5 5|1 2 3 4|	2D 45-Dart #53
1|5 5 4|3 2 1 5 5|	2C 46-Menetou #23
1|5 5 5|2 2 3 4 3 2 1|	3G 36-Parville #108
1|5 5 5 6|4 4 4 3 4|5 4 3 2 5|1	2G 37-Geoffroy #220
|1 5 5|6 6|3 3 4|	3F 62-Chamb-I #23
1|5 5 6 6 5 1|7 1 5 6|	3F 63-Chamb-II #18
|1 5 5|6 6 6 5 4|3 4 3 4|	3F 36-Parville #81
1 5 6 3 3 4 5 2 3 2 1 1	0C 7-Munich-1511f #10
1 5|6 3 4 5|3 2 1 1 5|6 5 4 3 4|	2A 37-Geoffroy #133
|1 5 6 3|4 5 3 3|	2C 55-Redon #15
1 5 6|3 4 5 4 3|3 2 2 1 5 4|	3D 63-Chamb-II #13
1|5 6 4|3 3 4 3 2|	3C 35-Bauyn-I #15
1|5 6|4 3|4 2 5|3|1 2|3 4|	3G 37-Geoffroy #106
|1 5 6|5 4 3|2 3 4|	3F 37-Geoffroy #163
1|5 6 5 4|3 4|	2C 64-Lebègue-I #41
|1 5 6|5 4 3|4 2 3|	3C 48-LaBarre-6 #31
1 5|6 5 6 ♭7 6 5 4|3 2 1 2 3 4|	2F 37-Geoffroy #73
|1 5 6 6|5 4|	3F 35-Bauyn-I #84
|1 5 6|7 1 2|2 3 2|	3B♭ 35-Bauyn-I #127
|1 5 6 7 1|7 1 7|	2G 35-Bauyn-III #83
|1 5 ♭6|♭7 1 6|4 3 2|5 4 3|	3C 37-Geoffroy #14
|1|6|5 5|5 2 3 4	3F 38-Gen-2348/53 #22
|1 6 5 6 4|5 6|	3F 35-Bauyn-I #85
|1 7 1 2 1|5 6|5 4 3|	3G 45-Dart #35
|1 71|2 2 3 1|4 3|	3C 36-Parville #126
|1 7 1 2 3 1|5 1 5 5|	2G 36-Parville #122
|1 7 1|2|3 4 3 2 1|5|	3C 45-Dart #42
1 7 1 2|3 4 5 5 5|5 17	2C 51-LaBarre-11 p 210

|1 7 1|5 1|2 3|	3D	45-Dart #16
|1 7 1|5 5 6|5 6 4|	3F	65-Lebègue-II #32
|1 7 1 5 6 5 4|3 4|	3D	62-Chamb-I #17
1 7 6 5 4ˑ3 2 3 1 2 3	0G	36-Parville #87
1 7 6|5 4 3 2|5 1 2 3 2	3D	64-Lebègue-I #9
|1 7 6 5 4 3|4 2 5|3 2 3 4	3B♭	22a-Roper #67
1 7 6 5 4|3 4 3 2 5|3 1 7 6 4|	2C	37-Geoffroy #20
|1 7 6|5 4 3|4 5 6|2 5 3|	3F	37-Geoffroy #72
1 7 6|5|5 5 6 7 1 2 3|	3C	35-Bauyn-I #23
1 7 6|5 5 6 3 4|5 5 4 3|	3F	35-Bauyn-II #71
1 7 6|5 5 6 7|1 2 3 3 2|	3C	62-Chamb-I #9
|1 7 6|5 5 5|6 7|1 5|1 7 6|	2C	55-Redon #19
|1 7 6 5|6 3|4 2 5|3 4 2 3 1|	3D	37-Geoffroy #40
|1 7 6 5 6|4 3|3 4 5 3 2|	3G	33-Rés-89ter #42
1 7 6 5 6 4 6 5 6 5 4 3 4 3 2 1	0C	48-LaBarre-6 #29
|1 7 6 5|6 5 4 3|4 2 5|3 4 3 2 1|	3G	37-Geoffroy #222
|1 7 6 5 6 5 4|3 4 3 2 1 2 3 4|	2C	5-Munich-1503*l* #11
1 7 6|5 6 5 4 3 4 5|6 1 2 3|4	3C	35-Bauyn-II #16
1 7 6|5|6 6 5 4|3 4 5|	3C	35-Bauyn-III #55
|1 7 6 ♭7 1|6 6 1 5 5|	3G	68-d'Anglebert #9
|1 ♭7 1|6 7 1|1 1 7|	3D	35-Bauyn-II #62
2|2 3 2 1 7 6 7|1 5	3C	35-Bauyn-I #9
2 2|3 4 2 1|7 7 2 2|3 2 1 7|6 6	2A	37-Geoffroy #144
2 3 4 5 5|5 4 5|	3D	68-d'Anglebert #57
2 3 4|5 5 6 5|2 4 5 2 3 #4 5|	3G	68-d'Anglebert #7
2 3 4|5 5 6 5 4|3 6 5 4 3 2 1	3C	36-Parville #63
2 3 4|5 6 5 4 3 4 5 1 1|	2G	68-d'Anglebert #2
2 7 5 1 7 1 2	0C	7-Munich-1511f #1
3 1|2 7 1 6|7 7 1 1|	2C	46-Menetou #3
3 1|5 2 3|1 6 4|	3C	36-Parville #66
3 1 5 3 1 5 5 2 3 4 5 4 4 3	0C	39-Vm7-6307-1 #2
3 1 5 4 7 2 3 6 1	0C	35-Bauyn-II #10
|3 1 5|5 2 4|3 1 3|	3C	48-LaBarre-6 #34
|3 1 5|5 4 3|4 5 4 3|2|	3F	37-Geoffroy #210
3 2 1 1 3 3 4 5 3 3	0C	7-Munich-1511f #24
3 2 1|2 1 7|1 7 6|7 1 7|3 4 3|	3D	37-Geoffroy #232
3 2 1|2 2 7|1 2|1 1 7	3D	22a-Roper #15
|3 2 1|3 4 5|5|5 6 7|	3G	35-Bauyn-I #97
|3 2 1|5 2|3 4 3 2 1|	3A	64-Lebègue-I #35
|3 2 1|5 4 3|2 2 3|	3C	46-Menetou #32
|3 2 1|5 4 3|2 3 1|	3C	46-Menetou #48
3 2 1|5 4 3 2 3 4|3 2 1 3 2 1|	2F	37-Geoffroy #168
|3 2 1 5 5|5 5 4 3|2 2 2 3 4|3 1|	2C	37-Geoffroy #184

|3 2 1 5 6 7|1 7 1 2|3 7 1 6 #4|5	3F	35-Bauyn-II #76
|3 2 1 5|6 7 1 7|6 5 4|	3F	35-Bauyn-I #81
|3|2|1|7 1|1|	3C	46-Menetou #12
3 2 1 7 1 2 3 4 2 2	0C	7-Munich-1511f #26
|3|2|1|7|6|3 4|5 5 #4|5|	3B♭	35-Bauyn-I #126
|3 2 2|2 1 7|1 2 3 4|5 2 2|2|	3F	35-Bauyn-II #80
|3 2 2 3 4|2 1 2 2|	2F	35-Bauyn-I #74
3|2 2 7|1 1 4|4 4 3|	3C	46-Menetou #22
|3 2 3|1 1 1 7|	3C	33-Rés-89ter #18
|3|2 3 1|4 2 5|3 1 2|3|	3C	35-Bauyn-II #29
|3 2 3|1 5|5 4 3|	3C	45-Dart #36
|3 2 3 1|5|6 5 4|3 2 3 4 3|	3C	37-Geoffroy #18
|3 2 3|1 7 1|5 6 5|	3G	62-Chamb-I #28
|3 2 3 4|2 2 3|1 7 1 2|7 7|	2C	37-Geoffroy #231
3 2 3 4|3 1	2F	55-Redon #17
3 2 3 4 3 4 5 3 2	0C	7-Munich-1511f #14
|3 2 3|4 4|2 3 4 2|3 1|	2G	54-Gen-2350/57 #1
|3 2 3 4 5|6 6|5 4 5 6 5|	3C	36-Parville #132
|3|2 7 1 2|3 2 3 1 3|2 1 7 1 2|	2G	37-Geoffroy #102
|3 3 1|5 5 2|3 4 3 2 1|2 3 2|	3F	37-Geoffroy #75
|3 3 1 5|5 3 1|5 1 2|	3F	35-Bauyn-II #77
3|3 1 5 5|5 5 1 2|7 1 2 3 3 2|	3A	37-Geoffroy #131
3|3 1 5 5|5 6 #5 #5|6 3 3 2 2 1|	3C	35-Bauyn-II #18
|3 3 2|1 3|2 1 7|1|	3G	65-Lebègue-II #44
3|3 2 1|5 4 3|	3F	64-Lebègue-I #49
3|3 2|1 7|1|	3C	18-Ch-Ch-1236 #32
|3 3 2|2 1 7 1 5 6|4 3 3 3 6|	3C	35-Bauyn-II #21
3 3|2 2 5 5|3 3 4 4|4 3 2 1|	2C	39-Vm7-6307-1 #10
3 3 2 3 3 2 3 2 3 4	0C	7-Munich-1511f #3
3 3|3 2 1 5|1 1 3 3|4 3 2 1 3 2	2G	37-Geoffroy #108
3 3 3 2 1 5 4 3 6 5 6 7	0C	7-Munich-1511f #23
3|3 3 2 3 4|5 1 2 3 3 2|	3C	63-Chamb-II #3
|3 3 3 3 4 5|1 2 3 2 1|3 4 5 #4 2	3C	60-Playford #71
3 3|3 4 2 1|1 2 1 7|	3G	68-d'Anglebert #8
|3 3 3|4|3 3 4|	3F	46-Menetou #103
3|3 3 4 5|1 5 6 7|1 1 7 6 5 6 5	2F	37-Geoffroy #69
|3 3 3 4 5|2 2 2 3|	2C	46-Menetou #87
3 3 3 5 3 2 3 1	0C	6-Munich-1511e #2
|3 3 4|2 2 3 1 1 7|7|6 3 3 4|	3C	35-Bauyn-II #20
|3 3 4|2 2 3|1 7 1 2|	3F	64-Lebègue-I #50
|3 3 4|2 2 3|4 4 5|	3A	65-Lebègue-II #24
3|3 4 3 2 1 5 4 5|3 2 1 5 5 6 7	2G	65-Lebègue-II #35
3|3 4 3 2 1 5 5|5 3 4 5 6 5 4 3	3F	37-Geoffroy #206

3|3 4 3 2 1 5 6 7|	2F 64-Lebègue-I #46
3|3 4 3 2 2 1|1 1 5 5 6 ♭7|4 3 4	3C 37-Geoffroy #13
3|3 4|3 4 5|1 1 5|6 7 1|1 2 7|	3G 37-Geoffroy #99
3|3 4 4|5 5 4 3|	3C 35-Bauyn-I #16
3|3|4 5|1|2 3|6 7 1|7 1|	3F 37-Geoffroy #77
3|3 4 5 2|3 1 5 5|	3F 62-Chamb-I #22
|3 3 4|5 3 4|5 6|	3F 35-Bauyn-I #83
3|3 4|5 3 6 7|	2C 33-Rés-89ter #11
|3 3 4 5|4 2 5|	3D 45-Dart #32
|3 3 4|5 4 3 2|1 2 3|2|3 2 1 7|	3C 37-Geoffroy #189
|3 3 4|5 4 3 2|3 1 2|7|	3C 9-Ihre-284 #49
3|3 4 5 4 3 4 3 2|	2C 64-Lebègue-I #37
|3 3 4|5 5 1|1 6 2|	3F 63-Chamb-II #19
3|3 4 5 5 4|3|2 2 2	3C 17-Rogers #23
|3 3 4 5 5|♯4 5 6 ♯4 5 5|3 3 4 5 5|	2G 54-Gen-2350/57 #10
|3 3 4|5 6 5|1 2 3|2 1|	3A 37-Geoffroy #132
3|3 5 4 3 2 2 2|1 5 6 4 3 2 5 4|	2C 63-Chamb-II #1
|3 4 2|2 3 1|1 2 1|	3C 35-Bauyn-II #27
3 4|2 2 3|1 6 7|1 1 7|	3G 65-Lebègue-II #38
3 4|2 2 5|1 1 2|1 7|	3D 64-Lebègue-I #12
3 4|2 5|1 1 2|	2F 46-Menetou #21
3 4|2 5 7|1 4 6|7 1 2|	3G 37-Geoffroy #233
|3 4 3 2 1|5 6 5|6 7 1|	3G 68-d'Anglebert #11
|3 4 3 2 1|5 6 7|1 7 6 1|	3G 46-Menetou #116
|3 4 3|2 3 2 1|2 2|	3C 45-Dart #64
3 4|3 4 5 5|1 2 3 4|3 4 5 5|	2G 37-Geoffroy #103
|3 4 3 4 5 6|4 3 4 5 4 5|3 5 5|	3G 68-d'Anglebert #13
|3 4 5|1 2 3|4 5 4 3 2|	3F 45-Dart #33
3 4 5 2 2|2|1 1 1 7|1 712	3A 37-Geoffroy #142
3 4 5|2 3 1 7 6|7 1 7 6|	2C 22a-Roper #27
|3 4 5|2 3 2 1|7 1|	3G 64-Lebègue-I #27
|3 4|5 2 3|4 3|	3C 36-Parville #118
3 4|5 2 4 3 2 1|7 5 1|	2C 33-Rés-89ter #8
3 4|5 2 5|1 1 2|7 6 5|	3D 36-Parville #29
3 4|5 3 2|1 1|1 2 3	3C 35-Bauyn-III #65
3 4|5 3 2 1 5|1 7 6 5|	2D 37-Geoffroy #35
|3 4 5 3|2 3 1|2 1 2 3 2|	3C 46-Menetou #59
|3 4 5 3|4 2 5|3 7 1|2 1 2 3 2|	3B♭ 37-Geoffroy #150
3 4|5|3 4 3 2|1 2 3 2|	3G 2-Witzendorff #99
|3 4 5|4|2 3 4	3G 43-Gen-2354 #4
|3 4 5|4 2 5|1 1 2|	3G 46-Menetou #17
3 4 5|4 3 2 3 1|2 5 1 7 6 1|	2A 37-Geoffroy #137
3 4|5 4 3|2 3 4|3 2 1|	3A 37-Geoffroy #143

3 4 5|4 3|2 7|	3C	33-Rés-89ter #17
|3 4 5|4|3 3 4|2 2|	3C	46-Menetou #5
|3 4 5 4 4|3|5 6 7 1	3C	35-Bauyn-I #10
|3 4 5|4 4 5|3 3 4|	3C	46-Menetou #15
3 4|5 5|1 2 3|4 3|2 3 4|5 5 5|	3G	37-Geoffroy #107
|3 4 5|5 1 2|7 1 7 6|	3C	35-Bauyn-II #22
|3 4 5|5 3|6 5 4 3|2 1|	3C	37-Geoffroy #188
|3 4 5 5 4 3|2	3D	35-Bauyn-I #45
3 4|5 5 4 3 4 2 3|1 1 1|	2F	54-Gen-2350/57 #34
|3 4 5|5 4 3|6 7 1|1 7 1|	3C	35-Bauyn-III #60
|3 4 5|5 5 6 7|1 1 7|7|	3C	35-Bauyn-II #25
|3 4 5 5 6|5 5	3D	35-Bauyn-I #47
3 4|5 6|4 4 3|	3F	46-Menetou #34
|3 4 5 6|5 1 1 6 2|	2F	62-Chamb-I #19
|3 4|5 6 5|4 2 5|3 4 3 2 1|	3C	48-LaBarre-6 #32
3 4|5 6 5 4 3|2 2 3 4|3 2 1 7 1|	2A	37-Geoffroy #139
3 4 5 6|5 4 3 2 4|3 1 3 4 5 6|	2A	37-Geoffroy #134
|3 4 5 6 5 4|3 4 5 6	3F	35-Bauyn-I #77
|3 4 5 6|5|4 6 5|5 4 3|	3C	35-Bauyn-I #28
|3 4 5|6 7 1|2 3 4|3 2|3 4 5|	3B♭	37-Geoffroy #151
|3 4 5 6 7|1 5 3 1|4	3C	35-Bauyn-I #14
|3 4 5|6 ♭7 6 5 4|3 2 3 4 3 4|	3G	37-Geoffroy #236
|3 4 5|6 ♭7 6|5 6 4|	3F	46-Menetou #104
3 4|5 6 ♭7|6 6 7 1 2|7 7 1 2 3	2F	37-Geoffroy #80
|3 4 5 7|1 5 3 1|4 5 3	3C	35-Bauyn-I #14
|3 4 5|7 2 1 2|3 4 5|7 2 1|	2A	37-Geoffroy #138
3 5|1 2 3 4|2 2 4 4|	2G	46-Menetou #91
|3 5 1 3|2|3 1 6 2|7 1 2 5|	2G	37-Geoffroy #225
|3 5 1 3 3|2 5 2|5 1 2|	3D	35-Bauyn-II #60
3 5 1 4 7 2 5 7 1 3	0C	33-Rés-89ter #1
3 5 1 5 6 3 4 2 ♭7	0C	35-Bauyn-II #9
3|5 1|7 5 1 2|	3G	19-Heardson #65
|3 7 5 5|7 1 2 3 4|	2D	48-LaBarre-6 #35
4 3 5 1|5 3 5 1|	0C	64-Lebègue-I #36
|5 1 1 1 1 5 1 1	0C	6-Munich-1511e #3
5|1 1 2 3 4 5|3 2 1 5|	2C	36-Parville #133
5|1 2|3 1 3 4 5|4 3|2 1 2 3	2C	22a-Roper #8
5 1 2|3 1 3 4 5 4|3 2 3 2|	2C	62-Chamb-I #7
5|1 2 3 2 1|5	2G	47-Gen-2356 #14
|5 1 2|3 2 3|3 3 5|	3F	35-Bauyn-I #80
|5 1 2 3 3 2|2 3 4 5|	3C	35-Bauyn-I #12
5 1 2 3 4 3 2 2 2	0C	6-Munich-1511e #14
5 1 2 3 4 3 3 2 1 2	0C	6-Munich-1511e #15

5|1 2 3 4|5 3|	2C 55-Redon #13
5 1 2 3 4 5 4 3	0C 6-Munich-1511e #13
5|1 2|3 4 5 5 4 3|2 1|	3C 36-Parville #111
5| 1 2 3 5|5 3 6 6 5|	2C 48-LaBarre-6 #33
|5 1 2|7 7|6 5 5 4|	3G 65-Lebègue-II #37
5 1 3 4 5 2 3 7 1 5 7 3	0A 35-Bauyn-II #8
|5 1 4 5|3 2|	2C 35-Bauyn-III #62
5|1 5 1 1 2 3 2|1 5 5 4 3 2 1 3|	3C 63-Chamb-II #5
5|1 5 3 5|1 5 3 1|2 3 4 3 2 3|	2D 42-Vm7-6307-2 #11
5|1 5 6 3 4|5 5 6 7|	2G 65-Lebègue-II #41
5|1 5 6 3 4 6 5 4|3 1 5 5 5 6 4	3G 68-d'Anglebert #4
|5 1|6 2|3 4|2 2|	3C 36-Parville #125
5 1 6 7 1 2 3 2 2	0C 7-Munich-1511f #20
5 1|7 1 2 3|1 2 3 4|	3A 65-Lebègue-II #27
5 1|7 1 2 3|2 2 3 6|7 5 1 2 7|	2F 37-Geoffroy #74
5|1 7 1 2|7 6 5 5|	2C 55-Redon #14
5 1|7 1 6 5 4|	2D 64-Lebègue-I #14
5 1|7 6 5 4|3 3 4 3|2 5 6 4 3|	2D 37-Geoffroy #39
|5 1 7 7|1 2 3 4 3 1|	2F 55-Redon #9
5 1|7 7 1|6 4 4|4 3 4 5|	3G 46-Menetou #9
5 2|3 1 3|2 5 6|7 1 2 7|1 5	2F 37-Geoffroy #76
|5 2 3 3 2 1|7 5 1 5 6 6 5 4|3 1	2C 35-Bauyn-II #15
5|3 1 2 2|3 1 5|3 1 2 3|1|	2G 37-Geoffroy #101
|5 3 1 2|3 3 2 1|7 1 7 6 7|	2C 48-LaBarre-6 #30
|5 3|1 2 3 4|5 5 7 3 2|2	3F 37-Geoffroy #207
5|3 1 4 3|2 7 3|	2C 46-Menetou #10
|5 3 1|4|3 4 5 6|2 2|	3C 46-Menetou #6
5 3 1|5 5|6 7 1 2|1 7|5 6 7|1 1	2F 39-Vm7-6307-1 #9
|5 3 2 1|5 6 7|1|	3C 5-Munich-1503l #9
|5 3 2|2 1|1 2 3|4 3|4 5 6|	3C 35-Bauyn-I #18
5|3 2 3 1 3|2 2 5|1 7 6 2|7 5 5|	2C 37-Geoffroy #19
5|3 3 2 1|5 5 6	3F 62-Chamb-I #20
5|3 3 3 3 5|1 1 1 1 3|	2C 46-Menetou #108
|5 3 3|4|3 2 1|	3C 46-Menetou #46
|5 3 4|2 2 3|1 4 5|	3F 65-Lebègue-II #31
|5 3 4|2 2|3 2 1 7 1|7 5	3C 37-Geoffroy #187
5 3|4 2 3 1|2 2 5 3|	2C 46-Menetou #2
|5 3 4|2|3 4 3 2 1|	3C 46-Menetou #7
5|3 4 3 1 2 3|2 5|1 2 1 6 7 1|	3G 37-Geoffroy #234
5 3|4 3 2 1|2 5 5 3|6 5 4 3 2 1	2B♭ 37-Geoffroy #148
5|3 4 3 2 1|5 5 6 6 7 1|	3F 62-Chamb-I #20
5|3 4 3|2 3|1 2|	3B♭ 36-Parville #137
5|3 4 5 1 1 2|7 1 2 3|	3G 68-d'Anglebert #3

5|3 4 5 1 1 2|7 3 2 1|	3G 35-Bauyn-II #86
|5 3 4|5 1|5 6 4|	3G 65-Lebègue-II #39
5|3 4 5 1 7 1|2 5 1	3F 35-Bauyn-I #70
5|3 4 5 2 3 1|2 7 5 3|2 3 1	3F 37-Geoffroy #211
5|3 4 5 3|1 2 3 4|	2C 46-Menetou #51
5|3 4 5|4 5 3|2 3 2 1|	3D 68-d'Anglebert #54
|5 3 4|5 5 6 7|1 1 7 1|	2C 5-Munich-1503*l* #4
|5 3 4 5 6|5 1|4 2 3|3 4 2 3 4|	3G 37-Geoffroy #237
5|3 4 5 6|5 5 4 3|	2G 64-Lebègue-I #25
5|3 4 5 6 7 1|7	3C 35-Bauyn-I #6
5 3 5 1 6 7 1 2 1 7 6 5	0D 22a-Roper #16
5|3|5 3 4|3 2|1 5|	3C 64-Lebègue-I #40
|5 3|6 4|2 5|3 1 2 3 4|5 3|	3G 37-Geoffroy #97
|5 3 6|5 4 3 3 4 3|2 2 3 1|	3F 35-Bauyn-II #75
|5 3 6 5|5 4 3 3 4|	2F 55-Redon #5
|5 3 6 7|1 2|3 2 1 1|	3F 35-Bauyn-II #79
5 4|3 1 2 3|2 2 1 7|1 5 6 3 4|	2D 37-Geoffroy #44
5 4|3 1 2 7|1 1 2|3 4 2 5|	2D 37-Geoffroy #42
5 4 3 1 5 6 2 #4 5 7 5 4	0G 36-Parville #107
5 4|3 2 1 1 ♭7|6 5 4 3|	3G 35-Bauyn-II #88
|5 4 3 2 1 2|3 3 4 2 2|	2G 68-d'Anglebert #10
|5 4 3 2 1|2 3 4|3 2 1 2 7 1|2|	3F 37-Geoffroy #209
5 4|3 2 1|7 1|2|3 3|2 1|7|	3G 37-Geoffroy #100
5 4|3 2 1 7 1|2 5|6 7|7 1 2	3G 62-Chamb-I #30
5|4 3 2 1|7 6 7 5 6|7 1 2 7|	2F 37-Geoffroy #78
|5|4|3 2|2 1|	3F 35-Bauyn-I #78
5 4|3 2 3 1|2 2 5 6|7 1 2 7|1|	2G 37-Geoffroy #104
|5 4 3|2 3|1 2 3|	3C 64-Lebègue-I #44
|5 4 3|2 3 1|2 5|1 2|	3C 46-Menetou #50
|5 4 3 2 3|7 1 2 5|1 2 3 2 1|	2G 55-Redon #22
5 4|3 3 3 2|1 1 5 4|3 2 1 2 3|1|	2D 37-Geoffroy #46
5 4|3 4 2|1 1 5|6 5 4|3 1 2|	3C 37-Geoffroy #21
5 4|3 4 3 2 1 7|1 1 3|4 5 6 7|1	2F 35-Bauyn-II #73
5 4|3 4 3|2 3 1 1|	2B♭ 65-Lebègue-II #15
|5 4 3|4 3 2|3 2 3 1|5 4 3|	3F 37-Geoffroy #167
5 4|3 4 5 1 2 7|1 5 1 2|	3D 46-Menetou #99
5 4|3 4 5 1 7 1|2 5 1 2 3	3F 35-Bauyn-I #71
5 4|3 4|5 3 6|5|	3F 65-Lebègue-II #30
|5 4 3|4 5 6|2 3 4|3 2 1|	3C 37-Geoffroy #22
|5 4 3 6|4 3 4 2|3 4 5 4 3|2 2|	3C 37-Geoffroy #17
5 4 3|7 1 2 1|	3C 33-Rés-89ter #12
5 4 5 6|5 1 4 2|3 1 5 4 5 6|	2G 37-Geoffroy #94
|5 4 5 6 5|3 4 2|3 2 3 4 3|	3C 46-Menetou #33

|5|4 6|5 4 5|3 2 3 4|	3D 68-d'Anglebert #56
|5 5 1 1|1 1 4 5|	2C 46-Menetou #58
|5 5|1 1|2 3|2 2 |5 5|1 1|	3G 37-Geoffroy #109
5|5 1 1 2|7 7 3 6 4 4|3 3 6 2 3	3C 35-Bauyn-II #19
5|5 1 1 5|6 6 5 4 3 4|	2G 59a-Handmaide #13
5|5 1 2 2|3 3 4 3 2 2 1|	3C 65-Lebègue-I #38
5|5 1 4 5|3 2 3 7|1 2 1 6 1 2|7	3B♭ 37-Geoffroy #146
|5 5 1|6 6 2|7 1 2|	3G 63-Chamb-II #29
|5 5 1|7 1 2|3 3|2 2|	3C 35-Bauyn-II #24
|5 5 1|7 1|5 5 6|	3F 35-Bauyn-I #82
5|5 1|7 5|1 2 1 1|3 4 5 ♭7|	3G 19-Heardson #65
5|5 1 7 6 5 4 3 4 5|3 2 1 7 1 2	2F 65-Lebègue-II #28
5|5 1 7 6|5 5 6 3 4 5|3 2 1 3 4	3C 37-Geoffroy #185
5|5 1 7 6|5 5 6 3 4 5|3 2 5 4 3	3F 64-Lebègue-I #48
5|5 1 7 6 5 6 ♭7 6 5 4|3 2 3 4 5	2F 37-Geoffroy #205
|5 5 1|7 7 1|1 2 3|	3C 7-Munich-1511f #5
5|5 1 ♭7 6 5 5|6 5 4 3 4|5 3 6	3E 37-Geoffroy #59
5 5|2 3 3|2 2 3 4 3|2 1 7 1 2 7|	2G 37-Geoffroy #105
|5 5 2|5 5 4|4 5 4|	3C 33-Rés-89ter #14
5|5 3 1 1|1 ♭7 6 5|6	3C 35-Bauyn-I #24
5 5|3 1 2 3 2 3 4|2 1 5 5|3 1 2	2C 40-Rés-476 #36
5|5 3 1 5|5 5 6 5 4|	3G 33-Rés-89ter #35
5|5 3 2 1 5|5 6 5 4|3 3 4 4 5 4|	3G 63-Chamb-II #28
|5 5 3 2 1|5 5|6 5 5 4|3 3 3 4|	2C 46-Menetou #1
5 5|3 3 1 2 3 4|2 2 5 5|3 #4 5 5	2F 37-Geoffroy #208
5|5 3 3|4 4|4 5 5 4|	3C 33-Rés-89ter #15
5|5 3 4 3 2 1|7 2|2 3 4 3|	3F 35-Bauyn-II #70
5|5 3|4 4 3|	3A 65-Lebègue-II #25
|5 5 3 4|5 1 1|1 2 3 1|	2C 54-Gen-2350/57 #2
5|5 3 4 5 4 2 1 2|3 4 3 5 1 2 1	2E 37-Geoffroy #58
5|5 3 4 5|6 6 5 4|	3C 35-Bauyn-III #53
5|5 3 6 5 4 3|3 3 4 3 2 1|5	3C 37-Geoffroy #186
|5 5 3|6 5|4 4 3|2 1|	3G 46-Menetou #14
5|5 4 3 2 1 2 2|3 3	3D 37-Geoffroy #36
5|5 4 3 2|3 2 1|7 1 2	3C 54-Gen-2350/57 #13
|5|5 4 3 2 3 3|3 2 1 1 2 3|	3C 35-Bauyn-III #90
5|5 4 3 2 3 5 4 3 2|	2F 63-Chamb-II #16
5 5 4 3 3 2 1 2 3 1 7 6 5	0G 5-Munich-1503l #8
|5 5|4|3 4 2|3 2 1|5 5|4 4|	3F 37-Geoffroy #165
5|5 4 3 4 3 2 5|1 ♭7 6 ♭7 6 5 6 1|	2B♭ 37-Geoffroy #145
5|5 4 3 4 3 2 5|3|	3G 63-Chamb-II #25
5|5 4 3 4 4|3 5 6 7 1 7 6 7|	3G 65-Lebègue-II #36

5 5 4|3 4 5 1 1|1 1 4 4|	2C	46-Menetou #57
|5 5 4 3 5|1 2|3 4 3 4 3 2 1|2 5	2C	36-Parville #123
|5|5 4 3|6 6 1 5|5 4 3|	3C	33-Rés-89ter #7
5 5 4 3 6 7 1 1 7 1	0C	7-Munich-1511f #4
5|5 4 4 3|3 2 2 1|7 2 1 7 6 6 5|5	3G	36-Parville #97
5|5 4 4 3|3 2 2 1|7 7 3 7 1 1 7|	3C	64-Lebègue-I #39
|5 5 4|4 3|3 3 4|3 5 4 3 2|	3D	35-Bauyn-II #61
5|5 4 4 3|3 4 5 4 3|2 2 3 4 3 2|	3G	35-Bauyn-II #91
|5 5 4|4 5 3|6 5 4|3 2 3|5 5|	3E	37-Geoffroy #60
5|5 4 5 3|2 1 3 4 5|	3F	62-Chamb-I #21
|5 5 4 5|3 3 2 3|	2G	65-Lebègue-II #42
|5 5 4|5 4 4 4 3|3 2|	3A	35-Bauyn-II #114
|5|5 4 5|6 6|	3C	45-Dart #43
5|5 4 6 5 4|3 3 4 5|	2C	51-LaBarre-11 p 207
|5 5 5|1 6|1 1 2 3|	3G	33-Rés-89ter #41
5|5 5 4 3|2 2|3|	3C	9-Ihre-284 #48
|5 5|5 4 3 2|3 2 1 7	3C	35-Bauyn-I #25
|5 5 5 4 3 2 4|3 4 5 1|	2C	35-Bauyn-III #56
|5 5|5 5|1 2 1|	3G	38-Gen-2348/53 #37
5|5 5 5 1 5|6 6 2 2 1|	2F	46-Menetou #18
|5|5 5 5 4|3 1|	3C	35-Bauyn-III #64
|5 5 5|5|4 3 2 2|2|5|5|	3F	37-Geoffroy #79
|5 5|5 5 4|4 5 4|	3C	35-Bauyn-III #51
|5 5 5|5 4|4 4 3 4 5|	3G	35-Bauyn-II #87
|5 5 5|5 5 5|5 5 #4|5 5 5|	3G	35-Bauyn-II #89
|5|5|5|5|5|5 6|2 3|1|	3F	37-Geoffroy #166
|5 5|5 5 5|6 5|4 3 2 5|3|	3G	45-Dart #31
|5 5 5|5|6 6 6|	3C	6-Munich-1511e #8
5|5 5 6 3 4 3 2 3 4|3 2 1	2G	28-Brussels-926 *l* 64v
|5 5 5|6 4|3 2 2|	3G	68-d'Anglebert #6
|5 5 5|6 5 5 4|3 1 7 1|	3C	35-Bauyn-II #23
|5 5 5|6|5 5 #4|5 4 3|	3C	35-Bauyn-II #26
5|5 5 6 7 1 3 2 1|	2C	33-Rés-89ter #1a
5|5 6 2 1|1 1 7 6 ♭7 4 3|	3F	37-Geoffroy #70
|5 5 6|4 3|2 3 4|	3G	64-Lebègue-I #26
5|5 6 4 3|3 3 4 5|	3G	35-Bauyn-II #84
|5 5 6 4 3 4|5 6 7 1|	2C	35-Bauyn-III #34
|5 5 6|4 4 5 3 3 2|2 3 1 7|1	3F	35-Bauyn-II #74
5|5 6 5 3 4 3 4 5|5 4|3 3 2 3 1	2C	37-Geoffroy #12
5|5 6 5 4 3|3 3 4 5|6 6	3G	24-Babell #253
5|5 6 5 4|3 3 4 5 4 3|	3G	64-Lebègue-I #23
5|5 6 5 4|3 3 4 5 6 4 3|2 1	3D	37-Geoffroy #37
5|5 6 5 4 3 4 4|3 3 5 6 7|	3D	68-d'Anglebert #52

5|5 6 5 4 3 5 4 3 2|1 1	2F 35-Bauyn-I #61
5|5 6 5 4|3 5 4 3 2 4 3 2 1 3|	3C 51-LaBarre-11 p 209
5 5 6 5 4 3 6 6 5|3 4 5 1 2 3 3	0C 7-Munich-1511f #27
5|5 6 5 4 5 3|3	3F 38-Gen-2348/53 #15
5|5 6 5 4 5|3 3 2 1 1 2|	3A 65-Lebègue-II #23
5|5 6 6|7 5 1 1 2|	3D 63-Chamb-II #14
5|5 6 7 1 1 2|3 1 3	3G 35-Bauyn-I #87
|5 5 6 7 1 2|3 3 3 4|	2F 46-Menetou #94
5|5 6 7 1 2|7 5 1 7 6|5	3G 35-Bauyn-II #90a
|5 5 6 7 1 5|1 7 1 2 3 3|	2C 64-Lebègue-I #43
|5 5 6 7 1 5 6 5 4|3 4|	2G 35-Bauyn-II #83
5|5 6 ♭7 5 4|4 5 4 3 4|	3G 68-d'Anglebert #5
|5 5 6 ♭7 6|4 3 2 5 3 2 1|5 5	3C 40-Rés-476 #37
5|5 7 1 2 3 4 2 3|1 5 6 7 1 1 5|	2A 65-Lebègue-II #22
|5 5 7|7 1 2 1|5 1 6|5 4 3|	3G 37-Geoffroy #93
5 6|4 3 2 3|3 1 5 6|4 3 2 3 4|3|	2C 37-Geoffroy #192
5 6|4 3 2 3 4|3 2 1 5 6|4 3 2 3	2G 37-Geoffroy #95
5|6 4 5 5|6 4 5 4 3|2 2|3 2 1 2	3G 42-Vm7-6307-2 #1
5 6 4 7 7 1 5 3 1	0F 36-Parville #106
|5 6 5|1 2|3 4|5 3 1|	3C 46-Menetou #37
|5 6 5|3 4 2|3 1 5|3 1 5|	3F 46-Menetou #35
|5 6 5|3 4 2|3 2 3 1|	3G 65-Lebègue-II #40
|5 6|5 3 4|5 4 5 6 5|5 6|	3A 37-Geoffroy #135
5 6|5 4 3 1 2|7 1 6 5|	2G 65-Lebègue-II #43
|5 6 5 4|3 2|1 7 1 2 3 4 3|2 1 7	2C 40-Rés-476 #40
|5 6 5 4 3 4 2|1 1 2 3 4 5 3|	2B♭ 35-Bauyn-II #119
5 6 5 4|3 4 2 2|3 2 1 1 7|	2A 46-Menetou #106
|5 6 5 4 3|4 2|3 4 3 2 1|2 2 3 2|	3E 37-Geoffroy #149
|5 6 5 4 3|4 2 5|3 4 3 2 1 2|2 2|	3A 37-Geoffroy #136
5|6 5 4 3 4|5 4 3 2 2|3 5	3F 35-Bauyn-I #69
|5 6 5 5 1 2|3|2 2 5 3 3 #4|	3C 35-Bauyn-I #21
|5 6 5|5 4 3|5 6 5 4 3|2 1|	3C 22a-Roper #52
|5|6|5 5|5 2 3 4|5 6 ♭7|	3F 35-Bauyn-I #86
|5 6 5 6 1|3 4 5	3G 59a-Handmaide #15
|5 6 5 6|5 5|1 2 1 2|	3G 35-Bauyn-I #93
|5 6 5|6 7 6 7 6 5|	3C 45-Dart #21
5|6 6 4|5 4 5 6 5|6 6 4|5|	3C 46-Menetou #49
|5 6 6 5|5 4 3 4|5 6 5 4 3|	3C 21-Rés-1186bis #11
5|6 6 7 1 5 5|5 6 5 4 3|	3F 63-Chamb-II #17
5 6 7|1 1 7 6|5 5	3D 35-Bauyn-I #49
5 6 7|1 1 7 6 5 6 4|3 3	2C 35-Bauyn-I #2
5 6 7|1 2 3|1 3 #4 4|	3D 4-Lynar #62
5|6 7 1 2 3|2|1 5 1 7|1|	3F 35-Bauyn-II #78

|5 6 7|1|2 3 4|	3G 35-Bauyn-III #68
5 6 7|1 2 5 6|3 5 6|	2D 35-Bauyn-I #44
5 6 7|1 2 7|3	3B♭ 35-Bauyn-I #125
5 6 7 1 5 3 ♭7 6 5 4 3 4 2 7	0C 35-Bauyn-II #11
5 6 7|1 5 4 3 2|3|	3D 38-Gen-2348/53 #30
5 6 7|1 5 4 3 3 6 6|	3C 33-Rés-89ter #13
5 6 7|1 5 5 6 5 4|3 2 1	3D 35-Bauyn-I #51
5 6 7|1 5 5 6 7|7 7 1 2	3C 55-Redon #23
5 6 7|1 5 6 3 4 4 5 2|3 3 2 1 7	2F 35-Bauyn-II #67
5 6 7 1 5 6|5 5	3F 35-Bauyn-I #75
5 6 7|1 6|7 1 2	3F 38-Gen-2348/53 #19
5 6 7|1 7 1 2|1 5	3D 35-Bauyn-I #54
5 6 7|1 7 6 5 4|5 4 4 3 2 1|	2F 35-Bauyn-II #66
5 6 7|1 7 6|5 5 4	3D 38-Gen-2348/53 #31
5 6 7 3 4 5 4 3 5 1	0C 36-Parville #105
5|6 7 5|6 7 5|6 7 1|	3C 35-Bauyn-I #7
5 6 7 7 1 5 3 1 4 5 1	0G 33-Rés-89ter #32
5 6 7 7 1 5 3 1|6	0G 68-d'Anglebert #1
5 7 1 2 3 1 5 2 2 3 4 7 4	0D 35-Bauyn-II #2
5 7 1 3|1 2 3 5|4 3 5 1|	0F 64-Lebègue-I #45
6 5 4|3 1 5 5 6 7|1 7 1 2|	3F 35-Bauyn-II #68
6 5 4|3 4 5 1 2|1	3F 35-Bauyn-I #63
6 5 4|3 4 5 5 6 5|5	3C 35-Bauyn-I #89
6 5 4|5 3 4 5 1 2|3	3G 35-Bauyn-I #90
7 1 2 3|2 3 4 5 4 3 2|	2C 9-Ihre-284 #47
7 1 2|3 3 2|1 2 1	3D 35-Bauyn-I #48
7 1 2|3 3 2 1|5 5	2G 28-Brussels-926 l 65r
7 1 2|3|3 2|2 2 3 4|5 4|	2F 35-Bauyn-II #81
7 1 2|3 3 4 5|2 2 4 3 2|1 7 1 2|	3D 37-Geoffroy #38
7 1 2|3 4 3 2 1|7 7 1 2 2|	3F 35-Bauyn-I #68
7 1 2 5 1 3 1 2 3	0F 35-Bauyn-II #13

Major, Second Strain

1 1|1 5 6 6|	3G 36-Parville #129
|1 1 2 1 7|	3D 35-Bauyn-I #54
1 1|5 5 6 ♭7 6 5|4 5 6 6|	2F 46-Menetou #110
1|1 6 7 1|2 2 1|	2C 33-Rés-89ter #11
|1 2 3 1|6 2 7 5|	2C 55-Redon #15
|1 2 3 2 1|2|	3F 35-Bauyn-I #85
1 2 3|2 1 2 3 4 3|	2C 36-Parville #67
|1 2 3|2 1 7|1 2 7|	3C 35-Bauyn-III #60

1 2|3 3 1 1|4 4 3 2|	2C	54-Gen-2350/57 #11
1 2 3 3 2 1 2 1 7 6 5 1 5	0C	6-Munich-1511e #4
1 2 3 3 2 1 2 1 7 6|5 2 2	0C	6-Munich-1511e #3
1 2 3 3 2 3 2 1 7 1	0C	7-Munich-1511f #23
|1 2 3|3 4 5|5 4 5|	3G	35-Bauyn-III #68
|1 2 3 4|2 7 1 2|7 5 1 2 3 4|	2A	37-Geoffroy #134
|1 2 3|4 3 2|3 1 2|	3C	36-Parville #126
1|2 3 4|3 4 5|6 ♭7 6 5|	3G	63-Chamb-II #30
|1 2 3 4 5|5 4 5 6|	2F	54-Gen-2350/57 #34
1 2|3 4 5 5|6|	3G	62-Chamb-I #30
|1 2 3 6|#5|	2C	35-Bauyn-III #62
1 5 3 1 5 6 ♭7 6	0F	35-Bauyn-II #12
|1 5 3 4 2 1|7 2	3F	35-Bauyn-II #76
|1 5 5|6 5 4 3|	3G	46-Menetou #116
|1 5|6 7|1 2|7 5|	3C	22a-Roper #7
|1 7 1 2 3 2 1|	2G	68-d'Anglebert #10
1 7|1 4 3|6 7 1 2|	3C	35-Bauyn-III #65
1 7|1 5|6 ♭7|	3G	22a-Roper #31
|1 7 1 5|7|5 6 ♭7 6 5 4|3|	3F	37-Geoffroy #209
|1|7 6|4 6|	3C	33-Rés-89ter #14
1|7 6 5 4|3 4 3 2 3 4|5 3 1	2G	Celle p 94
|1 7|6 6 6 5 4|3	3F	35-Bauyn-II #72
|2 1 2 3|2 2 2 3|	2G	65-Lebègue-II #42
|2 1 2 3|2 5 2 1 2 3|2 3 4 5 6 5	2C	40-Rés-476 #36
|2 1 2 3 4|3 2 3 4 5|1 2 3	3C	46-Menetou #33
|2 1 2 3 4 3|2 5 2 2	2C	22a-Roper #1
|2 1 2|3 4 5|1 2 7|6 5|1 7 6|	3C	39-Vm7-6307-1 #3
|2 1 2|7|5 5 4 5|	3A	65-Lebègue-II #24
|2 1 7 1 2 3|	3G	32-Oldham #9
2 1|7 1 2 3|2|	3F	64-Lebègue-I #49
2 1|7 1 2 5 6 7|1|	3D	62-Chamb-I #18
2 1|7 1 2 5 6 7|1 2 3|6 7 1 7 1	3B♭	37-Geoffroy #152
|2 1 2 1 7|6 6 1 7 6|#5 3 2|	3C	33-Rés-89ter #9a
|2 1 7 2|5 1 7 6 7 7 6|#5	2C	37-Geoffroy #20
2 1|7 6 5|1 2|3|5 4|3 2 1|	3G	37-Geoffroy #99
2 1|7 6 5 1 7|6 6 5 4 1 4 3	2G	65-Lebègue-II #43
2 1|7 6 5 1 7|6 ♭7 6|	2A	37-Geoffroy #133
2 1|7 6|5 4|3|	3F	65-Lebègue-II #30
2 1|7 6 5 #4|5	2C	35-Bauyn-I #3
|2 1 7 6 7 5|1|6 5 6 7 7 6|	3F	65-Lebègue-II #33
|2 1 7 6 7|5 1 6|7 1|2 1 2 3 2|	3D	37-Geoffroy #40
|2 2 1|2 2 3 4 5 4|	3F	35-Bauyn-I #67

2|2 1 2 3 2 1|	3A 65-Lebègue-II #23
2|2 1 2 3|3 7 1 7 6	3C 63-Chamb-II #2
2|2 1 2 3 4 5|3	3F 35-Bauyn-II #68
2|2 1 7|1|1 7|	3C 5-Munich-1503*l* #9
2 2 1 7 1 2 3 1 7 6 5 5 6 4 3	0C 7-Munich-1511f #10
2|2 1 7 1 6 1 7 5 4 5 4|	3A 35-Bauyn-II #113
2|2 1 7 6 2|7 3 1 7|6	3E 37-Geoffroy #59
2|2 1 7 6 5 1 7|6 7 7 2|#5 #4 3	3C 37-Geoffroy #186
2|2 1 7 6 5 4 3 4 5|	2G 65-Lebègue-II #35
2|2 1 7 6 5 4 4|	3G 64-Lebègue-I #23
2|2 1 7 6 5 5 4|	3C 51-LaBarre-11 p 209
2|2 1|7 6 5 6|5 4	3C 18-Ch-Ch-1236 #32
2|2 1 7 6 5 6 7|1 5 6 5 4 3|	3D 37-Geoffroy #37
2|2 2 1|2 3 4	3F 38-Gen-2348/53 #15
2 2|2 1 7 1 2 3 4|3 2 1 7 6 5|	2F 37-Geoffroy #73
2|2 2 2|1 4 3|2 1 2|	3G 36-Parville #108
2 2|2 2 3 4 5 1 2|3 1 7|6	3C 35-Bauyn-II #17
2 2|2 2 3 4 5 4|3	3C 35-Bauyn-I #25
2 2|2 2 3 4 5 5 5 4 3 2 3 4 5|	2E 37-Geoffroy #58
2 2 2|3|1 17|	3F 35-Bauyn-I #80
2 2 2 3 1 2 5 1 7 6 6	0C 6-Munich-1511e #2
|2 2 2|3|1 4 5|3 3|4 5 6 6|	3C 37-Geoffroy #189
|2 2 2|3|1 4 5|3|6 ♭7 6 5	3A 37-Geoffroy #132
2|2 2 3 2 1 2 2 1|7 6 5 1 1 7|	3F 65-Lebègue-II #29
|2 2 2|3 2|1 2 2 1|7|7 1 1|1	3C 37-Geoffroy #188
|2 2 2|3|2 1 7 1 1 7|	3F 33-Rés-89ter #22
2 2|2 3 2 1 7 1 2|	2D 68-d'Anglebert #50
2|2 2 3 2 1 7|6 4 3|2 3 #4	3C 17-Rogers #23
|2 2 2|3 2 1 7|6 #5 1|2	3C 35-Bauyn-II #24
2|2 2 3|2 #1 #1|2 3 4|	3C 9-Ihre-284 #48
|2 2 2|3|3 3 4|	3D 35-Bauyn-I #53
|2 2 2|3 3 3 5|4 3 2 1 7 6|	3F 62-Chamb-I #23
2 2|2 3 4 2|2 3 1 6|	2C 46-Menetou #3
|2 2 2|3 4 3 2 1 7|6 6 6|	3D 42-Vm7-6307-2 #12
|2 2|2 3|4 5|2 2|2 5|2 5|4 3|	3G 37-Geoffroy #109
2|2 2 3 4|5 4 3	3D 38-Gen-2348/53 #30
2|2 2 3 4 5 4 3 2 3 3 2 1|7	2C 35-Bauyn-I #2
|2 2 2|3 4 5|4 4|3 3|	3G 63-Chamb-II #29
2|2 2 3 4 5 5 6|#4	3G 65-Lebègue-II #36
|2 2 2|3 4 5 6|	3D 68-d'Anglebert #53
|2 2 2|3 6 7|1 7 6|#5|6 #4 #4|	3C 35-Bauyn-I #18
2|2 2 3 7 1|2 1 2 5|	3D 63-Chamb-II #12

2 2 2|♭3 4|5 2 2 2|3 4|	2D 26-Bull #18
|2 2 2|5 1 2|3 4|	3C 35-Bauyn-I #17
2 2|2 7 1 2 3|	3G 35-Bauyn-I #90
2 2|2 7 1 2|3	3G 35-Bauyn-I #87
|2 2 3|1 1 2|2 1 7|	3G 62-Chamb-I #28
2|2 3 1 2|7 7 3|	2C 46-Menetou #10
2|2 3|1 7|1 6 2|7 2 3 4|	3G 37-Geoffroy #106
2|2 3 2 1 6 7 6 7|	3C 53-Oldham-2 p 107
|2 2 3 2 1 7 1 2|	2C 35-Bauyn-I #1
2|2 3 2 1 7 1 6 7|	3C 33-Rés-89ter #2
2|2 3 2 1 7|1 7 6 6 7 1|2	2D 64-Lebègue-I #13
2|2 3 2 1|7 5 1 7|	3C 33-Rés-89ter #15
2|2|3 2 1 7|6|4 3|2 3 4|5	3C 17-Rogers #95
2|2 3 2 1 7 6 5 4 4 3|3 1 1 1	2F 37-Geoffroy #69
2|2 3 2 1 7 6 7|1 5 7 6	3C 8-Hintze #15
2|2 3 2 1|7 7 1 6 7 6|	3C 35-Bauyn-I #11
|2 2|3|2 1 7|7|1 7 1 2|	3F 35-Bauyn-II #75
2|2 3 2 7 1 2|5 5 6 5 4 3 4 5|	2A 37-Geoffroy #130
|2 2 3 2 7 1 2|7 6 7 1	2C 32-Oldham #22
2|2|3 3 2|1|2 2 1|2 7	3C 35-Bauyn-III #55
|2 2 3 3 2|1 2 3 2|	2D 64-Lebègue-I #14
|2 2 3|3 3 4 4 5 4 3|	3D 63-Chamb-II #15
2|2 3 4 2 1|7 5 1 7|6	3G 37-Geoffroy #92
2|2 3 4 2 4 3 4 3 2 1|	2A 65-Lebègue-II #22
|2 2 3 4 3|1 7 6 2 7 6 5|2 2	3C 40-Rés-476 #37
2|2 3 4 3|2 2 3 1|	2C 46-Menetou #51
|2 2 3|4|3 3 2|	3C 5-Munich-1503l #7
|2 2 3|4 3|3 3 6|	3F 35-Bauyn-I #82
2 2 3 4|3 3 4 5 1 1 2 3|	3C 46-Menetou #57
|2 2 3|4|3 4 3 2 1|	3G 43-Gen-2354 #4
2|2 3 4|4 4 5|3|4 3 2|♯1	3C 54-Gen-2350/57 #13
|2 2 3|4 4 5|3 3 3 2|3 3 2 1|	3D 37-Geoffroy #38
|2 2 3 4 4 5 6 5 4|	3B♭ 46-Menetou #115
|2 2 3 4 5|4 3|3 2 3|4|3	3B♭ 35-Bauyn-I #126
2|2 3 4 5|4 3 3 4 5 6|7 ♯5	3C 63-Chamb-II #3
|2 2 3|4 5 5|6 7 5 4|	3G 46-Menetou #17
|2 2 3|4 5|6 7 1|	3G 46-Menetou #14
2|2 3 6 7|♯5	3C 35-Bauyn-I #8
2|2 3 7 1 5 6|4 3 3 4 5|	3D 35-Bauyn-II #59
|2 2 5|1 7 1|6 5 4|	3F 37-Geoffroy #163
|2 2 5|3 4 5|2 3 1|	3C 36-Parville #124
2|2 5 4 3 1 1|	3G 63-Chamb-II #26

2|2 5 4 3 2 2|3 1 2 3 4 5|6 ♭7 6	3C 37-Geoffroy #13
2|2 5 4|3 3 4 5|6 ♭7 5 4	3F 35-Bauyn-I #68
|2 2 5|4 3 4 2 6 7|♯5	3F 35-Bauyn-II #74
2|2 5 4 3|6 6 4 5	3F 63-Chamb-II #18
2|2 5 4 5|3 3 4 5 4 5 5|6	3A 37-Geoffroy #131
2|2 5 4 5|3 3 4 5 5|6 6 7 1 2 3|	3C 37-Geoffroy #185
|2 2 5|♯4 3 4|♭7 6 5 ♯1 2 3	3G 37-Geoffroy #93
2|2 5 5 4|	3F 64-Lebègue-I #48
2|2 5 5|5 5 4 3|3 4 5 3 6 7|	3C 35-Bauyn-II #18
2|2 5 6 4 3|3	3G 32-Oldham #111
|2 2 5|6 5 4 3 2 1|7 1 2 3 4	3G 65-Lebègue-II #40
2|2 5 6 7 1 2|3 1 2 3|4 5 4 3 2	3D 37-Geoffroy #36
2|2 5 6 7|1 5 6 7 1 7|6 5	3F 35-Bauyn-I #77
2|2 5 6 7 7|1 1 2 3 1 7|6 7 1 2|	3F 37-Geoffroy #70
2|2 6 7 1 1 7|1 1 5 6|	3G 36-Parville #97
2|2 7 1 2|3 1 2 3|4 3 5 4 3 2|	3B♭ 37-Geoffroy #146
2|2 7 1 2 3 2 1 7|6 6 2 3 1|	2C 55-Redon #18
|2 2 7 1 2|7 5 3 4 5|	2G 36-Parville #122
2 2|7 5 1 ♭7 1 ♭7|6 6 ♭7 6 5 6|	2F 37-Geoffroy #208
2 2 7 5 5 3 1 1	0C 7-Munich-1511f #24
|2 3|1 1 2|7 1|	3G 64-Lebègue-I #26
|2 3 1|4 4 3|2 3 1|	3C 45-Dart #36
2 3|1 6 6 2 1|7 5 5 1 7|	2C 5-Munich-1503l #15
2 3|1 7 7 1 2 3 2 3 1|	3D 68-d'Anglebert #57
|2 3|2|1|1 1 7|6 7|1 5|	3G 35-Bauyn-I #97
2 3 2 1 2|7 1 2 1 7 1|6	2F 37-Geoffroy #205
2|3 2 1 2|7 5 1 7|	2C 22a-Roper #8
2|3 2 1 7 6 6|2 1 7 5|	2C 55-Redon #11
2|3 2 2|1 7 2|	3A 65-Lebègue-II #25
2 3 2|2 3 4 5 4 3|3	3C 35-Bauyn-I #14
|2 3 2|3 4 3 2 3 1|	3C 45-Dart #21
2 3|2 5 4|	3G 64-Lebègue-I #24
|2 3 2|6 5 6 7 1 6|7 1|	3D 64-Lebègue-I #11
|2 3 2 6 7 1|2 3 2 3|	3C 64-Lebègue-I #42
2 3 2 6|7 1 2 5 1 2 3 1|6 4 3 4	2G 37-Geoffroy #94
|2 3 2|7 1 2|5 6 5 6|7|	3F 37-Geoffroy #212
|2 3 2 7 1|2 6 7|1	3C 35-Bauyn-I #10
2|3|4 2|2 ♯1|	3C 35-Bauyn-III #64
|2 3 4 2|3 2 1|7 6 7|1 7 1 2 1|	3B♭ 37-Geoffroy #150
|2 3 4|3 2 1|4 5 6|5|	3G 37-Geoffroy #98
|2 3|4 3|2 1 |7 5|2 2|	3C 36-Parville #125
2 3|4 3 2 3 2 1|7 7 1 2 2 5|	2D 37-Geoffroy #42

|2 3 4|3 3|3 2 1|	3C 46-Menetou #15
|2 3|4 3 4 2|3 2 1|7 6 7 5|	3G 37-Geoffroy #96
|2 3 4|3 4 3|	3C 46-Menetou #7
|2 3 4|3 4 5|1 2 3|	3C 46-Menetou #46
|2 3 4|3 6|5 5 6|	3C 46-Menetou #57
|2 3 4|4 5 3|1 7 6|	3E 37-Geoffroy #60
2 3|4 4 5 6 5 4|3 1 1|	2G 64-Lebègue-I #25
|2 3|4 5 3|1 7 6|	3D 35-Bauyn-II #60
|2 3 4 5 3|2 1|7 1 2	3G 62-Chamb-I #29
2 3|4 5|3 3 3|6 6 7|	3F 46-Menetou #103
2 3 4|5 4 3 2 2 1|	3F 35-Bauyn-I #71
2 3 4|5 4 3 4 3|	2G 63-Chamb-II #24
2 3 4|5 4 3 4 3 2|	2C 63-Chamb-II #1
2 3 4|5 4 3 4 3 2 2 1|	3G 68-d'Anglebert #4
|2 3 4|5 4 3 #4 #5 6 7 1|	3C 33-Rés-89ter #12
2 3 4|5 4 3 6 5 6|	2F 63-Chamb-II #16
2 3 4|5 4 4|	3G 33-Rés-89ter #35
2 3 4|5 4 4|3 3|5 6 7 1 7 1|	3G 63-Chamb-II #28
|2 3 4|5 6 5 4 3|	3G 68-d'Anglebert #14
2 3 #4 5 6 7 1|2 3 2 1 3 2 1 7 6	2F 65-Lebègue-II #28
2|3 6 7 1 2 1|	3C 35-Bauyn-I #15
2|3 7 1 2 6 6|	3D 63-Chamb-II #13
2 ♭3 4|5	2D 26-Bull #19
|2 4 3 2 1|7 6 7 5|1 2 3 3|6 6|	3G 37-Geoffroy #222
|2 5 4|3 2 1|5 1 ♭7|6 5 4	3F 35-Bauyn-II #70
2 5 4 3 2 2 1|7 1|	3F 35-Bauyn-I #70
|2 5 4 3 2 4|3 4 2	2C 35-Bauyn-III #34
|2 5 4|3 3 3|3 3 3|	3C 6-Munich-1511e #8
2 5 4|3 3 4 3 4 5|	2A 46-Menetou #106
|2 5 4|3 4 5|5 2 3 4 5|	3C 35-Bauyn-II #25
|2 5 4|4 3|1 2 3|6 7 #5|	3F 37-Geoffroy #72
2|7 1 2|1 2 7|6 7 6 5|	3D 68-d'Anglebert #54
|2 7 1|2 3|2 4 3 2 1|	3F 65-Lebègue-II #32
2|7 1 2 3|2 6 6 7|	3C 35-Bauyn-I #26
2|7 1 2 5 2 7 1 2|7 7 5|	3F 35-Bauyn-II #77
2|7 1 2|5 5|2 3 4|3 2 1|4 5 6|	3D 37-Geoffroy #45
2 7 1|2 7 6 5|	2C 35-Bauyn-III #85
|2 7 1|6 6|5 5 5 6 4 3|	3D 64-Lebègue-I #10
|2 7 3|1 3 2 5|2 3 2 1|	2C 5-Munich-1503*l* #4
2 7 3 1 4 2 5 3	0C 7-Munich-1511f #17
|2 7 3 2 1 6 2 1|7 1 7 6 7	2C 55-Redon #4
|2 7 5|1|7 1 2 3	3C 46-Menetou #6
2|7 5 6 7|1 6 7 6 5|	3F 62-Chamb-I #20

|2 7 6|5 5 5 6 4 3|3 3 2 3|	3C 35-Bauyn-II #22
2 7 6 5|6 7 1 6 5 4|	3D 35-Bauyn-I #47
2|7 6 6 7 1|2 6 6 7 1|	2C 55-Redon #14
2|7 6 7 5 6 7|1 5 4 5 2|	3G 68-d'Anglebert #16
2|7 7 1 2 5|5 7 1|2 3 2 3|1 3|	2D 37-Geoffroy #35
|2 7 7 1 2|5 7|1 2 2 3|3 2|	3C 37-Geoffroy #187
|3 1|2 1 7|6 1 7 5 6 5|	3G 37-Geoffroy #97
|3 1 2 3 4 5|4 5 3 2|	2C 46-Menetou #108
3 1 2 3 6 7 1 7 1	0C 7-Munich-1511f #17
3 1|2 7 1 1|7 7 2 1|	2C 46-Menetou #2
|3 1 3|2 3|1 6 2|	3C 48-LaBarre-6 #34
|3 1 4 3|2 1 7 1|	2F 55-Redon #4
3 2 1 2 2 3 2 1 2 3	0C 7-Munich-1511f #20
3 2 1|2 7 5 1 1 7|1 6 5 5 6|	3C 35-Bauyn-II #19
3 2 1|2 7 7 1 2|3 5 6 5 6 7|	3F 35-Bauyn-II #69
|3 2 1 3|2 1 2 7|1 7 6 2|7	3C 37-Geoffroy #17
|3 2 1 3|2|1 6 7 1|7|	2G 37-Geoffroy #225
|3 2 1|5 6 4 3|2 2|	3A 35-Bauyn-II #114
3 2 1|7 1 2 2 3 4 5 4|3 3 #4	2B♭ 35-Bauyn-II #119
3 2 1|7 1 2 3 2 2 #1|	3D 68-d'Anglebert #51
3 2 1|7 1 2 3 3 4|	3C 64-Lebègue-I #38
3 2 1|7 1 2 3 4 4 3|	3G 35-Bauyn-II #84
3 2 1|7 1 2 3 6 7 1|	2C 5-Munich-1503l #11
3 2 1|7 1 2 5 6 4 5|	2C 35-Bauyn-III #56
3 2 1|7 1 2 5 6 5 4|3	3C 35-Bauyn-III #53
3 2 1|7 1 2 5 6 7|1 1 2 3|	3G 35-Bauyn-II #91
3 2 1|7 1 2 5 6 7|1|6 5 4 3	3D 35-Bauyn-I #58
3 2 1|7 1 2 5 6 7|1 1 7 6|	3B♭ 35-Bauyn-II #120
3 2 1|7 1 2 5 6 7|1 2 2 2|3 3	3G 68-d'Anglebert #3
3 2 1 7 1 2 7 6 5	0C 7-Munich-1511f #4
3 2 1 7 1 #4 6|#3 4	2F 35-Bauyn-II #67
|3 2 1 7 6 5|6 4 5 4	3G 59a-Handmaide #15
3 2 1|7 6 5 6 7 1 1|	3G 68-d'Anglebert #5
3 2 1|7 7 1 2|3 2 1 7 1|	2F 35-Bauyn-II #66
3 2 1|7 7 1 2 3 4 3 2 1|	2G 35-Bauyn-II #83
3 2 1|7 7 1 2 5 5|	3C 32-Oldham #4
3 2 1|7 7 6 5 5 #4|	3D 64-Lebègue-I #9
|3|2 2 3|1 1 2|7 5|2 5|	3C 35-Bauyn-II #29
|3|2|2 3 1|7 6|#1|	3F 35-Bauyn-I #78
|3 2 3 1|2 1 7|1 7 1 5|	3F 37-Geoffroy #167
|3 2 3|1 2|7 1|	3D 45-Dart #16
|3 2 3 4 3|1 4|3 4 5|	3G 45-Dart #35
3 3|1 1 4 3 2 1|	2C 47-Gen-2356 #17

|3 3 1|2 3 2|7 6 7|1 2 3 4|	3F 37-Geoffroy #73
|3 3|2 4 3 2 1|7 6 7 5|3 3 3|	3G 37-Geoffroy #236
|3 3 3 4|2 2 3 2|	3G 68-d'Anglebert #6
|3 3 3|4 5|6|	3F 46-Menetou #34
|3 3 4 3 2|1 2|	3C 45-Dart #41
|3 3 4|5 5 6|7 1 6|	3F 46-Menetou #35
3 3|#4 #4 #5 #5|6 6 7 1|	2B♭ 36-Parville #136
3 3|#4 5 6 5|#4 2	2C 22a-Roper #27
3 4|2 3 1 7 6|2 7 3 4|2	2G 37-Geoffroy #95
|3 4|2 7 1|2 1 2 3 2|3 4|2	3A 37-Geoffroy #135
|3 4 3 1 |2 3 2|7 6 7 5|1 2 1|	3C 37-Geoffroy #18
|3 4 3 2 1|2 3 2 1 7|1 2 3 7 6|	3G 68-d'Anglebert #11
|3 4 3 2 1|2 7 1|2 3 4|	3C 36-Parville #118
|3 4 3|2 1|7 1|	3C 46-Menetou #37
|3 4 3 2 #1 #1|2 3 2 1 7 7|	2C 64-Lebègue-I #43
|3 4 3|2 3|1 2 1 7 6|	3C 64-Lebègue-I #44
|3 4 3|2 3|4 5 6 3|	3F 37-Geoffroy #165
|3 4 3|2 5 3|1 1 2|	3F 55-Redon #21
|3 4 3 4 5|2 3 4|1 2 1 2 3|	3A 37-Geoffroy #136
|3 4 5|2 1 2|3 4 3 2 1|	3F 45-Dart #33
3 4 5|2 1|7 1 2|	2C 51-LaBarre-11 p 210
3 4|5 2 2 3 2|1 7 1 6 7 1|2	2C 40-Rés-476 #42
|3 4 5|2 3 4 3 2 1|7	2F 37-Geoffroy #168
3 4|5 3 2 1|2 1 7 6 5 1|	2C 55-Redon #13
3 4 5 3 4 5 1	0C 7-Munich-1511f #1
|3 4 5|3 4 5|4 3 2 1	3G 54-Gen-2350/57 #4
|3 4 5 3|6 5 6 5 4 3|	2C 36-Parville #123
|3 4 5|4 3|2 1|	3C 46-Menetou #50
3 4|5 4 3 2|3 6|#5 3 6|	3G 2-Witzendorff #99
|3 4 5|4 5 3 6 6 7|	3C 46-Menetou #48
3 4 5 5 3 2 2 5	0C 6-Munich-1511e #1
3 4 5|5 4 4|3	3C 35-Bauyn-I #16
|3 4 5 6|4 3 2|	3C 36-Parville #131
|3 4 5|6 5|4 5 4 3 2|	3A 64-Lebègue-I #35
3|#4 5 6 7|5 #4 3 4 3|	2C 36-Parville #133
3 #4 #5|6 6 6 7 1 2 2 2 1|	2C 33-Rés-89ter #16
|3 5 4 3 2|1 7 1|2 2 3 4|	3G 37-Geoffroy #237
|4 4|3 2 3 4|	3G 68-d'Anglebert #13
4|4 3 4|5 6 5 4	3F 35-Bauyn-I #75
4 5 6|7 6|5 4 3|	2D 35-Bauyn-I #44
#4 5 6|7 1 2 1 7 6 5 6 3 4|	2F 64-Lebègue-I #46
|#4 7 7 1 2 5 5 2 3 4|3|	3F 35-Bauyn-II #12

5 1 1 1 1 5 1	0C 7-Munich-1511f #14
|5 1 1 7|6 4 4 3 2 1|	2C 46-Menetou #23
5|1 2 3 1|2 6|2 1 7 1|	2C 55-Redon #19
|5 1 2 3 4 3|2 3 2 1 2 1|	3F 35-Bauyn-I #84
5|1 2 4 3 2 1|5 4 5 3 3|	2C 33-Rés-89ter #8
5 1 5 5 1 5 5 1	0C 6-Munich-1511e #13
|5 1 7 1|6 2 7 6 5|	2F 64-Lebègue-I #51
|5 1 7 6 5 4|3 4|	3D 35-Bauyn-I #57
|5 2 2|5 3 4 5|	2D 45-Dart #53
5 2 3 1 7 1|2 3 4	2G 35-Bauyn-III #92
|5 2 3|2 3|2 3 1|	3G 65-Lebègue-II #39
|5 2 3|4|3 1 7|	3G 65-Lebègue-II #37
5 2 3 4 3 2 1 2 3 4 3 4 3	2G 5-Munich-1503l #8
5 2 3 4 3 2 1|7|	2C 51-LaBarre-11 p 207
5 2|3 4 3 2 1|7 5 1|	3B♭ 36-Parville #130
|5 2 3|4 4 3|2 1 2|	3F 35-Bauyn-I #81
5 2 3|4 4 4|3 3 3|4 3 4 3 2 1|	2C 37-Geoffroy #184
5|2 3 4 4 5|3 1 6 7|	2G 65-Lebègue-II #41
5|2 4 5|3 6|#5 6 7 1|7	2G 42-Vm7-6307-2 #3
|5 2 5 4|3 4 3 4 5|4 3 2 3|	3C 46-Menetou #16
|5 2 7 6 5|6 7 1 6	3D 38-Gen-2348/53 #32
|5 2 7 7 6|5 2 7 2 1|	3C 33-Rés-89ter #20a
5|3 3 3 5|1 1 2 3|4 4 3|	3C 46-Menetou #49
|5 3 3|4 5 6 7|	3C 46-Menetou #90
5 3 4|2 1 7 1|	2B♭ 35-Bauyn-I #124
|5 4 3|2 1|7 1 2|3 2|	3G 32-Oldham #21
5 4 3|2 1 7 1 2 3|3 2 1	3G 63-Chamb-II #27
5 4 3 2 1 7|1 4 3 2 1 7 6|	2C 33-Rés-89ter #9
5 4 3 2|1 7 6 6 7|5 5 6 7	2C 35-Bauyn-I #4
5 4 3|2 2 3 1 4 5|3 2 3 4	3G 35-Bauyn-II #86
5 4 3|2 2 3 4 3 3 2 1 7 1|2 1 7	2G 37-Geoffroy #91
5 4 3|2 2 3 4 5 4|3 4 5 4 3|	2C 35-Bauyn-II #15
5 4 3|2 2 3 4 5 5 4|	3D 35-Bauyn-I #45
5 4 3|2 2 3 4 5 6 7|1	3C 35-Bauyn-II #16
5 4 3 2 3 2 1|7 1 2|	2C 35-Bauyn-III #86
5 4 3|2 3 2 #1 #1|	3C 64-Lebègue-I #39
5 4 3|2 3 4 4 5 6 5 4|	3F 64-Lebègue-I #47
5 4 3 2 3 4 5|3 2 3|1 2 3 4 3|	3F 35-Bauyn-II #79
5 4 3|2 3 7 1 2 2 1 7|	2D 35-Bauyn-II #58
5 4 3|2 3 4 5|3 2 3 1 2 3|	2C 48-LaBarre-6 #30
5|4 3 2|4 3 2 1|2 2 2|	3G 38-Gen-2348/53 #35
5 4 3|3 3 2 1 4 3|4 1 2	3G 35-Bauyn-I #89
5 4|3 3 4 2 2 3|4 3 4 5|	2A 65-Lebègue-II #26

|5 4 3|3 3 4 5 6 7|#5 6 6 3|	3C	35-Bauyn-II #21
|5 4 3|4 2 1|7 7|	3C	46-Menetou #32
5 4|3 4 3 2 3 2|	3G	19-Heardson #65
5 4 3|4 4 3 2 3 4 3 2 1|	2C	46-Menetou #87
|5 4 3|6 5 6|5 1|	3G	64-Lebègue-I #27
5 4 5 2 3 4|2 2 3|	3A	35-Bauyn-II #115
5 4 5 2 4|3 2 3 7 1 2|1 7 1	3D	37-Geoffroy #41
|5|4 5 3|2 1|	3C	47-Gen-2356 #13
|5 4 5 3|3 2|	3C	35-Bauyn-III #90
|5|4 5 3|3 4 3 2|	3C	33-Rés-89ter #4
|5 4 5|6 6|5 4 3 2|3 1	2G	54-Gen-2350/57 #1
5 5|1 1 7 6 6|2 7 7|3 2 3 1 7|	2D	37-Geoffroy #39
|5 5 1|7 7 1|	3F	46-Menetou #104
5 5 2 3 4 3 4 2	0C	7-Munich-1511f #3
5|5 2 3 4 4 3|	3F	36-Parville #83
5|5 2 3 4 5 4|3	3D	38-Gen-2348/53 #27
5 5 3 1 1 6 4 4	0G	7-Munich-1511f #24
5|5 3 4 5|6 5 6 4 1	2G	54-Gen-2350/57 #3
|5 5 4 3 2 1|7 1|	3D	62-Chamb-I #17
5|5 4|3 3 2|	3C	33-Rés-89ter #17
|5|5 4 3|4 3|	3C	45-Dart #43
5|5 4 3 4 4 3|3 5 6 7 1 7|6 5	3F	37-Geoffroy #71
5|5 4 4 3|3 2 1|4 3 4 5	2G	43-Gen-2354 #3
5|5 4 4 3|3 3 2 2 1|7 6 5 1 7 1|	3F	37-Geoffroy #206
|5 5 4|4 3|3 4 2|	3C	35-Bauyn-III #52
|5|5 4 4|3 3|5 6 7 1 7 1|	3G	35-Bauyn-I #91
|5 5 4 4 4 3|3 4 5 2 3|	3C	60-Playford #71
5|5 4 5 4 3|2 2 3 4 5 4 3|	3G	35-Bauyn-II #90
5|5 5 4 3 2 2 3 4 3 3 2 1|	2Bb	37-Geoffroy #145
5 5 5 4|3 3 3 4 3 2 2|	2C	46-Menetou #1
5|5|5 4 3|4 5 6|5 4 3|	3F	37-Geoffroy #77
5|5 5|5 5|5 4|	3C	35-Bauyn-I #7
5 5|5 5 6 7|1 6 #4 #4|	2G	46-Menetou #91
|5 5 6 3|4 5 3|	3C	46-Menetou #89
5|5 6 4 3 6 #5|	3C	63-Chamb-II #5
|5 5|6 4|5 3|	3C	9-Ihre-284 #49
5|5|6 7 1 2 7|	3D	4-Lynar #62
5 5|6 7 1 2|7 7 1 1|2 2 3 3 2|	2C	37-Geoffroy #192
5|#5 #5 #5 7|3 3 4|	2F	46-Menetou #21
|5 6 4 3 2|5 6 4 3 3 4|	3C	35-Bauyn-I #21
5 6|4 3 4 2 5 4|3 3 5|6 6 2	2F	37-Geoffroy #74
|5 6 4|3 6 #5|1 2 3|	3C	7-Munich-1511f #5
5 6 5|1 1 2 3 4 3|	3F	46-Menetou #94

5 6 5 4 3 1 2 3 4	0G	6-Munich-1511e #5
5 6 5 4|3 2 3 4 5 1 2 3 4|	3D	48-LaBarre-6 #35
|5 6 5 4 3|4 3|2 1 2 3 2|	3C	36-Parville #132
5 6|5 4 3 4 5| 6 6 5 6|	2A	37-Geoffroy #139
5|6 5 6 7 1 2|7 5 1|	3G	68-d'Anglebert #12
|5 6 6|7 1|1 2|	3G	32-Oldham #20
5 6|7 1 1|2 1 7 3 2 1|	2C	33-Rés-89ter #10
5 6 7 1 1|2 2	2G	59a-Handmaide #13
|5 6 7|1 2 1 7 1|6 1 7 6|	3C	48-LaBarre-6 #31
5 6|7 1 2 2 5|	3D	63-Chamb-II #14
5 6|7 1 2 3 2 1|7 1 2 5 1 7|	3D	35-Bauyn-I #48
5 6|7 1 2 3 2|1 7 1 2 5 6|	3A	65-Lebègue-II #27
|5 6 7 1 2 3|4|3 4 3 2 1|	3B♭	65-Lebègue-II #16
5 6 7 1 2 3|4|3 #4 5 3 6|	3B♭	22a-Roper #67
5|6 7 1 2|7 7 2|3 6 #5|	2F	35-Bauyn-II #73
5 6 7|1 5 4 3 2 1 2 3 4 5|	2G	28-Brussels-926 l 64v
|5 6 7|1 5 4 3 2 1|5 5 4 3|	3G	35-Bauyn-II #85
5 6 7|1 5|5 6 5 4|	3G	19-Heardson #69
|5 6 7|1 5|6 5 4|3|3 2 3 4|	2F	55-Redon #17
|5 6 7 1 5|6 5 4 5 3|	2F	55-Redon #9
|5 6 7|1|6 7 1|	3F	65-Lebègue-II #31
|5 6 7|1 7 1 2 1|	3G	45-Dart #50
5 6 7|1 7 1|6 7 1|2 2|7 7 3|	3C	37-Geoffroy #22
|5 6 7|1 7 6|5 4 3|2 5|	3F	37-Geoffroy #210
5 6 7|1 ♭7 6 5 4 3|#4 5|	2F	35-Bauyn-II #81
|5 6 7 7|1 2 1 7|	3C	35-Bauyn-I #12
5 6|7 7 1 2 3 4|	3D	46-Menetou #99
|5 6|7 7 1|2 3 6 7|1 2|	3G	63-Chamb-II #25
|5 6 7 7|7 1 2	3D	35-Bauyn-I #52
|5 6 ♭7 1 5 5|6 ♭7 5|	3F	38-Gen-2348/53 #11
|5 7 1|2 1 7 6|7 1 6|	3F	63-Chamb-II #19
6 5 4 5 5 6 5 4 5 6	0G	7-Munich-1511f #20
|6 5|7 1 2|2 2 3 6 7 1|	3C	35-Bauyn-I #19
|6 6|5 1 2 3 1 4 4 3 4|	3C	33-Rés-89ter #18
6 7|1 1 1 2 3|7 5 4|3 2 4 3	2A	37-Geoffroy #144
6 7 1|1 2 2 2 1 7 6 5 5|	2G	68-d'Anglebert #2
6 7 1|2 1 2 3 2 1|	2G	24-Babell #252
6 7 1|2 1 3 2 1 3 2 1 #4 5 6|	2E	37-Geoffroy #34
6 7 1|2 1 7|1 6 6 7 1|7 6 #5 #5	2G	28-Brussels-926 l 65r
6 7 1|2 1 7 6 5 5 4 3 2 3 4 5|	2C	37-Geoffroy #12
6 7 1 2 1|7 6 5 5 #4|	2C	62-Chamb-I #7
6 7 1|2 1 ♭7 6|2 5 4	2G	35-Bauyn-III #83

6 7 1|2 1 ♭7 6|6 6 5   3D 68-d'Anglebert #52
6 7 1|2 2 1 7 1|6 #4   3D 35-Bauyn-I #46
6 7 1|2 2 1 7 6|7 1 2| 3G 35-Bauyn-II #90a
6 7 1|2 2 2 3 4| 3C 36-Parville #62
6 7 1 2 2|2 5 1 2|7 7   3G 35-Bauyn-II #88
|6 7 1|2 2 2 7 1 2|3 3 3| 3F 62-Chamb-I #23
6 7 1|2 2 3 2 1|7| 3F 35-Bauyn-II #71
6 7 1|2 2 3 4 3 2 1 7| 2C 64-Lebègue-I #37
6 7 1|2 2 3 4|5   3C 62-Chamb-I #9
6 7 1|2 2 3|#4 2 5| 2D 63-Chamb-II #11
6 7 1|2 3 2 1 7 6 1 7 2| 2C 33-Rés-89ter #1a
6 7 1|2 3 2 1 7 6 5 1|1 7 6| 3D 35-Bauyn-I #51
6 7 1|2 3 2 1|7 6 5 4|3 2 2G 35-Bauyn-II #82
6 7 1|2 3 2 1 7 6 7|1   3C 36-Parville #61
6 7 1|2 5 4 5 4 3 4| 3G 68-d'Anglebert #7
6 7 1|2 5 6 7|1 2 3 4 5 6 5 4 3 3C 36-Parville #63
6 7 1|2 5 6 7 1 ♭7 6| 3D 68-d'Anglebert #52
6 7 1|2 7 2 1| 3G 35-Bauyn-II #90a
7 1|2 1 7 6 5|5 5 5 3 4|5 4 2G 37-Geoffroy #220
|7 1 2 1|7 7 1| 3C 46-Menetou #5
|7 1 2 2 2 2|2| 3B♭ 35-Bauyn-I #127
|7 1 2 2|2 2 3| 3G 35-Bauyn-II #87
|7 1 2 2|2|2 3 4| 3D 35-Bauyn-II #61
7 1|2 2|2 3 1|2 4|3 1 2| 3G 37-Geoffroy #107
7 1|2 2|2 3|4 3 2 1|2 1 7 6 5| 2D 42-Vm7-6307-2 #11
7 1 2 2 2 3 4 5 5 5   0C 7-Munich-1511f #19
|7 1 2|2 2 5 5 6| 3G 33-Rés-89ter #41
7 1 2|2 3 2 1|1 6 7 1| 2F 37-Geoffroy #80
7 1|2 2|3 3| 3C 36-Parville #111
|7 1 2|3 1|4 3 2 1 7 6|#5| 3C 37-Geoffroy #14
7 1|2 3 2|1 1 2 3|4 5 3C 35-Bauyn-I #24
7|1 2 3 2 1|2 2 1 7| 2C 64-Lebègue-I #41
7 1 2|3 2 1 2 3 2 1| 3D 35-Bauyn-I #49
|7 1|2 3 4|3 2 1|2 5| 3C 48-LaBarre-6 #32
7 1|2 3 4 5 4| 3G 35-Bauyn-I #100
7 1|2 3 4|5 6 7 ♭7|4 5 3| 3C 37-Geoffroy #21
|7 1 2|5|4 3 4 5|3| 3B♭ 37-Geoffroy #147
|7 1 2|5 6 7 1 1 7|7 1 1 7| 3C 35-Bauyn-II #23
|7 1 2|5 6 7 1 7 6| 2F 62-Chamb-I #19
|7 1 2|6 6 6|7 6 5 #4 3 6| 3G 35-Bauyn-I #93
7 1|2 7 1 2|3 1 3 4| 2C 48-LaBarre-6 #33
|7 1 2 7 1 7|6 5   2C 9-Ihre-284 #47

7|1 5 6 5 4|3 6 7	3F 35-Bauyn-I #76
|7 1|6 6 6 7|#5 #5 #5|5 6 5|	3F 39-Vm7-6307-1 #9
|7 1 7 1 2|5|	3G 33-Rés-89ter #42
7|3 2 1|2 7|1 6 6|	3B♭ 36-Parville #137
7|3 3 3|2 1 7|6 2 2|	3C 46-Menetou #47
|7 6|6|6 5|	3C 35-Bauyn-III #51
|7 7 1 2|1 6 2|	2D 45-Dart #32
7|7 1 2 2 3|4 3|4 3 2 #1	3C 35-Bauyn-I #27
7|7 1 2 3 1 7|	3B♭ 35-Bauyn-I #125
7 7|1 2 3 4|3 3 #4 5 6 6|	2B♭ 65-Lebègue-II #15
|7 7 1|2 3|4 3|	3F 46-Menetou #36
7|7 1 5 6|5 4 3	3C 35-Bauyn-I #6
7 7|1 5 6 5 4 3|	3F 63-Chamb-II #17
|7 7 1|6 6|	3F 64-Lebègue-I #50
7|7 1 6 7|#5 6 7 3	3F 35-Bauyn-I #69
7|7 1 7 6 5 6 7|	3F 35-Bauyn-I #63
|7 7|1 7 6 7|#5 6	3C 35-Bauyn-II #20
7 7 3 2|#1 6 5 4 3 2|	2C 46-Menetou #58
7|7 3 6 #5|6 1 7 6|	3F 62-Chamb-I #21
7|7 5 1 7|6 3 4 5 6 7|	3F 62-Chamb-I #22
7|7 5 6 7|1	3F 35-Bauyn-I #65
|7 7 6 5|1 7 1 2|1 ♭7 6 5|6 6 6	3F 37-Geoffroy #207
|7 7 7 1 2 1 7|6	3F 38-Gen-2348/53 #19
7 7|7 1 2 1 7 6|	3C 63-Chamb-II #4
7 7|7 1 2 2|	3C 35-Bauyn-III #63
7 7|7 1 2|3 2 2|2 2 1 2 1 7	3G 68-d'Anglebert #8
7 7|7 2 1 7 1 2 2 3|3 2 1 7 6 6|	3C 33-Rés-89ter #6

Minor, First Strain

|1 1|1|1 1 #7|	3d 35-Bauyn-II #55
1 1|1 1 2 3 2 1|	3d 64-Lebègue-I #3
1 1|1 1 7 6 5 7 5 7 6 6|	2g 41-Thomelin #1
|1 1 1 1 #7 1|2 2 2 3|1 1 4|#7	3d 37-Geoffroy #197
1|1|1 2 3 1 5 5 1 2|	2g 36-Parville #135
1|1 1 2|3 2 1 #7 1 2|1 1 1 7|	2c 37-Geoffroy #1
|1 1 1 2 3|2 2 5|5 #6 5 #4 5 #6|	3g 37-Geoffroy #84
1 1|1 2 3 7 1 5|6	2d 67-Gigault p 16
|1 1 1 2|#7 #7 1|5 4 5|3 2 1|	3d 35-Bauyn-II #50
1|1 1 5 7 6 5 6 4 6 5 4 3 2|	2c 37-Geoffroy #2
1|1 1 7 6 5 4 5 6 4 5 2|3 2 1 2	2a 37-Geoffroy #110

1|1 1 7 6 5 5 3 4|2 5 4 3 4 2 3	2d 48-LaBarre-6 #25
1|1 1 7 6 5 6 4 5|	2d 64-Lebègue-I #2
1|1 1 7 6 5 6 4 5|3 6 5 5 1 2|	2e 35-Bauyn-II #63
|1 1 1|7 6 5|6 7 6 5|	3d 45-Dart #61
|1 1 1|7 6 5|7 6	3a 1-Copenhagen-376 #40
|1 1 1|7|6 6 7|	3d 36-Parville #18
|1 1 1|7 #6 5 #6 7 6 5|4 4 5|	3d 29-Chigi #32
1 1|1 7 #6 7 7|7 1 5 6|	3a 33-Rés-89ter #20
|1 1 1|7 7 7|1 7|6|4 3|	3a 66-Perrine #25
|1 1 1|7 7 7|6 5 5|	3g 68-d'Anglebert #22
1|1 1 7 7 7 6|5 5 6 5 4 3|	2d 5-Munich-1503*l* #13
1|1 1 #7 1 2 2|3 4 5|	3d 17-Rogers #21
1|1 1 #7|1 5 2|	3a 66-Perrine #20
1|1 1 #7 2 1 5 5|6 7 6 5 5 5 6 7|	2c 37-Geoffroy #230
|1 1 1|#7 #6 #7|1 1|	3d 68-d'Anglebert #49
|1 1 1|#7 7|7 #6 5|6 2 3|2 1|	3a 37-Geoffroy #229
|1 1 1|#7 #7 #7|1 1 1|	3d 34-Gen-2357[A] #1
1|1 2 1 2 #7 5 1 #7|1 1 2 3 4 5 6|	3d 16-Cosyn #100
1|1 2 1 #7 1|1 5 6 5 4 3 2|3	3c 37-Geoffroy #3
1|1 2 2|3 3 4 5 4 3|	3a 64-Lebègue-I #30
1|1 2 3 1 2 1|#7 1 2 1 #7	3a 16-Cosyn #87
1|1 2 3|1 2 1|#7 1 4 7 6|	3d 66-Perrine #17
1|1 2 3 1 2 #7|1 1 7 6 5 6 4 5|3	2d 37-Geoffroy #23
1|1 2 3 1 3 4|5 5 4 3	2a 58-Dumont-1652 *l* 36v
1|1 2 3 1 3 4|5 5 5 #6 7 1 2|	2d 36-Parville #14
1|1 2 3 2|1 1 7 6|	2d 3-Berlin-40623 #72
1|1 2|3 2 1 2 1 #7|1 1 7 6|5 6 4	3a 37-Geoffroy #126
|1 1 2 3 2 1|5 5 4 3|	2g 36-Parville #121
1|1 2 3 2 1 5 5|5 5 1 2|3 7 1 5	3a 37-Geoffroy #111
1|1 2 3 2 1 7 6|7	3a 22a-Roper #32
1|1 2 3|2 3 4|5 #6 7|	3d 5-Munich-1503*l* #2
1|1 2 3 3 2|1 1 7 6|	2d 27-Gresse #21
1|1 2 3 3 2|1 2 3 2 7 6|	2a 5-Munich-1503*l* #12
1|1 2 3 3 2 1|#7	2a 35-Bauyn-III #40
|1 1 2 3 3|4 4 3 3 4|	2g 68-d'Anglebert #29
1|1 2 3 4 2 1|#7 1 2 5 1 7|	3c 37-Geoffroy #8
1|1 2 3 4 2 3 1 2|7 5|	3d 4-Lynar #64
1|1 2 3 4 3 1 3 4|5	2d 35-Bauyn-III #57
1|1 2 3 4 3 4|5 3 5	3d 35-Bauyn-III #58
1|1 2 3 4 5|4 3 2 3	2a 35-Bauyn-III #38
1|1 2|3 4|5 4|3 7|6 6 5|	3d 66-Perrine #14

|1 1 2 3 4 5|4 5 3 2 1|	3d	4-Lynar #63
|1 1 2 3|7 #6 7 5 #6|7 7 7 1 7 1 ♭2|	3a	37-Geoffroy #113
1|1 2 3 7 7 6|5	3a	47-Gen-2356 #9
1|1 2 5 4|3 2 1 7 6 5|	3d	16-Cosyn #44
1 1 2 #7 1 2 2	0d	7-Munich-1511f #12
1|1 2 #7 1 2|3	3d	22a-Roper #55
1|1 2 #7|1 5 5|6 4 5|	3d	6-Munich-1511e #6
|1 1 2|#7 #7 #7|#7 1 1|2 2 2|2 3 3|	3d	46-Menetou #88
1|1 3 1 5|5 #7 1 2|	3d	35-Bauyn-II #41
1|1 3 2 1 7 1|6 6 7 ♭5 ♭5 ♭5 6|	2b	37-Geoffroy #153
1|1 3 2 1 #7 1 2|3 1 3 4 5 #6|	2a	36-Parville #54
1|1 3 2 1 #7 #6 7 6 5|6 6 7 1 5 5	2e	37-Geoffroy #47
1|1 3 2 3 3 1 5|5 4 5 #6	3g	68-d'Anglebert #19
1|1 3|2 3 7 7 1|	3g	36-Parville #41
1|1 3|2 3 7 7 1 #6 7|	3g	68-d'Anglebert #21
1|1 3 4 5 4 5|4|	2c	35-Bauyn-II #30
1|1 3 4 5 6|7 6 6|	3e	35-Bauyn-II #64
|1 1 5 3|2 2 3|1 1 1 2 #6	2g	36-Parville #42
1|1 5 4 3 2|3 4 3 2 1 2 2 1|#7 1	3a	37-Geoffroy #112
1|1 5 4 #3|#3 #3 4 5|6 5 1 7|	3d	35-Bauyn-II #40
1|1 5 4 5|3 1	3d	35-Bauyn-III #46
1|1 5 4 5|3 1 2 2|	3d	68-d'Anglebert #40
1|1 5 4 5|3 3 4 5 1 2|	3d	65-Lebègue-II #2
|1 1 5|5 4 3 2|3 3|	3d	63-Chamb-II #10
1|1 5 6 5 4|3 4 3 2 1 1 7|	3d	63-Chamb-II #8
|1|1 6|1 3|	2a	35-Bauyn-III #42
1|1 7 1 7 6 7|5	3g	68-d'Anglebert #24
1 1 7 5 5	0a	7-Munich-1511f #29
1|1 7 6 5|	3d	32-Oldham-2
|1 1|7 6 5|4 5 3 4|	3d	5-Munich-1503*l* #14
|1 1 7 6 5 5 4 3|2 1 2 3|	2a	35-Bauyn-III #93
1|1 7 6 5 6 4 5 2|	2a	37-Geoffroy #110
|1 1 7 6|5 6|7 7|	2a	35-Bauyn-III #79
|1 1 7 6 5 6|7 7 7 7 6 5|	2a	46-Menetou #98
1|1 7 6|5 7 1|	3d	62-Chamb-I #12
1 1 7 #6 5 4 5	0d	7-Munich-1511f #15
1|1 7 7 6|5 5 4 4|4 3 2 1|1	3d	35-Bauyn-I #33
1|1 7|7 6|5 5 4 4|4 5 4 3 2 3 3	3b	37-Geoffroy #154
1|1 #7 1 2|2 1 7 #6	3d	17-Rogers #27
1|1 #7 1 2|3 2 2 1|	3g	65-Lebègue-II #8
|1 1 #7|1 2 3|2 3 4 3 2 1	3d	46-Menetou #25

|1 1 #7 1 2|5 5 4 5 2 3|	2g 46-Menetou #61
1|1 #7 1 5 6 7|5 4	2d 16-Cosyn #99
|1 1 #7 1 #7 1 5 6 4|	2d 66-Perrine #7
|1 2 1|5 6 7|6 7 1|	3f 37-Geoffroy #67
|1 2 1|#7 #6 5|3 4 3|	3d 48-LaBarre-6 #38
|1 2 2|3|4 3 2 3 4 4 5|	3a 22a-Roper #33
1 2|3 1 2 4|5 5 4 3|	2g 45-Dart #66
|1 2 3|1 4 5 6|5 4 5 2|	3a 64-Lebègue-I #33
|1 2 3 1|5 1 #7|	2d 55-Redon #6
1 2 3 1|5 4 5 3 2|3 2 1 1 7 1 5|	2g 46-Menetou #105
|1 2|3 1 5|5 4 3|	2e 35-Bauyn-III #36
|1 2 3 1 7|7 6 5 4|5 2 1|1 7 6|	2d 66-Perrine #19
|1 2 3|2 1 1|1 1 1|	3d 54-Gen-2350/57 #27
|1 2 3|2 1|1 2 3|	3d 6-Munich-1511e #10
|1 2 3 2|1 1 7 6|	2a 1-Copenhagen-376 #39
1 2|3 2 1|2 3 2|1 #7 1|#7 1 2|	3g 37-Geoffroy #88
|1 2 3|2 1|2 #7|1 1|	3f 37-Geoffroy #66
1 2|3 2 1 3 4|5	3g 35-Bauyn-I #105
1 2 3 2 1|5 5 4 5 2|3 3 4 5 4 3|	2e 37-Geoffroy #56
|1 2 3 2 1|7 5 7|5 5 4|	2d 54-Gen-2350/57 #29
|1 2 3 2 1|#7 1 1 1 7 5 #6|	2d 5-Munich-1503l #5
|1 2 3 2 1|#7 1 1 2 5|	2d 68-d'Anglebert #46
1 2|3 2 1|#7 1 2|	3a 45-Dart #51
1 2|3 2 1 #7|1 2 3 2 1 2|	3g 46-Menetou #24
|1 2|3 2 1|#7 1 2|5|	3g 36-Parville #127
|1 2 3|2 1|#7 1|2 5 #6 7|1 #7 1|	3d 54-Gen-2350/57 #32
|1 2 3|2 2 3 1 7 6|5 4 4 7|	3d 35-Bauyn-II #45
|1 2 3|2 3 1|1 1 1|	3d 16-Cosyn #101
|1 2|3 2 3 1|5 4 5|3 4 3 2 3|	3c 37-Geoffroy #6
1 2|3 2 3|1 #7 1|	3g 36-Parville #128
1 2|3 2 3 4 5 6|5|	3d 35-Bauyn-II #52
|1 2 3 3 2|1 2 3 1 7 6|5	2a 35-Bauyn-III #84
1 2|3 3 2 1 2 3 2 3 4|3 3 2 3 4|	3g 68-d'Anglebert #26
1 2|3 3 4|2 3 2|	3d 65-Lebègue-II #4
|1 2 3|3 4 5|5|	3a 35-Bauyn-I #120
1 2|3 3 4|5 6|	3g 63-Chamb-II #23
|1 2 3|3 4 5 7 7 1|	3d 35-Bauyn-I #40
|1 2 3|3 #7 1|1 7 1 6 7|5|	3a 16-Cosyn #87a
1 2 3 4 2 1 #7 1	0d 7-Munich-1511f #28
1 2|3 4 3 2 1 2|1 2 3 4 5 #6	2g 54-Gen-2350/57 #23

1 2|3 4 3 2 1 2|1 #7 1 2 3 4 5 4|	3d 4-Lynar #67
1 2|3 4 3 2 3 1|#7 #7 1 2|3 4 3	2a 37-Geoffroy #228
|1 2 3|4 3 2|3 4 5|#7 1 2 5|	3d 37-Geoffroy #204
|1 2 3 4 3 2 5|3 1 2|3 4 5 6 5|	3a 35-Bauyn-II #111
1 2|3 4 4|5 5 5 5 5 #6|	3g 62-Chamb-I #25
1 2 3 4 5 2 3 1 2	0d 7-Munich-1511f #11
|1 2 3 4|5 4|3 2 1|1	2a 62-Chamb-I #1
1 2 3 4 5 4 5 3 2 5 5 4 5	0d 7-Munich-1511f #2
1 2 3 4|5 5 6 4|5 5 5 1 2 3 4|	2a 35-Parville #52
1 2 3 4|5 5 6 6 6|5 5 4 3 4 5|	2d 36-Parville #23
1 2|3 4 5 5 #6 7 1 2 1|#7 1 7 6|	3d 62-Chamb-I #14
|1 2 3 4 5 6|4 5 3 1|1 2 3 4 5 5	2a 37-Geoffroy #119
|1 2 3|4 5 6|5 4 3|2 3 1|#7 1 2|	3a 37-Geoffroy #129
1 2 3 4|5 6 5 4 4|	2a 65-Lebègue-II #20
1 2|3|4 5|#7|1 2|5 1|	3g 37-Geoffroy #87
|1 2 3|5 6 7|3 4 5|4 3|	3d 35-Bauyn-II #56
1 2 5 #6 7 #6 5	0d 7-Munich-1511f #9
1|2 #7 3|4|	3d 66-Perrine #6
|1 2|#7 #6 #7|1 #7 1|	3g 68-d'Anglebert #36
|1 2 #7|7 1 #6 5 4|	3a 37-Geoffroy #127
1|3 2 1|5 5 1|7 5 #6|	3g 35-Bauyn-I #104
1|3 2 3 4|5	2a 56-Mersenne
|1 3 2 4 3 5|2 3 1|1 1 1|	3d 16-Cosyn #101
|1 3 4|2 2|5 5 #4 #5|	3d 65-Lebègue-II #3
1|3 4 5|4 2 3|3 1|	3a 36-Parville #119
1 3 4|5 4 3 4 5 4 3 2|3 5 #6 7|	3d 68-d'Anglebert #44
|1|3 4 5|4 5 2|	3d 36-Parville #24
1|3 4|5 4 5 6 5 1|	2g 36-Parville #139
|1 3 4 5 6|7	3e 35-Bauyn-II #64
1 3 5 1 3 4	0c 36-Parville #69
1 3 5 1 3 5 3 1 5 3 2 3 4 5 4 4	0d 45-Dart #58
1 3 5 4 5 2 3 #7 1 2 #7 4	0g 35-Bauyn-II #3
1|5 1 1 #7|1 5|3 4|	3d 36-Parville #17
1 5|1 2 2 1|#7 #7 2 3|	2d 46-Menetou #28
1 5 1 2|3 4|	3g 35-Bauyn-I #106
|1 5 1|2 3 4|	3a 45-Dart #47
|1 5 1|7 6 5|4 5 3|	3d 43-Gen-2354 #5
1|5 1 #7 1|2 5 3 2 1 7 6|	3d 64-Lebègue-I #4
|1 5 1|#7 #6 5 4 5|	2g 46-Menetou #107
|1 5 2 3|2 3 1 1 2 3|	2d 55-Redon #2

Incipit	Code	Source
1 5 3 1 5 #6|7 5 7 6|	2d	59-Dumont-1657 / 31v
1 5|3 2 1 3 2 1|	2g	45-Dart #45
|1 5|3 2 1|5 1|	3g	46-Menetou #86
|1 5 3 2|1 7 1 2 1|7 #6 7 1 7|	2d	54-Gen-2350/57 #30
1|5 3 2 3 #7	2g	42-Vm7-6307-2 #7
1 5|3 4 3|2 2 5 1|7 3 2 2 1|1|	2b	37-Geoffroy #157
1 5|3 4|5 1 2#7|	2d	46-Menetou #29
1|5 4 1 #7|1 5 2 4|	3d	33-Rés-89ter #25
1 5|4 3 2 3 4|5 #7 1 2|	2d	37-Geoffroy #29
1|5 4 3 4 5|3 1 5|	3g	68-d'Anglebert #25
|1 5|4 3 4|5 5 5|	3g	68-d'Anglebert #31
1 5|4 5 2 3 5 1|7 1 5 6|	3d	64-Lebègue-I #8
1|5 4 5 3 1 3 1 2 5 #6|	3a	35-Bauyn-I #122
1|5 4 5|3 2 1|#7|	3a	46-Menetou #19
|1 5 5|3 4 5 1 1|6 6 6 7 4|	2g	46-Menetou #13
1 5|5 5 4 5|3 2 3 4 2|5 4 3 2 2|	2a	39-Vm7-6307-1 #11
|1 5 5|6 5|	2d	59-Dumont-1657 / 32v
|1 5 5|6 #6|4 4 4 5|	3d	64-Lebègue-I #5
|1 5 5|6 7 5 4 4|	3d	35-Bauyn-I #41
1 5 6 #3 4 2 3 #7 1 #6	0d	35-Bauyn-II #1
|1 5 6 #3 4 5|5 2 3 #7 1 2|	3d	35-Bauyn-II #123
|1 5 6|4 4 5 4|3 4 4 3|2 1|1 5 6|	3e	37-Geoffroy #53
|1 5 6 5 4|3 2 1 5 #6|	2g	36-Parville #43
1 5|6 5 4 3 2 5 4|3 2 1 6 5|	2a	46-Menetou #31
1|5 6 5 4 4|3 3	3a	32-Oldham #107
|1 5 6 6 5 4|3 1 5 #6|	2g	68-d'Anglebert #35
|1 5 6 7|6 5 4 3|	2a	46-Menetou #45
|1 5 #6|7 1|#7 1|	3d	65-Lebègue-II #5
|1 5 #6|7 6 5|4 5 3|	3d	5-Munich-1503l #3
|1 5 #6|7 7|7 1 6 5|	3e	35-Bauyn-II #65
|1 5 #6|7 7 7|6 6 6|	3d	68-d'Anglebert #43
|1 5 #6|#7 1 2|3 2 1|2 1 7 #6 5|	3d	37-Geoffroy #199
|1 5 7 6 5 4|3 5 4|5 5 4 5 4 3|	2a	66-Perrine #24
1 5 #7|1 5 5 4|3 4	3a	66-Perrine #23
1 7 1 2 1	0d	6-Munich-1511e #9
1 7 1|3 3 2|1 7|7 6|	3d	35-Bauyn-III #17
|1 7 1|5 4 3|4 2 5|3 4 3 2 1|	3g	37-Geoffroy #86
|1 7 1|5 6|4 5|3 2 1|3 3 4|	3a	37-Geoffroy #121
|1 7 1 5 6 4|5 6 5 4 3 2|3 2 1|	3d	37-Geoffroy #203
|1 7 1 5|6 6 6 7|	2a	56-Menetou #113

1 7 1|6 5 4 3 2 1|5 3 2 3|	3a 46-Menetou #44
|1 7 6|5 4 2 3|2 1|	3d 35-Bauyn-II #44
|1 7 6 5 4|3 2	2d 35-Bauyn-III #82
1 7 6 5 4 3 2 1 1 2 3 #7	0d 36-Parville #1
|1 7 6|5 4 3|4 2 5|3 4 3 2 1|1|	3e 37-Geoffroy #52
|1 7 6 5|4 6 6 7|1 1 2 3|	2a 54-Gen-2350/57 #26
1 7 6|5 5 4 3 2 5 4|	2d 66-Perrine #2
|1 7 6 5 5|5 4	2d 35-Bauyn-III #94
|1 7 6 5 6 3 4|5 4 3	2a 35-Bauyn-I #111
|1 7 6 5 6 4|5	2d 66-Perrine #10
1 7 6|5 6 7 4|5 4 4 3|	3d 63-Chamb-II #9
1|7 6 5 6 7 5|	2g 45-Dart #48
|1|7|6 6 5|	3a 35-Bauyn-I #119
|1 #7 1 1 #7 1 #7 1 5 6 4|	2d 66-Perrine #7
|1 #7 1|2 2 2|3 3 4 3|	3d 68-d'Anglebert #47
1 #7 1 2 2 3 3 2 1	0d 7-Munich-1511f #25
|1 #7 1|2 3 1|2 1 2 3 2 3|1 #7 1|	3a 37-Geoffroy #127
|1 #7 1 2|3 2|2 7 1 2|	3g 68-d'Anglebert #27
1 #7|1 2 3 4|2 2 5 6|4 3 2 3	2a 37-Geoffroy #116
1 #7|1 2 3 4|2 3 2 1 2 #7 1|2 3	2d 37-Geoffroy #27
1|#7 1 2|5 4 3|4 3 2|	3d 6-Munich-1511e #7
|1 #7 1|3 3 2|1 7|7 6|	3d 35-Bauyn-III #17
|1 #7|1 3|4 5|5 2|2 3|	2e 35-Bauyn-III #35
|1 #7 1|5 1|2 3|2 3 2 3|	3d 37-Geoffroy #200
1 #7|1 5 4 5|3 7|1 2 3 2 3 4	3d 66-Perrine #5
|1 #7 1 5 6 5 4|5 1 2 3 4|	2d 33-Rés-89ter #28
1|#7|1|7 6|5 5 4|	3d 33-Rés-89ter #26
1 #7 2|1 5 4 5|3 3 2 4|3 6 5 5 #6|	3d 66-Perrine #4
2 1 2|3 4 5 5 #6 7 1 2|#7	3e 35-Bauyn-I #37
2 1 3 5 2 1 3 5 2 4 3 5 4 6	0d 45-Dart #30
2 1 #7|1 1|2 5 5 4 5|3 3 2 1|	3d 19-Heardson #46
|2 3 2|1 2 #7 1|	2g 68-d'Anglebert #30
2|3 2 1|2 #7|1 1 #7 1|	3g 35-Bauyn-II #122
2|3 2 1 #7|1 2|	2g 36-Parville #44
|2 3 2|3|2|1 1|	2a 35-Bauyn-III #43
2 3 4 2 5 3 4 #6 #3 4 5 7 1 7	0g 68-d'Anglebert #17
2|3 4 5 5|5 4 3 4|	2a 55-Redon #1
2 3 4|5 5 5 5|5	2a 47-Gen-2356 #10
2 3 4 5|5 6 5 4 3|	3d 68-d'Anglebert #45
3 1 2 3 2 1 7 3	0a 7-Munich-1511f #7

|3 1 2 3 4|5 5 6|4 4 5|	3d	46-Menetou #109
3|1 2 #7|1 2|	3d	46-Menetou #41
|3 1 2|#7|1 5 #6|	3a	32-Oldham #16
|3 1 5|3 1 5|5 1|	3g	63-Chamb-II #21
3 1|5 4 3 2 3 4|3 2 1	2g	37-Geoffroy #215
|3 1 5 5 1 2|#7|	3g	62-Chamb-I #27
|3|1|5 5 5|	3a	35-Bauyn-I #117
3 1|5 6 4 3|2 2 5 4 3 2|1	2a	37-Geoffroy #120
|3 1 #7|1 5 6|5 4 7|	3g	36-Parville #138
3 2|1 1 1 #7|1 1 2|	2d	6-Munich-1511e #12
|3 2 1|1 7 1 5 6 #7|7 #6 5 5 5 6|	3d	35-Bauyn-II #46
|3 2 1|2 1 #7|1 2 1|#7|1|	3g	37-Geoffroy #90
3 2|1 2 2 1 #7 1|2 5 3 2|1 2 2 1	2d	37-Geoffroy #198
3 2|1 2 2 1|#7 5 1 5|6 5 4 5|3	2d	37-Geoffroy #31
|3 2|1 2|3 #7|1 2|3 2|1 2|	3g	37-Geoffroy #216
|3 2|1|2 #7 1|2 3 2|3 2|	3b	37-Geoffroy #156
|3 2 1|5|1 3 2 1|#7 #6 #7|1 1 5|	3d	37-Geoffroy #28
|3 2 1|5 2 3|4 2|	3d	35-Bauyn-II #54
3 2|1 5 4 3|2 1 7 #6 5|1	2d	64-Lebègue-I #6
|3 2 1|5 4 3|	2a	36-Parville #140
3 2 1|5 5 5|1 1 2|#7 #7|	3g	46-Menetou #62
|3 2 1|5 5 5 6|4 4 3 4 5|	3g	68-d'Anglebert #23
3 2|1 5 6 4 3|2 2 5 4 3 2|3	2d	37-Geoffroy #26
|3 2 1|5 6|4 5|	3a	64-Lebègue-I #34
|3 2 1|5 6 5|4 5 #6|7 1 7|	3a	34-Gen-2357 [A]
|3 2 1|5 #6 7 5|1 1 2|#7 #6 5 4 3 2|	3a	46-Menetou #96
3 2|1 7 1 7 6 5|6 5 5 6|7 6 5	2e	37-Geoffroy #50
3 2 1|7 6 5|6 5 4|3 2 3|	3c	37-Geoffroy #10
|3 2 1 7 6 5|6|5 5 5 4 3 4|5|	3d	37-Geoffroy #11
|3 2 1|#7 1 2|	3d	45-Dart #24
|3 2 1|#7 1 2|3 4 5|5 4 5|	3b	37-Geoffroy #155
|3 2 1|#7 #7 1 5 6|4 3 2|1	2d	35-Bauyn-II #37
|3 2 3|1 2 #7|1 5|3 2 3|	3d	36-Parville #112
3 2 3 4 5 4 3 2 1 2 3	0d	7-Munich-1511f #16
|3 2 3 4 5 6 5|4 5 3 2|	2g	65-Lebègue-II #10
|3 3 1|3 2 3|4 4 1 2|3 2	3g	22a-Roper #64
3|3 2 1|3 2 1|#7 1 2 5|	3d	8-Hintze #11
|3 3 2|1|5 5 5|	3a	62-Chamb-I #5
|3 3|2 2|1 1 1|#7|	3a	37-Geoffroy #128
|3 3 2|2 3 1|7 1 6|6 5 6 5|	3c	37-Geoffroy #4

|3 3 2|2 3 1|7 1 #6|6 7 1 5|	3d	37-Geoffroy #25
|3 3|2 2|5 5|	3g	54-Gen-2350/57 #24
|3 3 2 3|1 1 7 1|6 5 6 6 5|5	2a	37-Geoffroy #195
3|3 2 3 2|1 1 7 6 5|	3b	35-Bauyn-II #117
3|3 2 3 2 1 5 5 4|3 3 4 3 2 2 3	2d	37-Geoffroy #196
3|3 2 3 4 4|5 5 4 5 6|	3a	35-Bauyn-II #106
|3 3 3 2 1|4 4 5 4 3 2|	2d	46-Menetou #27
3|3 3 2 1 5 5 4 2|	2g	64-Lebègue-I #16
|3 3 3|2 1 7 6 5|	2g	35-Bauyn-I #108
|3 3 3 2 1|#7 1 2|3 2	3d	17-Rogers #22
|3 3 3|2 2 3 2|1 1 2 1|	3d	16-Cosyn #101
|3 3 3 2 4|4 5 4|	3a	66-Perrine #21
|3 3 3|3|2 3 2 1|	3a	32-Oldham #5
|3 3 3 4|2 2 2 2 3 4|5 5 5 6|	3d	68-d'Anglebert #42
3 3 3 4 5|1 1 1|	2a	46-Menetou #56
|3 3 3 4 5|1 7 1 5|	2d	68-d'Anglebert #48
|3 3 4|2 2|1 1 2|	3a	35-Bauyn-II #110
|3 3 4|2 2 3|5 5 6|	3d	35-Bauyn-II #49
3|3 4 3 2 1 5 5 4|3 2 5 5 #6 #7 1	2d	62-Chamb-I #11
3|3 4 5 1 7 1|6 5 5 #6 7|	3g	68-d'Anglebert #20
3 3|4 5 4 3|2 #7 1 2|3 4 2 1|1|	2a	46-Menetou #93
3|3 4 5 6|5 5|	3d	63-Chamb-II #7
|3 4 2|1|2 3 4 3 2 3 2|	3a	62-Chamb-I #6
3 4|2 2 3|1 1 2|	3a	32-Oldham #15
|3 4 3 2 1 2 3 4|5 4 5 #6	2g	54-Gen-2354/57 #5
|3 4 3 2 1 5 4 5|3 1 4 3 2 3 1 2|	2a	35-Bauyn-II #101
|3 4 3 2 1 5 5 4|3 2 3 5 #6 #7 1 #7|	2d	36-Parville #21
|3 4 3|2 1|#7 1|	3d	64-Lebègue-I #7
|3 4 3 2 3 #7 #7 1 2|1 1 7|	3c	35-Bauyn-II #33
|3 4 3|5|#7 1 2|	3a	32-Oldham #18
|3 4|5 1 1 2 1|#7|	2d	35-Bauyn-III #44
|3 4 5 1 2 #7|1	3d	66-Perrine #3
|3 4 5|3 1|1 2 3|#7 5|	3d	35-Bauyn-III #49
3 4|5 4 3 2 2|3 3 3|2 1 #7 1 2|#7	3a	40-Rés-476 #41
3 4 5|4 3 2|2 3 4|	2a	46-Menetou #38
3 4|5 4 3|2|3 4 5|	3g	68-d'Anglebert #34
|3 4 5|4 5 2|3 4 3 2 1|	3g	65-Lebègue-II #13
|3 4 5|4 5 3|2 3 1|	3c	46-Menetou #11
|3 4 5|4 5 4 3 2|3 2 1|	3g	36-Parville #134
|3 4 5 5 1|2 1 #7 6|	2g	35-Bauyn-I #102
3 4|5 5 2 2|4 3 2 1|	2a	46-Menetou #26

|3 4 5|5 3|6 7 5|	3d 1-Copenhagen-376 #48a
|3 4 5 5|4 4 5	3a 35-Bauyn-II #109
3 4|5 5 5 4|5 1 7 6|	2d 54-Gen-2350/57 #9
3 4|5 5 5 5|6 4 3 2 5|3	2g 42-Vm7-6307-2 #2
|3 4 5|5 6 5 4 4|	3d 35-Bauyn-I #43
|3 4 5 5 6 7|5 #6 5 #6	2a 32-Oldham #106
|3 4 5|6 4 4|4 5 3|	3a 46-Menetou #55
3 4|5 6 5|4 3 2|3 2 1|1 2|3 4 5|	3g 37-Geoffroy #219
3 5 1 1 7 6 5	0e 35-Bauyn-II #14
3 5 1|2 2 1 2|3 2 3 1 7 6 5 4 5	0d 36-Parville #3
3 5 1 3 5 1 3 2 5 2	0a 35-Bauyn-II #7
3 5 1 3 5 1 5 3 5 1 2 #7 2	0d 22a -Roper #54
3 5 1 7 3 7 6 2 3 5 4 3	0g 35-Bauyn-II #5
3 5 3 5 1 5 3 5 2 3 1 3 5 3 1	0a 35-Bauyn-II #6
3 5 3 5 1 5 3 5 2 3 1 3 5	0a 36-Parville #144
3 5 6|7 7 1 1 1 7 6|	2a 45-Dart #37
4 3 2|1 5 #6 7 7 6|5	3a 35-Bauyn-I #113
4 3 2|3 4 5 4|3 2|	2b 35-Bauyn-II #116
4 3 5 1 4 3 5 1	0d 64-Lebègue-I #1
|5 1 1 1|1 7 7 7|	2g 68-d'Anglebert #32
5|1 1 1 5|6 6 5|	2a 46-Menetou #42
|5 1 1|7 #6 5|5 5 4|	3d 33-Rés-89ter #27
|5 1 1|#7 #7 #7 1|5 1 7|	3a 66-Perrine #27
5|1 2 2 1|#7 1 5|6 5 4 5|	2e 37-Geoffroy #54
|5 1 2|3 2 1|#7|1 2 3|7 1 7|	3a 35-Bauyn-I #121
5|1 2 3 2 1 #7|1 5 #6	3d 35-Bauyn-I #35
|5 1 2 3 2 1|#7 5 3 2 1 2 1|	3d 4-Lynar #68
5|1 2 3|2 3 1|1 1 1|	3d 18-Ch-Ch-1236 #6
5|1 2 3|2 3 1|2|5 5|1 2 3|	3d 37-Geoffroy #201
|5 1 2|3 2 3 1|#7 1 5 4|	3d 35-Bauyn-II #47
5|1 2 3 2 3 4|#7 5 1 7|6 7 5 6 4	3e 37-Geoffroy #48
5|1 2 3|3 4 5|6 5 4 3 2 4|3 1	3a 2-Witzendorff #94
|5 1 2|3 4 5|	3g 45-Dart #49
5 1 3 5|5 1 3 5|1 5 1|	0g 64-Lebègue-I #15
|5 1 3|#7 2 5|#6 5 4|3 2 3|	3b 37-Geoffroy #158
5 1|4 2 3 #7 1|2 2 5 7|6	2a 37-Geoffroy #115
|5 1 5|4 4 5|4 3 2 2|	3g 68-d'Anglebert #28
|5 1 7 5 1 2|3 2 1 7 6 7|	3d 62-Chamb-I #16
5 1|7 6 5 6 5 4|5 3 4 2|3 4 5 6	3d 37-Geoffroy #202
5|1 7 6 5 6 5 4|5 #7 1 2 3 2 3 4|	3a 62-Chamb-I #2
|5 1 7 6 5 6|6 5 4 6|5 4 3 2 3 2	2g 37-Geoffroy #85

5 1|7 #6 5 #6 7|#6 5 6|5 5 4|	3g	65-Lebègue-II #12
5 1|#7 1 2 3|2 2 5 5|1 7 6 5 4|5|	2e	37-Geoffroy #51
|5 1 #7 1|2 3 2|5 3 6 5|4 5 5|	2a	37-Geoffroy #118
5 1 #7 1 2 3 3	0d	7-Munich-1511f #8
5|1 #7 1 2 3 4|2 1 7 6 5 4|	2d	55-Redon #12
|5 1|#7 1 2 3 4|2 5 6|4 3 2 2 1	3c	37-Geoffroy #7
5 1|#7 1 2 3 4 3|2 2 5 1|	2a	37-Geoffroy #124
5|1 #7|1 5|1 2 3 2 1|	2d	48-LaBarre-6 #28
|5 1 #7 1 7|6 6 5 4	2e	35-Bauyn-III #80
|5 1 #7 5 1 2|3 2 1 2|	2d	20-Ch-Ch-378 #3
5 1|#7 5 1 2 3 2 3	0d	7-Munich-1511f #13
5 1|#7 #6 5 3 2 1|5 4 5|	3d	46-Menetou #30
5 1|#7 #6 5 3 4|	2g	46-Menetou #112
|5 2|1 3 4 3|2 1|1 1 1 #7|1|	3d	66-Perrine #18
|5 2|3 #7 1 2|3 3 5 1|#7	2g	64-Lebègue-I #21
5 2|3 #7 1|2 3 4|3 2 3 1|	3f	37-Geoffroy #65
|5 2 4|3 2 1|#7 1 2 3 4|3 1 1|	2a	37-Geoffroy #125
|5 2 5 5 #6 #7|1 #7 1 2 2|	2g	46-Menetou #83
5|3 1 3|2 #3|4 5 4 3 2|	3a	22a-Roper #34
5|3 1 5|1 1 3|7 1 6 7|	2g	51-LaBarre-11 p 211
5|3 1 6 7|5 4 3 5|	2a	36-Parville #51
|5 3 2|1|3 2 3|	3g	35-Bauyn-II #96
5|3 2 1|5 1 4 5 6|	3e	35-Bauyn-I #59
5|3 2 1|5 7|1 2 3|	3a	36-Parville #56
5|3 2 3 4|2 5|1 4 2 5|3 1 3|	2g	42-Vm7-6307-2 #10
|5 3|2 3 4|5 4 5 6|	3g	65-Lebègue-I #22
|5 3 4 2|3 1 2 2|5 3 4 5|	2a	37-Geoffroy #226
|5 3 4|5 6|5 6 4|	3a	65-Lebègue-II #21
|5 3 5|1 4 2|	3a	45-Dart #46
5|3 5|1 5|6 5 4 3|	2d	48-LaBarre-6 #27
|5 3 5|4 4 5 2|3 3 2|	3g	65-Lebègue-II #9
|5 4 2|3|1 4 #3|4|	3d	35-Bauyn-II #48
5 4 3 2|1 1 2 3 2 1|2 5 1	2a	37-Geoffroy #114
|5 4 3 2 1 1 2|#7	3d	32-Oldham #31
5 4|3 2 1|1 5 4 3 2 1|1 1 1|	3g	37-Geoffroy #217
|5 4 3 2|1 2 #7|	3d	46-Menetou #111
5 4|3 2|1 3 2|1 2 3 1|5 1 2|	3d	66-Perrine #13
5 4|3 2 1 6 7|5 5 3 2	2d	36-Parville #11
|5 4 3 2 1|#7 1 2|	3g	35-Bauyn-III #89
5 4|3 2 3 1|	2c	45-Dart #57

|5 4 3|2 3 1|♯7 1 2|5 ♯6 ♯7|	3g	37-Geoffroy #89
5 4 3 3 4|5|	3g	35-Bauyn-I #103
|5 4 3|4 2|3 1|	3a	36-Parville #53
|5 4 3 4 4|5	3g	38-Gen-2348/53 #1
5 4|3 4 5|1 1 7|6 7 1|5	3d	37-Geoffroy #30
|5 4 ♯3 2 3|4 ♯3|	2g	35-Bauyn-II #92
|5 4 4|4 3 2|1 2 3 4|5 4 4|	3d	35-Bauyn-II #57
|5 4 4|4 ♯3 4 5|6 5|5 4 5|	3d	35-Bauyn-II #51
|5 4 5 1 2 3 1|♯7 1 5 6|	2g	63-Chamb-II #20
|5 4 5 2|3 2 3 1|2 3 4|♯7 1 2 5|	3a	37-Geoffroy #123
|5 4 5|3 2|2 3 3 2|	3c	35-Bauyn-II #34
|5 4 5|3 2|3 4 4|	3a	46-Menetou #43
5 4 5|3 3 4|5 5 1|5 ♯7	3d	66-Perrine #1
|5 4 5 3 4|2 2 3 4 2|3 4 5 1 1 4	2d	66-Perrine #12
5 4 5 6|4 4 3 4 5|2 2 3 4 5|	3a	22a-Roper #14
|5 5 1|2 2 3|1 1 2|	3a	65-Lebègue-II #19
|5 5 1 2|3 2 1 ♯7 1|	2c	45-Dart #56
5|5 1 2 3 2 1|♯7 ♯7 1 ♯6 7 6|	3a	35-Bauyn-II #104
|5 5 1|4 4|5 6 3 4 2|3 3|2 2 2|	3f	37-Geoffroy #63
5 5 1 6|7 6|	3d	66-Perrine #9
5 5 1 ♯6 5 4	0d	7-Munich-1511f #11
|5 5 1|7 5 1|♯7 1 2|	3d	32-Oldham #6
|5 5 1|7 6 5|6 7 1|	3d	35-Bauyn-III #48
|5 5 1|7 6 5|3 1 2|2 1 ♯7|	3e	37-Geoffroy #49
|5 5 1 7 6 5|6 5 4	3a	38-Gen-2348/53 #8
5 5|1 7 6 7|5 5 4 4|	2g	65-Lebègue-II #14
5|5 1|♯7 1 2 3 2|	3d	66-Perrine #15
|5 5 1|♯7|1|2|3 3 4|2 2 3	3d	62-Chamb-I #15
|5 5 1|♯7 ♯7 1|2 2 3|	3d	5-Munich-1503*l* #6
|5 5 1|♯7 ♯7|1 2 3|2|3 1 1|	3a	64-Lebègue-I #32
|5 5 1|♯7 ♯7|1 2|3 3|5 5 1|♯7 ♯7|1 2	3g	46-Menetou #101
|5 5 1|♯7 ♯7 ♯7|1 2 3|	3d	46-Menetou #53
5|5 2 3 2|1	3a	47-Gen-2356 #2
5|5 2 3|♯7 1 2|♯7 5|	3a	7-Munich-1511f #6
5|5 3 1 5|5 1|	3d	36-Parville #16
5 5|3 2 3 1 1 2|♯7 5 4 3|	3g	68-d'Anglebert #33
5 5 3|4 4 5|3 3 4|	2a	46-Menetou #40
5|5 3 4 4|5 5 ♯6	3a	35-Bauyn-I #114
5|5 3 4 5|4 5 3 4|	3g	65-Lebègue-II #11
5|5 3 4 5 6 6 5 4|5	2g	65-Lebègue-II #6

5|5 3 4 5 6 7 6 5 4 3 2 1|	2g 65-Lebègue-II #7
|5 5 3|6|4 2 5|	3g 46-Menetou #4
|5|5 3|6 5|4|	3e 22-Ch-Ch-1117 #2
5|5 4 3 2 1 2 3|#7 1 2 3|4 5 4 5	3g 37-Geoffroy #123
5|5 4 3 2 1 2|#7 1 2 2|3 2 3 4 4	3g 37-Geoffroy #82
5|5 4 3 2 1 3 2 1|#7	2d 35-Bauyn-III #81
5|5 4 3 2 1 3 4|3 5	3a 35-Bauyn-I #115
5|5 4 3 2 1 5 5|5 5 #6 7|	3g 64-Lebègue-I #18
5|5 4|3 2|1 5|6 5 6 7 6|5	3d 54-Gen-2350/57 #7
5|5 4 3 2 1 6 7|5 5 #6 7 1 2|	3a 64-Lebègue-I #31
|5 5 4 3|2 1 7|1 7 6 5 6 7 5|	2a 35-Bauyn-II #100
5|5 4 3 2 1 7 6|5 #6 #6|	3a 62-Chamb-I #3
5|5 4 3|2 1 #7 1 2|	2a 54-Gen-2350/57 #15
5|5 4 3 3 4 5 1 3|2 3 4 4|	3a 65-Lebègue-II #18
5|5 4 3|3 4 5|5 4 3 2|	3a 54-Gen-2350/57 #14
5|5 4 3 4 2 5|1 3|6 5 6 4 5 3|2|	3g 37-Geoffroy #218
5|5 4 3 4 4|5|	3g 63-Chamb-II #22
5 5|4 4 5 4 3 2|3 2 3|1 #7 1 2 2	2c 37-Geoffroy #5
5|5 4 5 2|3 2 3 #7|1 5 4 3 2 1|#7	3f 37-Geoffroy #62
5|5 4 5 4 3|2 5 #6|	2d 54-Gen-2350/57 #21
5|5 4 5 3 1|1 7 1 2|	3d 68-d'Anglebert #41
5|5 4 5 4 3 2 1 1 7 5|6 7 6 5	2g 68-d'Anglebert #18
5|5 4 5 6|5 4 3 2	3a 35-Bauyn-III #72
|5 5 5|1 1|1 1 1|5	2d 35-Bauyn-I #42
5|5 5 1 2|#7 1 7 #6 5|6 5 4 5	3g 37-Geoffroy #83
5 5|5 1 3 2 1|#7	3d 17-Rogers #26
5|5|5 2 2|	3a 66-Perrine #26
5 5|5 2 3 2 1 2 1 2 3|#7 #7	3a 32-Oldham #108
5 5|5 4 3 2 1 1 2|#7	3d 35-Bauyn-III #45
5|5 5 4 3 2|1 2 3 3|	2d 55-Redon #7
|5 5 5 4 3 2|3 2 2|	2g 62-Chamb-I #24
|5 5 5 4|3 2 3 5|	2a 66-Perrine #22
|5 5|5 4 3 3 3 3|4 3 7 6|	3a 35-Bauyn-II #108
|5 5 5 4|3 4 4 4 5 3|	2g 1-Copenhagen-376 #51
|5 5 5|4 4|3 2 1|1 #7 1 |2 2	3c 66-Perrine #29
|5|5|5 4|4 3 2 1|7 7|#6	2a 35-Bauyn-III 37
5|5 5 4|5 1 2 3 2|	3a 32-Oldham #26
|5 5|5 5|4 2|	2a 26-Bull #17
|5 5 5|5 4|#3 4 5|	3c 35-Bauyn-II #32
|5 5 5|5 4|5 1|2	3g 35-Bauyn-II #94
|5 5 5|5|4 5 4 3|	3a 35-Bauyn-III #71

|5 5 5 5|5 4 3|5 6 4 7|	2a	35-Bauyn-II #103
|5 5 5 5|5 4 4 2 4|3	3c	66-Perrine #30
|5 5 5|5 5 5|5 4|4 5|2 #3|4	3g	62-Chamb-I #26
|5 5 5|5 5 5|5 4 4 5|3 2|2 3 4|	3d	33-Rés-89ter #30
|5 5 5|5 5|6 6 7|	3b	35-Bauyn-II #118
5|5 5|6 5 5 4|3 1|1 7 6 5 6 7|	3d	35-Bauyn-III #88
|5 5 5|6 6|2 2 3 1|	3g	64-Lebègue-I #20
5|5 5 6 7|1 1 2 #7|	3d	19-Heardson #64
5|5 5 6 7|1 2 3 3	3a	38-Gen-2348/53 #7
5|5 5 #6 7 1 #7 1 2|	2d	63-Chamb-II #6
5|5 5 #6 #7|1 #7 1 2|3 2 3	2g	37-Geoffroy #81
5|5 6 4 3|5 4 3 2	3d	35-Bauyn-III #47
5|5 6 4 4|2 5 6 7 6 5|4 3 2 1|	3a	35-Bauyn-II #105
5|5 6 4 5|3 4 2 1 5|	3d	4-Lynar #69
|5 5 6|5 1 7 6|5 3 4 5|5 5 4 3|	2d	66-Perrine #11
5|5 6 5 4 3 2 3 4|5 1 1 1 1 7 1	2d	65-Lebègue-II #1
5|5 6 5|4 3 2|3 4 5|6 2 3|2 1	3a	55-Redon #3
5|5 6 5 4|3 4 3|	2g	54-Gen-2350/57 #28
5|5 6 5 4 3 4 5 2 1|	2g	64-Lebègue-I #17
5|5 6 5 4 3 4|5 5 4 3 2 1 5 5|	3d	62-Chamb-I #13
5|5 6 5 4 5 4 3 2 2 1|#7	2a	28-Brussels-926 l 66r
|5 5 6 5 4|5 5 #6 #7|	3d	35-Bauyn-I #32
5|5 6 5 4 7|5 5 7 6 5|	3g	64-Lebègue-I #19
5|5 6 6|5 1 2 3 2 1|	3a	35-Bauyn-III #70
|5 5 6|6|5 5 4|5|	3g	35-Bauyn-II #95
|5 5 6 6 5 4|5 5 #6 #7|	3d	35-Bauyn-I #32
5|5 #6 5 7 #6 |5 4 3 2 3 4|	3d	4-Lynar #66
5|5 #6 7 1|7 1 #6|5|	3d	29-Chigi #31
5|5 #6 7 1|#7 1 2 2|3 7 7 1 ♭2 7 6|	3d	37-Geoffroy #24
5 5 #6 7|1 #7 1 2|3 4 3	2d	35-Bauyn-I #29
5|5 #6 7|#6 7 1|7|	3a	36-Parville #55
5|5 #7 1 2 3 4 5 4 3|	2a	65-Lebègue-II #17
|5 6 4 3|2 3 1 2 #7 5|1 #7 1 2 3 2	2a	37-Geoffroy #117
5|6 4 5|3 3 6|5 1 2|	3a	36-Parville #120
5 6|4 5 4 3 1|2 2 5 6|	2f	37-Geoffroy #64
5 6|5|4|3 2|	3g	35-Bauyn-II #99
|5 6 5|4 3 2|3 2 1|#7 2 5|5 6 5|	3a	37-Geoffroy #227
|5 6 5|4 3 2|3 3|	3g	36-Parville #110
|5 6 5 4|3 3|3 2 2 2 1 1|	2f#	35-Bauyn-II #121

|5 6|5 4|3 4|	3a	46-Menetou #8
|5 6 5|4 5|3 2|2|	3d	'35-Bauyn-II #53
5 6|6 3 4 5|5 4 3 4 2|3|	3d	37-Geoffroy #32
5|6 6|5 4 3|2 2 5|	3a	46-Menetou #54
5 6 7|1 1 5 5|5 4 5 6 7 7|	3a	35-Bauyn-II #107
5 6|7 7 3 6|5 5 4 5 #6|7 7 #6|	2g	46-Menetou #84
|5 #6|#4|5|5 #6 7|	3d	45-Dart #38
5 #6 #6|#6 5 #6 #6|#6 7 1 #6	2c	54-Gen-2350/57 #25
5 #6 7 1 5 3 1|6 3 2 #7 5 3 1|	2d	45-Dart #54
|5 #6 7 1 7 #6|5 4 3|3 4|	3d	54-Gen-2350/57 #31
5 #6|7 5 1 1|#7 1 1|	2d	54-Gen-2350/57 #22
5 #6 #7|1 1 1 7 #6 5 6 4 5|3 4 5 5	2d	68-d'Anglebert #39
5 #6 #7|1 2 1|2 2 3|	3d	45-Dart #62
5 #6 #7|1 2 3 1 7 6|5 5 6 5 4|	2d	36-Parville #15
5 #6 #7|1 2 3 2 1 2|#7 #6 5 1 1 #7|	3d	35-Bauyn-II #42
5 #6 #7|1 2 3 2 3 4 5 5 1 4 5 6 7|	2d	35-Bauyn-II #36
|5 #6 #7 1 2|#7 1 2 3 4	2d	35-Bauyn-III #33
5 #6 #7 1 5 7 6 5 4 5 2 3 4 5	0d	33-Rés-89ter #23
5 #6 #7|1 7 6 5 4 5|6 5 4|	2d	35-Bauyn-II #35
5 #6 #7|1 #7 1 2 3 4 5|5 1 7 #6	3d	35-Bauyn-II #43
5 #6 #7|1 #7 1 #7|1 2 3 4|	3d	66-Perrine #8
|5 7 #6 5|4 5 6 5 4 3|2|	3f	37-Geoffroy #68
5 #7 1 2 3 1 7 1 #3 5 #6	0g	35-Bauyn-II #4
6 5 2|3 4 3 #7|1 5 4 3|2 3 2 #6|	3c	37-Geoffroy #9
7 3 4 5 6 5 5 4 3 4	0a	6-Munich-1511e #15
#7 1 2|3 2 1 7 6|5 1 #7|1	3d	35-Bauyn-II #38
#7 1 2|3 2 3 4 5 1 1 #7|	2a	35-Bauyn-II #102
#7 1 2|3 2 3 4|5 4 3 3 2|	3g	35-Bauyn-II #93
#7 1 2|3 3 2 1 1 2|#7 #7 5 #6 #7|	3c	35-Bauyn-II #31
#7 1 2|3 3 4|2 2	3g	32-Oldham #109
#7 1 2|3 3 4 5 1 1 1|1 1 2 3 #7 1	2f	37-Geoffroy #61
#7 1 2|3 4 4|4 3 2 1|	3d	35-Bauyn-II #39
#7 1 2 3 4 5 4 4	0a	64-Lebègue-I #28

Minor, Second Strain

1 1|1 1 1 1 5|6 4 5 6|7 7 7 1 7	2g	42-Vm7-6307-2 #2
|1 1 2 1 7|6 6 7 1 6|	2g	54-Gen-2350/57 #33
|1 1 5|1 1 2 3|1 1 2 3|	3d	46-Menetou #111

|1 1|#6 #6|7 7|	3g	54-Gen-2350/57 #24
1 2|1 5 #6 #7 1|#6 #6 2 3|	2f	37-Geoffroy #64
|1 2 1 7 6 4|5 4 5 3 2|	3g	35-Bauyn-II #3
1|2 3 1 2 1 7 #6|	3g	54-Gen-2350/57 #24
1 2|3 1 2 3 4 2 3 4|5 4 3 4 5	2g	54-Gen-2350/57 #28
|1 2 3 2 1|7 7 6|5 5 4 3 4|	2d	54-Gen-2350/57 #9
|1 2|3 2 3|4 2 3|	3g	68-d'Anglebert #36
|1|2|3 3 4 5 3|4 2 1|	3d	4-Lynar #63
1 2 3 4|5 4|	3g	35-Bauyn-III #89
|1 2 3 4|5 4 3 2|3 4 3 2 1 2 1 2	2g	68-d'Anglebert #30
1 2 3 4 5 4 3 2 3	0d	7-Munich-1511f #2
1 2|3 4 5 5|2 3 2|	2g	36-Parville #44
1 2 3 4 5 5 4 5	0d	7-Munich-1511f #8
1 2|3 4 5 5 6 6 7 1 2 1|	3d	32-Oldham #13
1 2 3|4 5 6 7 6|5	3a	47-Gen-2356 #9
1 2 3 4|5 #6 5 #6 7 1|4 5 4 5 #6 7	3d	4-Lynar #68
1 3 2 1 5 2|3 2 1 7 #6 5|	3d	35-Bauyn-II #1
1 4 5 2 3 #7 1 5 6	0g	35-Bauyn-II #3
|1 5 3 2 3 1|#7 1 2 5|	3g	68-d'Anglebert #32
|1 5 5 5|4 4 3 3 3 4 5|	2g	68-d'Anglebert #29
1 5 6|5 6 2 3 2 3 4|	2a	35-Bauyn-III #93
|1 5 #6|7|1 1 2|	3d	35-Bauyn-I #43
|1 5 #6|7 7|7 3|	3d	6-Munich-1511e #7
|1 #6|7 5|	3d	4-Lynar #66
|1 7 1 2 1 7|6 5 4 7|	2g	54-Gen-2350/57 #5
|1 7 1 2 3 2 3 4|5	3a	35-Bauyn-II #107
|1 #7 1|2 3|2 1 2 3|	2d	48-LaBarre-6 #27
1|#7 #6 #7 1 1|2 3|	2g	45-Dart #67
2 1|2 3 2 1 2|#7 6	2c	66-Perrine #30
|2 1 2 3 4 2|5 5 6 4 4 5|	2g	65-Lebègue-II #10
2 1|2 5 5 7 #6 1|7 6 7|	2d	6-Munich-1511e #12
|2 1 2|#7|5 5 4 5 2|	3d	68-d'Anglebert #43
|2 1 7 #6|7|1 2|3|	3a	32-Oldham #18
2 1|#7 5 1 2|3 1 4 3|	2c	45-Dart #57
2|2 1 2 3 2 1|	2d	64-Lebègue-I #2
2|2 1 #7 1 2|3	2d	66-Perrine #10
2 2|2 1 2 #7|	3g	68-d'Angelbert #19
2|2 2 1 #7 2|5	2d	66-Perrine #12
|2 2 2 2|2|3 4 4|5|	3d	35-Bauyn-II #56
|2 2 2|2 3|1 1 1|	3d	45-Dart #61

2 2|2 2 3 4 5 2 3|

2 2|2 2 3 4 5 2 3 3|

|2 2 2 3|1 1 2|

2 2|2 3 2 1 #7|1 7 #6 7 6

2|2 2 3 2 1|#7 1 #7 #6|5 #6

|2 2 2 3 2 3 1 3|

|2 2 2|3 3 6|5 4 3 2 1 7|

2|2 2 3 #71 2|

2 2|2 5 5 #6|

2 2|2 #7 1 2|3 1 2 3 4|

|2 2 3|1 1|7 1 7 6 5|6 5 4|7 6 5

2|2 3 1 2 7 7 #6|

2|2 3|1 2 #7 1 2 |#7|

|2 2 3 1 3|2 5 5 7 4 6|

2 2|3 1 4 1|

|2 2 3 1|4 5 2 1 7|

2|2 3 2 1|2 5 4 3|

2|2 3 2 1 2|#7 1 7 6|

2 2|3 2 1 4 1|

2 2|3 2 1 5 4 #3|4 1 1|3 2 1 7 #6

2|2 3 2|1 7 1|#7 1 7|

2|2 3 2 1|7 6 5|

2|2 3 2 1 #7 1 2|3 3 4 5 6 5|

2|2 3 2 1 #7 1 2|

2|2 3 2 1 #7 1 2|#7 5 4 3|

2|2 3 2 1|#7 1 5 #6|7 1 7|6 5|

2|2 3 2 1|#7 #6 #7|1 2 1|7 6 5|4

2|2 3 2 #7 1 2|#7

2 2|3 3 2 1 4|2 1 7 3 2|

|2 2 3 3|3|3 4 2|

|2 2 3|3 3 4|4 5 4 3

2 2|3 3 #3 #3|4 5 6 5 5|

2|2 3 4 2 1|#7 5 1 7|#6

2 2|3 4 3 2 1 1|1 7 7|

2 2|3 4 3 2 1 2|

|2 2|3 4 3 2 1|7 7 1|

|2 2|3 4 3 2 1| #7|

2|2 3 4 3 2 7 #6 5|

|2 2 3 4 5 1 2|

3a   35-Bauyn-I #113

3c   35-Bauyn-II #31

3d   65-Lebègue-II #3

2g   68-d'Anglebert #18

3d   17-Rogers #27

2d   66-Perrine #7

3d   37-Geoffroy #197

3a   35-Bauyn-II #106

3a   35-Bauyn-I #114

2a   39-Vm7-6307-1 #11

3e   37-Geoffroy #52

3g   68-d'Anglebert #21

3a   37-Geoffroy #126

2d   33-Rés-89ter #28

2a   49-RésF-933 #13

2a   37-Geoffroy #118

3d   63-Chamb-II #8

3d   64-Lebègue-I #3

2a   35-Bauyn-III #50

2c   37-Geoffroy #5

3a   32-Oldham #15

2e   35-Bauyn-II #63

3g   37-Geoffroy #82

3d   36-Parville #16

3a   64-Lebègue-I #30

3d   62-Chamb-I #12

3d   66-Perrine #14

3d   24-Babell #224

2e   37-Geoffroy #50

3b   35-Bauyn-II #118

3a   35-Bauyn-I #118

2g   68-d'Anglebert #35

3d   37-Geoffroy #24

3a   33-Rés-89ter #20

2d   64-Lebègue-I #6

3d   5-Munich-1503*l* #6

3a   22a-Roper #34

2d   55-Redon #12

2g   62-Chamb-I #24

2|2 3 4 5 3 2|	3d	32-Oldham #2
|2 2 3 4|5 4|#3 4 5|	2g	35-Bauyn-II #92
2 2 3 4|5 #6 #7 1|2 3 4|	2d	36-Parville #1
|2 2 3 4 5 #7 1 2|	2g	35-Bauyn-I #107
2|2 3 #7|1	3d	35-Bauyn-III #45
|2 2 #3|4 4|3 3 4|	3a	65-Lebègue-II #19
2|2 4 3 2 1 2 1|#7	3d	22a-Roper #55
2|2 5 1 2 7|	3d	35-Bauyn-II #52
|2 2 5|3 2 1|4 5 5|6 5 4|	3d	37-Geoffroy #28
|2 2 5|#3 #3|	3a	46-Menetou #19
|2 2 5|#3 4 5|6 7 1|4|	3g	37-Geoffroy #86
2|2 5 4|3 1 2 3|	3d	66-Perrine #15
|2 2 5 4 3 2 1|6 7 6 5 4 4|	2g	37-Geoffroy #85
|2 2 5|4 5|3 2 3|	3a	64-Lebègue-I #34
2 2|5 4 6 5 2 4|3 3 1 4 3|	2a	37-Geoffroy #115
|2 2 5 5|#3 #3 4 5|	2c	45-Dart #56
2|2 5 5 4|3 1 7 6 5 5|	3b	37-Geoffroy #154
|2 2 5|5 4 #3 4 4 3|2 5 6 5|	2a	66-Perrine #24
2|2 5 5 #6|7	3a	35-Bauyn-I #122
|2 2 5 6|#3 1 1|4 4 5|6	3g	37-Geoffroy #84
2|2 5 6 5 4 3 2 1|#7 1 2 5 1 #7|	3f	37-Geoffroy #62
2|2 5 #6|7 #6|7 7 1 2|	3a	35-Bauyn-II #105
2|2 5 #6 #7|1 2 1 7 6 5 4	3d	62-Chamb-I #13
2|2 5 #6 #7 1 2|3 3 2 1 7 6 5 5	3c	37-Geoffroy #8
2 2 7 5 2|2 2 3 4 5 4|	3a	55-Redon #3
|2 2 #7 1 2|3 2 1 7 6 5|4 4 7 6|	3g	36-Parville #138
2|2 #7 5 1|	3d	35-Bauyn-II #41
2 2|#7 7 1 2 5 2 #1|2 #6 #6 #4	2c	37-Geoffroy #230
|2 3 1|1 2 1 #7|1 b2 1 7 6 5|5 4	3c	37-Geoffroy #4
|2 3|1 2 3|2 6 1|7 1|	3b	37-Geoffroy #156
2 3|1 2 3 4 3 2 1|#7 5 2 3|	2d	37-Geoffroy #27
|2 3 1|4 3 2 1|#7 1|2 3 2|	3d	37-Geoffroy #200
2 3 1|#7 1 2|5 #6	2d	35-Bauyn-III #82
2 3 2 1 2|#7 1 7|6 #7 1 #7|	2d	35-Bauyn-III #33
|2 3 2 1 2|#7 #6 5 5 5 5 4|	3a	35-Bauyn-II #111
2 3 2 1|5|	2a	36-Parville #54
2|3 2 1|#7|1 7 6|5 1 7|	3a	36-Parville #56
|2 3 2 1 #7 5 4 3|	3c	35-Bauyn-II #33
|2 3 2 2 3 4|2 1 1 1 2 7 7 7 #6|	2f#	35-Bauyn-II #121

|2|3 2 3|4 2 3|4 5|	3g	36-Parville #143
2|3 3 #3|4 4|	2a	36-Parville #51
|2 3 4|1 1|7 7 1|#6 #6|	3e	37-Geoffroy #49
|2 3 4 2|3 2|1 2 3|#7 1 2 3 4 2|	3f	37-Geoffroy #65
2 3 4|2 3 4 5 6 7|	3b	35-Bauyn-II #117
|2 3 4 2 5 3|4 5 6 7 6|	2a	1-Copenhagen-376 #50
2 3 4|3 1 2 3 2 1|	2d	36-Parville #14
|2 3 4|3 2 1|#7|	3d	35-Bauyn-III #49
2 3 4|3 3 2 1 #7 5 5 4|	2g	64-Lebègue-I #17
|2 3|4 3 4 2|3 2 1|#7 #6 #7 5|	3c	37-Geoffroy #6
|2 3 4|4 3 2|1 2 3|1 7|	3a	7-Munich-1511f #6
|2 3|4 4|4 3|2 2|	3a	46-Menetou #8
2 3 4|5|1 1 7|	3d	66-Perrine #4
2 3 4|5 1 2 3 4 4|	2d	35-Bauyn-II #36
2 3 4 5 2 3|2	2a	5-Munich-1503l #12
2 3 4 5 2|3 #7 1 2 5 1|	2d	59-Dumont-1657 l 31v
2 3 4|5 4 3 2|1 3 2 1|#7	3d	18-Ch-Ch-1236 #3
|2 3 4|5 4 3 2|3 2 1|	3g	63-Chamb-II #21
2 3 4|5 4|#3 4 5|6 7 1|	2g	35-Bauyn-II #92
2 3 4|5 4 4 3|	3a	35-Bauyn-III #70
2 3 4|5 4 5 6 7 5 1 7 1 7 6 5|	2g	65-Lebègue-II #7
2 3 4|5 5 4 3 2 3 2 1 7 6 5|	2d	48-LaBarre-6 #25
2 3 4|5 5 4 3 2 3|2	3a	35-Bauyn-III #72
2 3 4|5 5 4 3 2 3 3 2|2 5 #6 7 #7	3d	35-Bauyn-II #38
2 3 4|5 5 4 5 3 4 2 1|#7 1 2 3	3d	17-Rogers #21
|2 3 4|5 5 6 5|	3d	68-d'Anglebert #47
2 3 4|5 5 #6 7 #6 #6 7 1 #7 #7 1 2|	2e	37-Geoffroy #47
|2 3 4|5 6|4 5|3	3d	35-Bauyn-II #51
2 3 4|5 6 7 6 5 4 3|	2a	64-Lebègue-I #29
2 3 4|5 6 7 6 5 6 7|	2d	65-Lebègue-II #1
2 3 4 5 #6|7 1 7 7 7|7 1 7 6 5 3	3d	4-Lynar #69
2 3 4 5 #6 7 1|#7 1 7 6 5 4 3 2|	2a	65-Lebègue-II #17
2 3 4|#7 1 2 5 4 3 2|	2d	36-Parville #15
2 3 4|#7|3 1 #7|1|	3c	37-Geoffroy #9
|2 3|#7 1 2|5 1|	3g	46-Menetou #86
|2 4 5|3 2 1|2 3 4 3 2 1|	3d	46-Menetou #25
|2 5 2|2 1 7|7 7 7|	3d	36-Parville #24
2 5|2 3 1 #7|	3d	64-Lebègue-I #8
|2 5 2|3 2|	2e	35-Bauyn-III #36
2 5|#3 2 1 2 #3|	2g	64-Lebègue-I #21

2 5|#3 2 1|6 5 6|	3d	46-Menetou #30
2 5|#3 #3 4 5|6 4 7 6 5|	2a	46-Menetou #31
|2 5 4 3 4 3 2 1|	2d	59-Dumont-1657 *l* 32v
|2 5 4|#3 #3 4 4 #3|4 #6 7 6|	3d	35-Bauyn-II #46
|2 5 4|#3 4 5|6 6 5|4 3 2|	3d	37-Geoffroy #199
|2 5 4 5|#3 2 #3|	3d	68-d'Anglebert #42
|2 5|4 5 6|	2a	35-Bauyn-III #37
|2 5 6|#3 2 1|1 5|6 6 7|	3e	37-Geoffroy #53
|2 #7 1|2 3|2 3 1|	3a	65-Lebègue-II #21
|2 #7 #6|5 5|6 7 1 7 6 5|	3d	62-Chamb-I #15
3 1 5 3|2 3 2 1 #7 5|	3a	16-Cosyn #87
|3 2 1|2 1 #7|♭2 1 7|1 7 6 5|	3d	37-Geoffroy #25
|3 2 1 2 3 1|4|5 4 3 2 1 7|	3d	65-Lebègue-II #5
3 2 1 7|1 2 3|	3a	62-Chamb-I #3
|3 2 1 7 1 7 6|5 5 6 5 6|	2a	35-Bauyn-I #110
3 2 1|7 1 7 6 5 6 5 4 3 4 5|4	3d	35-Bauyn-II #42
3 2 1|7 6 5 1 7 6|5	2d	35-Bauyn-III #81
3 2 1|7 6 5 #6 7 1|2	3a	32-Oldham #108
3 2 1|7 #6 7 7 1 2|	3a	32-Oldham #107
3 2 1 7 #6|#7|2 3 1 2 #7|1|	2c	37-Geoffroy #1
|3 2 1 7 7 6|5	2d	66-Perrine #19
3 2 1|#7 1 2 3|	2d	35-Bauyn-III #94
3 2 1|#7 1 2|3|	3d	35-Bauyn-III #88
3 2 1|#7 1 2 3 2 5 4 5|	2a	58-Dumont-1656 *l* 36v
3 2 1|#7 1 2 3 3|2 1 2 3 4	3d	35-Bauyn-I #33
3 2 1|#7 1 2 3 4|2 3 2 2|	2e	35-Bauyn-III #80
3 2 1|#7 1 2|7 5|1 6 7	3d	35-Bauyn-II #54
3 2 1 #7 5 1|1 7	2g	41-Thomelin #1
3 2 1|#7 5 2 4 3 5 1 2 1 #7	2c	37-Geoffroy #2
3 2 1|#7 #6 5 4 5 4 5 3 2 1|	2g	65-Lebègue-II #6
3 2 1|#7 #6 5 5 4 4 5|	3a	22a-Roper #32
3 2 1|#7 #7 1 2 3 2|	2d	63-Chamb-II #6
3 2 1|#7 #7 1 5 6 7 6 5|4	3a	35-Bauyn-II #104
3 2 2 3 4|#7 1 2 1 2 3 4	2d	37-Geoffroy #196
|3 2 3|1 4 3 2 1|#7 1|	3a	46-Menetou #43
3 2 3 4 5 2 1 2 3 4	0d	7-Munich-1511f #28
3|2 4 3 2|1 3 2 1|#7|	3d	5-Munich-1503*l* #10
3|3 1|4 5 3 4|2 7|	3d	29-Chigi #31
|3 3 2 1|7 1 2|3	3g	35-Bauyn-I #103

3|3 3 2 1 7 1 2|	3g	63-Chamb-II #22
|3 3 3|2 2|3 1 2 #7|	3d	54-Gen-2350/57 #27
|3 3 3|2 2 3 2|1 1 2 1|	3d	16-Cosyn #101
|3 3 3|2 3 2|1 1 2 1|	3d	18-Ch-Ch-1236 #6
|3 3 3|3 #3|4 4|	3g	68-d'Anglebert #31
3 3|3 4 5 6|4 4 2 5|	2d	46-Menetou #29
3|3 4 5|3 2 3|	3g	45-Dart #40
3|3 4 5 4 5|3|	3d	66-Perrine #1
3 3 4 5 5 4 3 4 4 5 #6	0d	7-Munich-1511f #13
|3 3|4|5 6 4|	3d	36-Parville #18
|3 3 6|4 4|7 7 3|	3g	46-Menetou #4
|3 3 7 1 5 6|7|	3g	35-Bauyn-I #106
3|3 #7 1 2 6 6 6 7 1|5 5	2b	37-Geoffroy #153
|3 #3 #3|4 5 6|4 7 6 5|	3g	68-d'Anglebert #28
|3 #3 #3|4 5 6|5 6 7 5|	3g	68-d'Anglebert #34
|3 4|2 7|6 7 5|4 3|	3d	35-Bauyn-II #53
|3 4 3|2 4 3 2|1 3 2 1|	3d	48-LaBarre-6 #38
3|4 3 4 5 6 4|	2g	45-Dart #48
|3 4 5 1 7 6|5	3a	35-Bauyn-I #111
|3 4 5 2 3 7|1 2 3 4|	2d	67-Gigault p 16
|3 4 5 3|3 2 3|	3d	33-Rés-89ter #29
|3 4 5|4 4 5 3 2|2 5 #6 7|	3d	35-Bauyn-II #45
3 4|5 4 5|1 6 5|	3a	45-Dart #51
3 4|5 4 5|3 2 3 2 3|1	3d	65-Lebègue-II #4
|3 4 5 4|5 #6 7|	2d	68-d'Anglebert #46
|3 4 5|4 7 6 5|	2a	36-Parville #140
3 4|5 5 4 5|	2g	65-Lebègue-II #14
3 4|5 5 #6 7 5 4 5 4|3 1 3 2|	2d	27-Gresse #21
3|4 5 6 5|4 3 4 2|	2g	36-Parville #114
3|4 5 6 5|4 3 4 2|3 2 3 4 5 #6|	2d	48-LaBarre-6 #28
3 4|5 #6 7 1|#7	3g	65-Lebègue-II #11
3 5 1 1 7 #6	0a	35-Bauyn-II #6
|3 5 5|6 7 1 7|6 5 4 4|	3g	36-Parville #134
|3 5 6 7 5 1|7	3g	35-Bauyn-I #105
|3|#6|#7 1 2|	3a	35-Bauyn-I #119
|3 7 1|2 3 4|4 3 2|	3a	35-Bauyn-I #120
|3 7 1|5 5 7|	3d	35-Bauyn-III #17
3|7 5 3 7|5 3 7 5|	2g	51-LaBarre-11 p 211
|3 7 7|1 1|6 ♭2 1|1 7|	3d	35-Bauyn-II #44
4 2 1 2 7 1 2 3 3	0d	7-Munich-1511f #9
|4 4 5 3|3|4 3|	2a	56-Mersenne

4 5 2
4 5 6|7 1 2|3 2 2|
4 5 #6|7 6 5|5 5 5 1|
4 7 1 2 3 4 1 #7 5
5|1 1 #6|7 #4 5|
5|1 2 3|3 2|1 1 4|
|5 1 2|#3|4 4 #3|
5|1 3 4|5 2 #7|
5 1 #6	7 1	2 3 4
5 1	7 6 5	6 4 5	5 4 3	6 7 5
5 1	7 #6 5	6 4
5 2	3 1 6 5	4 4 5 6 7 6	5 6 7 1
5 2	3 1 6 5	4 5 6	#7 5 1 4 4 3
5 2 3 1 #7 1	2 5
5 2 3 1	#7 1 2 3 2
5 2	3 4 2	1 7
5 2 3 4 3 2	3 2 2 3
5 2 3	#7 1 2 5 #6 7	1
5	2 5 4 5 3 1 6 6	5 4 1 7 #6 4 7
5 2 #7 #6 5	1 7 #6 4	7 6 5 4
5 3 7	7 6 5
5	#3 2 #3 1	4 3 4
5	#3 #3 #3 #3	4 4 4 #3
5 #3	4 5 6 4 2
5 4 3 2 1 2 2 1	#7
5 4 3	2 1 2 3 2 1	#7
5 4 3	2 1 #7 1 2 2
5 4 3	2 2 1 7	#6 2 #7 #6 5
5 4 3	2 2 3 #7 1 1 7 6	5 6 7
5 4 3	2 2 3 #7 1 #7	1 5 6 7 1 7 6
5 4 3	2 2 4 3 2 1 #7 1	1
5 4 3	2 3 1
5 4 3 2 3 1 2	3 3	#3 #3 #3 4 5
5 4 3 2 3 1	4 5 6	7 6 5 4 5 4 3
5 4 3|2 3 2|1 2 3 4 2 2
5 4 3 2 3 2 1
5 4 3| 3 2 1 4|2 1 7 7 6 5 4|
5 4 3 2|3 2 1 4 5 4 1|
5 4 3|2 3 2 1 #7 1 2|3 3 3 2 1|

0d	36-Parville #1
2b	35-Bauyn-II #116
2d	35-Bauyn-I #42
0d	7-Munich-1511f #9
3a	46-Menetou #42
3e	35-Bauyn-I #59
3d	63-Chamb-II #10
3d	66-Perrine #6
3d	5-Munich-1503*l* #3
3g	33-Rés-89ter #38
3g	36-Parville #127
2a	37-Geoffroy #114
2b	37-Geoffroy #157
2d	20-Ch-Ch-378 #3
3g	62-Chamb-I #27
3g	63-Chamb-II #23
3g	46-Menetou #83
3g	35-Bauyn-II #93
2g	36-Parville #135
2a	37-Geoffroy #117
3a	45-Dart #47
3a	36-Parville #119
2g	46-Menetou #107
2a	46-Menetou #26
3d	35-Bauyn-I #35
2a	35-Bauyn-III #40
3d	68-d'Anglebert #41
2d	35-Bauyn-III #44
2a	35-Bauyn-II #100
2d	35-Bauyn-II #35
3e	37-Geoffroy #48
3d	36-Parville #112
3a	37-Geoffroy #113
2a	37-Geoffroy #119
2g	64-Lebègue-I #16
0a	6-Munich-1511e #15
3g	65-Lebègue-I #19
2g	46-Menetou #105
3d	35-Bauyn-II #43

5 4 3|2 3 2 1 #7 1 2|3 4 5 6|	2a	35-Bauyn-II #101
5 4 3 2 3|2 3 4 5|	3a	46-Menetou #113
5 4 3|2 3 4 5 4 3 2|	2a	32-Oldham #106
5 4 3|2 3 4 5 6 7|	3d	35-Bauyn-II #39
5 4 3 2 3 4|#7 1 2 3 2|3 2 3	2g	37-Geoffroy #81
|5 4 3 2 3|6	2d	66-Perrine #2
|5 4 3 2 3 #7 1|2|	2a	62-Chamb-I #6
|5 4 3 2|4 3 2 1|5 6 5 4 3 2 1 #7|	3d	45-Dart #62
|5 4 3 2 4 3 2 3 4|2 2 3 3 #3 #3|	2a	46-Menetou #98
|5|4 3 4 4|	2a	66-Perrine #22
5 4 3|7 6 5 6 6 5|5 5 6|4 4 4	2a	37-Geoffroy #195
5 4|#3 #3 #3 #3|	2g	42-Vm7-6307-2 #10
|5|4 #3|4 4|2 3 2 1 7	3g	35-Bauyn-II #94
5 4|#3 4 5 6|5 #6 7 #6 7 1|	3g	46-Menetou #24
|5 4 5 3 2 3|1 4 4 4 5 3|	3d	46-Menetou #27
|5 4 5 4 3|7 2 3 2 1|	2a	46-Menetou #45
5 4|5 5 4 3 2 3|	3a	35-Bauyn-I #112
5|4 5 6 7 5 4 5 3 4|2 7 1 2 3|	3d	4-Lynar #67
|5 4 5|#7 1 2 3 4 2|3 4|	3a	64-Lebègue-I #33
|5 5 1 1|#6 #6|7 7|	2d	55-Redon #7
5 5|1 1 7 6 5|	2a	37-Geoffroy #116
5 5|1 1 #7 1 2|3|2 3 1|	3g	36-Parville #121
5 5|1 2 1|5 #6 7|#6 5 4|	3g	37-Geoffroy #217
|5 5 1 2 1 7|	2g	46-Menetou #61
5 5|1 2 7|#6 4 4 3|2	2d	37-Geoffroy #26
5 5|1|6 6 5|	3d	46-Menetou #41
|5 5 1|#6 2|#7 1|2 3 2|5 5 1|	3a	37-Geoffroy #122
5 5 1 #6 5 4	0d	7-Munich-1511f #11
|5 5 1|#6 #7 1|	3d	45-Dart #24
5|5 1 7 6 5 5 4	3g	68-d'Anglebert #25
5|5 1 #7 #6 #7|	3d	66-Perrine #3
5|5 2 3 2|	3a	36-Parville #145
5|5 2 3 4 3 2|	2c	35-Bauyn-II #30
5 5 2|3 4 5 6 5 4|	3a	46-Menetou #44
5|5 2 4|3 1 2|	3d	66-Perrine #8
5 5|3 6 6 6 5|4 4 4|	2a	46-Menetou #38
5|5 4 3 2|1 7 1 2|	2a	55-Redon #1
5|5 4 3 2|1 7 #6|7|	3a	36-Parville #5
5|5 4 3|2 2 3|2 3	3d	66-Perrine #18
|5 5 4 3|2 2 3 4|3 2 1|#7 #7 1 2|	3f	37-Geoffroy #67

5 5 4 3 2|3 3 3 2 1 #7|1 1 1 7 6	2e 37-Geoffroy #56
5|5 4 3 2 4 3|2 1|	2d 35-Bauyn-III #57
5|5 4 3|3 4 5|5 4 3 2|	3a 54-Gen-2350/57 #14
5|5 4 4 3|2	3d 35-Bauyn-III #47
5|5 4 5 6 7 6|	3g 62-Chamb-I #25
5 5 4 5 #6 7 5	0d 6-Munich-1511e #9
5|5 5 2 4|#3 1 2 #3 1 5 4 3|	2g 1-Copenhagen-376 #51
5|5 5 4 3|2 2 3|	3d 66-Perrine #18
|5 5|5 4 4|4 5 6|	3d 43-Gen-2354 #5
5|5 5 4 5|3 7 6|5 3 2 3 1 1|	3d 66-Perrine #17
|5 5 5 #4 5|5 6 7 5 6 5	3d 17-Rogers #22
|5 5 5|5 2 3|	3a 32-Oldham #5
|5 5 5 5|4 4 5|	3g 68-d'Anglebert #22
5 5|5 5 5 4 3 2 3 1 2|	2d 68-d'Anglebert #39
|5 5 5|5 5 5|4 3 2 1 3 3 3|	3a 66-Perrine #25
|5 5 5|5 5 5|4 4 5|	3d 66-Perrine #16
5 5|5 5 #6 #7|1	3d 35-Bauyn-III #46
|5 5 5 6|4 3 4 2|5 4 3 2|	3a 22a-Roper #33
|5 5 5 6|4 4 #3 4 5|6 6 6 7|	3a 35-Bauyn-II #110
5|5 5 6 5 4 4 3|	3a 64-Lebègue-I #31
5|5 5 6|7 7 5|3 3 6|	3a 36-Parville #120
|5 5 5 #6|7 5 4 4|5 5 5 3|4 2 3|	2a 37-Geoffroy #226
5 5|5 #6 7 5 #6 #7|1	3d 8-Hintze #11
|5 5 6|4 3 2|	3g 45-Dart #49
5 5 6 4 4 5 3 3 2	3d 35-Bauyn-I #40
|5 5 6|4 4 5|3 3 4	3a 35-Bauyn-II #65
|5 5 6 4 4 7|7 7 #6	3a 35-Bauyn-II #109
|5 5 6 5|4|4 #3 4|	3d 35-Bauyn-III #48
5 5|6 6 5 4 3|2 1 7 7 1|4	2a 37-Geoffroy #120
5|5 6 7 1 4 4|4 2 3 4 5 6|	3e 35-Bauyn-II #64
5|5 6 7 3 4 5|4 5|6 7 1 7 1 6|	3g 37-Geoffroy #218
5|5 6 7 3 4 5|6	3g 68-d'Anglebert #20
|5 5 6 7|#3 #3 #3 4 5|	3f 37-Geoffroy #63
5|5 6 7 5 5 4|5 3 3 2	2d 16-Cosyn #99
5|5 6 7|5 6|4	3g 36-Parville #110
|5 5 6|7 5|6 6 5 6|	3a 46-Menetou #54
5|5 6 7 7 6 5|4	3a 38-Gen-2348/53 #7
5|5 6 7|7 6 5 4 5|7 1 7|	3d 19-Heardson #64
|5 5 6|7 7|7 1|	3g 46-Menetou #101
5 5|#6 #6 #7 1|#7 #7 1 2 1 2 #7|1 5 5|	3g 36-Parville #42
5|5 #6 7|1 1 #7	3d 66-Perrine #9

5|5 #6 7|3 6|	3a 66-Perrine #26
5|5 #6 7|5 1 2|#7|	3d 6-Munich-1511e #6
5|5 #6 7 5 1 2|#7 1 2	3d 35-Bauyn-III #58
5|5 #6 7|5 4 3 4 2|3 4 4 5|	3d 33-Rés-89ter #25
5|5 #6 7 5 #6 7|	3a 65-Lebègue-II #18
5|5 #6 7 6 5 4 3|	3d 63-Chamb-II #9
|5 5 #6|7 #7|1 2|	3a 32-Oldham #16
|5 5 #6 #7 1|2 #3 4 3 4 5	2g 35-Bauyn-I #102
5|5 7 6|5 4 3|	3a 66-Perrine #21
5 6|#3 4 #3 4 5 4 3|2 3 2|1 2 3 4	2d 37-Geoffroy #198
5 6|4 4 5|#3 #3 4|5 4 5 6 7 5|	3a 40-Rés-476 #41
|5 6 4|4 7|5 4 3 2|	3g 35-Bauyn-I #104
5 6 4|5|	3c 66-Perrine #29
|5 6 5 4 3 1 2 3 4 5 4 3|	2d 5-Munich-1503l #13
5 6 5 4 3 2 1|#7 1 #7 1 1 2 1 2 3	2a 37-Geoffroy #110
|5 6 5 4 3|2 2|	3d 46-Menetou #109
|5 6 5|4 3 4 2|	2g 54-Gen-2350/57 #23
|5 6 5 4|3|6 7 6 5|	3e 22-Ch-Ch-1117 #2
5|6 5 4 5 1|3 4 3 2 1 #7	3a 35-Bauyn-II #6
|5 6 5 4 5 2|3 4 3 2 3 1|#7|	3d 37-Geoffroy #203
5 6 5 6|4 4 b2 1 7 6 5 4|	3g 36-Parville #115
|5 6 7|1 2 1 7|#6 7 1|	3d 1-Copenhagen-376 #48a
5 6|7 1|2 3 4|5 4 3 2 3 2 1	3d 4-Lynar #65
|5 6 7|1 5 #6 2|	3d 19-Heardson #46
|5 6 7 1 7 6 5|	3d 4-Lynar #64
|5 6 7|3 3 3|	3a 46-Menetou #55
|5 6 7|3 4 5|	3a 45-Dart #46
5 6 7 5 4 3|4 5|	3d 35-Bauyn-I #36
|5 6|7 5|6 4|	3a 36-Parville #53
|5 6 7 6 5 4 3|4|	3d 62-Chamb-I #16
5 6 7 6 5 4 5|3 2 3 1 5	2a 1-Copenhagen-376 #39
|5 6 7|6 5 4|5 6 5|1 4 5|	3b 37-Geoffroy #155
|5 6 7 7 1 1 #7|1	3d 17-Rogers #26
|5 6 7 7 1 2|	2g 63-Chamb-II #20
|5 6 7|7 6 5 4 6|5 6 5 4 3|	3g 65-Lebègue-II #13
5|#6 5|4 7|	2g 36-Parville #139
5 #6|7|1|2|3 4|5 4 3 2|	3d 18-Ch-Ch-1236 #1
5 #6 7 1 2|3 5 6	3a 35-Bauyn-I #115
5 #6|7 1 2|#4 5 #6|7 #6|	3g 36-Parville #128
|5 #6 7 1 7 #6|5 4 3|3 4|	3d 54-Gen-2350/57 #31

5 #6 7 1 #7|1 2 3 4 4|5	2d 24-Babell #184
|5 #6 7|4 7|1 2 3|	3d 64-Lebègue-I #7
5 #6|7 5|4 5|6 4 3 2|3	3d 66-Perrine #13
|5 #6 7 5|6 5 4|5 3 4|	3d 5-Munich-1503l #2
5 #6|7 5 6 5|4 5 3 4|	2d 55-Redon #2
|5 #6 7|#6 5 4|5 4 3|	3c 46-Menetou #11
|5 #6 7|#6 7 1|#7 1|	3d 29-Chigi #32
5 #6 7 #6 7|5 4|3 4 5|4 5|	3a 66-Perrine #20
5 #6 7 7 1 2 3 3|	2d 55-Redon #6
5 #6|7 7 1 6 5|6 4 7 2|	2e 37-Geoffroy #51
|5 #6 7|7 #6 #7|1 7 #6|#6 5|	3d 35-Bauyn-II #50
5 #6|7 7 7 1|2 7 2 2|1 7 #6 5|	2g 42-Vm7-6307-2 #7
5 #6|7 7 7 1|#6 5 6 6 6	3g 68-d'Anglebert #26
5 #6 #7|1 1 7 1 2 1 7|	3d 68-d'Anglebert #44
5 #6 #7 1 2|3 3 4 5 5|	3d 68-d'Anglebert #48
5 #6 #7 1 #7|1 2 3 4	2d 62-Chamb-I #11
|5 7|4 6|5 5 6|7|	3a 16-Cosyn #87A
5 #7 1|2 1 #6 #7 1 2|	3g 68-d'Anglebert #24
|5 #7 1 2 3 4|2 3 2 1|	3d 35-Bauyn-II #123
5|#7 1 2 5 #6 7|	3g 35-Bauyn-II #93
6 5 4|3 2 1 #7 1|	3g 64-Lebègue-I #18
6 5 4 3 2 3 4 3 2 1|	2a 35-Bauyn-II #102
6 7 1|2 2 2 2|2	2a 47-Gen-2356 #10
|#6 #6 7|5 #4 5|#6 7 #6 7 5	3d 45-Dart #38
#6 7 1 2 2|2 3 2 1 7 #6 7|	3d 68-d'Anglebert #45
#6 #7 1|2 3 2 4 3 5 4 6 5 4 3 2|3	2f 37-Geoffroy #61
#6 #7 1|2 5 2 5 2|3 #3 4 5|	2a 35-Bauyn-II #103
|#6 #7 1 2 #7 1|#7 #6 5|5 #6	3d 35-Bauyn-II #37
|7 1 2|2|4 5 6|	3d 5-Munich-1503l #14
7 1 2 2 4 5 #6 #6 3 4 5 5	3d 7-Munich-1511f #15
|7 1 2 3 2 3|1 2 3 4 3 2|	2d 5-Munich-1503l #5
7 1 2|3 3 2 1 7 1 7 6|5	2a 62-Chamb-I #1
7|1 2 3 3 2 4 3 2|	3d 62-Chamb-I #14
7 1 2|3 4 5 1 2 1|	3a 62-Chamb-I #4
7 1 2|3 7 1 5 6|	3a 32-Oldham #26
7 1 2|3 7 1 7 6 5|	3d 63-Chamb-II #7
|7 1|6 5|2 3 4 3 2 1|	2e 35-Bauyn-III #35
|7 1 7|6 6|5|	3a 35-Bauyn-I #121
7 1|7 6 7 1 7 1|	2g 45-Dart #45

|7 3 2|1 1|2 2 2 #3|	3d 64-Lebègue-I #5
7|3 4 5|3 4 3|#7 5 5|	3a 2-Witzendorff #94
|7 3 5|4 4 5 4|3 3 2|	3a 64-Lebègue-I #32
|7 5|6 4|5 4 3 2 1|	3d 6-Munich-1511e #10
7 6 5 2 3 4	0d 7-Munich-1511f #18
7 6 5|4 2 5 4 3 2 3 4|2	3d 18-Ch-Ch-1236 #47
7 6 5 4 |7 3|	2a 35-Bauyn-III #42
|7 6|5 5 1 7|#6 7 7 6|	3g 64-Lebègue-I #22
7 6|5 5 4 3 2 3|4	3a 62-Chamb-I #2
|7 6 5|6 5 4|5 4 3 2 1|	3d 22a-Roper #56
7 6 5|6 5 4 5 4 3|2 5 3 6|	3a 46-Menetou #56
7 6|5 6 5 45 4|3 4 3 2 1 2|	2d 3-Berlin-40623 #72
7 6 5|6 5 4|6 3 2 1|♭2 1 7|	3d 37-Geoffroy #30
|7 #6 5 3 2|1 2 1 #7|1 5 #6 7|	3d 35-Bauyn-II #47
7|7 1|1 1 #7|	3a 66-Perrine #28
7|7 1 2 3|2 3 4 5|4 5 1 2|	3d 65-Lebègue-II #2
|7 7 1 2 3 2 3 4|5 4 5 6|	3a 35-Bauyn-II #107
|7 7 1 2 3 3|2 4 3 2|	3d 35-Bauyn-I #32
|7|7 1 2|3 3 4|	3a 35-Bauyn-I #117
7|7 1 5 6 6 5|5 5 6 5 4 3|2	3a 37-Geoffroy #112
7|7 1 7 6 5|4 3 4 5|6 7 5 1	3g 37-Geoffroy #213
7|7 1 7 6 5 6 6 5	3d 65-Lebègue-I #4
7|7 1 7 6 5 6 7|5 4 3 7 7|1 4 2	3a 37-Geoffroy #111
|7 7 3|2 2 3 2|1 4 5|	3e 35-Bauyn-II #65
7|7 4 5 6 6 5|5 6 4 5|6 7 5	3c 37-Geoffroy #3
|7 7 6|5 5 #6|7 #7|	3d 33-Rés-89ter #27
7|7 6 5 6 6 5|5 5 #6 7|1 7 6	3g 37-Geoffroy #83
7|7 6 6 5|5 5 5 #6|7	3d 35-Bauyn-II #40
|7 7|7 1 2|3 3 4|	3a 62-Chamb-I #5
|7 7|7 1 2 3|4 1 2|	2g 35-Bauyn-I #108
7|7|7 1 7 6 5 5 6 7 4 5 3|4	2d 37-Geoffroy #23
7|7 7 1 7 6 5|6 6 5 4 5 4|	3g 65-Lebègue-II #8
7 7|7 5 1|1 #7|	3d 33-Rés-89ter #26
7 7|7 5 6 7|	2d 36-Parville #11
7 7|7 5 6 7|1 1 7 6 6|	2d 46-Menetou #28
7|7 7 6|5 4|	3a 66-Perrine #23
|7|7 7 6|5 4 5|	2a 35-Bauyn-III #79
7|7 7 6 5 6|5	2a 35-Bauyn-III #38
|7 7 7|7 1 7 #6|5 3 4|	3c 35-Bauyn-II #32
7 7 7|7 4 5 6 6 5|	3a 35-Bauyn-III #71
|7 7 7|7 6 5|3 3 4|	3g 68-d'Anglebert #23

|7 7 7|7|#6 7 #6 5|	3g	64-Lebègue-I #20
|7 7 7|7|7 6 5|	3g	35-Bauyn-II #96
7 7 7|7 7 7|6 6 6|	3d	35-Bauyn-II #49
|7 #7 1 2|5 5 6 5|4 5 5 4|	3g	65-Lebègue-II #9
|#7 1 2|2 2 3|	3d	32-Oldham #6
|#7 1 2 3 1 1|2 5 6 7	3a	38-Gen-2348/53 #8
#7 1 2 3|4 2 5 4 3 2|	2a	65-Lebègue-II #20
|#7 1 2|3 4 3 2|1 1|7 1 2 3 2 1|	3d	35-Bauyn-I #41
|#7 1 2|3 4 3 2 1 1|7 7 1 7 6|	3a	35-Bauyn-II #108
|#7 1 2|5 #6 #7|5 1 7 #6|	3d	66-Perrine #5
|#7 #7 1|2 3|3 2 3|1 1 2 3|	3a	37-Geoffroy #121
#7|#7 1 2 5 1 7|	3d	68-d'Anglebert #40
#7 #7|1 5 6 6|4 7 3|	2g	46-Menetou #112

APPENDIX C

WORK LISTS

The lists which follow provide eleven detailed indexes to the works of selected composers. Except for Lebègue, all of the major composers of seventeenth-century French harpsichord music are included. Lebègue is omitted because all of the works which can be definitely attributed to him are contained in *64-Lebègue-I* and *65-Lebègue-II;* the inventories for those two sources serve, then, as an index.

In addition, work lists for Gaultier, Lully and Tresure are provided, although they are here not considered to be seventeenth-century French harpsichord composers. Their works are nevertheless represented in sufficient numbers in the Catalog inventories to warrant an index. In these three cases, the indexes are not complete, as only the works found in sources which are discussed in this study are cited. In all cases, the numerals refer to the numbering systems used in the inventories in the Catalog.

In the cases of Gaultier and La Barre, it is impossible to assign all of the works to specific composers. The works of the composers with the same family name are given in a single list, with specific attributions indicated where possible.

Work List 1: d'Anglebert

Abbreviations:

D   Double by d'Anglebert of a work by another composer.

T   Transcription by d'Anglebert of a work by another composer.

		68-d'Anglebert	33-Rés-89ter	32-Oldham	36-Parville	35-Bauyn-III	45-Dart	51-LaBarre-11	46-Menetou	24-Babell	12-Walther	15-Berlin-30206
1	Prélude (G)	1	32	..	..	..	..	..	..	..	..	..
2	Allemande (G)	2	..	..	..	..	..	..	..	..	..	..
3	Courante (G)	3	..	..	..	..	..	..	..	..	..	..
3a	Double (G)	3a	..	..	..	..	..	..	..	..	..	..
4	Courante (G)	4	..	..	..	..	..	..	..	..	..	..
5	Courante (G)	5	..	..	..	..	..	..	..	..	..	..
6	Sarabande (G)	6	..	..	..	..	..	..	..	..	..	..
7	Gigue (G)	7	..	..	..	..	..	..	..	..	..	..
8	Gaillarde (G)	8	38	..	..	..	..	..	..	..	..	..
9	Chaconne (G)	9	..	..	..	..	..	..	..	..	..	..
10	Gavotte (G)	10	39	..	..	..	..	..	..	..	..	..
11	Menuet (G)	11	40	..	..	..	..	..	..	..	..	..
T12	Ouverture (G)	12	..	..	..	..	..	..	..	..	..	..
T13	Ritournelle (G)	13	..	..	..	..	..	..	..	..	..	..
T14	Menuet (G)	14	..	..	109	..	..	205	..	..	..	..
T15	Chaconne (G)	15	..	..	..	..	..	..	..	..	..	..
16	Gigue (G)	16	37	..	..	..	..	..	..	..	..	..
17	Prélude (g)	17	42a	..	..	..	..	..	..	..	..	..
18	Allemande (g)	18	..	..	..	..	..	..	..	..	..	..
19	Courante (g)	19	..	..	..	..	..	..	..	..	..	..
20	Courante (g)	20	..	..	..	..	..	..	..	..	..	..
T21	Courante (g)	21	42d	..	41	..	..	..	117	..	..	..
21a	Double (g)	21a	42e	..	41a	..	..	..	..	..	..	..
22	Sarabande (g)	22	..	..	..	..	..	..	..	..	..	..
T23	Sarabande (g)	23	..	..	141	..	..	..	..	..	..	..
24	Gigue (g)	24	..	..	..	..	..	..	..	..	..	..
T25	Gigue (g)	25	..	..	..	..	..	..	..	..	..	..
26	Gaillarde (g)	26	..	12	..	..	..	..	..	..	..	..
27	Passacaille (g)	27	44	..	..	..	..	..	..	..	..	..
T28	Menuet (g)	28	..	..	..	..	..	..	..	..	..	..

		68-d'Anglebert	33-Rés-89ter	32-Oldham	36-Parville	35-Bauyn-III	45-Dart	51-LaBarre-11	46-Menetou	24-Babell	12-Walther	15-Berlin-30206
29	Gavotte (g)	29	..	..	..	..	..	..	..	..	..	..
30	Gavotte (g)	30	..	..	..	..	..	..	..	..	..	..
31	Le Bergere Anette (g)	31	..	..	142	..	..	..	..	..	..	..
T32	Ouverture (g)	32	42b	..	..	..	..	..	..	..	..	..
T33	Les Sourdines (g)	33	..	..	..	..	..	..	..	..	..	..
T34	Les Songes agréables (g)	34	43	..	..	..	..	..	..	..	..	..
T35	Air d'Appolon (g)	35	..	..	..	..	..	..	..	..	..	..
36	Menuet de Poitou (g)	36	..	..	143	..	..	..	..	..	..	..
T37	Passacaille (g)	37	..	..	..	..	..	..	..	..	..	..
38	Prélude (d)	38	23	..	..	..	..	..	..	..	..	..
39	Allemande (d)	39	..	..	..	..	..	..	..	..	x	..
40	Courante (d)	40	..	..	..	..	..	..	..	..	x	..
40a	Double (d)	40a	..	..	..	..	..	..	..	..	x	..
41	Courante (d)	41	..	..	..	..	..	..	..	..	x	..
42	Sarabande (d)	42	..	..	..	..	..	..	..	..	x	..
43	Sarabande (d)	43	24	..	..	..	..	..	..	..	x	..
44	Gigue (d)	44	..	..	..	..	..	..	..	..	x	..
45	Gaillarde (d)	45	..	..	..	..	..	..	..	..	x	..
46	Gavotte (d)	46	..	..	..	..	..	..	..	..	..	..
47	Menuet (d)	47	..	..	..	..	..	..	..	..	..	..
T48	Ouverture (d)	48	..	..	..	..	..	..	..	..	..	..
49	Folies d'Espagne (d)	49	21	..	..	..	..	..	..	..	..	40
50	Allemande (D)	50	..	..	..	..	..	..	..	..	..	..
51	Courante (D)	51	..	..	..	..	..	..	..	..	..	..
52	Courante (D)	52	..	..	..	..	..	..	..	..	..	..
53	Sarabande (D)	53	..	..	..	..	..	..	..	..	..	..
54	Gigue (D)	54	..	..	..	..	..	..	..	..	..	..
T55	Chaconne (D)	55	..	..	..	..	..	206	..	..	..	..
56	Chaconne (D)	56	..	..	..	..	..	..	..	..	..	..
57	Tombeau (D)	57	..	..	..	..	..	..	..	..	..	..
58	Prélude (C)	..	1	..	..	..	..	..	..	..	..	..
59	Allemande (C)	..	1a	..	..	..	..	..	..	..	..	..
D60	(Courante) (C)	..	2a	..	..	..	..	..	..	..	..	..
D61	(Courante) (C)	..	3a	..	..	..	..	..	..	..	..	..
T62	Sarabande (C)	..	4	..	..	..	..	..	..	..	..	..
D62a	Double (C)	..	4a	..	..	..	..	..	..	..	..	..
D63	(Gigue) (C)	..	5a	..	..	..	..	..	..	..	..	..
64	Gaillarde (C)	..	6	..	..	63	..	..	..	..	..	..
64a	Double (C)	..	6a	..	..	..	..	..	..	..	..	..
65	Chaconne (C)	..	7	..	65	..	39	212 229	..	204	..	..

		68-d'Anglebert	33-Rés-89ter	32-Oldham	36-Parville	35-Bauyn-III	45-Dart	51-LaBarre-11	46-Menetou	24-Babell	12-Walther	15-Berlin-30206
T66	Bourrée (C)	..	8	..	..	..	..	..	..	..	..	..
T67	Les Démons (C)	..	9	..	..	..	..	..	..	..	..	..
T68	Les Démons (C)	..	9a	..	..	..	..	..	..	..	..	..
T69	Marche (C)	..	10	..	..	..	..	..	..	..	..	..
T70	Gigue (C)	..	11	..	..	..	..	..	..	..	..	..
T71	Courante (C)	..	12	..	..	..	..	..	..	..	..	..
T72	Courante (C)	..	13	..	..	..	..	..	..	..	..	..
T73	Sarabande (C)	..	14	..	..	..	..	..	..	..	..	..
T74	Courante (C)	..	15	..	..	..	..	..	..	..	..	..
T75	Allemande (C)	..	16	..	..	..	..	..	..	..	..	..
T76	Courante (C)	..	17	..	..	..	..	..	..	..	..	..
T77	Chaconne (C)	..	18	..	..	..	..	..	..	..	..	..
78	Gaillarde (a)	..	20	..	..	..	..	..	..	..	..	..
D79	(Sarabande) (F)	..	22a	..	..	..	..	..	..	..	..	..
T80	Courante (d)	..	25	..	17	..	..	..	..	..	..	..
T81	Courante (d)	..	26	..	..	..	..	..	..	..	..	..
T82	Sarabande (d)	..	27	..	..	..	..	..	..	..	..	..
T83	Gigue (d)	..	28	..	..	..	..	..	..	..	..	..
T84	Courante (d)	..	29	..	..	..	..	..	..	..	..	..
T85	Sarabande (d)	..	30	..	..	..	..	..	..	..	..	..
D86	(Allemande) (G)	..	33a	..	..	..	..	..	..	..	..	..
D87	(Courante) (G)	..	34a	..	..	..	..	..	..	..	..	..
D88	(Courante) (G)	..	35a	..	..	..	..	..	..	..	..	..
D89	(Sarabande) (G)	..	36a	..	..	..	..	..	..	..	..	..
D90	(Sarabande) (G)	..	41a	..	..	..	..	..	..	..	..	..
T91	Sarabande (G)	..	42	..	..	..	..	..	..	..	..	..
T92	Ouverture (g)	..	42c	..	..	..	..	..	..	..	..	..
93	Courante (C)	..	..	4	..	..	..	..	..	..	..	..

Work List 2: Chambonnières

Abbreviations:

? Uncertain attribution

#		Brunold-Tessier	62-Chamb-I	63-Chamb-II	32-Oldham	35-Bauyn-I	36-Parville	38-Gen-2348/53	47-Gen-2356	45-Dart	60-Playford	33-Rés-89ter	55-Redon	52-Rés-2671	53-Oldham-2	2-Witzendorff	5-Munich-1503ℓ	8-Hintze	18-Ch-Ch-1236	23-Tenbury	24-Babell	44-LaPierre	22a-Roper	35-Bauyn-II
1	Allemande (a)	1	1		29	110																		
2	Courante (a)	2	2		30	112																		
2a	Double (a)	2a	2a		30a	112a																		
3	Courante (a)	3	3		27	116	3																	
4	Courante (a)	4	4				5																	
5	Sarabande (a)	5	5			117											94							
6	Gaillarde (a)	6	6			123																		
7	Allemande la Dunquerque (C)	7	7			3																		
8	Courante Iris (C)	8	8			9	61		12			2	23		107				15	3	58 34A	18	58	
9	Courante (C)	9	9			23	62					3												
10	Sarabande de la reyne (C)	10	10			19																		
11	Allemande la loureuse (d)	11	11		23	30	21													184				
12	Courante la toute belle (d)	12	12		10	31	19																	
13	Courante de madame (d)	13	13		11	34	20																	
14	Courante (d)	14	14		13	37																		
15	Sarabande (d)	15	15			38														220				
16	Les Barricades (d)	16	16			36																		
17	Gigue la madelainette (d)	17	17			56									14									
18	Gigue (d)	18	18			58																		
19	Allemande (F)	19	19			60																		
20	Courante (F)	20 101	20			65																		
21	Courante (F)	21	21			66																		
22	Courante (F)	22	22			62	18																	
23	Sarabande (F)	23	23			79	81																	
24	Pavane (g)	24	24			107																		
25	Courante (g)	25	25																					
26	Sarabande (g, a)	26 133	26		25	118																		
27	Courante (g)	27	27																					
28	Sarabande (G)	28	28			95																		
29	Gigue la villageoise (G)	29	29			98		38																
30	Canarie (G)	30	30			99	96	25																
31	Allemande (C)	31		1		5																		
32	Courante (C)	32		2																				
33	Courante (C)	33		3		13																		
34	Gaillarde (C)	34 75		4		20																		
35	Gigue la verdinguette (C)	35		5		22				5														
36	Allemande (d)	36		6		29		39																
37	Courante (d)	37		7																				
38	Courante (d)	38		8																				
39	Courante (d)	39		9																				
40•	Sarabande (d)	40		10		39																		
41	Allemande (D)	41		11																				
42	Courante (D)	42		12				28																
43	Courante (D)	43		13		55		29																
44	Courante (D)	44		14		50																		
45	Sarabande (D)	45		15		53																		
46	Allemande (F)	46		16		61																		
47	Courante (F)	47		17		76		10																
48	Courante (F)	48		18		72		20																
49	Sarabande (F)	49		19		17																		
50	Pavane (F)	50		20		109																		

#	Title	Brunold-Tessier	62-Chamb-I	63-Chamb-II	32-Oldham	35-Bauyn-I	36-Farville	38-Gen-2348/53	47-Gen-2356	45-Dart	60-Playford	33-Rés-89ter	55-Redon	52-Rés-2671	53-Oldham-2	2-Witzendorff	5-Munich-1503ℓ	8-Hintze	18-Ch-Ch-1236	23-Tenbury	24-Babell	44-LaPierre	22a-Roper	35-Bauyn-II
51	Gigue (g)	51	..	21	..	..	..	..	..	..	..	..	..	..	..	..	..	..	..	..	248	..	..	..
52	Courante (g)	52	..	22	..	103	..	1	..	..	..	..	..	..	..	..	..	..	..	..	..	..	..	..
53	Gigue (g)	53	..	23	..	..	..	..	..	..	..	..	..	..	..	..	..	..	..	..	..	..	..	..
54	Allemande (G)	54	..	24	..	..	..	..	..	..	..	..	..	..	..	..	..	..	..	..	..	..	..	..
55	Gigue (G)	55	..	25	..	..	..	..	..	..	..	..	..	..	..	..	..	..	..	..	..	..	..	..
56	Courante (G)	56	..	26	19	92	92	36	..	..	..	34	..	..	..	..	..	..	..	40	87	..	..	..
57	Courante (G)	57	..	27	9	88	90	36	..	..	..	35	..	..	..	..	..	..	..	..	..	..	..	..
58	Courante (G)	58	..	28	7	91	91	33	..	..	..	35	..	..	..	..	..	..	..	..	..	..	42	..
59	Sarabande jeunes zéphirs (G)	59	..	29	8	96	93	..	55	..	..	36	..	..	..	..	1	..	..	..	..	..	..	..
60	Menuet (G)	60	..	30	..	..	..	..	..	..	..	..	..	..	..	..	..	..	..	..	..	..	..	..
61	Sarabande (d)	85	..	..	14	40	..	..	..	..	..	..	..	..	..	..	..	..	..	..	..	..	..	..
62	Le Printemps (a)	142	..	..	15/15a	..	145	..	2	..	..	..	..	..	..	..	..	..	..	..	..	..	..	..
63	Sarabande (a)	..	..	..	16	..	..	..	..	..	..	..	..	..	..	..	..	..	..	..	..	..	..	..
64	Gigue (a)	..	..	..	18	..	..	..	..	..	..	..	..	..	..	..	..	..	..	..	..	..	..	..
65	Sarabande (G)	..	..	..	20	..	..	..	..	..	..	..	..	..	..	..	..	..	..	..	..	..	..	..
66	L'Estourdie (G)	..	..	..	21	..	..	..	..	..	..	..	..	..	..	..	..	..	..	..	..	..	..	..
67	Allemande le moutier (C)	61	..	..	22	1	60	..	..	..	..	..	..	..	..	..	..	..	..	..	200	..	..	..
68	Gaillarde (B♭)	141	..	..	24	127	..	..	..	..	..	..	..	..	..	..	..	..	..	..	..	..	..	..
68a	Double (B♭)	141	..	..	24a	127a	..	..	..	..	..	..	..	..	..	..	..	..	..	..	..	..	..	..
69	Courante (a)	..	..	..	26	..	..	..	..	..	..	..	..	..	..	..	..	..	..	..	..	..	..	..
70	Gigue la vetille (a)	137	..	..	28	122	..	..	8	..	..	..	..	..	..	..	..	..	..	..	..	..	..	..
71	Allemande (C)	62	..	..	..	2	..	..	..	..	..	..	..	..	..	..	..	..	..	..	..	..	..	..
72	Allemande (C)	63	..	..	..	4	..	..	..	..	..	..	..	..	..	..	..	..	..	..	..	..	..	..
73	Courante (C)	64	..	..	..	6/94	..	..	..	..	..	..	..	..	..	..	..	..	..	..	..	..	..	..
74	Courante la sotise (C)	65	..	..	..	7	148	..	..	..	..	..	..	..	..	..	..	..	..	..	206	..	..	..
75	Courante (C)	66	..	..	..	8	..	..	..	..	..	..	..	..	..	..	..	..	..	..	..	..	..	..
76	Courante (C)	67	..	..	..	10	..	..	..	..	..	..	..	..	..	..	..	..	..	..	..	..	..	..
77	Courante (C)	68	..	..	..	11	..	..	..	..	..	..	..	..	..	..	..	..	..	..	..	..	..	..
78	Courante (C)	69	..	..	..	12	..	..	..	..	..	..	..	..	..	..	..	..	..	..	..	..	..	..
79	Courante (C)	70	..	..	..	14	..	..	..	..	..	..	..	..	..	..	..	..	..	..	..	..	..	..
80	Courante (C)	71	..	..	..	15	..	..	..	..	..	..	..	..	..	..	..	..	..	..	..	..	..	..
81	Courante (C)	72	..	..	..	16	..	..	..	..	..	..	..	..	..	..	..	..	..	..	..	..	..	..
82	Sarabande (C)	73	..	..	..	17	..	..	..	..	..	..	..	..	..	..	..	..	..	..	..	..	..	..
?83	Sarabande (C)	74	..	..	..	18	..	..	..	..	..	..	..	..	..	..	..	..	..	..	..	..	..	28
84	Gigue (C)	76	..	..	..	21	..	..	..	..	..	..	..	..	..	..	..	..	..	..	..	..	..	..
85	Courante (C)	77	..	..	..	24	..	..	..	..	..	..	..	..	..	..	..	..	..	..	..	..	..	..
86	Courante (C)	78	..	..	..	25	..	..	..	..	..	..	..	..	..	..	..	..	..	..	..	..	..	..
87	Courante (C)	79	..	..	..	26	..	..	..	..	..	..	..	..	..	..	..	..	..	..	..	..	..	..
88	Courante (C)	80	..	..	..	27	..	..	..	..	..	..	..	..	..	..	..	..	..	..	..	..	..	..
89	Chaconne (C)	81	..	..	..	28	..	..	..	..	..	..	..	..	..	..	..	..	..	..	..	..	..	..
90	Courante (d)	82	..	..	..	32	..	..	..	..	..	..	..	..	..	..	..	..	..	..	..	..	..	..
91	Courante (d)	83	..	..	..	33	..	..	..	..	..	..	..	..	..	..	..	..	..	..	..	..	..	..
92	Courante (d)	84	..	..	..	35	..	..	..	..	..	..	..	..	..	..	..	..	..	3	186	..	..	..
92a	Double (d)	84	..	..	..	35a	..	..	..	..	..	..	..	..	..	..	..	..	..	..	..	..	..	..
93	Sarabande (d)	86	..	..	..	41	..	..	..	..	..	..	..	..	..	..	..	..	..	..	..	..	..	..
94	Pavane (d)	87	..	..	..	42	..	..	..	..	..	..	..	..	..	..	..	..	..	..	..	..	..	..
95	Sarabande (d)	88	..	..	..	43	..	..	..	..	..	..	..	..	..	..	..	..	..	..	..	..	..	..
96	Allemande la mignonne (D)	89	..	..	..	44	..	..	..	..	..	..	..	..	..	..	..	..	..	..	..	..	..	..
97	Courante (D)	90	..	..	..	45	..	27	..	..	..	..	..	..	..	..	..	..	..	..	..	..	..	..
98	Courante (D)	91	..	..	..	46	..	..	..	..	..	..	..	..	..	..	..	..	..	..	..	..	..	..
99	Courante (D)	92	..	..	..	47	..	32	..	..	..	..	..	..	..	..	..	..	..	..	..	..	..	..
100	Courante (D)	93	..	..	..	48	..	..	..	..	..	..	..	..	..	..	..	..	..	..	..	..	..	..
101	Courante (D)	94	..	..	..	49	..	31	..	..	..	..	..	..	..	..	..	..	..	..	..	..	..	..
102	Courante (D)	95	..	..	..	51	..	..	..	..	..	..	..	..	..	..	..	..	..	..	..	..	..	..
103	Sarabande (D)	96	..	..	..	52	..	26	..	..	..	..	..	..	..	..	..	..	..	..	..	..	..	..
104	Courante (D)	97	..	..	..	54	..	..	..	..	..	..	..	..	..	..	..	..	..	..	..	..	..	..
105	Gigue bruscanbille (D)	98	..	..	..	57	..	..	..	..	..	..	..	..	..	..	..	..	..	..	..	..	..	..
106	Gigue (e)	99	..	..	..	59	34	..	..	..	..	..	..	..	..	..	..	..	..	..	..	..	..	..
107	Courante (F)	100	..	..	..	63/64/73	9	..	..	..	..	..	..	..	..	..	..	..	..	..	..	..	..	..

No.	Title	Brunold-Tessier	62-Chamb-I	63-Chamb-II	32-Oldham	35-Bauyn-I	36-Parville	38-Gen-2348/53	47-Gen-2356	45-Dart	60-Playford	33-Rés-89ter	55-Redon	52-Rés-2671	53-Oldham-2	2-Witzendorff	5-Munich-1503ℓ	8-Hintze	18-Ch-Ch-1236	23-Tenbury	24-Babell	44-LaPierre	22a-Roper	35-Bauyn-II
108	Courante (F)	102	..	..	..	67	..	..	..	..	..	..	..	..	..	..	..	..	..	..	..	..	..	..
109	Courante (F)	103	..	..	..	68	..	..	..	..	..	..	..	..	..	..	..	..	..	..	..	..	..	..
110	Courante (F)	104	..	..	..	69	..	14	..	..	..	..	..	..	..	..	..	..	..	..	..	..	..	..
111	Courante (F)	105	..	..	..	70 / 71	79 / 82	..	..	..	..	..	..	..	..	..	..	..	..	..	..	..	..	..
112	Rondeau (F)	106	..	..	..	74	..	21	..	..	..	..	..	..	..	..	..	..	..	..	..	..	..	..
113	Courante (F)	107	..	..	..	75	..	..	..	..	..	..	..	..	..	..	..	..	..	..	..	..	..	..
114	Courante (F)	108	..	..	..	77	..	..	..	..	..	..	..	..	..	..	..	..	..	..	..	..	..	..
115	Sarabande (F)	109	..	..	..	78	..	..	..	..	..	..	..	..	..	..	..	..	..	..	..	..	..	..
116	Sarabande (Volte) o beau jardin (F)	110	..	..	..	80	80	..	..	..	..	22	..	..	..	..	..	..	..	..	..	..	..	..
117	Sarabande (F)	111	..	..	..	81	..	16	..	..	..	..	..	..	..	..	..	..	..	..	..	..	..	..
118	Sarabande (F)	112	..	..	..	82	..	..	..	..	..	..	..	..	..	..	..	..	..	..	..	..	..	..
119	Chaconne (F)	113	..	..	..	83	86	..	..	..	..	..	..	..	..	..	..	..	..	..	..	..	..	..
120	Brusque (F)	114	..	..	..	84	..	12	..	..	..	..	..	..	..	..	..	..	..	..	..	..	..	..
121	Brusque (F)	115	..	..	..	85	..	13	..	..	..	..	..	..	..	..	..	..	..	..	..	..	..	..
122	Chaconne (F)	116	..	..	..	86	..	22	..	..	..	..	..	..	..	..	..	..	..	..	..	..	..	..
123	Courante (G)	117	..	..	..	87	..	..	..	..	..	..	..	..	..	..	..	..	..	..	..	..	..	..
124	Courante (G)	118	..	..	..	89	..	..	..	..	..	..	..	..	..	..	..	..	..	..	..	..	..	..
125	Courante (G)	119	..	..	..	90	..	..	..	..	..	..	..	..	..	..	..	..	..	..	..	..	..	..
126	Sarabande (G)	120	..	..	..	93	..	37	..	..	..	..	..	..	..	..	..	..	..	..	..	..	..	..
127	Sarabande (G)	121	..	..	..	97	94	..	..	..	..	..	..	..	..	..	..	..	..	..	..	..	..	..
128	Gigue (G)	122	..	..	..	100	95	..	..	..	..	..	..	..	..	..	..	..	..	..	..	..	..	..
129	Chaconne (G)	123	..	..	..	101	..	..	..	..	..	..	..	..	..	..	..	..	..	..	..	..	..	..
130	Allemande l'affligée (g)	124	..	..	..	102	..	..	..	..	..	..	..	..	..	..	..	..	..	..	..	..	..	..
131	Sarabande (g)	125	..	..	..	104	40	..	..	..	..	..	..	..	..	..	..	..	..	..	..	..	..	..
132	Gigue (g)	126	..	..	..	105	..	..	..	..	..	..	..	..	..	..	..	..	..	..	..	..	..	..
133	Gigue (g)	127	..	..	..	106	..	..	..	..	..	..	..	..	..	..	..	..	..	..	..	..	..	..
134	Favane (g)	128	..	..	..	108	..	..	..	..	..	..	..	..	..	..	..	..	..	..	..	..	..	..
135	La Drollerie (a)	129	..	..	..	111	..	..	..	..	..	..	..	..	..	..	..	..	..	..	..	..	..	..
136	Courante (a)	130	..	..	..	113	..	..	..	..	..	..	..	..	..	..	..	..	..	..	..	..	..	..
137	Courante (a)	131	..	..	..	114	..	..	..	..	..	..	..	..	..	..	..	..	..	..	..	..	..	..
138	Courante (a)	132	..	..	..	115	..	..	..	..	..	..	..	..	..	..	..	..	..	..	..	..	..	..
139	Sarabande (a)	134	..	..	..	119	..	4	..	..	..	..	..	..	..	..	..	..	..	..	..	..	..	..
140	Sarabande (a)	135	..	..	..	120	..	6	..	..	..	..	..	..	..	..	..	..	..	..	..	..	..	..
141	Sarabande (a)	136	..	..	..	121	..	..	..	..	..	..	..	..	..	..	..	..	..	..	..	..	..	..
142	Allemande (B♭)	138	..	..	..	124	..	..	..	..	..	..	..	..	..	..	..	..	..	..	..	..	..	..
143	Courante (B♭)	139	..	..	..	125	..	..	..	..	..	..	..	..	..	..	..	..	..	..	..	..	..	..
144	Sarabande (B♭)	140	..	..	..	126	..	..	..	..	..	..	..	..	..	..	..	..	..	..	..	..	..	..
145	Courante (C)	..	..	..	..	..	63	..	..	..	..	..	..	..	..	..	..	..	..	..	..	..	..	..
146	Sarabande (d)	..	..	..	..	..	..	..	..	61	..	..	..	..	..	..	..	..	..	..	..	..	..	..
147	Courante (d)	..	..	..	..	..	..	..	..	62	..	..	..	..	..	..	..	..	..	..	..	..	..	..
148	Sarabande (C)	..	..	..	..	..	..	..	..	..	71	..	..	..	..	..	..	..	..	..	..	..	..	..

<u>**Work List 3**</u>: <u>**Louis Couperin**</u>

Abbreviations:

? Uncertain attribution.

D Double by Couperin of a work by another composer.

No.		35-Bauyn-II	36-Parville	32-Oldham	33-Rés-89ter	35-Bauyn-I	35-Bauyn-III	47-Gen-2356	38-Gen-2348/53	40-Rés-476	45-Dart	49-RésF-933	23-Tenbury	24-Babell	31-Madrid-1360
1	Prélude (d)	1	2	..	..	..	..	..	..	..	..	..	..	..	..
2	Prélude (D)	2	25	..	..	..	..	..	..	..	..	..	..	..	..
3	Prélude (g)	3	35	..	..	..	..	..	..	..	..	..	..	..	..
4	Prélude (g)	4	..	..	..	..	..	..	..	..	..	..	..	..	..
5	Prélude (g)	5	..	..	..	..	..	..	..	..	..	..	..	..	..
6	Préluae (a)	6	45	..	..	..	..	..	..	..	..	..	..	..	..
7	Prélude (a)	7	46	..	..	..	..	..	..	..	..	..	..	..	..
8	Prélude (A)	8	..	..	..	..	..	..	..	..	..	..	..	..	..
9	Prélude (C)	9	..	..	..	..	..	..	..	..	..	..	..	..	..
10	Prélude (C)	10	58	..	..	..	..	..	..	..	..	..	..	..	..
11	Prélude (C)	11	59	..	..	..	..	..	..	..	..	..	..	..	..
12	Prélude (F)	12	75	..	..	..	..	..	..	..	..	..	..	..	..
13	Prélude (F)	13	76	..	..	..	..	..	..	..	..	..	..	..	..
14	Prélude (e)	14	101	..	..	..	..	..	..	..	..	..	..	..	..
15	Allemande (C)	15	..	..	..	..	..	..	..	..	..	..	..	..	..
16	Courante (C)	16	..	..	..	..	..	..	..	..	..	..	..	..	..
17	Courante (C)	17	..	..	..	..	..	..	..	..	..	..	..	..	..
18	Courante (C)	18	..	..	..	..	..	..	..	..	..	..	..	..	..
19	Courante (C)	19	..	..	..	..	..	..	..	..	..	..	..	..	..
20	Sarabande (C)	20	..	..	..	..	..	..	..	..	..	..	..	..	..
21	Sarabande (C)	21	..	..	..	..	..	..	..	..	..	..	..	..	..
22	Sarabande (C)	22	..	..	..	..	..	..	..	..	..	..	..	..	..
23	Sarabande (C)	23	..	..	..	..	..	..	..	..	..	..	..	..	..
24	Sarabande (C)	24	..	..	..	..	..	..	..	..	..	..	..	..	..
25	Sarabande (C)	25	..	..	..	..	..	..	..	..	..	..	..	..	..
26	Chaconne (C)	26	..	..	..	..	..	..	..	..	..	..	..	..	..
27	Passacaille (C)	27	..	..	..	..	..	..	..	..	..	..	..	..	..
?28	Sarabande (C)	28	..	..	18	..	..	..	..	..	..	..	..	..	..
29	Menuet (C)	29	..	..	..	..	..	..	..	..	..	..	..	..	..
30	Allemande la précieuse (c)	30	70	..	..	..	..	..	..	..	..	..	..	..	..
31	Courante (c)	31	71	..	..	..	..	..	..	..	..	..	..	..	..
32	Sarabande (c)	32	72	..	..	..	..	..	..	..	..	..	..	..	..
33	Gigue (c)	33	73	..	..	..	..	..	..	..	..	..	..	..	..
34	Chaconne la bergeronette (c)	34	74	..	..	..	..	..	..	..	..	..	..	..	..

		35-Bauyn-II	36-Parville	32-Oldham	33-Rés-89ter	35-Bauyn-I	35-Bauyn-III	47-Gen-2356	38-Gen-2348/53	40-Rés-476	45-Dart	49-Rés-933	23-Tenbury	24-Babell	31-Madrid-1360
35	Allemande (d)	35	..	..	..	..	..	..	..	..	..	..	..	..	..
36	Allemande (d)	36	4	..	..	..	..	..	..	..	..	..	..	..	..
37	Pièce de 3 sortes de mouvements (d)	37	..	..	..	..	..	..	..	..	..	..	..	..	..
38	Courante (d)	38	..	..	..	..	..	..	..	..	..	..	..	..	..
39	Courante (d)	39	10	..	..	..	..	..	..	..	..	..	..	..	..
40	Courante (d)	40	..	..	..	..	..	..	..	..	..	..	..	..	..
41	Courante (d)	41	5	..	..	..	..	..	..	..	..	..	..	222	..
42	Courante (d)	42	..	..	..	..	..	..	..	..	..	..	..	..	..
43	Courante (d)	43	..	..	..	..	..	..	..	..	..	..	..	..	..
44	Sarabande (d)	44	..	..	..	..	..	..	..	..	..	..	..	..	..
45	Sarabande (d)	45	..	..	..	..	..	..	..	..	..	..	..	..	..
46	Sarabande (d)	46	..	..	..	..	..	..	..	..	..	..	..	..	..
47	Sarabande (d)	47	..	..	..	..	..	..	..	..	..	..	..	..	..
48	Sarabande (d)	48	..	..	..	..	..	..	..	..	..	..	..	..	..
49	Sarabande (d)	49	6	..	..	..	..	..	..	..	..	..	..	..	..
50	Sarabande (d)	50	..	..	..	..	..	..	..	..	..	..	..	..	..
51	Sarabande (d)	51	.:	..	..	..	..	..	..	..	..	..	..	..	..
52	Canarie (d)	52	8	..	..	..	..	..	..	..	..	..	..	..	..
53	Volte (d)	53	..	..	..	..	..	..	..	..	..	..	..	..	..
54	La Pastourelle (d)	54	9	..	..	..	..	..	..	..	..	..	..	..	..
55	Chaconne (d)	55	12	..	..	..	..	..	..	..	..	..	..	..	..
56	Sarabande (d)	56	..	..	..	..	..	..	..	..	..	..	..	..	..
57	Chaconne la complaignante (d)	57	13	..	..	..	..	..	..	..	..	..	..	..	..
58	Allemande (D)	58	26	..	..	..	..	..	..	..	..	..	..	..	..
59	Courante (D)	59	..	..	..	..	..	..	..	..	..	..	..	..	..
60	Sarabande (D)	60	28	..	..	..	..	..	..	..	..	..	..	..	..
61	Gaillarde (D)	61	..	..	..	..	..	..	..	..	..	..	..	..	..
62	Chaconne (D)	62	27	..	..	..	..	..	..	..	..	..	..	..	..
63	Allemande de la paix (e)	63	30	..	..	..	..	..	..	..	..	..	..	..	..
64	Courante (e)	64	31	..	..	..	..	..	..	..	..	..	..	..	..
65	Sarabande (e)	65	32	..	..	..	..	..	..	..	..	..	..	..	..
66	Allemande (F)	66	..	..	..	..	..	..	..	..	..	..	..	..	..
67	Allemande grave (F)	67	77	..	..	..	..	..	..	..	..	..	..	..	..
68	Courante (F)	68	78	..	..	..	..	..	..	..	..	..	..	..	..
69	Courante (F)	69	..	..	..	..	..	..	..	..	..	..	..	..	..
70	Courante (F)	70	..	..	..	..	..	..	..	..	..	..	..	..	..
71	Courante (F)	71	..	..	..	..	..	..	..	..	..	..	..	..	..
72	Sarabande (F)	72	85	..	..	..	..	..	..	..	..	..	..	..	..
73	Branle de Basque (F)	73	..	..	..	..	..	..	..	..	..	..	..	..	..
74	Sarabande (F)	74	..	..	..	..	..	..	..	..	..	..	..	..	..
75	Sarabande (F)	75	..	..	..	..	..	..	..	..	..	..	..	..	..
76	Gigue (F)	76	..	..	..	..	..	..	..	..	..	..	..	..	..
77	Gaillarde (F)	77	84	..	..	..	..	..	..	..	..	..	..	..	..
78	Chaconne (F)	78	..	..	..	..	..	..	..	..	..	..	..	..	..

		35-Bauyn-II	36-Parville	32-Oldham	33-Rés-89ter	35-Bauyn-I	35-Bauyn-III	47-Gen-2356	38-Gen-2348/53	40-Rés-476	45-Dart	49-Rés.F-933	23-Tenbury	24-Babell	31-Madrid-1360
79	Gigue (F)	79	..	..	..	..	..	..	..	..	..	..	..	..	..
80	Chaconne (F)	80	..	..	..	..	..	..	..	..	..	..	..	..	..
81	Tombeau (F)	81	..	..	..	..	..	..	..	..	..	..	..	..	..
82	Allemande (G)	82	88	..	33	..	..	5	..	..	..	..	..	252	..
83	Allemande (G)	83	..	..	..	..	..	..	..	..	..	..	..	..	..
84	Courante (G)	84	89	..	..	..	..	..	..	..	..	..	..	253	..
85	Courante (G)	85	..	..	..	..	..	..	..	..	..	..	..	..	..
86	Courante (G)	86	..	..	..	..	..	..	..	..	..	..	..	..	..
87	Sarabande (G)	87	98	..	..	..	..	..	..	..	..	..	..	254	..
88	Gaillarde (G)	88	100	..	..	..	..	..	..	..	..	..	..	..	..
89	Chaconne (G)	89	99	..	..	..	..	..	..	..	..	..	..	..	..
90	Courante (G)	90	..	..	..	..	..	..	23	..	..	..	..	..	..
91	Courante (G)	90a	..	..	..	..	..	..	24	..	..	..	..	..	..
92	Courante (G)	91	..	..	..	..	..	..	..	..	..	..	..	..	..
93	Allemande (g)	92	36	..	..	..	..	..	..	..	..	..	..	..	..
94	Courante (g)	93	37	..	..	..	..	..	..	..	..	..	..	..	..
95	Sarabande (g)	94	..	..	..	..	..	..	2	..	..	..	..	..	..
96	Passacaille (g)	95	39	..	..	..	..	..	..	..	..	..	..	..	..
97	Sarabande (g)	96	38	..	..	..	..	..	..	..	..	..	..	..	..
98	Passacaille (g)	99	..	..	..	..	..	..	..	..	..	..	..	..	..
99	Allemande (a)	100	..	..	..	..	..	..	..	..	..	..	..	..	..
100	Allemande (a)	101	..	..	..	..	..	..	..	..	..	..	..	..	..
101	Allemande (a)	102	47	..	..	..	..	3	..	29	..	..	..	..	..
102	La Piémontoise (a)	103	..	..	..	..	..	..	..	..	..	..	..	..	..
103	Courante (a)	104	..	..	..	..	..	..	..	..	..	..	..	..	..
104	Courante (a)	105	..	..	..	..	..	..	..	..	..	..	..	..	..
105	Courante la mignonne (a)	106	48	..	..	..	..	4	..	..	..	..	..	..	..
106	Courante (a)	107	..	..	..	..	..	..	..	..	..	..	..	..	..
107	Sarabande (a)	108	..	..	..	..	..	..	..	..	..	..	..	..	..
108	Sarabande (a)	109	..	..	..	..	..	..	..	..	..	..	..	..	..
109	Sarabande (a)	110	50	109	..	..	..	..	..	..	..	..	..	..	..
110	Sarabande (a)	111	..	..	..	..	..	..	..	..	..	..	..	..	..
?111	Menuet de Poitou (a)	112	53	..	..	78	..	..	..	..	..	..	..	..	..
D111a	Double (a)	112a	53a	..	..	78a	..	..	..	..	..	..	..	..	..
112	Courante (A)	113	..	..	..	..	..	..	..	..	..	..	..	..	..
113	Sarabande en rondeau (A)	114	..	..	..	..	..	..	..	..	..	..	..	..	..
114	Gigue (A)	115	..	..	..	..	..	..	..	..	..	..	..	..	..
115	Allemande (b)	116	102	..	..	..	..	..	..	..	..	..	..	..	..
116	Courante (b)	117	103	..	..	..	..	..	..	..	..	..	..	..	..
117	Sarabande (b)	118	104	..	..	..	..	..	..	..	..	..	..	..	..
118	Allemande (Bb)	119	..	..	..	..	..	..	..	..	..	..	..	..	..
119	Courante (Bb)	120	..	..	..	..	..	..	..	..	..	..	..	..	..
120	Pavane (f#)	121	..	..	..	..	..	..	..	..	..	..	..	..	..
121	Chaconne (g)	122	..	..	..	..	..	..	..	..	..	..	..	..	..

		35-Bauyn-II	36-Parville	32-Oldham	33-Rés-89ter	35-Bauyn-I	35-Bauyn-III	47-Gen-2356	38-Geu-2348/53	40-Rés-476	45-Dart	49-RésF-933	23-Tenbury	24-Babell	31-Madrid-1360
122	Gigue (d)	123	7	..	..	..	..	6	..	..	..	..	..	..	..
?123	Prélude (d)	..	1	..	..	..	..	..	..	..	..	..	..	..	..
124	Gavotte (d)	..	11	..	..	..	..	..	..	..	..	..	..	..	..
D125	(Gavotte) (a)	..	52a	..	..	..	50a	..	..	..	..	13a	12a	59a	41a
D126	(Allemande) (C)	..	60a	..	..	1a	..	..	..	..	..	..	..	..	..
D127	(Rigaudon) (C)	..	67a	..	..	..	..	..	..	..	..	..	..	..	..
128	Prélude (c)	..	69	..	..	..	..	..	..	..	..	..	..	..	..
129	Prélude (G)	..	87	..	..	..	..	..	..	..	..	..	..	..	..
?130	Prélude (a)	..	144	..	..	..	..	..	..	..	..	..	..	..	..
D131	(Gavotte) (C)	..	146	..	..	..	54a	..	..	..	..	..	..	..	..
132	Allemande (a)	..	..	106	..	..	..	..	..	..	..	..	..	..	..
133	Courante (a)	..	..	107	..	..	..	..	..	..	..	..	..	..	..
134	Courante (a)	..	..	108	..	..	..	..	..	..	..	..	..	..	..
?135	Chaconne (G) (Louis Couperin?)	..	..	..	..	..	..	..	..	..	31	..	..	..	..

Work List 4: Dumont

		58-Dumont-1652	59-Dumont-1657	61-Dumont-1668	35-Bauyn-III	5-Munich-1503ℓ
1	Allemande grave (C)	x	..	..	86	..
2	Allemande (d)	..	x	..	..	..
3	Allemande grave (d)	..	x	..	..	..
4	Allemande (a)	..	..	x	..	..
5	Allemande (C)	..	..	..	56	..
6	Allemande (d)	..	..	..	57	..
7	Courante (d)	..	..	..	58	..
					87	
8	Allemande (d)	..	..	..	81	..
9	Allemande (a)	..	..	..	84	12
10	Allemande (C)	..	..	..	85	..
11	Pavane (d)	..	..	..	94	..
12	Allemande (C)	..	..	..	..	11
13	Allemande lente (d)	..	..	..	..	13

Work List 5: Gaultier

Abbreviations:

D   Denis Gaultier "le jeune" (1595/03-1672)
E   Ennemond Gaultier "le vieux" (ca. 1575-1651)
DE Work variously attributed to both Denis and Ennemond Gaultier
P   Pierre Gaultier "de Marseilles" (1643/4-1697)

		66-Perrine	33-Rés-89ter	35-Bauyn-III	36-Parville	45-Dart	24-Babell	14-Schwerin-619	4-Lynar	9-Ihre-284	Stockholm-2	Stockholm-176	Skara	Ottobeuren	Darmstadt-17	Darmstadt-18	31-Madrid-1360	51-LaBarre-11	55-Redon
E1	Courante l'immartelle (d)	1	29	..	..	40	226	..	..	..	32	4v	20	142	..	..	..	..	..
E2	Allemande, Tombeau de Mézangeau (d)	2	..	..	..	..	..	..	..	..	..	..	..	..	..	..	..	..	..
E3	Allemande/Gigue, Testament (d)	3	..	..	..	..	..	..	..	..	..	..	..	..	..	..	..	..	..
E4	Courante (d)	4	..	..	..	..	..	..	..	..	..	..	..	..	..	..	..	..	..
E5	Courante (d)	5	..	..	..	..	..	..	..	..	..	..	..	..	..	..	..	..	..
E6	Canarie (d)	6	..	..	..	..	..	..	..	..	..	..	..	..	..	..	..	..	..
E7	Allemande la poste (d)	7	28	..	..	..	..	..	..	..	..	..	..	..	..	..	..	..	..
E8	Courante (d)	8	..	..	..	..	..	..	..	..	..	..	..	..	..	..	..	..	..
E9	Courante (d)	9	..	..	..	..	..	..	..	..	..	..	..	..	..	..	..	..	..
E10	Gigue (Carillon) (d)	10	..	..	..	..	..	..	..	..	..	..	..	..	..	..	..	..	..
D11	Fantaisie (d)	11	..	..	..	..	..	..	..	..	..	..	..	..	..	..	..	..	..
D12	Gigue (d)	12	..	..	..	..	..	..	..	..	..	..	..	..	..	..	..	..	..
D13	Courante (d)	13	..	..	..	..	..	..	..	..	..	..	..	..	..	..	..	..	..
D14	Courante la royale (d)	14	..	..	..	..	..	..	..	..	..	..	..	..	..	..	..	..	..
D15	Courante (d)	15	..	..	..	..	..	..	..	..	..	..	..	..	..	..	..	..	..
D16	Sarabande (d)	16	30	..	..	..	..	..	..	..	..	..	..	..	..	..	..	..	..
DE17	Courante la Lyonaise (d)	17	..	..	..	..	..	..	..	..	..	..	..	..	..	..	..	..	..
DE18	Courante le canon (d)	18	..	..	..	..	..	..	..	..	34	5v	..	..	..	..	..	..	..
D19	Allemande grave, Tombeau (d)	19	..	..	..	..	..	..	..	..	..	..	..	..	..	..	..	..	..
E20	Courante/volte les larmes (a)	20	25	..	17	..	..	..	..	..	..	..	..	..	..	..	..	..	..
E21	Courante (a)	21	..	..	..	..	..	..	..	..	..	..	..	..	..	..	..	..	..
D22	Pavane (a)	22	..	..	..	..	..	..	..	..	..	..	..	..	..	..	..	..	..
D23	Courante (a)	23	..	..	..	..	..	..	..	..	..	..	..	..	..	..	..	..	..
DE24	Allemande, Tombeau de l'enclos (a)	24	..	..	..	..	..	..	..	..	..	..	..	..	..	8v	..	..	..
D25	Sarabande (a)	25	..	..	..	..	..	..	..	..	..	..	..	..	..	..	..	..	..
D26	Courante la belle ténébreuse (a)	26	..	..	..	..	..	..	..	..	..	..	..	..	..	..	..	..	..
D27	Chaconne/Sarabande (a)	27	..	..	..	..	..	..	..	..	..	..	..	..	..	..	..	..	..
E28	Courante la petite bergère (a, d)	28	26	..	..	..	..	..	..	..	..	..	..	..	..	..	..	..	..
E29	Sarabande (c)	29	..	..	..	..	..	..	..	..	..	..	..	..	..	..	..	..	..
E30	Pièce (c)	30	..	..	..	..	..	..	..	..	..	..	..	..	..	..	..	..	..
E31	Gigue (C)	..	11	..	..	..	..	..	..	..	..	..	..	..	..	..	..	..	..
E32	Courante (C)	..	12	..	..	..	..	..	..	..	..	..	..	..	..	..	..	..	..
E33	Courante la superbe (C)	..	13	..	..	..	..	..	..	..	..	..	..	..	..	..	..	..	..
E34	Courante (C)	..	15	..	..	..	..	..	..	..	..	..	..	..	..	..	..	..	..
E35	Allemande la vestemponade (C)	..	16	..	..	..	..	..	..	..	..	..	..	..	..	..	..	..	..
E36	Courante (C)	..	17	..	..	..	..	..	..	..	..	..	..	..	..	..	..	..	..
E37	Chaconne (C)	..	18	..	..	..	..	..	..	..	..	..	..	..	..	..	..	..	..
E38	Sarabande (d)	..	27	..	..	..	..	..	..	..	..	..	..	..	..	..	..	..	..
39	Sarabande (C)	..	..	64	..	..	..	..	..	..	..	..	..	..	..	..	..	..	..
40	Canarie (C)	..	..	65	..	..	..	..	..	..	..	..	..	..	..	..	..	..	..
P41	Les Plaisirs (g)	..	..	..	138	44	..	54 57	..	..	..	..	..	..	..	..	..	..	..
42	Rigaudon (a)	..	..	..	140	..	..	..	..	..	..	..	..	..	..	..	..	..	..
E43	Courante la belle homicide (a/d)	..	..	..	..	..	162	..	..	..	30	10v	..	..	..	..	..	..	..
44	Courante (d)	..	..	..	..	..	..	66	..	..	..	..	..	..	..	..	..	..	..
45	Allemande (G)	..	..	..	..	..	..	..	..	98	..	..	..	..	..	..	..	..	..
46	Sarabande (d)	..	..	..	..	..	..	..	..	..	..	..	..	..	21	..	..	..	..
47	Allemande (d)	..	..	..	..	..	..	..	..	..	..	..	..	..	22	..	..	..	..
48	Courante (d)	..	..	..	..	..	..	..	..	..	..	..	..	..	23	..	15v	..	..
49	Allemande la brave (d)	..	..	..	..	..	..	..	..	..	..	..	..	..	..	141	..	..	..

		66-Ferrine	33-Rés-89ter	35-Bauyn-III	36-Farville	45-Dart	24-Babell	14-Schwerin-619	4-Lynar	9-Ihre-284	Stockholm-2	Stockholm-176	Skara	Ottobeuren	Darmstadt-17	Darmstadt-18	31-Madrid-1360	51-LaBarre-11	55-Redon
50	Sarabande la courieuse (d)	..	..	..	..	..	..	..	..	..	..	..	..	142	..	..	..	..	..
51	Gigue l'estourdie (d)	..	..	..	..	..	..	..	..	..	..	..	..	143	..	..	..	..	..
52	Allemande l'industrie (F)	..	..	..	..	..	..	..	..	..	..	..	..	152	..	..	..	..	..
53	Allemande la bergère (G)	..	..	..	..	..	..	..	..	..	..	..	..	158	..	..	..	..	..
D54	Courante l'incomparable (G)	..	..	..	..	..	..	..	..	..	..	..	..	159	..	..	..	..	..
55	Sarabande la délicate (G)	..	..	..	..	..	..	..	..	..	..	..	..	159	..	..	..	..	..
56	Marche	..	..	..	..	..	..	..	..	..	..	..	..	..	..	..	37	..	..
75	Gigue (C)	..	..	..	..	..	..	..	..	..	..	..	..	..	..	..	..	..	4

Work List 6: Hardel

		35-Bauyn-III	36-Parville	32-Oldham	45-Dart	49-RésF-933	23-Tenbury	24-Babell	31-Madrid-1360	25-Bod-426	44-LaPierre	St-Georges
1	Allemande (d)	44	22	..	..	..	..	219	..	..	52	..
2	Courante (d)	45	..	31	..	..	..	..	..	..	54	..
3	Courante (d)	46	..	..	..	..	..	..	..	.•	..	..
4	Courante (d)	47	..	..	..	..	..	..	..	..	..	..
5	Sarabande (d)	48	..	..	..	..	..	221	..	..	..	..
6	Gigue (d)	49	..	..	..	..	..	147	..	..	..	..
7	Gavotte (a)	50	52	..	60	13	12	159	41	20	..	51

Work List 7: La Barre

Abbreviations:

? Uncertain attribution

Title	17-Rogers	16-Cosyn	18-Ch-Ch-1236	19-Heardson	20-Ch-Ch-378	22-Ch-Ch-1177	4-Lynar	27-Gresse	9-Ihre-284	3-Berlin-40623	31-Madrid-1360	1-Copenhagen-376	29-Chigi	59a-Handmaide	Oxford-IB	Drexel-5609	8-Hintze	36-Parville	35-Bauyn-III	24-Babell	56-Mersenne
1 Corrant Beare (d)	21		33																		
2 Selebrand Beare (d)	22		34					23				231									
3 Corrant Beare (C)	23 95	114	31													43	12 39				
4 Corrant Beare (d)	26																				
5 Corrant Beare (d)	27																				
? 6 Coranto Mr Tresure (LaBarre, LaBar, Monsu della Bara, Mr Gibbons) (d)		44	1 8	46		65	22							30	x						
7 Mr Bares Allmaine (unavailable)		p 251																			
8 Monsier Bares Allmaine (a)		87																			
9 Coranto to itt (a)		87a																			
?10 Allmaine (d)		99																			
11 Corant Mr Bare (d)		100	47																		
?12 Sellabrand (d)		101	6																		
?13 Corant (C)			32																		
14 Corant Labar (d)			9	64																	
?15 Corant la Barr (Treser) (G)			65		2																
?16 Corant Labar (Tresor) (G)			69											14							
?17 Allmaine (G)														13							
?18 Saraband (G)														15							
19 Saraband La Barr (é)							2														
20 Courante de La barre (D)									62												
?21 Corante (d)									63												
22 Auttre Corant de la Barre (d)									64												
23 Almande LB (d)									21		72	39									
?24 Allemand (C)									47												
25 Courant La Bar (C)									48												
?26 Saraband (d)									49												
27 [Corente di Monsu della Bara] (d)													31								
28 Sarabanda del mS (d)												40	32								
29 Courant (d)																		11			
30 Tu crois ô beau soleil (diminutions by Pierre III) (d)																					x
31 Prelude de Monsieur de la Barre (d)																		3			
32 Allemande La Barre (d)																		14			
33 Allemande la Barre (d)																		15		223	
34 Courante La Barre (d)																		16		224	
35 Sarabande la barre (d)																		18		187	
36 Courante Mr dela Barre [Allemande] (a)																		54			
37 Courante de M de labarre (a)																		55	69		
38 Gigue de Mr de labarre (a)																		56			
39 Courante la barre (F)																		83			
40 Allemande/Gigue de Mr De la barre (d)				3															32 66		
41 Allemande/Gigue de Mr Joseph De la barre (C)																			34 61		
42 Courante de Mr De la barre (C)																		55			

Lebègue: see 64-Lebègue-I and 65-Lebègue-II

Work List 8: Lully

Chronological List of Stage Works:

1654   Ballet de Thétis et Pélée [Lully/Collasse]
1657   Ballet de l'amour malade
1661   Ballet de l'Impatience
1665   Ballet de la Naissance de Venus
1666   Ballet des muses
1668,
1675   Le Carnaval (Mascarade de Versailles)
1668   La Grotte de Versailles
1669   Ballet de Flore
1670   Les Amants magnifiques
1670   Le Bourgeois Gentilhomme, Ballet des Nations
1672   Les Fêtes de l'Amour et de Bacchus
1673   Cadmus et Hermione
1674   Alceste
1675   Thésée
1675   Le Carnaval [see 1668]
1676   Atys
1677   Isis
1678   Psyché
1679   Bellérophon
1680   Proserpine
1681   Le Triomphe de l'Amour
1682   Persée
1683   Phaéton
1684   Amadis
1685   Roland
1685   Idylle sur la paix
1685   Ballet du temple de la paix
1686   Armide
1686   Acis et Galathée
1687   Achille et Polixène

Achille et Polixène (1687)

I-5 Passacaille (A) | 24-Babell #280

Acis et Galathée (1686)

	14-Schwerin-619	24-Babell	68-d'Anglebert	36-Parville	49-RésF-933	23-Tenbury	51-LaBarre-11	45-Dart	22a-Roper	44-LaPierre
Prologue Air (C)	..	..	..	67	..	..	..	37	51 / 53	14 / 25A
II-5 Chaconne (D)	123	97	55	29	4	75	206	..		
III-9 Passacaille (d)	50	..	..	..	..	..	..	..		

Alceste (1674)

Complete vocal score	48-LaBarre-6 #23a
Ouverture (a)	40-Rés-476 #39; 46-Menetou #113
Prologue Rondeau la gloire (C)	40-Rés-476 #40
Menuet les divinitez des fleuves (C)	31-Madrid-1360 # 24/8
Quel Coeur sauvage (C)	31-Madrid-1360 #24/9
IV-1 Alcide est vainqueur (Bb)	27-Gresse #29

Amadis (1684)

	46-Menetou	36-Parville	42-Vm7-6307-2	49-RésF-933	24-Babell	10-Schwerin-617	Stoss	Copenhagen-396	44-LaPierre
Ouverture (g)	13	..	..	..	..	..	47v	..	..
Prologue Suivons l'amour (G)	14	..	9	..	..	..	..	x	23 / 57A
Second Air Gigue (g)	24	..	..	..	..	..	..	..	..
I-4 Marche pour le combat de la barrière (C)	23	..	..	..	..	..	..	..	..
Second Air trompettes (C)	16	..	..	..	..	..	..	..	..
II-1 Prelude Arcabonne (F)	18	..	..	..	..	..	..	..	..
II-4 Bois épais (F)	21	..	..	..	..	..	..	..	..
II-7 Vous ne devez plus attendre (g)	20 / 39	110	8	23	..	19	..	..	..
IV-6 Menuet pour les suivants d'Ugande (A)	17	..	..	..	..	..	..	..	..
Coeurs accablés (A)	15	..	..	..	..	..	..	..	..
V-5 Chaconne (C)	..	66	..	..	209	..	..	..	..

Les Amants magnifiques (1670)

I Danse des pêcheurs (F)	28-Brussels-926 ℓ 6r
I Danse de Neptune (F)	28-Brussels-926 ℓ 7r
I Les Suivants de Neptune (F)	28-Brussels-926 ℓ 8r

Ballet de l'amour malade (1657)

Ouverture (g)	Grimm ℓ 88v
1-x 2me Air pour les mesmes Jean Doucet (g)	36-Parville ₦24

Armide (1686)

	46-Menetou	14-Schwerin-619	24-Babell	31-Madrid-1360	68-d'Anglebert	36-Parville	49-RésF-933	23-Tenbury	Minorite
Ouverture (C)	57	..	..	..	..	..	..	..	..
Prologue Entrée (a)	..	65	..	..	..	..	..	..	..
Gavotte rondeau (a)	60	..	..	..	..	..	..	..	..
Entrée (C)	58	..	..	..	..	..	..	..	..
Menuet (C)	..	..	..	24/7	..	..	..	..	..
Menuet (C)	59	..	..	..	..	..	..	..	..
II-4 Second Air (sourdines) (g)	..	64	124	..	33	115 149	2	49	..
V-2 Passacaille (g)	..	63	138	27	37	..	1	..	44v

Atys (1676)

	36-Parville	46-Menetou	47-Gen-2356	39-Vm7-6307-1	40-Rés-476	24-Babell	14-Schwerin-619	Lüneburg-1198	68-d'Anglebert	33-Rés-89ter	Grimm
Ouverture (g)	..	..	..	..	..	243	..	..	..	..	..
Prologue Les Plaisirs à ses yeux (g)	..	..	..	..	41	..	.	..	..	..	..
Air pour la suite de Flore (G)	..	..	..	..	..	..	58	..	..	..	..
II-4 Entrée des zéphirs (g)	..	..	..	..	..	132	55	..	..	..	..
Que devant nous (g)	..	..	..	..	..	..	..	79	..	..	..
III-4 Les Songes agrábles (g)	117	114	..	..	..	131	53	..	34	43	..
Entrée des songes funestes (B♭)	..	..	..	..	..	..	85	..	..	..	80v
[Les Songes funestes (B♭)]	..	115	..	..	..	..	86	..	..	..	..
IV-5 La Beauté la plus severe (C)	..	..	17	10	..	..	..	..	..	..	..
Unlocated											
Menuet d'Atys (C)	118	..	..	..	..	..	..	..	..	..	..

Bellérophon (1679)

	46-Menetou	14-Schwerin-619	24-Babell	40-Rés-476	27-Gresse	Bod-576
Ouverture (C)	87	83	199	26	53	54
I-5 Marche des Amazons (C)	90	122	..	..	..	..
III-5 Le Malheur (G)	91	..	..	..	..	..
V-3 Trompettes (C)	89	..	..	..	..	..

Le Bourgeois Gentilhomme (1670)

	36-Parville	24-Babell	23-Tenbury	50-Paignon	51-LaBarre-11
Ballet des Nations 3 1er Air des Espagnols (B♭)	130	269	80	10	..
Ballet des Nations 4 Chaconne des Scaramouches (G)	..	258	..	..	1

Cadmus et Hermione (1673)	68-d'Anglebert #12
Prologue-3 Entrée de l'envie (C)	14-Schwerin-619 #78
III-6 Marche des sacrificateurs (C)	14-Schwerin-619 #75, 44-LaPierre p 48

Le Carnaval (Mascarade de Versailles) (1668, 1675)	
Ouverture (g)	68-d'Anglebert #32, 33-Rés-89ter #42b
III Les Maîtres à danser (B♭)	28-Brussels-926 ℓ 11r
Canaries (B♭)	28-Brussels-926 ℓ 12v
[Canarie] (C)	31-Madrid-1360 #31
V Chaconne d'Arlequin (G)	49-RésF-933
VII Air pour les mariez (B♭)	23-Tenbury #79, 24-Babell #268

Les Fêtes de l'Amour et de Bacchus (1672)	
Ouverture (g)	46-Menetou #83, 14-Schwerin-619 #52

Ballet de Flore (1669)	
Ouverture (d)	23-Tenbury #56, 24-Babell #143
XV Menuet	27-Gresse # 36-Parville #124 Terburg 9-Ihre-284 #88

La Grotte de Versailles (1668)

	36-Parville	14-Schwerin-619	46-Menetou	49-RésF-933	Minorite
Complete vocal score	..	..	..	..	..
Ouverture (g)	121	121	118	3	44r
Air des echos (G)	..	59	..	..	..

Idylle sur la paix (1685)

Complete vocal score   48-LaBarre-6 #1
Chantons Bergers (d)   46-Menetou #53

Ballet de l'impatience (1661)
II-1 Entrée (g) (Bel Iris [d])

28-Brussels-926 ℓ 3r
3-Berlin-40623 #1
11-Ryge #48
Rés-819-2 ℓ 72r
Terburg
Skara #35
Van-Eijl #25
Stockholm-228 ℓ 20v

Isis (1677)

	36-Parville	46-Menetou	42-Vm7-6307-2	40-Rés-476	24-Babell	14-Schwerin-619	33-Rés-89ter	Stoss	49-RésF-933	27-Gresse	45-Dart	22a-Roper
Ouverture (g)	42	85	5	35	128	51	42c	24v	24	..	..	..
Prologue-3												
Prélude des muses (g)	..	..	..	..	..	118	..	..	..	..	..	..
1r Air pour les muses (g)	..	61	6	..	130	..	..	..	..	..	52	..
2e Air pour les muses (g)	127	..	..	38	..	..	..	..	..	..	..	..
Air (trompettes)	..	..	..	36	..	74	..	..	..	..	..	28
II-7 Les Plaisirs les plus doux (d)	..	..	..	..	..	..	..	..	..	37	..	..
Aimez, profitez (d)	..	..	..	..	..	..	..	..	..	38	..	..
2e Air (g)	..	..	7	..	..	..	..	..	..	..	..	..
Que ces Lieux (g)	..	..	10	..	..	..	..	..	..	40	..	..
III-6 3e Air (C)	..	..	..	37	..	..	..	..	..	..	..	..

Ballet des muses (1666)

II-2 Chaconne (B♭, C, G)   14-Schwerin-619 #111
                                 36-Parville #116
                                 46-Menetou #116
                                 50-Paignon #12
                                 Minorite ℓ 50r

Ballet de la naissance de Vénus (1665)

II-6 Sarabande Dieu des en-   24-Babell #247,
     fers (g)   36-Parville #141,
                                 68-d'Anglebert #23

Persée (1682)

	46-Menetou	36-Parville	14-Schwerin-619	48-LaBarre-6	Lüneburg-1198	Madrid-1357	31-Madrid-1360	24-Babell
Ouverture (a)	98	..	66	..	..	..	..	152
Prologue Hautbois (passepied) (a)	97	120	..	..	..	..	..	..
IV-6 Gigue (D)	99	..	..	..	..	..	38	..
Nostre espoit alloit (D)	..	..	..	32	69	..	..	..
Que n'aimez vous (D)	..	..	..	..	..	51	..	..
V-8 Passacaille (a)	96	..	67	..	⊚	..	..	..

Phaéton (1683)

	46-Menetou	14-Schwerin-619	24-Babell	43-Gen-2354	68-d'Anglebert	Berlin-30363	44-LaPierre
Ouverture (C)	1	77	..	..	..	..	..
Prologue							
Troupe d'Astrée dansante (C)	6	..	..	..	..	..	..
Cherchons la paix (C)	5	..	..	..	..	..	..
Dans ces Lieux (a)	8	..	..	..	..	..	..
Plaisirs venez sans crainte (C)	10	..	..	..	..	..	..
I-7 Rondeau (C)	2	..	..	..	..	..	..
Le Plaisir est necessaire (C)	3	..	..	..	..	..	..
II-3 Que l'Incertitude (C)	22	..	..	..	..	..	..
II-5 Chaconne (G)	9	61	263	1	15	..	24 45A
III-4 Air pour Merops (d)	..	..	..	..	..	1r	..
IV-1 1r Air le printemps (g)	107	..	120	..	..	..	..
Second Air (g)	101	..	..	..	..	..	..
Dans ce Palais (g)	4	..	..	..	..	..	..

Proserpine (1680)

	46-Menetou	14-Schwerin-619	36-Parville	68-d'Anglebert	23-Tenbury	22a-Roper
Ouverture (d)	92	..	..	48	..	..
Prologue Air [la discorde] (D)	..	60	..	..	46	..
Menuet (d)	..	..	112	..	..	..
Air de trompettes (C)	..	..	..	..	..	1
II-8 Second Air (a)	93	..	..	..	..	..

Psyché (1678)

Ouverture (C)   14-Schwerin-619 #82, 24-Babell #57

V-4 1r Air pour les suivants de Mars (D)   36-Parville #123, #147, 39-Vm7-6307-1 #12

Roland (1685)

	46-Menetou	14-Schwerin-619	36-Parville	45-Dart	Lüneburg-1198	24-Babell	Stockholm-228	43-Gen-2354	68-d'Anglebert	44-LaPierre	22a-Roper
Ouverture (d)	27	49	..	..	..	182	..	..	..	..	..
Prologue-1 Menuet (F)	36	..	..	..	..	..	..	..	..	..	..
Menuet (F)	35	..	..	..	..	..	..	..	..	..	..
Prologue-2 Gigue (d)	30	..	..	..	..	..	..	..	..	..	..
Gavotte (d)	29	..	..	..	..	..	..	..	..	..	..
C'est l'amour (d)	28	..	..	..	64	183	9v	..	..	..	..
I-6 Marche (D)	..	..	..	..	..	217	..	..	..	..	..
Entre-acte (D)	..	..	..	..	..	218	..	..	..	..	..
II-5 Entrée gavotte (a)	31	..	..	..	..	..	..	..	..	..	..
Qui gouste de ces eaux (a)	38	..	..	..	..	..	..	..	..	..	..
IV-2 J'entens un bruit (C)	33	..	..	..	..	..	..	..	..	40	..
IV-3 Le Marié marche (C)	32	..	..	..	..	..	..	..	..	..	..
Menuet (C)	37	..	..	..	..	..	..	2	..	..	..
Menuet hautbois (C)	33	..	..	..	..	..	..	..	..	40	..
V-2 Symphonie (G)	..	..	..	..	..	..	..	..	13	..	..
Unlocated La Mariée (G)	..	62	122	34 65	..	..	..	..	..	..	19

Ballet du temple de la paix (1685)

	46-Menetou	14-Schwerin-619	28-Brussels-926	48-LaBarre-6	24-Babell	31-Madrid-1360
Complete vocal score	..	..	..	1	..	..
Ouverture (a)	56	68	63v	..	..	..
Prologue						
Preparons nous (a)	40	..	..	..	123	..
Entrée de bergers et bergères (a)	45	..	..	..	..	..
La Gloire luy suffit (a)	42	..	..	..	..	..
Gigue (a)	44	..	..	..	..	..
Menuet (a)	43	..	..	..	..	..
On conteroit plus tost (C)	47	..	..	..	..	..
Entrée des Basques (a)	..	76	..	33	..	..
Suivons l'aimable paix (C)	51 52	..	..	..	..	..
Canaries (C)	48	..	..	..	..	..
Passepied (C)	..	..	..	..	..	36
Hautbois [passepied] (C)	49	..	..	..	..	..
Menuet (C)	50	..	..	..	..	..
Le Paix revient (C)	46	..	..	..	..	..

Thésée (1675)

	40-Rés-476	36-Parville	14-Schwerin-619	25-Bod-426	24-Babell	33-Rés-89ter	23-Tenbury	Inglis	44-LaPierre
Prologue Trompettes (Mars)(C)	..	131	69	..	..	..	..	..	44 20A
Hautbois (C)	..	132	71	7	..	..	..	..	22A
I-8 Marche (C)	42	133	72	..	..	..	..	..	23A
Entrée des combatans (C)	..	..	73	..	..	..	..	..	..
III-3 Prelude (F)	..	..	..	..	233	..	..	..	..
III-6 Premier Air (F)	..	..	..	..	234	9	67	..	..
Second Air (F)	..	..	..	..	235	9a	..	14r	..
IV-7 Aimons, aimons tout nous (C)	..	111	..	..	..	..	..	..	..
L'Amour plaist (C)	..	125	..	..	..	..	..	..	..
Marche des Trompettes (un-located)	..	..	..	..	..	..	..	..	46

Ballet de Thétis et Pélée (1654)
Ouverture (D)   14-Schwerin-619 #42,
                                 23-Tenbury #17,
                                 48-LaBarre-6 #35

Le Triomphe de l'amour (1681)

	46-Menetou	14-Schwerin-619	24-Babell	36-Parville	68-d'Anglebert	Inglis	Stockholm-176	30-Cecilia
Ouverture (F)	94	84	231	..	..	..	..	..
2e Menuet pour les graces (F)	104	..	..	..	..	..	..	..
Gavotte pour Orithie et ses nymphes (g)	112	..	133	..	..	..	..	..
2e Air pour Endimion (g)	..	..	134	..	..	..	..	..
Chaconne pour les Indiens (C)	..	..	..	..	..	17v	..	..
Entrée d'Apollon (g)	100	56	129	43	35	..	14v	52r
1r Air pour la jeunesse (g)	..	..	135	128	..	..	..	..
2e Air pour les mêmes (g)	..	..	136	..	..	..	..	..

Miscellaneous Works

Plusieurs Pièces de symphonie (published, 1685)
  Menuet (C)   Lüneburg-1198 p 84

Trios pour le coucher du roy (Trios de la chambre du roi)
  Dans nos bois (C)   27-Gresse #20, #52,
                                 36-Parville #109,
                                 51-LaBarre-11 p 205,
                                 68-d'Anglebert #14
  La jeune Iris (C)   68-d'Anglebert #28

Pieces Attributed to Lully
but Unlocated in Stage Works

	68-d'Anglebert	36-Parville	33-Rés-89ter	46-Menetou	14-Schwerin-619	42-Vm7-6307-2	Berlin-30363
Courante (g)	21	41	42d	117	..	..	..
Gigue (g)	25	..	..	..	..	..	..
Passepied (G)	..	108	..	..	..	..	..
Allemande des fragments de M. Lully (D)	..	..	..	..	48	11	1r

Work List 9: Monnard

		35-Bauyn-III	32-Oldham	38-Gen-2348/53	23-Tenbury	24-Babell	6-Munich-1511e	31-Madrid-1360	30-Cecilia	44-LaPierre
1	Courante (C)	53 59	..	..	..	..	..	..	..	..
2	Sarabande (C)	60	..	34	4	56	11	23/648r	..	2
3	Courante (a)	72	3	..	..	..	..	..	..	..

Work List 10: Richard

		35-Bauyn-III	36-Parville	33-Rés-89ter	32-Oldham	47-Gen-2356
1	Allemande (d)	33	..	..	..	..
2	Allemande (a)	40	..	..	..	..
3	Courante (a)	70	49	..	..	..
4	Sarabande (a)	71	..	..	5	..
5	Allemande (d)	82	..	..	..	..
6	Allemande (G)	83	..	..	..	..
7	Courante (d)	88	..	..	..	..
8	Gigue (g)	89	..	..	..	..
9	Gigue (G)	92	..	..	..	..
10	Courante (G)	..	97	..	..	..
11	Sarabande (G)	..	..	41	..	..
12	Courante (a)	..	..	..	..	9

Work List 11: Tresure

Abbreviations:

   ? Uncertain attribution

		19-Heardson	18-Ch-Ch-1236	16-Cosyn	Skara	8-Hintze	27-Gresse	9-Ihre-284	Van-Eijl	Bod-576	24-Babell	20-Ch-Ch-378	4-Lynar	29-Chigi	Oxford-IB	59a-Handmaide
1	Corant Tresor (D)	9														
2	2 Corant Tresor (D)	10														
3	Corant Mr Treser (a)	57														
4	Corant [and Double] Tresor (a)	58														
5	Corant, division Treser (a)	59														
6	Courant Monsier Tresor (a)	60														
7	Coranto Treser (a)	61									161					
8	Allmaine Treser (d)	63														
?9	Corant Treser (la Barr) (G)	65														
?10	Corant Labar (Tresor)	69										2				
11	Coranto Tresor (e)	72														14
12	Coranto Tresor (e)	73														
?13	Coranto Mr Tresure (La Barre, LaBar, Monsu della Bara, Mr Gibbons) (d)	46	1	44			22						65	30	x	
14	Corant Jonas Tresure (G)		2													
15	Courant variola Jo. Tresure		8													
16	Ayre Jo: Tresure (d)		2a													
17	Corant J. Tresure (d)		4													
?18	Saraband (La Barre) (d)		5		3											
19	Coranto Mr. Tresure (d)		6	101												
20	Allamanda Joan Tresor (d)			89												
21	Sarabanda J.T. (d)				2											
22	Allemande plorant Jonas Tresor (e)				4											
23	Cour Jo. Tr: (e)					1										
?24	Sarabande (e)					2										
25	Almande. J.T. (G)					3										
?26	Courante (G)						17									
?27	Sarabande (G)						18									
?28	Almande (a)						19									
?29	Courante (a)						31									
30	Sarabande Tresor (a)						32									
?31	Jigge (a)						33	76								
32	Allemand Tresoor (a)						34									
?33	Courant (a)								4	36						
?34	Saraband (a)									38						
?35	Allmaine (G)									40						13
?36	Saraband (G)															15

APPENDIX D

LIST OF COMPOSERS

The following list presents the bibliographical justification of the biographical information which has been used throughout the study. Although many of the citations were derived from standard music reference books, the more obscure names can only be located after considerable searching throughout the literature, if at all.

A bibliographic citation is given in parentheses following each identification. The abbreviations are explained in the List of Abbreviations at the beginning of this volume. The concluding comment in each entry indicates which sources contain the works of the composer. For musicians who are here not considered to be seventeenth-century French harpsichord composers, the list of sources is not exhaustive; only those sources are cited which are discussed in this study. In appropriate cases, the reader is directed to Appendix C, where a list of works provides a more detailed index of the composer's music.

ABEL (Äbel, Ebel), David (d. 1639). North German organist (*Apel-HKM*). Pieces in *1-Copenhagen-376*.

AGNESI, Maria Teresa (1720-1795). Italian harpsichordist and composer (*MGG-S*). Pieces in *15-Berlin-30206*.

AGULIERA DE HEREDIA, Sebastián (b. 1570). (*Grove-5*). Pieces in *31-Madrid-1360*.

ALBINONI, Tomaso (1671-1750). Italian composer of stage and instrumental music (*MGG*). Pieces in *13-Möllersche*.

ALDRICH, Henry (1647-1710). English composer, dean of Christ Church, Oxford, beginning in 1689 (*Arkright catalog*). Scribe (?) of *20-Ch-Ch-378*.

d'ANDRIEU see DANDRIEU.

d'ANGLEBERT, Jean-Henri (1635-1691). (*Gilbert*). See work list, Appendix C.

ANSELME, Jean-Baptiste (fl. 1735). Composer of *Raton et Rossette*, a parody of Mondonville's *Titon et l'Aurore* (*Eitner*). Pieces in *51-LaBarre-11*.

ARDEL see HARDEL.

ARNÒ (Arnauld?), Pietro. Unidentified composer, possibly French. See *Vat-mus-569*.

ARTUS.   Unidentified composer of instrumental music, presumably French.   Probably not either Jean Artus le Borgne (fl. 1661-1684) who was a violin player and dancing master in the Versailles *écurie* (*Benoit*) or Arthur (Artus) Aux Cousteaux (d. ca. 1656) who was *maître* at St. Chapelle in Paris and who published psalms, noëls, etc. from 1631 to 1655 (*Fasquelle*).   Pieces by the unidentified Artus in *5-Munich-1503l, 7-Munich-1511f, 8-Hintze, 9-Ihre-284, 27-Gresse, 55-Redon, 59a-Handimaide, Celle* and *Cassel.*

AUBERT, Jacques "le vieux" (ca. 1689-1753).   Parisian court violinist and composer (*Fasquelle*).   Pieces in *53-Oldham-2.*

BABELL (Babel)
  -Charles (fl. 1697-1720).   Instrumentalist and arranger at the British court in The Hague and in London (cf. pp. 68-70, above).   Scribe of *23-Tenbury, 24-Babell, Newberry, Cummings* and *Bod-393.*   Compiler of *Trios-1* and *Trios-2.*
  -William (ca. 1690-1723).   Charles' son; London harpsichord virtuoso, composer and arranger (cf. pp. 68-70, above).   Owner of *23-Tenbury* and *24-Babell.*   Pieces in *49-RésF-933.*

BACH, Johann Sebastian (1685-1750).   Pieces in *12-Walther* and *13-Möllersche*; see also *24-Babell.*

BALES (Balles, Bates, Balls), Alphonso (fl. ca. 1635).   Musician for voices and lute at the English court (*De Lafontaine*).   Probably the composer of pieces in *17-Rogers*, although there was also a Richard Balls (d. ca. 1622) who was a public musician for voice in London (*Cofone*).

BALLARD.   Family name of a number of French musicians and publishers.   The following list of seventeenth-century members is based on Lesure (*MGG*), Rollin (*MGG-S*) and Pogue (*Grove-6*):
  -Robert I (1525-1588).   Founder of publishing firm with Le Roy.
  -Pierre I (1575/80-1639).   Son of Robert I, continuing the publishing house.
  -Robert II (1575-post 1650).   Brother of Pierre I, lutenist, lute teacher and composer.   Published lute books in 1611 and 1614.   Pieces in *4-Lynar*; cf. *Imhoff.*
  -Robert III (d. 1673).   Son of Pierre I, continued publishing house; usually cited as "Robert II" in lists which omit the lutenist, cited here as Robert II.
  -Christophe (1641-1715).   Son of Robert III, publisher.
  -Pierre II (d. 1703).   Brother of Christophe, publisher.
  -Jean-Baptiste Christophe (ca. 1663-1750).   Son of Christophe, publisher.

BAPTIST (Baptiste, etc.).   Identification in manuscripts which can signify either Lully or Draghi (as well as Loeillet, slightly later).

BARRETT, John (ca. 1674-ca. 1735).   English composer (*Caldwell*).   Pieces in *23-Tenbury* and *24-Babell.*

BEAUMON, Georg de.   Unidentified seventeenth-century (Flemish?) composer of organ music.   Pieces in *28-Brussels-926.*

BEER (Behr), Leonhard (fl. 1644-1651).   Leipzig organist (*Eitner*) whose initials are the same as La Barre, causing a misattribution of pieces in *27-Gresse.*

BÈGUE see LEBÈGUE.

BELLEVILLE, Jacques, Sieur de (fl. 1615/16; d. 1637/46). Ballet composer and director; 11 lute pieces were published by Ballard in 1631 and others are found in manuscript (*Souris-C*). No known harpsichord music. Cf. *Uppsala-409* and *Uppsala-134:22.*

BERFF, Georg. Organist from Deventer (The Netherlands) (*Noske*). Pieces in *Van-Eijl.*

BERTHET (Berthelet), Pierre (fl. 1695). Parisian singing teacher; published several *Leçons de musique* in 1695 and was included in several of Ballard's collections of airs (*Honegger*). Pieces in *48-LaBarre-6* and *51-LaBarre-11.*

BESARD (Besardus), Jean-Baptiste (ca. 1567-1625). French lutenist and composer who worked in Germany (*Fasquelle*). Pieces in *Berlin-40147.*

BLAINVILLE, Charles Henri (ca. 1711-ca. 1777). French composer of instrumental and vocal music, as well as theoretical works (*Fasquelle*). The composer represented in *51-LaBarre-11?*

BLANCROCHER, Charles Fleury de (ca. 1607-1652). French lutenist; only one known surviving work (*Rave, Massip*). Dedicatee of several *tombeaux*, including one by Louis Couperin in *35-Bauyn-II.*

BLANKENBURGH, Quirijn van (1647-ca. 1739). Dutch organist and composer (*Eitner*). Pieces in *24-Babell.*

BLOW, John (1649-1708) (*Caldwell*). Pieces in *21-Rés-1186bis* and *22-Ch-Ch-1177.*

BOCAN see CORDIER.

BÖHM, Georg (1661-1773) (*MGG*). Pieces in *13-Möllersche;* see also *8-Hintze.*

BOUSSET, Jean-Baptiste Drouart de (1662-1725). Parisian composer of airs (*Fétis*). Pieces in *51-LaBarre-11.*

BOYVIN, Jacques (ca. 1653-1706). Organist and composer in Rouen (*MGG*). Pieces in *28-Brussels-926.*

BRAUN, P. Unidentified (Belgian?) organ composer, probably fl. ca. 1670. Pieces in *28-Brussels-926.*

BREWER (Breuer), Thomas (b. 1611). Viol player and composer in London (*Grove-5*). Pieces in *17-Rogers.*

BROCKHUISEN, Barend. Dutch organist (*Noske*). Pieces in *Van Eijl.*

BRUHNS, Nicolaus (1665-1697). (*MGG*). Pieces in *13-Möllersche.*

BRUININCKS, Hamel. Unidentified. Pieces in *23-Tenbury* and *24-Babell.*

BRULLARD (Bruslard, Brulard, Brulare, Bruslart). Family name of several violinists at the French court, the most prominent of whom were:
-Vincent (m. 1630) "violin du chambre du roi" (*Jurgens*).
-Jacques (d. ca. 1670) "violin de chambre," 1664; succeeded to *24-violons de chambre* in 1670 (*Benoit*).
-Louis (d. ca. 1670). Career seems identical to that of Jacques (*Benoit*).
Pieces of Brullard (which one undetermined) in *9-Ihre-284.*

BRYNE (Bryan, Brian), Albetus (Albert) (ca. 1621-1671). English organist and composer (Cooper for *Grove-6*). Pieces in *18-Ch-Ch-1236, 19-Heardson, 22-Ch-Ch-1177* and *59a-Handmaide.*

BULL, John (ca. 1563-1628) (Caldwell). Pieces in *4-Lynar, 16-Cosyn, Lynar-A2* and *26-Bull*; cf. *19-Heardson* and *59a-Handmaide.*

BURETTE (Buret). Family name of several musicians in Paris:
-Claude (d. ca. 1700). Harpist and composer (*Fasquelle*). Pieces in *Burette-409.*
-Pierre Jean (1665-1747). Son of Claude, medical doctor and musical theorist (*Fasquelle*). Scribe of *Burette-407, -408, -409* and *-410.*
-Jacques (fl. 1692). Violinist at Versailles (*Benoit*).
-Bernard (fl. 1722-1726). Harpsichordist, teacher of Mlle de Charolois; published cantatas (*Fasquelle*).
Pieces by "Buret l'Aisne" (Claude?) in *47-Gen-2356.*

BUSTIJN (Bustyn), Pieter (Pierre) (fl. 1628). Organist in Middelburg (*Eitner*). Pieces in *12-Walther.*

BUT see DU BUT.

BUXTEHUDE, Dietrich (1637-1707). (*MGG*). Pieces in *11-Ryge, 12-Walther* and *13-Möllersche.*

BYRD, William (1543-1623) (*Grove-5*). Pieces in *4-Lynar, Lynar-A2, 17-Rogers* and *26-Bull.*

BYRON, William Lord (1669-1736). English composer (*Caldwell*). Pieces in *22a-Roper, 23-Tenbury* and *24-Babell.*

CABANILLES, Juan (1644-1712). (*MGG*). Pieces in *31-Madrid-1360* and *Madrid-1357.*

CAECILE, Sr. Unidentified. Piece in *22a-Roper.*

CAMPIAN (Campion), Thomas (1567-1620). English poet and composer (*Grove-5*). Works in *17-Rogers.*

CAMPRA, André (1660-1744). French opera composer (*Fasquelle*). Pieces and transcriptions in *45-Dart, 48-LaBarre-6, 49-Rés-933* and *Berlin-30363.*

CHABANCEAU see LA BARRE.

CHAMBONNIÈRES, Jacques Champion, sieur de (1601/2-1672). (D. Fuller for *Grove-6*). See work list, Appendix C.

CHAMPION. At least six musicians of this name were active in the sixteenth and seventeenth centuries (D. Fuller for *Grove-6*):
-Jacques I (d. post 1535). No known works.
-Nicolas I (fl. ca. 1526). No known keyboard music.
-Thomas "Mithou" (d. post 1580). Organist and spinet player; no known keyboard music.
-Jacques II "de La Chapelle" (ca. 1555-1642). Organist and spinet player. Pieces attributed to him in *26-Bull* and *Celle*.
-Jacques III "de Chambonnières." See CHAMBONNIÈRES.
-Nicolas II or Jehan-Nicolas "de La Chapelle" (1620/25-pre 1662). No known keyboard music.

CHANCY, François de (d. 1656). French court singer, lutenist and composer (*MGG*). Transcriptions in *54-Gen-2350/57*.

CHAPELLE (Chapel, etc.). See CHAMPION, Jacques II.

CHARPENTIER, Marc-Antoine (ca. 1634-1704). Parisian composer (*Honegger*). Transcriptions in *24-Babell*.

CHARREART, du. Perhaps a corruption of "Du Carroy" (q.v.). Pieces in Wolffheim.

CLARKE, Jeremiah (1673/4-1707). (*Caldwell*). Pieces in *22a-Roper, 23-Tenbury, 24-Babell, Clark-M678*.

CLÉRAMBAULT (Clairambault, etc.), Louis-Nicolas "le père" (1676-1749). (*MGG*). Pieces in *12-Walther* and *50-Paignon*.

COBB, John (fl. 1638-1653). English court organist and composer (*Pulver*). Pieces in *19-Heardson*.

COBERG, Johann Anton (Jean-Antoine) (1650-1708). Organist in Hanover (*Eitner, Fétis*). Pieces in *13-Möllersche*; cf. *Grimm*.

COLASSE see COLLASSE.

COLEMAN (Colman), Charles (pre 1636-1664). English viol player and composer (*Grove-5, Caldwell*). Pieces in *60-Playford*.

COLEMAN, Mark (fl. mid 17th c.). Perhaps related to Charles Coleman. (*Caldwell*). Piece in *18-Ch-Ch-1236*.

COLENSI. Unidentified. Pieces in *Stoss*.

COLIN, "Master." Unidentified music teacher in England. Piece in *25-Bod-426*.

COLIN DE BLAMONT (Collin), François (1690-1760). Composer at Versailles of vocal and stage music (*Honegger*). Transcriptions in *Berlin-30363*.

COLL see MARTIN Y COLL.

COLLASSE (Colasse), Pascal (1649-1709). Opera composer (*MGG*). Some of the works are partially by Lully (q.v.). Transcriptions in *14-Schwerin-619, 23-Tenbury* and *48-LaBarre-6*.

CONVERSI (Converso), Girolamo. Late sixteenth-century Italian madrigalist (*MGG-S*). Transcriptions in *Eÿsbock*.

CORDIER, Jacques "Bocan" (ca. 1580-1653). Viol player and dancer from Lorraine (*Fasquelle, Massip*). Mersenne named his "La Bocanne" tune after this composer. Transcriptions in *54-Gen-2350/57*.

CORELLI, Arcangelo (1653-1713). Pieces in *14-Scherwin-619, 24-Babell,* and *31-Madrid-1360*.

CORNET, Pierre (Pieter, Peter, Pietro) (fl. 1593-1626). Organist in Brussels, associate of Bull's (*MGG-S*). Pieces in *4-Lynar, 26-Bull*.

COSYN (Cosin, Cosens, Cossens), Benjamin (ca. 1570-post 1652). English organist and composer (*Grove-5, Caldwell*). Pieces in *16-Cosyn* and *19-Heardson*; scribe of *16-Cosyn*.

COUPERIN. The following members of the family were musicians in the seventeenth century (D. Fuller for *Grove-6*):
-Mathurin (1595-post 1623). Instrumentalist in Brie.
-Charles I (159?-pre 1662). Son of Mathurin; instrumentalist in Chaumes.
-Charles II (1638-1679). Organist, composer, but no works can be attributed. Cf. *Burette-407*.
-Louis (ca. 1626-1661). Son of Charles I. See work list, Appendix C.
-François I (ca. 1631-1708/12). Brother of Louis, keyboard player. No works can be attributed.
-François II "le Grand" (1668-1733). Although some of his harpsichord pieces were certainly written before 1700, he is here considered an eighteenth-century composer. Pieces in *30-Cecilia, 50-Paignon, 51-LaBarre-11, 52-Rés-2671, 53-Oldham-2, Berlin-30363, Cecilia*.

CROFT, William (1678-1727). English organist and composer (*Grove-5*). Pieces in *21-Rés-1186-bis* and *24-Babell*.

CROFURO. Misreading of TRESURE (q.v.).

DAMANCE (D'amance), Paul (ca. 1650-ca. 1700). Organist in Lisieux, Normandy (*MGG*). Pieces in *28-Brussels-926*.

DANDRIEU (d'Andrieu), Jean François (ca. 1682-1738). (*MGG*). pieces in *12-Walther, 14-Schwerin-619, 50-Paignon, 51-LaBarre-11* and *53-Oldham-2*.

DANGLEBERT see ANGLEBERT.

DE GRIGNY see GRINGY.

DE LA BARRE see LA BARRE

DENIS, Jean (d. 1672). Spinet builder (*Honegger*). Piece in *57-Denis*.

DEOPARD see DIEUPART

DESFONTAINES, Jean (ca. 1658-post 1732). Composer of many airs published by Ballard from 1692-1731 (*Fasquelle, Curtis-Berkeley*). Pieces in *51-LaBarre-11*.

DESMARETS (Desmaretz, Desmarais), Henri (1662-1741). Court composer and musician in Paris (*MGG, Fasquelle*). Pieces in *51-LaBarre-11*.

DESTOUCHES, André Cardinal (1672-1749). French opera composer (*Fasquelle*). Pieces in *49-RésF-933, 51-LaBarre-11, Berlin-30363, Bod-425*.

DES VOYES. Unidentified. Pieces in *51-LaBarre-11*.

DIESSENER (Disineer, Desznier, etc.), Gerhard (fl. 1660-1673). Composer in Kassel who evidently emigrated to London ca. 1673 (*MGG*). Pieces in *22-Ch-Ch-1177*.

DIEUPART, Charles or François or both (post 1667(?)-ca. 1740). French violinist, harpsichordist and composer, active mainly in London (D. Fuller for *Grove-6*). Excluded from this Catalog as an eighteenth-century composer. Pieces in *12-Walther, 23-Tenbury, 24-Babell* and *Berlin-8551*.

DORSERŸ. Unidentified. Pieces in *Darmstadt-17*.

DOWLAND, John (1563-1626) (*Grove-5*). Pieces in *Eÿsbock*.

DRAGHI, Giovanni Battista (b. ca. 1640). Composer of Italian birth who worked in London from as early as 1667, sometimes confused with Lully, as both were referred to as "Baptiste" in manuscripts (*Grove-5*). Pieces in *22-Ch-Ch-1177, 23-Tenbury, 24-Babell, Clark-D173, Inglis*.

DROUART see BOUSSET.

DUBREUIL, Jean (1710-1775). Parisian music teacher and harpsichordist (*MGG-S*). Pieces in *51-LaBarre-11*.

DU BUISSON (d. 1710). One of many composers of this name (first name unknown); Parisian composer of airs (*MGG*). Pieces in *51-LaBarre-11*.

DU BUT. Family name of at least five musicans (Joël Dugot for *Grove-6*):
- -"Toussain Dubut" mentioned as "joueur d'instruments" in Paris, 1599.
- -"Dubut," violinist in Paris in 1636.

-Pierre. Lutenist in Paris in 1644, perhaps the "père" Dubut mentioned by René Milleran ca. 1690 as the foremost seventeenth-century lutenist.
-Louis. Lutenist in 1644.
-Nicolas (1638-post 1692). Parisian instrument maker (and lutenist?) in 1671. Perhaps one of the two sons of Pierre.
Transcriptions (which Du But uncertain) in *Stockholm-176* and *Stockholm-228*.

DU CAURROY (du Carroy), Eustache (1549-1609). Parisian composer of vocal and instrumental music (*MGG*). Perhaps the "du Charreart" in *Wolffheim*.

DÜBEN, Gustaf (1624-1690). Important organist and composer in Stockholm and Uppsala (*MGG*). Composed and transcribed pieces in *Skara* and *Uppsala-409*.

DUFAUT (Dufault) (fl. 1631-1699). First name unknown; French lutenist, student of the Gaultiers, probably in England by 1670 (*Souris-D*). Transcriptions in *18-Ch-Ch-1236* and *Uppsala-409*.

DUMANOIR, Guillaume (1615-ca. 1690). Violinist and composer at the Paris court (*Fasquelle*). Transcriptions in *9-Ihre-284*, *28-Brussels-926* and *Uppsala-409*.

DUMONT, Henry (1610-1684). Organist, harpsichordist and composer of Belgian birth who worked in Paris from ca. 1638 (*Fasquelle*). See work list, Appendix C.

DUPLESSIS "l'ainé" (fl. 1704-1748). Parisian violinist at the opera *(Fétis)*. Pieces in *51-LaBarre-11*.

EBEL see ABEL.

EBNER, Wolfgang (1612-1665). South German organist (*MGG*). Pieces in *Ottobeuren*.

ECCLES, John (1668-1735). English composer *(Caldwell)*. Pieces in *22a-Roper*, *23-Tenbury* and *24-Babell*.

EDELMANN, Moritz (d. 1680). North German organist (*Eitner*). Pieces in *13-Möllersche*.

ELLIS, William (ca. 1620-1674). Oxford composer and compiler *(Caldwell)*. Compiler and scribe (in part?) of *18-Ch-Ch-1236*; possibly the "W.E." in *Ch-Ch-1113*.

ERBACH, Christian (ca. 1570-1635). South German organist and composer (*MGG*). Pieces in *4-Lynar* and *Lynar-A2*.

ERBEN, Johann Balthasar (1626-1686). Organist in Danzig (*MGG-S*); the same name is found in Weimar (fl. 1657) (*Breig*). Pieces in *8-Hintze*.

ESTENDORFFER, Pater Anton Pad. (1670-1711). South German organist and composer (*Tilsen*). Scribe and composer in *Ottobeuren*.

ESTY (?), Guelheur (?). Unidentified. Piece in *55-Redon*.

FABRICIUS, Werner (1633-1679). North German organist, composer (*MGG*). Pieces in *13-Möllersche.*

FACY (Facey, etc.), Hugh (fl. 1618-1620). English organist and composer (*Grove-5-S*). Pieces in *19-Heardson.*

FARINEL (Farinelli), Michael (1649-post 1697). French violinist who married a harpsichordist, Marie-Anne Cambert and was at the English court from 1675-1679, at Versailles in 1688 and then in Grenoble and Toulouse until after 1697 (*Fasquelle*). Pieces in *21-Rés-1186bis, 45-Dart* and *RCM.*

FARNABY. Family name of two English harpsichordists and composers (*Caldwell*):
-Giles (ca. 1560-1640).
-Richard (b. ca. 1590), son of Giles.
Pieces in *4-Lynar, 26-Bull.*

FAVIER.
-Jacques (fl. 1664-1689). Member of 24 violins at Versailles (*Benoit*).
-Jean (d. pre 1719). His son, also one of the 24 violins (*Benoit*).
Piece probably by Jean in *44-LaPierre* and Vm7-3555.

FERRABOSCO.
-Alfonso II (ca. 1575-1628). English composer of Italian parentage, who wrote no known original keyboard music (*Grove-5*). Pieces in *18-Ch-Ch-1236* and *26-Bull.*
-John (1626-1682). Son of Alfonso II (*Caldwell*). Pieces in *18-Ch-Ch-1236.*

FERRETTI, Giovanni (b. ca. 1540). Italian composer (*MGG*). Pieces in *Eÿsbock.*

FINGER, Gottfried (Godfrey) (ca. 1660-post 1723). Moravian composer, resident in England ca. 1685-ca. 1703 (*Caldwell*). Pieces in *23-Tenbury.*

FIOCCO, Pietro Antonio (Pierre-Antoine) (ca. 1650-1714). Italian composer of sacred and secular vocal music who worked in Brussels (*Grove-5*). Pieces in *24-Babell.*

FISCHER, Johann Caspar Ferdinand (d. 1746). (*MGG*). Pieces in *Minorite.*

FLOR, Christian (1626-1697). Organist in Lüneburg and elsewhere (*MGG*). Pieces in *13-Möllersche.*

FORCER, Francis (ca. 1650-1705). English composer (*Caldwell*). Pieces in *23-Tenbury, 24-Babell.*

FORMILOE. Unidentified (English?) composer. Pieces in *16-Cosyn.*

FOUCART (Fuckart), Jacques (Jacob) (fl. 1626). French violinist who was engaged by the Prince of Denmark (*Mersenne, Elling*). Pieces in *Kabinet* and *Leningrad.*

FRESCOBALDI, Girolamo (1583-1643) (*MGG*). Pieces in *29-Chigi, 30-Cecilia, 31-Madrid-1360, 32-Oldham, 35-Bauyn-III* and *Rés-819-2.*

FROBERGER, Johann Jakob (1616-1667) (*MGG*). Pieces in *5-Munich-15031, 8-Hintze, 10-Schwerin-617, 24-Babell, 27-Gresse, 35-Bauyn-III, 36-Parville, 47-Gen-2356, Berlin-40147, Van Eijl, Stoss, Rés-819-2, Ottobeuren, Grimm, Minorite.*

GABRIELI, Giovanni (ca. 1555-1612). (*MGG*). Pieces in *4-Lynar* and *Lynar-A2.*

GALUPPI, Baldassare (1706-1785). Pieces in *15-Berlin-30206.*

GAULTIER (Gautier). At least five composers wioth this family name were active in the seventeenth century (*Souris-G, Fasquelle, Honegger*):
-Ennemond "le vieux de Lyon" (ca. 1575-1651). Lutenist.
-Denis "le jeune de Paris" (1597/03-1672). Lutenist, cousin of Ennemond.
-Jacques "d'Angleterre" (fl. 1617-1648). Lutenist, active in England from ca. 1617.
-Pierre "d'Orléans" (fl. 1635). Lutenist. Also known as "de Rome."
-Pierre "de Marseilles" (1643/4-1697). Harpsichordist, organist and founder of the opera at Marseilles. No original keyboard music can be found, but some instrumental works are found in keyboard transcriptions.
See work list (which Gaultier is often unclear), Appendix C.

GEOFFROY, Jean Nicolas (d. 1694). Organist in Paris and then Perpignan (D. Fuller for *Grove-6*). Pieces in *37-Geoffroy. 40-Rés-476* was once "attributed" to Geoffroy and is now frequently known as the "Geoffroy organ book," but it has nothing to do with this composer.

GIBBONS.
-Orlando (1583-1625). (*Grove-5*). Pieces in *4-Lynar, 16-Cosyn, 17-Rogers, 19-Heardson, 20-Ch-Ch-378, 21-Rés-1186bis, 26-Bull* and *Lynar-A2.*
-Christopher (1615-1676). (*Grove-5*). Son of Orlando, composer. Pieces in *19-Heardson.*

GIBBS, Richard (fl. 1622-1635). English organist and composer (*Grove-5*). Pieces in *19-Heardson, 22-Ch-Ch-1177, 59a-Handmaide* and *Inglis.*

GIGAULT, Nicolas (1624/5-1707). Parisian organist and harpsichordist (*MGG*). Pieces in *67-Gigault.*

GILLIER (Gilliers). Pierre "l'Aîné" (b. 1665). Published a book of airs and symphonies from operas in 1697 (*Fasquelle*). Pieces in *24-Babell.*

GODARD (Godardum), Robert. Mid sixteenth-century composer and organist of the cathedral at Bauvais (*MGG*). No known keyboard works, but transcriptions from vocal works in *Eÿsbock.*

GODEAU, Antoine (1605-1672). French bishop who wrote several texts which were set to music by Louis XIII and others, published by Ballard (*Fasquelle*). Cf. *25-Bod-426.*

GRECO, Gaetano (ca. 1657-ca. 1728). Neapolitan composer (*Grove-5*). Cf. *30-Cecilia.*

GRESSE, J B (i.e., Jacob?). Unidentified (Dutch?) composer. Pieces in *27-Gresse.*

GRIGNY, Nicolas de (1672-1703). Organist and composer in Reims (*Honegger*). There is no known harpsichord music, but pieces are misattributed to him in *Berlin-8551*.

GRIMM (Grim), Christian (fl. 1699). Organist in Demmin (northern Germany) (*Frotscher*). Scribe and composer in *Grimm*.

GUÉDRON (Guesdron), Pierre (d. 1620/21). French composer of secular vocal music (*Fasquelle*). Transcriptions in *54-Gen-2350/57*.

GUERRE see LA GUERRE.

GUMPRECHT, Johann (fl. 1688). Lutenist from Strasbourg (*Fasquelle*). Transcriptions in *Darmstadt-17* and *Nuremberg*.

HAMEL see BRUININCKS.

HANDEL, George Frideric (Georg Friedrich Händel) (1685-1759) (*Grove-5*). Transcriptions in *24-Babell* and *Minorite*.

HARDEL (Hardelle, Ardel). Family name of several instrument makers and at least one composer (D. Fuller for *Grove-6*):
-Gilles (fl. 1611). "Maître facteur d'instruments."
-Guillaume (d. ca. 1676). Son of Gilles; instrument maker (lutes?).
-François (b. 1642). Son of Guillaume (?).
-Jacques (fl. 1663-1676; d. pre 1680). Son of Guillaume (?), "officier de la duchesse d'Orléans," probably the composer of the harpsichord and lute works and the student of Chambonnières. See work list, Appendix C.

HART, Philip (ca. 1676-1749). English composer (*Caldwell*). Pieces in *Inglis*.

HAUβMANN (Hausmann, Husmann), Valentin (d. 1611/14). German organist and composer who settled in Nuremberg (*MGG*). Pieces in *Linz*.

HAYM (Haim, Aimo), Nicolas Francis (Nicola Francesco) (ca. 1679-1729). Italian composer of German parentage who worked in London from 1704 as a music teacher and Italian opera composer-impressario (*Eitner, Grove-5*). Transcriptions in *25-Bod-426*.

HEARDSON (Hirdson), Thomas (fl. 1640-1679). English composer (*Hendrie*). Presumed scribe of *19-Heardson*.

HENRECY. Unidentified, perhaps the same as the "Mr. Henry" in *Saizenay-I*. Piece in *Skara*.

HEREDIA see AGUILIERA DE HEREDIA.

HEYDORN, P (fl. 1693). Organist in Brussels known to Walther as a composer of organ music (*Eitner*). Pieces in *13-Möllersche*.

HILLER (Hüller), Johann Adam (1728-1804). Leipzig composer (*MGG*). Pieces in *15-Berlin-30206*.

IHRE, Thomas (b. 1659). Musician from Visby (Sweden) (*Lundgren*). Owner and scribe of *9-Ihre-284*.

IVES (Ive), Simon (1600-1662). English organist and composer (*Grove-5*). Pieces in *60-Playford*.

JACKSON, John (d. 1688). English composer (*Caldwell*). Piece in *59a-Handmaide*.

JACOB (Jacobus), Giovanni (fl. 1552). Lute composer from Milan (*Eitner*). Transcriptions in *Eÿsbock*.

JACOPINO (fl. early 17th c.). Neapolitan calypso singer (*Dart-HI*). Piece arranged in *59a-Handmaide*.

JACQUET see LA GUERRE.

JOHNSON, Robert II (ca. 1580-ca. 1633). English composer, son of John Johnson (d. 1594) (*Caldwell*). Pieces in *17-Rogers* and *Ch-Ch-1113*.

KAUFFMANN, Georg Friedrich (1679-1735). German composer (*MGG*). Pieces in *12-Walther*.

KELLER, Godfrey (Gottfried?) (fl. 1707). German music teacher and composer who settled in London towards the end of the seventeenth century (*Grove-5*). Pieces in *23-Tenbury*.

KELZ (Keltz, Kölz, Kolz, Cölsch), Matthias II (1634-pre 1694). Augsburg composer (*MGG*). Pieces in *Stoss*.

KERLL, Johann Kaspar (1627-1693). South German composer (*MGG*). Pieces in *8-Hintze, Stoss, Van-Eijl* and *Ottobeuren*.

KING, Robert (d. post 1728). English composer (*Caldwell*). Pieces in *21-Rés-1186bis, 23-Tenbury, 24-Babell* and *Clark-M678*.

KLAR, J. Unidentified. Pieces in *13-Möllersche*.

KREBS.
    -Johann Tobias I (1690-1762) (*MGG*). Scribe in *12-Walther*.
    -Johann Ludwig (1713-1780). His son (*MGG*). Scribe and pieces in *12-Walther*.

KRIEGER, Adam (1634-1666). Composer and keyboard player in Leipzig and Dresden (*MGG*). Pieces in *3-Berlin-40623* and *Berlin-40147*.

LA BARRE (Chabanceau de la Barre). The following list of identified musicians of this complicated family is based on Bowers for *Grove-6* and *Souris-V*:
-Pierre I (fl. 1567; d. 1600). Organist.

His sons:

-Claude (b. 1570). Organist, harpsichordist.
-Pierre II (1572-post 1626). Organist, lutenist.
-Jehan
-Germain (b. 1579). Organist.
-Pierre III (1592-1656). Identified as "joueur d'épinette" in his 1614 marriage contract; referred to as "La Barre le jeune." Composer of diminutions in *56-Mersenne* and possibly other pieces attributed to La Barre.

Third generation:

-Sebastien
-Charles-Henri (ca. 1625-ca. 1670). Harpsichordist.
-Benjamin
-Anne (1628-1688). Singer
-Joseph (1633-pre 1678). Composer of vocal and harpsichord music. At least one of the pieces in *35-Bauyn-III* is by this composer.
-Pierre IV (1634-pre 1710). Instrumentalist: lute and theorbo (and spinet?).

Eighteenth century:

-Michel (ca. 1675-1743). Flutist.
-[name unknown] (fl. post 1724). Organist, owner and scribe in the Berkeley collection of manuscripts.

See work list, Appendix C. Code names have been adopted here for the composer(s) on the basis of the circulation pattern of the pieces attributed to "La Barre" in manuscripts: the "English La Barre" (see *16-Cosyn* in the Commentary), the "Bauyn La Barre" (see *35-Bauyn* and *36-Parville* in the Commentary) and the "Berkeley La Barre" (see *48-LaBarre-6* in the Commentary). None of these designations can be linked with certaintly to a specific member of the family listed above.

LACOSTE (La Coste), Louis de (ca. 1675-post 1757). Parisian opera composer from the 1690's into the eighteenth century (*MGG, Fasquelle*). Pieces in *51-LaBarre-11*.

LA CROIX. Unidentified. Pieces in *Uppsala-409* and *Add-52363*.

LA GUERRE, Élisabeth Jacquet de (1659-1729). Parisian composer and harpsichordist who wrote compositions as early as 1677 and published harpsichord books in 1687 and 1707 (*Grove-5*). Unlocated 17th-c. pieces in *Jacquet*.

LAMBERT, Michel (ca. 1610-1696). Lutenist, singer composer with several publications (*MGG*). Pieces in *33-Rés-89ter*, *46-Menetou* and perhaps *Ottobeuren*.

LANCIANI, Flavio Carlo (fl. 1683-1706). Roman composer of operas and oratorios (*MGG*). Transcriptions in *Stoss.*

LANIER (Laniere, Lanaere, etc.), Nicolas (1588-1666). English singer, composer and painter of French descent. Pieces in *17-Rogers.*

LA PIERRE. Unidentified. Piece in *55-Redon.*

LASSO, Orlando di (1532-1594) (*MGG*). Transcriptions in *4-Lynar* and *Eÿsbock.*

LAWES.
-Henry (1595-1662). English composer, brother of William (*Pulver*). Pieces in *17-Rogers, 19-Heardson.*
-William (1602-1645). English composer (*Caldwell*). Pieces in *16-Cosyn, 18-Ch-Ch-1236, 59a-Handmaide* and *60-Playford.*

LEBÈGUE, Nicolas-Antoine (ca. 1631-1702). (Higginbottom for *Grove-6*). All of the known harpsichord works are in the published editions (*64-Lebègue-I* and *65-Lebègue-II*). Some of the anonymous pieces in *28-Brussels-926* and *48-LaBarre-6* could be by Lebègue. Concordances in *10-Schwerin-617, 11-Ryge, 12-Walther, 13-Möllersche, 14-Schwerin-619, 21-Rés-1186bis, 22a-Roper, 23-Tenbury, 24-Babell, 28-Brussels-926, 30-Cecilia, 35-Bauyn-III, 36-Parville, 45-Dart, 46-Menetou, 48-LaBarre-6* and *50-Paignon.*

LEBRET. Unidentified eighteenth-century composer. Pieces in *LeBret.*

LEGHI. Unidentified. Piece in *22a-Roper.*

LE ROUX, Gaspard (d. 1705/07). French harpsichordist (A. Fuller for *Grove-6*). Here considered an eighteenth-century composer because his works were published after 1700. Pieces in *12-Walther.*

LOBERT (?), de. Possibly a corruption of LAMBERT (q.v.); also read as "Cobert." Pieces in *Ottobeuren.*

LOCKE, Matthew (ca. 1622-1677) (*Caldwell*). Pieces in *19-Heardson, 22-Ch-Ch-1177, 59a-Handmaide* and *60-Playford.*

LOEILLET (Lullie, Lolliet). Family of Belgian musicians (*Honegger*):
-John (Jean) (1680-1730). Emigrated to England, sometimes confused with Jean-Baptiste.
-Jacques (1685-1746)
-Jean-Baptiste (b. 1688). Sometimes confused with Lully and Draghi beause all three were referred to as "Baptiste."
Pieces in *53-Oldham-2* (by Jean-Baptiste?); cf. *14-Schwerin-619.*

LOOSEMORE (Henry? d. 1670) (*Caldwell*). Pieces in *18-Ch-Ch-1236.*

LORENCY. Unidentified. Possibly the lutenist "Laurencinius di Roma" (Laurenzius, Lorencini da Linto), who was the teacher of Besard (ca. 1567-ca. 1625) (*Pohlmann*). Piece by Lorency in *35-Bauyn-III*.

LORENTZ, Johan II (ca. 1610-1689). Danish organist and composer (*MGG*). Pieces in *3-Berlin-40623* and *9-Ihre-284*.

LOWE, Edward (ca. 1610-1682). English organist and composer (*Grove-5*). Piece in *22-Ch-Ch-1177*.

LÜBECK, Vincent (1645/56-1740) (*MGG*). Pieces in *12-Walther*.

LULLY (Lulli), Jean-Baptiste (Giovanni Battista) (1632-1687). (*MGG*). It cannot be proven that there are any original harpsichord pieces by Lully, although not all of the harpsichord pieces attributed to him can be traced to an original model in the known stage and instrumental works. See work list, Appendix C.

MACQUE, Giovanni de (ca. 1550-1614). Flemish composer of Italian madrigals (*MGG, Grove-5*). Transcriptions in *26-Bull*.

MARAIS.
-Marin (1656-1728). French gambist (*Fasquelle*). Transcriptions in *33-Rés-89ter* and *24-Babell*.
-Roland (ca. 1680-ca. 1750). Son of Marin, also a gambist (*Fétis, MGG*). Transcriptions in *49-RésF-933*.

MARCHAND. Family name of a number of musicians, including several keyboard players (D. Fuller for *Grove-6*). The most famous was:
-Louis (1669-1732). His music is considered here to be of the eighteenth century because it was published after 1700.
Pieces (which Marchand is not always certain) in *12-Walther, 14-Schwerin-619, 45-Dart, 51-LaBarre-11* and *52-Rés-2671*.

MARENZIO, Luca (1553/54-1599) (*MGG*). Transcriptions in *4-Lynar*.

MARTIN Y COLL, Antonio (fl. 1706-1734). Spanish organist and composer (*MGG*). Compiler of *31-Madrid-1360* and *Madrid-1357*.

MELANTE. Anagrammatic pseudonym of TELEMANN (q.v.).

MELL, Davis (1604-post 1661). English violinist (*Grove-5*). Piece in *59a-Handmaide*.

MENETOU, Françoise-Charlotte deSenneterne (de) (b. ca. 1680). Child who sang (and composed?) airs for Louis XIV in 1689 (*Curtis-Berkeley*). Pieces in *46-Menetou*.

MERCURE (Merceur, Mercour, Mercury). Name of at least two French lutenists active in the first half of the seventeenth century (Cooper for *Grove-6*, *Rollin*).
-John (ca. 1580/90-pre 1660). Born in France, emigrated to England probably during the reign of Charles I; was established at the English court by 1641. No

known lute music survives, but transcriptions in *17-Rogers, 19-Heardson, 18-Ch-Ch-1236, Bod-220* and *Stockholm-228.*
-"d'Orléans" ("Aurelianensis"). Lute works published in Strasbourg and elsewhere in the early decades of the century. Transcription in *Linz.*

MERULA, Tarquino (d. post 1652) (*MGG*). Pieces in *Lynar-A2.*

MESANGEAU (Mézangeau), René (d. ca. 1638). French lutenist. (*Fasquelle, Souris-M*). Transcriptions in *1-Copenhagen-376, 2-Witzendorff, 33-Rés-89ter* and *35-Bauyn-III.*

MESSAUS, Gulielmus (1585-1640). Composer in Antwerp and associate of Bull's (*MGG*). Scribe of *26-Bull.*

MONDONVILLE, Jean-Joseph Cassanéa de (1711-1772) (*MGG*). Transcriptions in *51-LaBarre-11.*

MONNARD. Name of at least three musicians in seventeenth-century Paris (*Fasquelle*):
-Charles. Lutenist.
-Emery (b. ca. 1611). Organist at the Église des Innocents until 1639, at St. Laurent in 1642.
-Nicolas. Brother of Emery, organist at Jacobins in 1624, at St. Eustache (1634-1646). See work list (which Monnard is not certain), Appendix C.

MONTELAN, Claude-Rachel de (1646-1738). Argenteuil composer (*Curtis-Berkeley*). Pieces in *44-LaPierre* and *51-LaBarre-11.*

MORGAN. Unidentified seventeenth-century English (Welsh?) composer of incidental stage music, some of whose works were misattributed to Purcell (*Grove-5*). Piece in *23-Tenbury.*

MOSS, John (fl. 1663-1684). English viol player (*Grove-5*). Piece in *59a-Handmaide.*

MOUTON, Charles (d. ca. 1699 or ca. 1710). French lutenist whose biography is confused, but who was very prominent (his portrait hangs in the Louvre). Last master of the French lute school, with 94 known lute pieces (*Rave*). Transcriptions in *Stockholm-176.*

MUFFAT, Georg (1653-1704). (*MGG*). Pieces in *24-Babell, Ottobeuren, Minorite.*

NEUFVILLE (Neufoille), Johann Jakob (Jacob de) (1684-1712). Nuremberg composer (*MGG*). Pieces in *12-Walther.*

NIVERS, Guillaume-Gabriel (1632-1714). Parisian organist, harpsichordist, composer (*MGG*). No harpsichord music is known to survive. Possibly the transcriber of the Lully pieces in *40-Rés-476.* Organ pieces in *12-Walther, 28-Brussels-926* and *40-Rés-476.*

ORLANDI. Unidentified eighteenth-century composer. Perhaps one of the ones listed in *Eitner.* Pieces in *15-Berlin-30206.*

OSSU. Unidentified. Pieces in *23-Tenbury*.

PACHELBEL, Johann (1653-1706). (*MGG*). Pieces in *11-Ryge, 13-Möllersche* and *Grimm*.

PAISIBLE (Peasable), James (Jacques) (ca. 1650-ca. 1721). French wind player, singer and composer who was resident in England from 1674 to 1688 and returned again several times years later (1693?) (M. Antoine in *Recherches-15, Grove-5*). Also known as "the younger" (*Caldwell*). Pieces in *24-Babell*.

PASQUINI. Name of two Italian composers (*MGG*):
-Ercole (d. 1608/20). Pieces in *30-Cecilia*.
-Bernardo (1637-1710). Pieces in *Stoss, Minorite*.

PEPUSCH, John Christopher (1667-1752). English composer of German birth, resident in London from ca. 1700 (*Grove-5*). Owned a large library which included *26-Bull* and other lost sources of music attributed to "Chapelle" (i.e., Champion?). Pieces in *24-Babell*.

PERRINE (d. post 1698). First name unknown. Parisian lute teacher, the first to abandon tablature in favor of score notation (*MGG*). See *66-Perrine*.

PESENTI, Martino (ca. 1600-1647/48). Venetian harpsichordist and composer (*MGG*). Pieces in *Berlin-40147*.

PEUERL (Bäuerl, Peyerl), Paul (ca. 1570/80-post 1625). Nuremberg organist and composer (*MGG*). Pieces in *Linz*.

PEZ (Petz, Betz, Beez), Johann Christoph (1664-1716). South German composer (*MGG*). Instrumental pieces in *13-Möllersche* and *Grimm*.

PHILIPS, Peter (1560/61-1628). (*MGG*). Pieces in *4-Lynar, 19-Heardson* and *Eÿsbock*.

PINEL. Name of at least seven seventeenth-century lutenists (Dugot for *Grove-6, Rave, Fasquelle*):
-Pierre (fl. 1641). Father or uncle of Germain.
-Germain (d. 1661). The most prominent Pinel, assumed to be the composer of the 60-odd lute pieces which survive. Was a lutenist, theorbo player and composer at Versailles.
-Jean-Baptiste ⎫
-Séraphin ⎬ Sons of Germain. All lutenists, but not known to
-Jean ⎭ have been composers.
-François (ca. 1635-1709). Lutenist at Versailles from 1667; relationship to the Pinel family unknown.
Transcriptions (from original works presumably by Germain) in *1-Copenhagen-376, 5-Munich-15031, 7-Munich-1511f, 33-Rés-89ter, 35-Bauyn-III, 36-Parville, 47-Gen-2356, Skara* and *Ottobeuren*.

POGLIETTI (Boglietti), Alessandro (d. 1683). Organist, presumably of Italian birth, active in Vienna (*MGG*). Pieces in *Ottobeuren*.

PORTER, Philip. Unidentified. Pieces in *17-Rogers.*

PORTMAN, Richard (d. ca. 1655). Pupil of Orlando Gibbons, organist of Westminster Abey (*Caldwell*). Pieces in *22-Ch-Ch-1177.*

PRATT, Thomas. Unidentified 17th c. English composer. Piece(s) in *59a-Handmaide.*

PRICE, Robert. Unidentified seventeenth-century composer (*Caldwell*). Pieces in *18-Ch-Ch-1236* and *21-Rés-1186bis.*

PURCELL.
-Daniel (ca. 1660-1717). Brother of Henry (*Grove-5*). Piece in *23-Tenbury.*
-Henry (1659-1695) (*Grove-5*). Pieces in *21-Rés-1186bis, 22-Ch-Ch-1177, 22a-Roper, 23-Tenbury, 24-Babell, Clark-D173* and *Clark-M678.*

RACQUET (Raquette, etc.), Charles (1597-1664). Organist of Notre Dame in Paris, collaborated with Mersenne in writing the *Harmonie universelle* (*MGG*). No known harpsichord music, but an organ piece in *56-Mersenne.*

RADEKE (Radeck, Radecker), Johann Rudolf (fl. 1633-34). Organist active in Denmark (*Dickinson, Eitner*). Pieces in *Voightländer.*

RAMEAU, Jean-Philippe (1683-1764). (*Fasquelle*). Pieces in *14-Schwerin-619, 51-LaBarre-11* and *52-Rés-2671.*

RAMER. Unidentified. Pieces in *Ottobeuren.*

REBEL, Jean-Ferry (1666-1747). Parisian composer of instrumental music (*MGG*). Pieces in *51-LaBarre-11.*

REICH, Pater Honarat (1677-1732). Scribe of *Ottobeuren* (*Tilsen*).

REINCKEN (Reinken, Reinike), Johann (Jan) Adam (1623-1722). North German composer and organist (*MGG*). Pieces in *11-Ryge* and *13-Möllersche.*

REUTTER, Georg the elder (1656-1738). Viennese composer (*MGG*). Pieces in *Minorite.*

RICHARD. Name of at least three seventeenth-century French composers (Higginbottom for *Grove-6, Fasquelle, Jurgens*):
-Pierre (fl. 1600). Organist and harpsichordist in Paris. No known works.
-Étienne (ca. 1621-1669). Parisian organist, harpsichordist and viol player at court. Presumed to be the composer of all of the known harpsichord works.
-François (ca. 1580-1650). Lutenist (and composer?) at Versailles, not known to be related to Étienne. See work list (all by Étienne?), Appendix C.

RICHTER, Ferdinand Tobias (ca. 1649-1711). Viennese organist and composer (*MGG*). Pieces in *Minorite.*

RITTER, Christian (fl. 1666-1725). North German organist (*MGG*). Pieces in *13-Möllersche.*

ROBERDAY, François II (1624-1680). Parisian silversmith and composer who borrowed themes from Louis Couperin, among others (*Ferrard*). No known harpsichord works. See *Roberday*.

ROBERTS, John. English seventeenth-century composer (*Caldwell*). Pieces in *18-Ch-Ch-1236*, *19-Heardson*, *22-Ch-Ch-1177*.

ROGERS, Benjamin (1614-1698). English composer (*Caldwell*). Pieces in *18-Ch-Ch-1236*, *19-Heardson* and *59a-Handmaide*.

ROSSI, Luigi (1598-1653). Italian musician at the French court in 1646/7-1649, known as "Sr Luigi" (or variant thereof) (*Fasquelle*). Only known keyboard piece in *23-Tenbury*, *24-Babell*, *35-Bauyn-III* and *36-Parville*.

ROUSSEAU, Jean-Jacques (1712-1778). French philosopher and composer (*Fasquelle*). Transcriptions in *51-LaBarre-11* and *53-Oldham-2*.

SANDLEY, Benjamin. Unidentified seventeenth-century English composer (*Caldwell*). Pieces in *27-Gresse* and *59a-Handmaide*.

SCARLATTI.
-(Pietro) Alessandro (1660-1725) (*MGG*). Transcriptions in *25-Bod-426*.
-Domenico (1685-1757) (*MGG*). Piece in *52-Rés-2671*.

SCHALE, Christian Friedrich (1713-1800). Berlin Violoncellist, organist and composer (*MGG*). Pieces in *15-Berlin-30206*.

SCHEDLICH (Schädlich), David (1607-1687). Nuremberg composer (*MGG*). Pieces in *Imhoff*, *Berlin-40147*.

SCHEIDEMANN, Heinrich (ca. 1596-1663). Organist and composer in Hamburg (*MGG*). Pieces in *9-Ihre-284*, *Drallius*, *Leningrad*, *Celle*, *Voigtländer* and *Van-Eijl*.

SCHEIDT, Samuel (1587-1654). Organist and composer in Halle (Saale) (*MGG*). Piece in *Voigtländer*.

SCHILDT, Melchior (1592/3-1667). Hannover organist and composer (*MGG*). Pieces in *Voigtländer*.

SCHOP, Albert (b. 1632). Son of Johann, student of Scheidemann, organist in Hamburg (*MGG*). Pieces in *3-Berlin-40623* and *Van-Eijl*.

SERINI, Giovanni Batista (ca. 1710-post 1756). Composer in Bückenburg (*MGG*). Pieces in *15-Berlin-30206*.

SHORE, John (ca. 1662-1752). English trumpet player, lutenist and composer (*Grove-5*). Pieces in *22a-Roper*, *23-Tenbury*.

SMITH, John Christopher II (1712-1795). English composer of German birth (*Grove-5*). Pieces in *24-Babell*.

SPARR, Gustaff Larsson (1625-1689). Swedish musician (*Rudén*). Pieces in *Skara*.

STEENWICK, Gisbert van (d. 1679). Organist in Arnhem (Netherlands), compiler and pieces in *Van-Eijl* (*Noske*).

STEFFANI, Agostino (1654-1728). Italian composer active in northern Germany (*MGG*). Pieces in *13-Möllersche, 23-Tenbury* and *Grimm*.

ŠTĚPÁN (Steffan, Steffani, etc.), Josef Antonín (Guiseppe Antonio) (1726-1797). Bohemian keyboard player (*MGG*). Pieces in *15-Berlin-30206*.

STIL, Joh. Unidentified. Pieces in *13-Möllersche*.

STOOS (Stoss), Joan. Unidentified (German?) composer, perhaps related to the "N. Stoss" who composed a violin sonata in the eighteenth century (*Eitner*). Pieces in *Rost, Stoss*.

STRADELLA, Alessandro (1644-1682). (*MGG*). Pieces in *30-Cecilia*.

STRAUβ, Christoph (ca. 1575-1631). Viennese organist and composer (*MGG*). Pieces in *Linz*.

STRENGTHFIELD, Thomas (fl. pre 1656). Unidentified (*Caldwell*). Pieces in *17-Rogers*.

STRIE, D. Undentified. Pieces in *3-Berlin-40623*.

STRIGGIO, Alessandro the elder (ca. 1535-1589/95). Lutenist, organist, madrigalist (*MGG*). Pieces in *4-Lynar*.

STROBEL (Strobelt). Family name of three German lutenists active in Strasbourg and Darmstadt (*MGG*):
-Valentin I (ca. 1580-1640).
-Valentin II (1611-post 1669). Son of Valentin I.
-Johan Valentin (1643-1688). Son of Valentin II.
Transcriptions (of works by Valentin I or II) in *Berlin-40147, Darmstadt-17, Stockholm-176* and *Stockholm-228*.

SUFFRET. Unidentified French composer, perhaps the "S......" who published a number of motets in Paris. Pieces in *51-LaBarre-11*.

SWEELINCK, Jan Pieterszoon (1562-1621) (*MGG*). Pieces in *4-Lynar* and *26-Bull*; cf. *Celle*.

TALLIS, Thomas (ca. 1505-1585) (*Caldwell*). Pieces in *16-Cosyn* and *26-Bull*.

TELEMANN (Melante [anagrammatic pseudonym]), Georg Philipp (1681-1767) (*MGG*). Pieces in *12-Walther, 21-Rés-1186bis, 49-RésF-933* and *Grimm*.

THOMELIN, Jacques-Denis (ca. 1640-1693). Parisian organist at a number of churches, then at the royal chapel from 1678 (*Fasquelle, MGG*). Pieces in *28-Brussels-926* and *41-Thomelin.*

TOLLET, Thomas (fl. 1668-1699). Irish musician and composer (*Grove-5*). Pieces in *24-Babell.*

TOMKINS, Thomas (1572-1656) (*Grove-5, Caldwell*). Pieces in *19-Heardson.*

TRESURE (Tresor, Treser), Jonas (fl. 1650-1660?). Unidentified composer. Apparently considered to be French in England; often confused with La Barre and John Mercure. Although he is here not considered to be a French composer, a work list is provided, Appendix C. See Commentary to *19-Heardson.*

UMSTATT, Joseph (d. 1762). South German composer (*MGG*). Pieces in *15-Berlin-30206.*

URREDA, Johannes (fl. 1476-1480). Spanish composer (*MGG*). Cf. *Madrid-1357.*

VALOIS. Unidentified. Pieces in *23-Tenbury* and *24-Babell.*

VERACINI. Name of at least three Italian composers (*MGG*):
-Francesco di Niccolò (1638-1720). Known for sonatas da camera.
-Antonio (1659-1733). Son of Francesco, also composed sonatas da camera.
-Fr. Maria (1690-1768). Student of Pasquini. Pieces (which Veracini is unclear) in *14-Schwerin-619.*

VERDIER. Parisian family of musicians, including at least two who worked in Stockholm (*MGG*):
-Robert I (fl. 1620). Wind player.
-Robert II (fl. 1661). Perhaps the same as Robert I.
-Michel (fl. 1668-1690). Maître at St. Julien des Menétriers.
-Abel (fl. 1641-1647). Wind and violin player.
-Edme (fl. 1671). Listed among "concertans de la suite d'Apollon" in a ballet performance.
-Pierre I (d. 1697). Active in Paris and Stockholm as instrument player.
-Pierre II (d. post 1706). Worked in Stockholm, mostly as ballet composer. Transcriptions (of pieces by Pierre II?) in *45-Dart, Stockholm-228* and *Uppsala-409.*

VINCENT (fl. 1606-1643). Unidentified lutenist, composer and teacher. May be the Vincent who played with Louis Couperin in ballets de cour in 1657 and 1661. A number of lute pieces survive (*Fasquelle*, Bourligueux for *Grove-6*). Perhaps the composer represented in *35-Bauyn-III.*

WAGENSEIL, Georg Christoph (1715-1777) (*MGG*). Pieces in *15-Berlin-30206.*

WALTHER, Johann Gottfried (1684-1748). (*MGG*). Scribe of *12-Walther.*

WECKMANN, Matthias (1621-1674). Organist and composer in Hamburg from 1655 (*MGG*). Probably the scribe of *8-Hintze* and *Lüneburg-147,* and certainly of *Lüneburg-207:6;* erroneously considered the scribe of *4-Lynar.*

WILSON, John (1595-1674). Lutenist, viol player and composer at the English court (*Grove-5*). Pieces in *17-Rogers*.

WOODSON, Leonard (d. 1641). English organist and composer (*Grove-5*). Pieces in *4-Lynar*.

YOUNG, William (d. 1671). English viol player and composer for that instrument who worked on the continent (*Grove-5*). Probably the Young in *16-Cosyn*.

ZACH, Johann (1699-1773). Bohemian composer (*MGG*). Pieces in *15-Berlin-30206*.

ZACHARIÄ, Justus Friedrich Wilhelm (1726-1777). German composer, author (*MGG*). Pieces in *15-Berlin-30206*.

ZACHOW, (Zachau), Friedrich Wilhelm (1663-1712). North German composer (*MGG*). Pieces in *13-Möllersche*.

ZIANI, Pietro Andrea (ca. 1620-1684). Italian composer (*Caldwell*). Pieces in *24-Babell*.

BIBLIOGRAPHY A

Manuscript Music

All musical manuscripts which were consulted for this study are listed here with the exception of Lully opera scores (see Meredith Ellis, "The Sources of Jean-Baptiste Lully's Secular Music," *Recherches* 8 (1968): 89-130; 9 (1969): 21-25). Manuscript documents are listed in section C of the Bibliography, "Literature."

The manuscripts are arranged by location: country, city, library and shelf number. Each entry is given a brief annotation consisting (when applicable) of the approximate date of the source, the medium for which it was written and the code which has been assigned to it in the present study.

AUSTRIA

Linz; Oberösterreiches Landesmuseum (*olim* Museum Francisco-Carolinim)

MS 16 Inc. 9467	1611-1613, keyboard; *Linz.*

Vienna; Minoritenkonvent, Klosterbibliothek & Archiv

MS 741	post 1724, keyboard.
MS 743	1708-17??, keyboard; *Minorite.*

Vienna; Österreichische Nationalbibliothek, Musiksammlung

MS 16,798	1699, keyboard; *Grimm.*
MS 18,491	1649, keyboard; *Imhoff.*

BELGIUM

Brussels; Bibliothèque royale Albert 1er (Koninklijke Bibliothek Albert I), département de manuscrits

MS III 899	17th c., German keyboard
MS III 900	ca. 1660?, Belgian keyboard; *Beatrix.*
MS III 926	post 1670, Belgian keyboard; *28-Brussels-926.*
MS III 1037	ca. 1680, lute and motets.

Brussels; Conservatoire royal de musique, bibliothèque

26.651	19th c. ms copy of *62-Chamb-I* and *63-Chamb-II.*
cf XY 24.106	18th c. unlocated Philidor ms; *Brussels-24.106.*
cf XY 27.220	17th c. unlocated Chambonnières ms; *Brussels-27.220.*
s.s.	Copy of *Faille* by Charles Van den Borren.

DENMARK

Copenhagen; Det kongelige Bibliotek, Haandskrift Afd.

Additamenta 396 4o	post 1684, keyboard; *Copenhagen-396.*
Gl. Kgl. Saml. Nr. 376, Fol.	1629-ca. 1650, keyboard; *1-Copenhagen-376.*
Ny kgl Saml MS 1997 2o	1637, keyboard, "Obmans ms."
Thott 292 8o	1699-1702, keyboard; *Thott*

Ibid., Musikafdelingen

Mu 6610.2631	post 1642, keyboard; *Voigtländer.*
Mu 6806.1399	ca. 1700?, keyboard; *11-Ryge.*

FRANCE

Besançon; Bibliothèque municipale

No 279152, 279153	1699, lute; *Saizenay-I, Saizenay-II.*

Clermont-Ferrand; Archives départementales du Puy-de-Dome

2 E 976 57	1661, harpsichord; *55-Redon.*

Paris; Bibliothèque de l'arsenal

s.s (*olim* M 410/24)	Unlocated "méthode de clavecin."
MS 935 (*olim* M [Carton 4] n.c.)	18th c., harpsichord.
M 957 1-12	Miscellaneous mss and printed sources; exercises, rules of transposition, chansons, fragments.
MS 6784	18th c., harpsichord with some instrumental.
MS 6820	18th c., harpsichord, "Thiebaut ms."

Paris; Bibliothèque nationale, département de la musique

Rés F 933 (*olim* Conservatoire de musique)	post 1715, harpsichord; *49-RésF-933.*
Rés Vma ms 7$^{(1-2)}$	1731, chansons; *Rés-Vma-ms-7/2.*
Rés Vma ms 854	1645-1680, airs de cour, à boire.
Rés Vmb ms 7	ca. 1680, lute, "Barbe ms."
Rés Vm^7 674, Vm^7 675 (*olim* Vm7 1852, Vm7 1862)	post 1658, harpsichord; *35-Bauyn.*
Rés 89ter (*olim* Conservatoire de musique 18223)	post 1677, harpsichord; *33-Rés-89ter.*
Rés 475 (*olim* Conservatoire de musique 24827).	post 1694, harpsichord; *37-Geoffroy.*
Rés 476 (*olim* Conservatoire de musique 24827 [*sic*]).	post 1679, organ and harpsichord; *40-Rés-476*
Rés-819$^{(2)}$ (*olim* Conservatoire de musique)	post 1661, German keyboard; *Rés-819-2.*
Rés 1185 (*olim* Conservatoire de musique 18548)	ca. 1613, 1652, English harpsichord; *16-Cosyn.*
Rés 1186 (*olim* Conservatoire de musique 16546)	17th c. English harpsichord.
Rés 1186bis$^{(1-2)}$	post ca. 1680 (part 2), English harpsichord; *21-Rés-1186bis.*
Rés 2094 (*olim* Conservatoire de musique 12 1861)	1677-1683, organ; *Thiéry.*
Rés 2671 (*olim* Conservatoire de musique 2389)	post 1742, harpsichord *52-Rés-2671.*
Vm^6 5	1691, violin ballet ms; *Veron.*
Vm^7 675	post 1686, lute.
Vm^7 1099	17th c., instrumental; *Rost.*
Vm^7 1817	1675?, German organ.
Vm^7 1817bis	ca. 1680?, harpsichord; *41-Thomelin.*
Vm^7 1818	post 1684, German harpsichord; *Stoss.*
Vm^7 1823	1688, French organ.
Vm^7 1852, Vm^7 1862	see: Rés Vm^7 674-675.
Vm^7 3555	18th c., violin ms.
Vm^7 4867	post 1715, violin ms; *Vm7-4867.*
Vm^7 6211 - 6212	mid 17th c., lute.
Vm^7 6307$^{(1)}$	post 1678, harpsichord, viol; *39-Vm7-6307-1.*
Vm^7 6307$^{(2)}$	post 1684, harpsichord; *42-Vm7-6307-2.*
Vm^8 1139	post 1724?, harpsichord; *St-Georges.*

Paris; Bibliothèque Sainte-Geneviève

MS 2348	post 1658?, harpsichord, organ; *38-Gen-2348/53.*
MS 2350	ca. 1630-1670, harpsichord, organ; *54-Gen-2350/57.*
MS 2353	post 1658?, organ; *38-Gen-2348/53.*
MS 2354	post 1685, harpsichord; *43-Gen-2354.*
MS 2356	ca. 1690?, harpsichord, organ; *47-Gen-2356.*

MS 2357	ca. 1690?, (part 1), harpsichord; *34-Gen-2357[A]*.
	ca. 1630-1670 (part 2), harpsichord; *54-Gen-2350/57*.
MS 2374	1716, harpsichord; *50-Paignon*.
MS 2382	18th c., harpsichord; *LeBret*.
MS 3168	17th c., instrumental.
MS 3169	17th c., instrumental.

Paris; Conservatoire national supérior de musique, bibliothèque

The mss formerly held by this library are now in the Bibliothèque nationale (Paris), département de la musique. The following old numbers are relevant to mss listed above:

Rés F 913	Rés F 913
2389 (crossed out)	Rés 2671
12,1861	Rés 2094
18,223	Rés 89ter
18,546	Rés 1186
18,548	Rés 1185
18,570	Rés 1186bis
24,827	Rés 475
24,827 [*sic*]	Rés 476

Paris; private collection: Estate of Madame de Chambure (Geneviève Thibault)

s.s.	1687, harpsichord; *44-LaPierre*.

Versailles; Bibliothèque municipale

Ms. Mus. 54 9	18th c., vocal.
Ms. Mus. 64, 65$^{1-3}$	18th c., vocal.
Ms. Mus. 139 - 143	18th c., instrumental; *Philidor*.

GERMANY (Federal Republic and Democratic Republic interfiled)

Berlin; Deutsche Staatsbibliothek, Musikabteilung (East Berlin); Staatsbibliothek der Stiftung preussischer Kulturbesitz, Musikabteilung (West Berlin). Locations for the mss are given after the shelf numbers: E (East Berlin), W (West Berlin) and U (unlocated).

Lübbenau Tabulaturen,	
Lynar A-1 [E]	ca. 1615-1650, keyboard; *4-Lynar,*
Lynar A-2 [E]	*Lynar-A2*.
Mus. Ms. P 801 [E]	ca. 1712-post 1731, keyboard; *12-Walther*.
Mus. Ms. 4112 [U]	17th c., "G.A.A. französiche Tanzsuiten."
Mus. Ms. 8551 [W]	ca. 1725?, keyboard; *Berlin-8551*.
Mus. Ms. 30,078 [E]	18th c., keyboard.
Mus. Ms. 30,206 [E]	ca. 1750-1770, keyboard; *15-Berlin-30206*.

Mus. Ms. 30,363 [E]	post 1723, keyboard; *Berlin-30363.*
Mus. Ms. 30,382 [E]	18th c., keyboard.
Mus. Ms. 40,034 [W]	1585, keyboard, "Löffelholtz tablature."
Mus. Ms. 40,035 [U]	18th c., keyboard, "Orgelbuch Joh. Val. Eckelt."
Mus. Ms. 40,068 [W]	1656, lute; *Rodenegg.*
Mus. Ms. 40,076 [U]	17th c., keyboard.
Mus. Ms. 40,147 [U]	ca. 1660-1680, keyboard; *Berlin-40147.*
Mus. Ms. 40,148 [U]	Modern partial transcription of *1-Copenhagen-376.*
Mus. Ms. 40,165 [W]	Modern copy of 1568 lute tablature.
Mus. Ms. 40,268 [W]	1715-1718, keyboard.
Mus. Ms. 40,600 [E]	17th c., lute.
Mus. Ms. 40,601 [E]	17th c., lute.
Mus. Ms. 40,621 [W]	ca. 1640, keyboard.
Mus. Ms. 40,622 [U]	1664-1684, cittern.
Mus. Ms. 40,623 [U]	1678, keyboard; *3-Berlin-40623.*
Mus. Ms. 40,624 [U]	post 1715, keyboard; *Berlin-40624.*
Mus. Ms. 40,644 [W]	1717-1719, keyboard; *13-Möllersche.*

Celle; Bomann Musik Bibliothek

MS 730	1662, keyboard; *Celle.*

Darmstadt; Hessische Landes- und Hochschulbibliothek, Musikabteilung

Mus. ms. 17 (*olim* MS 2897)	1672, keyboard; *Darmstadt-17.*
Mus. Ms. 18 (*olim* MS 2898)	1674, keyboard; *Darmstadt-18.*
Mus. Ms. 1198 (*olim* MS 2898/1)	16--, score in organ tablature; *Darmstadt-1198.*
MS 1655	1653, lute; destroyed in World War II, but photocopy available.

Leipzig; Musikbibliothek der Stadt Leipzig

Ms. II.6.16	ca. 1650, keyboard.
Ms. II.6.18	1650-1670, keyboard.
Ms. II.6.19	1681, keyboard.

Lüneburg; Ratsbücherei der Stadt Lüneburg, Musikabteilung

Mus. Ant. Pract. KN 146	1650, keyboard; *Drallius.*
Mus. Ant. Pract. KN 147	17th c., keyboard; *Lüneburg-147.*
Mus. Ant. Pract. KN 148	1655-1659, keyboard; *2-Witzendorff.*
Mus. Ant. Pract. KN 149	ca. 1670, keyboard.
Mus. Ant. Pract. KN 207:6	17th c., vocal; *Lüneburg-207:6.*
Mus. Ant. Pract. KN 1198	1687, keyboard; *Lüneburg-1198.*

Munich; Bayerische Staatsbibliothek, Musiksammlung

Mus. Ms. 1503k	17th c., French (?), organ; *Munich-1503k.*
Mus. Ms.1503*l*	ca. 1660?, harpsichord; *5-Munich-1503l.*
Mus. Ms. 1511e	ca. 1660?, harpsichord; *6-Munich-1511e.*
Mus. Ms. 1511f	ca. 1660?, harpsichord; *7-Munich-1511f.*
Mus. Ms. 1511g	17th c., melody-bass parts and/or score.
Mus. Ms. 1657	ca. 1637-1649, melodies.
Mus. Ms. 4112	1687, keyboard.

Nuremberg; Germanisches Nationalmuseum, Bibliothek

Hs. 31781	1699-1721, keyboard; *Nuremberg.*
Hs. 139600	17th c., lute.

Ottobeuren, Algau (Schwaben, Bayern); Benediktiner-Abtei, Musikarchiv und Bibliothek

MO 1037	1695, keyboard; *Ottobeuren.*

Schwerin; Wissenschaftliche Allgemeinbibliothek des Bezirkes Schwerin

Musik Hs. 617 (*olim* Anonyma D-2)	post 1684, harpsichord; *10-Schwerin-617.*
Musik Hs. 619 (*olim* Anonyma D-4; Klavierbuch 7)	ca. 1720?, harpsichord; *14-Schwerin-619.*
Musik Hs. 633	18th c., harpsichord.
Musik Hss. 635-636	late 18th c., large group of unrelated keyboard mss.
Musik Hs. 640	ca. 1670-1690?, angelique.

Wolfenbüttel; Herzog August Bibliothek

Ms. Cod. Guelf 1055	1641, keyboard.

Zweibrücken; Bibliothek Bipontina, Herzog-Wolfgang-Gymnasium

Anon. Tab. [s.s.]	ca. 1615, keyboard.

Zwickau; Ratschulbibliothek

Ms. Mus. C 6	ca. 1595, keyboard.

GREAT BRITAIN

Cambridge; Fitzwilliam Museum

ms 3-1956	ca. 1608-1640, lute; *Cherbury.*

Edinburg; National Library of Scotland

Inglis 94 MS 3343	ca. 1695, keyboard; *Inglis.*

London; British Library, Reference Division [British Museum], Department of Manuscripts

Additional 10337	1656, harpsichord, vocal; *17-Rogers.*
Additional 14336	17th c., motets.
Additional 16889	ca. 1615-1618, lute.
Additional 22099	1704-1707, keyboard.
Additional 23623	ca. 1629, keyboard; *26-Bull.*
Additional 29379	17th c., motets.
Additional 29485	ca. 1599, keyboard, "Susanne van Soldt ms."
Additional 30491, *l.* 23-206	early 17th c., Neapolitan keyboard, "Rossi ms."
Additional 31403	early 17th c., keyboard.
Additional 36661	17th c., keyboard.
Additional 38189	ca. 1690-1722, violin.
Additional 39569	1702, harpsichord; *24-Babell.*
Additional 41205	18th c., harpsichord, "Wm. A. Barrett ms."
Additional 52363	1704, keyboard.
Egerton 814	1744, chansons.
Egerton 2514	17th c., chansons.
Egerton 2959	17th c., harpsichord.
Sloane 1021	17th c., lute; *Sloane-1021.*
Sloane 2923	ca. 1683, lute.

Ibid., Music Room

R.M. 24.*l.*4	17th c., harpsichord (Cosyn holograph).

London; Royal College of Music Library

ms 835	modern copy, keyboard.
ms 2093	17th c., keyboard; *RCM.*

London; private collection: Estate of Thurston Dart, on permanent loan to the Faculty of Music, King's College, London.

s.s. (#2 on unpublished "Handlist of Manuscripts from the Dart Collection . . .")	post 1687, harpsichord; *45-Dart.*

London; private collection: Guy Oldham

s.s.	ca. 1650-1661, keyboard; *32-Oldham.*
s.s.	post 1752, harpsichord; *53-Oldham-2.*

Oxford; Bodleian Library

Ms. Mus. Sch. c. 61	18th c., instrumental
Ms. Mus. Sch. c. 94	1661, guitar.
Ms. Mus. Sch. c. 95	17th c., melody, vocal.
Ms. Mus. Sch. D. 220	1654, instrumental bass part; *Bod-220.*
Ms. Mus. Sch. E. 393	1700, vocal; *Bod-393.*
Ms. Mus. Sch. E. 398	17th c., treble-bass (Lully).
Ms. Mus. Sch. E. 419	1733, treble.
Ms. Mus. Sch. E. 425	post 1708, keyboard; *Bod-425.*
Ms. Mus. Sch. E. 426	post 1708, keyboard; *25-Bod-426.*
Ms. Mus. Sch. E. 443-E. 446	17th c., instrumental.
Ms. Mus. Sch. F. 573	17th c., melody-bass.
Ms. Mus. Sch. F. 576	post 1679, lute, vocal, harpsichord; *Bod-576.*
Ms. Mus. Sch. F. 578	17th c., lute, guitar.
Ms. Mus. Sch. G. 616-G. 618	17th c., lute, guitar.

Oxford; Christ Church Library

Mus. Ms. 378	ca. 1675-1710?, harpsichord; *20-Ch-Ch-378.*
Mus. Ms. 430	17th c., harpsichord.
Mus. Ms. 431	17th c., harpsichord.
Mus. Ms. 437	17th c., harpsichord.
Mus. Ms. 1003	17th c., harpsichord.
Mus. Ms. 1113	17th c., harpsichord; *Ch-Ch-1113.*
Mus. Ms. 1177	post 1680, harpsichord; *22-Ch-Ch-1177.*
Mus. Ms. 1179	17th c., harpsichord.
Mus. Ms. 1236	ca. 1650-1674, harpsichord; *18-Ch-Ch-1236.*

Oxford; private collection: Mrs. I. B.

s.s.	1652, keyboard; *Oxford-IB.*

Tenbury Wells (Worcestershire); St. Michael's College Library

MS 1508	1701, harpsichord, *23-Tenbury.*

HUNGARY

Sopron; Liszt Ferenc Muzeum

Tabulatur d. J.J. Starck	1689, keyboard.

ITALY

Bologna; Civico museo bibliografico musicale

Ms. AA/360	ca. 1640-1680, keyboard; *Bologna-360.*

Rome; Biblioteca Apostolica Vaticana

Ms. Chigi Q IV 24	ca. 1650?, keyboard, *29-Chigi.*
Ms. Chigi Q IV 27	ca. 1650?, keyboard, *Chigi-27.*
Ms. Vat. mus. 569	ca. 1660-1665, keyboard, *Vat-mus-569.*

Rome; Conservatorio di Musica Santa Cecilia, Biblioteca

MS A/400	ca. 1700?, keyboard; *30-Cecilia.*
MS no. 417.1	18th c., harpsichord.
MS no. 417.2	19th c., copy (Rameau).

NETHERLANDS

Amsterdam; Toonkunst-Bibliotheek

| 208 A 4 | 1671, harpsichord; *Van-Eijl.* |

Den Haag; Gemeente Museum

| 4 H 34 | 1665, keyboard. |
| 21 E 47 | 17th c., keyboard. |

Utrecht; Instituut voor Muziekwetenschap der Rijksuniversiteit te Utrecht

| MS q-1 | post 1669, harpsichord; *27-Gresse.* |
| M So-2 | 17th c., keyboard, "Campuysen ms." |

SPAIN

Madrid; Biblioteca nacional

M 815 (-G.-G^a-16)	1721, keyboard.
M 1250	18th c., keyboard.
Ms 1357	1706, keyboard; *Madrid-1357.*
Ms 1358	1707, keyboard.
Ms 1359	1708, keyboard.
Ms 1360	1709, keyboard; *31-Madrid-1360.*

SWEDEN

Norrköping; Stadsbiblioteket

| Finspong 9098 | 17th c., violin; *Finspong.* |

Skara; Stifts- och Landsbiblioteket, Högre Allmänne Läroverks Musiksamling

Skara 493b (nr 31)   1659-post 1661, keyboard; *Skara.*

Stockholm; Kungliga Biblioteket

S. 176	post 1681, keyboard; *Stockholm-176.*
S. 228	post 1685, keyboard; *Stockholm-228.*
S. 226a	1620, lute (photocopy of original in Skoklosters Bibliotek).

Stockholm; Kungliga Musikaliska Academiens Bibliotek

Tabl. 1	ca. 1600, keyboard; *Eÿsbock.*
Tabl. 2	ca. 1680?, keyboard; *Stockholm-2.*

Uppsala; Universitetsbiblioteket, Carolina Rediviva

Ihre 284	1679, harpsichord; *9-Ihre-284.*
IMhs 13:6a	17th c., instrumental.
IMhs 134:22	ca. 1650-1662?, instrumental score; *Uppsala-134:22.*
IMhs 408	1641, keyboard.
IMtab Nr 410 (1712)	1705-1727, keyboard.
MS 409	ca. 1650-1662, instrumental score; *Uppsala-409.*
MS 409:2	See IMhs 134:22.

SWITZERLAND

Basel; Öffentliche Bibliothek der Universität, Musiksammlung

Ms F.IX.53   17th c., lute.

UNITED STATES

Berkeley, California; University of California at Berkeley, Music Library

MS 765	post 1682, vocal; *LaBarre-1.*
MS 766	post 1685, vocal; *LaBarre-2.*
MS 767	post 1686, vocal; *LaBarre-3.*
MS 768	post 1688, vocal; *LaBarre-4.*
MS 769	post 1693, vocal; *LaBarre-5.*
MS 770	post 1697, harpsichord, vocal; *48-LaBarre-6.*
MS 771	post 1699, vocal; *LaBarre-7.*
MS 772	post 1703, vocal; *LaBarre-8.*
MS 773	post 1718, vocal; *LaBarre-9.*
MS 774	post 1719, vocal; *LaBarre-10.*
MS 775	post 1724, harpsichord, vocal; *51-LaBarre-11.*

MS 776	post 1685, organ (Lebègue).
MS 777	post ca. 1689, harpsichord; *46-Menetou.*
MS 778	post 1686, harpsichord; *36-Parville.*

Chicago, Newberry Library, Special Collections

Case MS VM2.3 E58r	ca. 1691, harpsichord; *22a-Roper.*
Case MS VM21 R295	mid-18th c., harpsichord, French.
Case MS VM145 L788	17th c., instrumental melodies.
Case MS VM350 B113t	ca. 1700, instrumental trios; *Newberry.*
Case MS 7Q 5	17th c., lute.

Los Angeles, California; University of California at Los Angeles, William Andrews Clark
Memorial Library

| D. 173 M4 H295 1690bd | 1690, harpsichord; *Clark-D173.* |
| M. 678 M4 H295 1710 | 1710, harpsichord; *Clark-M678.* |

New Haven, Connecticut; Yale University, John Herrick Jackson Music Library

| LM 5056 | 1680-1690, keyboard. |
| Ma 21 H 59 | ca. 1660-1674?, harpsichord; *8-Hintze.* |

New York, New York; New York Public Library, Library and Museum for the
Performing Arts, Music Division

Drexel MS 5609	Late 18th c., harpsichord, copied by Sir John Hawkins; *Drexel-5609.*
Drexel MS 5611	ca. 1664?, harpsichord; *19-Heardson.*
Drexel MS 5612	17th c., harpsichord.

South Bend, Indiana; private collection: Bruce Gustafson

| 6 | ca. 1700, 3 instrumental part-books, *Cummings.* |

Washington, D.C.; Library of Congress, Music Division

| M 21 M 185 [missing] | ca. 1700?, harpsichord. |

U. S. S. R.

Leningrad; Library of the Academy of Sciences

| MS QN 204 | 1650, keyboard; *Leningrad.* |

UNLOCATED (see also: Brussels Conservatoire; Berlin deutsche Staatsbibliothek;
Washington Library of Congress; discussions in Commentary of Huygens, Titon
du Tillet).

Burette, Pierre-Jean. *Catalogue de la bibliothèque de feu M. Burette*, 3 vols. Paris: G. Martin, 1748.

407	1695, harpsichord; *Burette-407*.
408	1695, harpsichord; *Burette-408*.
409	1695, harpsichord, harp; *Burette-409*.
410	n.d., harpsichord; *Burette-410*.

Écorcheville, Jules. *Catalogue des livres rares et précieux compossant la collection musicale de feu M. Jules Écorcheville.* Paris: Émile Paul, 1920.

304	ca. 1625, keyboard; *Faille*.

Hochschule für Musikerziehung und Kirchenmusik [former]

MS 5270	1675-1690, keyboard (cf. Riedel, *Quellen*, pp. 78-79).

Pirro, André. *Les Clavecinistes*. Paris: H. Laurens, 1924.

p. 44	17th c., keyboard; *Terburg*.

Wolffheim, Werner. *Versteigerung der Musikbibliothek des Herrn Dr. Werner Wolffheim.* 2 vols.   Berlin: Breslauer & Liepmannssohn, 1928-1929.

48	1630-1650?, keyboard; *Wolffheim*.

Ward, John. *Lives of the Professors of Gresham College.* London: 1740.

18	ca. 1629, keyboard.

BIBLIOGRAPHY B

Printed Music

Albert, Heinrich. *Dritter Theil der Arien oder Melodeyen (1640)*, Denkmäler deutscher Tonkunst: vol. 12. Ed. Eduard Bernoulli, rev. Hans Joachim Moser. Wiesbaden: Breitkoof & Härtel, 1958.

d'Anglebert, Jean-Henri. *Pieces de clavecin*. Paris: author, 1689.

————. *Pièces de clavecin*, Le Pupitre: no. 54. Ed. Kenneth Gilbert. Paris: Heugel, 1975.

————. *Pièces de clavecin*, Publications de la Société française de musicologie. Ed. Marguerite Roesgen-Champion. Paris: Droz, 1934.

Anonyme français du 17e siècle, le livre d'orgue de Marguerite Thiéry, l'Organiste liturgique: no. 25. Paris: Schola Cantorum, n.d.

Auxcousteaux, Artus. *Noëls et cantiques spirituels*. Paris: Robert Ballard, [1644].

————. *Second Livre de noëls*. Paris: Robert Ballard, 1644.

————. *Les Quatrains de Mr. Mathieu mis en musique à trois parties selon des douze modes*. Paris: Robert Ballard, 1643.

————. *Suite de la première partie des Quatrains*. Paris: Robert Ballard, 1652.

Babell, Charles, ed. *Trios de differents autheurs*. 2 vols. Amsterdam: Roger [1697, 1700].

Ballard, Robert. [*Premier Livre de luth*. Paris: P. Ballard, 1611.]

————. *Diverses Piesces mises sur le luth par R. Ballard*. Paris: P. Ballard, 1614.

————. *Premier Livre (1611)*. Ed. André Souris and Sylvie Spycket; intro. by Monique Rollin. Paris: Centre national de la recherche scientifique, 1963.

————. *Deuxième Livre (1614) et pièces diverses*. Ed. André Souris, Sylvie Spycket and Jacques Veyrier; intro. by Monique Rollin. Paris: Centre national de la recherche scientifique, 1964.

Bang, Claus Hansen. *Med lyst vil jeg begynde* [broadside]. N.p., 1639.

Besard, Jean-Baptiste. *Novus Partus, sive Concertationes Musicae*. Augsburg: 1617.

————. *Oeuvres pour luth seul*. Ed. André Souris; intro. by Monique Rollin. Paris: Centre national de la recherche scientifique, 1969.

Brade, William. *Newe lustige Volten, Couranten, Balletten, Padoanen, Galliarden, Masqueraden, auch allerley arth Newer Französischer Täntze.* Berlin: Martin Guth, 1621.

Bull, John. *Keyboard Music I*, Musica Britannica: no. 14. Ed. John Steele and Francis Cameron; intro. by Thurston Dart. London: Stainer and Bell, 1960.

_____. *Keyboard Music II*, Musica Britannica: no. 19. Ed. Thurston Dart. London: Stainer and Bell, 1963.

Buxtehude, Dietrich. *Klaviervaerker.* 2nd ed. Ed. Emilius Bangert. Copenhagen: Hansen, 1944.

Byrd, William. *Keyboard Music*, Musica Britannica: no. 28. Ed. Alan Brown. London: Stainer and Bell, 1971.

Cabanilles, Juan. *Musici organici Iohannis Cabanilles, Opera omnia*, vol. 1. Ed. Hygino Anglès. Barcelona: Biblioteca de Cataluña, 1927.

Campra, André. *L'Europe galante.* Paris: Ballard, 1697.

_____. *Les Festes vénitiennes.* Paris: Ballard, 1710.

Chaconnes et passacailles, Orgue et liturgie: 22. Ed. Noëlie Pierront. Paris: Schola cantorum, 1954.

Chambonnières, Jacques Champion. *Les Pieces de clauessin.* Paris: Jollain, 1670.

_____. *Les Pieces de Clauessin . . . Liure Second.* Paris: Jollain, [1670].

_____. *Oeuvres complètes*, Publications de la Société française de musicologie. Ed. Paul Brunold and André Tessier. Paris: Senart, 1925; reprint ed., New York: Broude Brothers, 1967.

_____. *Les deux Livres de clavecin.* Ed. Thurston Dart. Monaco: Oiseau Lyre, 1969.

A Choice Collection of Ayres for the Harpsichord or Spinet. London: Young, 1700.

Clém. de Bourges et N. de Grotte, fantaisies; Ch. Racquet oeuvres complètes; Denis Gautier, tombeau, l'Organiste liturgique: no. 29. Ed. Jean Bonfils. Paris: Schola Cantorum, n.d.

A Collection of Lessons and Aires for the Harpsichord or Spinnett compos'd by Mr. J. Eccles, Mr. D. Purcell and Others. London: I. Walsh and I. Hare, [1702].

Corelli, Arcangelo. *Suittes pour le clavecin.* 2 vols. Amsterdam: Roger, [ca. 1715].

Couperin, Louis. *Oeuvres complètes.* Ed. Paul Brunold. Paris: Oiseau Lyre, 1936.

_____. *Pièces de clavecin*. Ed. Paul Brunold, rev. Thurston Dart. Monaco: Oiseau Lyre, 1959.

_____. *Pièces de clavecin*, Le Pupitre: no. 18. Ed. Alan Curtis. Paris: Heugel, 1970.

Croft, William. *Complete Harpsichord Works*. 2 vols. Ed. Howard Ferguson and Christopher Hogwood. London: Stainer and Bell, 1974.

Dandrieu, Jean-François. *Livre de clavecin . . . dédie à Monsieur Robert*. Paris: author, Ribon, Roucault [ca. 1704].

_____. *Music for Harpsichord*. Ed. John White. University Park: Pennsylvania State University Press, 1965.

_____. *Livre de clavecin . . . organiste de St. Merry*. Paris: author, Foucault [ca. 1704].

_____. *Pièces de clavecin courtes et faciles*. Paris: author, Foucault [ca. 1704].

_____. *Premier Livre de pièces de clavecin*. Paris: author, 1724.

_____. *Second Livre de pièces de clavecin*. Paris: Boivin, 1728.

_____. *Troisième Livre de pièces de clavecin*. Paris: author et al., 1734.

_____. *Trois Livres de clavecin de jeunesse*, Publications de la Société française de musicologie 1:21.   Ed Brigitte François-Sappey.   Paris: Heugel, 1975.

_____. *Trois Livres de Clavecin*. Ed. Pauline Aubert and Brigitte François-Sappey. Paris: Schola Cantorum, 1973.

Destouches, André Cardinal. *Issé*. Paris: Ballard, 1708.

Dieupart. *Six Suites pour clavecin*. Ed. Paul Brunold. Paris: Oiseau Lyre, 1934.

Draghi, Giovanni Battista. *Six Select Suites of Lessons for the Harpsichord*. London: Walsh, [1707].

Dufaut. *Oeuvres*. Ed. André Souris; intro. by Monique Rollin. Paris: Centre national de la recherche scientifique, 1965.

Dumont, Henry. *Cantica sacra*. Paris: Robert Ballard, 1652; 2nd ed., 1662.

_____. *Meslanges*. Paris: Robert Ballard, 1657.

_____. *Motets a devx voix avec la basse-continve*. Paris: Robert Ballard, 1668.

_____. *L'Oeuvre pour clavier*, l'Organiste liturgique: no. 13.   Ed. Jean Bonfils. Paris: Schola   Cantorum, 1956.

Elizabeth Roger's Virginal Book, 1656, Corpus of Early Keyboard Music: no. 19.   Ed. George Sargent.   N.p.:   American Institute of Musicology, 1971.

Elizabeth Rogers Hir Virginall Booke. Ed. Charles J.F. Cofone. New York: Dover, 1975.

English Pastime Music, 1630-1660, Collegium Musicum: Ser. 2, vol. 4.   Ed. Martha Maas.   Madison: A-R Editions, 1974.

Eyck, Jacob van.   *Der Fluyten Lust-Hof, Vol Psalmen, Paduanen, Allemanden, Couranten, Balletten, Airs, etc.*   2. vols.   Amsterdam: Paulus Matthysz, 1646, 1654.

Frescobaldi, Girolamo.   *Orgel- und Klavierwerke.* 5 vols.   Ed. Pierre Pidoux.   Kassel: Bärenreiter, 1948-1953.

_____. *Keyboard Compositions Preserved in Manuscripts*, Corpus of Early Keyboard Music: no. 30.   3 vols.   Ed. Richard W. Shindle.   N.p.:   American Institute of Musicology, 1968.

Froberger, Johann Jakob.   *Orgel-und Klavierwerke*, Denkmäler der Tonkunst in Österreich IV/1:8, VI/2:13, X/2:21.   3 vols.   Graz: Akademische Druck- u. Verlagsanstalt, 1896; reprint ed., 1959.

Fuhrmann, Georg Leopold.   *Testudo Gallo-Germanica.* Nuremberg: Norici, 1615.

Gaultier, Denis.   *La Rhétorique des dieux et autres pièces de luth*, Publications de la Société fançaise de musicologie.   2 vols.   Ed. André Tessier.   Paris: Droz, 1932-1933.

Gaultier, Ennemond.   *Oeuvres du vieux Gautier.*   Ed. André Souris; intro. by Monique Rollin.   Paris: Centre national de la recherche scientifique, 1966.

Gaultier, Pierre [de Marseilles].   *Symphonies.* Paris: Ballard, 1707.

Gaultier, Pierre [d'Orléans].   *Les Oeuvres.* Rome: n.p., 1638.

Geoffroy, Jean Nicolas.   "A New Chapter in the History of the Clavecin Suite" by Pauline M. Campbell.   M.M. thesis, University of Illinois, 1967.

Gibbons, Orlando.   *Keyboard Music*, Musica Britannica: no. 20.   Ed. Gerald Hendrie. London: Stainer and Bell, 1962.

Gigault, Nicolas. *Livre de mvsiqve dediè à la très Ste. Vierge.* Paris: author, 1682.

_____. *Livre de musique pour l'orgue.* Paris: author 1685.

Gillier, Pierre [l'Aîné].   *Livre d'airs et de symphonies meslez de quelques fragments d'opéra.*   Paris: author, Foucoult, 1697.

Hammerschmidt, Andreas. *Erster Fleiss allerhand newer Paduanen, Galliarden, Balletten, Mascharaden, Françoischen Arien, Courentten, und Sarabanden.* Freiburg: Georg Beuther, 1639.

Hardel. ["Pièces de clavecin"]. Ed. Henri Quittard. *Revue musicale*, supplément, Nov. 15, 1906.

"Huit Pièces inédites." Ed. André Pirro. *Revue musicale*, supplément, Feb., 1921.

"Keyboard Tablatures of the Seventeenth Century in the Royal Library, Copenhagen." Ed. Alis Dickinson. Ph.D. dissertation, North Texas State University, 1974.

Kindermann, Johannes Erasmus. *Ausgewählte Werke*, Denkmäler der Tonkunst in Bayern 13: 21-24. Ed. Felix Schreiber. Leipzig: Breitkopf & Härtel, 1913-1924.

Kirchner, Athanatius. *Musurgia universalis.* Rome: n.p., 1650.

Klavierboek Anna Maria van Eijl, Monumenta Musica Neerlandica: no. 2. Ed. Frits Noske. Amersdam: Verenigung voor Nederlandse Muziekgeschiedenis, 1959.

Lebègue, Nicolas-Antoine. *Les Pieces de Clauessin.* Paris: Baillon, 1677.

_____. *Second Liure de clavesin.* Paris: Lescop, 1687.

_____. *Oeuvres de clavecin.* Ed. Norbert Dufourcq. Monaco: Oiseau Lyre, 1956.

Livre d'orgue attribué à J.M. Geoffroy, Le Pupitre: no. 53. Ed. Jean Bonfils. Paris: Heugel, 1974.

Locke, Matthew. *Keyboard Suites.* 2nd ed. Ed. Thurston Dart. London: Stainer and Bell, 1964.

Lorentz, Johann. *Klavierwerke.* Ed. Bo Lundgren. Lund: n.p., 1960.

Lully, Jean-Baptiste. For a listing of printed and manuscript opera scores, see: Meredith Ellis. "The Sources of Jean-Baptiste Lully's Secular Music." *Recherches* 8 (1968): 89-103.

_____. *Nine Seventeenth-Century Organ Transcriptions from the Operas of Lully.* Ed. Almonte Charles Howell, Jr. Lexington: University of Kentucky Press, 1963.

Manuscrit Bauyn [facsim ed.]. Preface by François Lesure. Geneva: Minkoff, 1977.

Marais, Marin. *Pièces à une et à deux violes.* Paris: author, [1686].

_____. *Pièces de violes.* Paris: author, [1701].

_____. *Pièces de violes.* Paris: author, [1711].

_____. *Pièces à une et à trois violes.* Paris: author, [1717].

_____. *Pièces de viole.* Paris: author, [1725].

_____. *Pièces en trio pour les flûtes, violon & dessus de viole.* Paris: author, [1692].

Marais, Roland. *1er. Livre de pièces de voile.* Paris: author, 1735.

Mercure. *Oeuvres des Mercure.* Ed. Monique Rollin and Jean-Michel Vaccaro. Paris: Centre national de la recherche scientifique, 1977.

Mesangeau, René. *Oeuvres.* Ed. André Souris; intro by Monique Rollin. Paris: Centre national de la recherche scientifique, 1971.

Muffat, Georg. *Apparatus musico-organisticus [1690].* Ed. S.F. Lange. Leipzig: Rieter-Biedermann, 1888.

Nederlandse Klaviermuziek uit de 16e en 17e eeuw, Monumenta Musica Neerlandica: no. 3. Ed. Alan Curtis. Amsterdam: Verenigung voor Nederlandse Muziekgeschiedenis, 1961.

Oeuvres de Chancy, Bouvier, Belleville, Dubuisson, Chevalier. Ed. André Souris; intro. by Monique Rollin. Paris: Centre national de la recherche scientifique, 1967.

Oeuvres de Vaumesnil, Edinthon, Perrichon, Raël, Montbuysson, La Grotte, Saman, La Barre. Ed. André Souris, Monique Rollin and Jean-Michel Vocars. Paris: Centre de la recherche scientifique, 1974.

L'Orgue parisien sous le règne de Louis XIV. Ed. Norbert Dufourcq. Copenhagen: Hansen, 1956.

Oud-nederlandsche Muziek uit het Muziekboek van Anna Maria van Eijl. Ed. Julius Röntgen. Amsterdam: Alsbach; Leipzig: Breitkopf & Härtel, 1918.

Oude en niuwe Hollantse Boeren-Lietes en Contradansen. 12 parts. Amsterdam: Roger, n.d.

Pachelbel, Johann. *Variationswerke, Hexachordum appolinis, 1699.* Ed. Hans Joachim Moser. Kassel: Bärenreiter, 1958.

Parthenia or the Maydenhead of the First Musicke that Euer Was Printed for the Virginalls. London: Evans, [ca. 1613].

Perrine. *Livre de musique pour le lut.* Paris: author, 1682.

_____. *Pieces de Luth en musique.* Paris: author, 1680.

Playford, John. *Musicks Hand-maide.* London: John Playford, 1663.

_____. *The First Part of Musick's Hand-maid Published by John Playford.* Ed. Thurston Dart. London: Stainer and Bell, 1969.

_____. *The Second Part of Musick's Hand-maid, Revised and Corrected by Henry Purcęll.* 2nd ed. Ed. Thurston Dart. London: Stainer and Bell, 1962.

_____. *Musick's Delight on the Cithren.* London: John Playford, 1666.

Praetorius, Michael. *Terpsichore (1612),* Gesamtausgabe der Musikalischen Werken von Michael Praetoris, Friedrich Blume, gen. ed.: vol. 15. Ed. Günther Oberst. Wolfenbüttel: Georg Kallmeyer Verlag, 1929.

Les Pré-classiques français, l'Organiste liturgigue: no. 18. Ed. Jean Bonfils. Paris: Schola Cantorum, 1957.

Les Pré-classiques français (supplément), l'Organiste liturgique: no. 31. Ed. Jean Bonfils. Paris: Schola Cantorum, n.d.

Les Pré-classiques français, La Barre, Gautier, Ballard, et anonymes, 8 courantes extraites du ms. Lynard Al de Lübbenau, l'Organiste liturgique: no. 58-59. Ed Jean Bonfils. Paris: Schola Cantorum 1967.

Purcell, Henry. *A Choice Collection of Lessons for the Harpsichord.* 3rd ed. London: Westminister, n.d.

Rameau, Jean-Philippe. *Premier Livre de pièces de clavecin.* Paris: author, 1706.

_____. *Nouvelles Suites de pièces de clavecin.* Paris: author, [1728].

_____. *Pièces de clavecin.* Ed. Camille Saint-Saëns. Paris: Durand, n.d.

Reincken, Johann Adam. *Collected Keyboard Works,* Corpus of Early Keyboard Music no. 16. Ed. Willi Apel. N.p.: American Institute of Musicology, 1967.

Roberday, François. *Fugues et caprices à 4 parties.* Paris: Sanlecque, 1660.

_____. *Fugues et caprices pour orgue,* Le Pupitre: no. 44. Ed. Jean Ferrard. Paris: Heugel, 1972.

Rogers, Benjamin. *Complete Keyboard Works.* Ed. Richard Rastall. London: Stainer and Bell, [1969].

Rossi, Luigi. *Il Palazzo incantato.* Facsim ed., New York: Garland, 1977.

_____. *Six Airs et une passacaille.* Ed. Henri Prunières. Paris: Senart, 1914.

Scheidemann, Heinrich. *Orgelwerke.* 3 vols. Ed. Gustav Fock and Werner Breig. Basel: Bärenreiter, 1967-1971.

Schmidt, Bernhard. *Tabulatur Buch.* Strassbourg: n.p., 1607.

The Second Book of the Ladys Banquet. London: Walsh & Hare, 1706.

The Second Book of the Harpsichord Master. London: Walsh, 1700.

Seventeenth-Century Keyboard Music in the Chigi MSS of the Vatican Library, Corpus of Early Keyboard Music: no. 32, vols, 1-3. Ed. Harry B. Lincoln. N.p., American Institute of Musicology, 1968.

Starter, Jan. *Friesche Lust-Hof.* Amsterdam: Dirck Pieterszoon Voscuyl, [1624].

Sweelinck, Jan Pieterszoon. [*Selected Works,*] Exempla Musica Neerlandica: 2. Ed. Jost Harro Schmidt. Amsterdam: Vereningung voor Nederlandse Muziekgeschiedenis, 1965.

The Third Book of the Harpsichord Master. London: Walsh & Hare, 1702.

'T Uitnement Kabinet vol Pavanen, Almanden, Sarabanden, Couranten, Balletten, Intraden, Airs, etc. Amsterdam: Paulus Matthysz, 1646, 1649.

Ursillo, Fabio. *VI Sonates en trio.* Paris: Le Clerc & Boivin, [1731].

Valerius, Adriaen. *Nederlantsche Gedenck-Clanck.* Haarlem: Valerius, 1626.

Vingt Suites d'orchestre du XVIIe siècle français. 2 vols. Ed. Jules Écorcheville. Paris: L.-Marcel Fortin, 1906.

Visée, Robert de. *Oeuvres complètes pour guitare,* Le Pupitre: no. 15. Ed. Robert W. Strizich. Paris: Heugel, 1969.

Voigtländer, Gabriel. *Erster Theil allerhand Oden vnnd Lieder.* Sorφ: n.p., 1642.

BIBLIOGRAPHY C

Literature

Library catalogs are alphabetized by the location of the library or the name of the collector, as appropriate.

Aber, Adolf (Jd). *Die Pflege der Musik unter den Wettinern und wettinischen Ernestinern.* Bückeburg & Leipzig: Siegel, 1921.

Adams, Robert Lee. "The Development of a Keyboard Idiom in England During the English Renaissance." Ph.D. dissertation, Washington University at St. Louis, 1960.

Aiguillon (France). Robert, Jean. "La Bibliothèque musicale du Château d'Aiguillon." *Recherches* 8 (1973): 56-63.

Anderson, Lyle John. "Cecilia A/400: Commentary, Thematic Index and Partial Edition." M.M. thesis, University of Wisconsin, Madison, 1977.

Anthony, James. *French Baroque Music from Beaujoyeulx to Rameau.* New York: Norton, 1973.

Apel, Willi. "The Collection of Photographic Reproductions at the Isham Memorial Library, Harvard University," *Musica disciplina* 1:1 (1946): pp. 68-73, 144-148, 235-238.

_____. *The History of Keyboard Music to 1700.* Translated and revised by Hans Tischler. Bloomington: Indiana University Press, 1972.

Atcherson, Walter T. "Symposium on Seventeenth-Century Music Theory: England." *Journal of Music Theory* 16: 1-2 (1972): pp. 6-15.

Auerbach, Erich. *Das französische Publikum des 17. Jahrhunderts.* Munich: Hueber, 1933.

Avignon (France). Paris. Bibliothèque nationale, département de la musique. Vmd ms 1. "Manuscrits (et quelques imprimés) concernant la musique à la bibliothèque d'Avignon."

Bähr, Johann. *Musicalische Discurse.* Nuremberg: P. C. Monath, 1719.

Ballard. Le Beau, Elisabeth. "La Bibliothèque musicale des éditeurs Ballard à Paris à la fin du XVIIe siècle." *XVIIe Siècle* 21-22 (1954): 456-462.

Barbour, J. Murray. *Tuning and Temperament: A Historical Survey.* East Lansing: Michigan State College Press, 1953.

Baron, John H.   "First Report on the Use of Computer Programming to Study the Secular Solo Songs in France from 1600-1660."   *Bericht über den internationalen musikwissenschaftlichen Kongress Bonn 1970.*   Edited by Carl Dahlhaus et al. Kassel: Bärenreiter, 1970, pp. 333-336.

Beechey, Gwilym.   "A New Source of 17th-Century Keyboard Music."   *Music & Letters* 50   (1969):   278-289.

Benoit, Marcelle.   "Une Dynastie de musiciens Versaillais: Les Marchand."   *Recherches* I   (1960):   99-129.

_____.   *Musiques de cour, chapelle, chambre, écurie: 1661-1733; documents recuilles,* La Vie musicale en France sous les rois Bourbons: no. 20.   Paris: A. & J. Picard, 1971.

_____.   *Versailles et les musiciens du roi, 1661-1733; étude institutionnelle et sociale.* Paris: A. & J.   Picard,   1971.

Berlin.   Blechschmidt, Eva Renate.   *Die Amalien-Bibliothek.*   Berlin: Merseburger, 1965.

_____.   Kast,   Paul.   *Die   Bach-Handschriften   der   Berliner   Staatsbibliothek.* Trossingen: Hohner,   1958.

Bloomington, Indiana.   *The Apel Collection of Early Keyboard Sources in Photographic Reproduction in the Indiana University Music Library.*   Bloomington: Indiana University Music Library, [195?] (Mimeographed.)

Boalch, Donald H.   *Makers of the Harpsichord and Clavichord, 1440-1840.*   Second edition.   Oxford: The Clarendon Press, 1974.

Boehme, Franz Magnus.   *Geschichte des Tanzes in Deutchland.*   Leipzig: Breitkopf & Härtel,   1886.

Borren, Charles van den.   "Einige Bermerkungen über das handschriftliche Klavierbuch (Nr.   376) der Königlichen Bibliothek zu Kopenhagen."   *Zeitschrift für Musikwissenschaft*   13   (1930-31):556-558.

_____.   "Le Livre de clavier de Vincentius de la Faille (1625)."   *Mélanges de Musicologie offerts à Lionel de la Laurencie.*   Paris: Droz, 1933, pp. 85-96.

_____.   *The Sources of Keyboard Music in England.*   Translated by James E. Matthew.   New York: Novello, 1914.

Borroff, Edith.   *An Introduction to Elisabeth-Claude Jacquet de la Guerre.*   New York: Institute of Mediaeval Music, 1966.

Bouquet, Marie-Thérèse.   *Musique et musiciens à Annecy, les Maîtrises 1630-1789.* Annecy: Academie Salesienne;   Paris: Picard, 1970.

Boulay, Laurence. "La Musique instrumentale de Marin Marais." *La Revue musicale* 226 (1955): 61-75.

Bouvet, Charles. *Une Dynastie de musiciens français: les Couperin, organistes de l'église Saint-Gervais.* Paris: Delagrave, 1919.

Boyvin, Jacques. *Traité abrégé de l'accompagnement.* Paris: Ballard, 1700.

Branner, Shirley P. "The Harpsichord Music of Jacques Champion de Chambonnières." M.A. thesis. Yale University, 1954.

Breig, Werner. "Die Lübbenauer Tabulaturen Lynar A1 und A2." *Archiv für Musikwissenschaft* 25 (1968): 96-117, 223-236.

_____. "Zu den handscriftlich überlieferten Liedvariationen von Samuel Scheidt." *Die Musikforschung* 22 (1969): 318-328.

Brenet, Michel [Marie Bobillier]. *Les Concerts en France sous l'Ancien Régime.* Paris: Fischbacher, 1900.

_____. "La Librairie musicale en France de 1653 à 1790, d'après les registres de privilèges." *Sammelbände der Internationalen Musikgesellschaft* 8 (April-June, 1907):401-466.

Briquet, Charles M. *Les Filigranes, dictionnaire historique des marques du papier.* Paris, 1907. Facsimile ed., with supplement, edited by Allan Steveson. 3 vols. Amsterdam: The Paper Publication Society, 1968.

Brossard, Sébastien de. "Catalogue des livres de musique théorique et pratique, vocalle et instrumentale . . . qui sont dans le cabinet du Sr. Sébastien de Brossard," 1724. Bibliotheque nationale (Paris), department de la musique. Rés Vm8 20; fair copy of autograph, rès Vm8 21.

_____. *Dictionnaire de musique.* Third edition. Amsterdam: Roger, 1705.

Brossard, Yolande de. *Musiciens de Paris, 1535-1792.* Paris: Picard, 1965.

_____. "Musique et bourgeoisie au dix-septième siècle d'après les Gazettes de Loret et de Robinet." *Recherches* I (1960):47-49.

Brunner, Renate. "Die deutsche Liebhaber-Klavierbücher des 17. Jahrhunderts." Dissertation, Universität Freiburg/Br., forthcoming.

Brunold, Paul. *François Couperin.* Translated by J.B. Hanson. Monaco: Lyrebird Press, 1949.

_____. "Trois Livres de pièces de clavecin de J.F. Dandrieu." *Revue de musicologie* 43 (August, 1932): 147-151.

Brussels. Bibliothèque royale de Belgique. *Catalogue de la bibliothèque de F. J. Fétis, acquise par l'état Belge.* Brussels: C. Muquardt. 1877.

_____. Huys, Bernard. *Catalogue des imprimés musicaux des XVe, XVIe et XVIIe siècles, fonds général.* Brussels: Bibliothèque royale de Belgique, 1965.

_____. *Quinze Années d'acquisitions* [1954-1968], *de la pose de la première pierre à l'inauguration officielle de la bibliothèque royale Albert 1er.* Brussels: Bibliothèque royale Albert 1er, 1969.

Bukofzer, Manfred. *Music in the Baroque Era.* New York: Norton, 1947.

Burette, Pierre-Jean. *Catalogue de la bibliothèque de feu M. Burette.* 3 volumes. Paris: G. Martin, 1748.

Caldwell, John. *English Keyboard Music Before the Nineteenth Century.* New York: Praeger, 1973.

Caluori, Eleanor. *Luigi Rossi.* Cantata Index Series 3. Wellesley: Wellesley College, 1965.

Campbell, Pauline M. "A New Chapter in the History of the Clavecin Suite: Jean Nicolas Geoffroy." M.M. thesis, University of Illinois, 1967.

Castro Escudero, José. "Additions à l'article de D. Devoto sur 'La Sarabande'," *Revue de musicologie* 47 (1961):119-125.

Churchill, William A. *Watermarks in Paper in Holland, England, France, etc. in the XVII and XVIII Centuries and Their Interconnection.* Amsterdam: Menno Hertzberger, 1935.

Citron, Pierre. "Autour des folies françaises." *La Revue musicale*, numéro spécial 226 (n.d.):89-96.

Clercx, Suzanne. *Le Baroque et la musique.* Brussels: Éditions de la Librairie encyclopédique, 1948.

Cohen, Albert. "A Study of Instrumental Ensemble Practice in Seventeenth-Century France." *Galpin Society Journal* 15 (March, 1962):3-17.

Cooper, Barry A.R. "Albertus Bryne's Keyboard Music." *Musical Times* 113 (1972):142-143.

_____. "English Solo Keyboard Music of the Middle and Late Baroque." D.Phil. thesis. Oxford University, 1974.

_____. "The Keyboard Suite in England Before the Restoration." *Music & Letters* 53:3 (1972), pp. 309-319.

Corrette, Michel. *Le Maître de clavecin.* Paris: author, 1753.

Cortot, Alfred. *Bibliothèque Alfred Cortot, catalogue.* Argenteuil: R. Coulouma, 1936.

Curtis, Alan. "Jan Reinken and a Dutch Source for Sweelinck's Keyboard Works." *Tijdschrift der Vereeniging Nederlandse Muziekgeschiedenis* 20:1-2 (1964-65), pp. 45-56.

_____. "Musique classique française à Berkeley; pièces inédites de Louis Couperin, Lebègue, La Barre, etc." *Revue de musicologie* 56:2 (1970):   pp. 123-164.

_____. *Sweelinck's Keyboard Music; A Study of English Elements in 17th-Century Dutch Composition.* Leiden: University Press, 1969.

Danckert, Werner. *Geschichte der Gigue.* Leipzig: Kistner & Siegel, 1924.

Darmstadt. Noack, Friedrich. "Die Tabulaturen der hessischen Landesbibliothek zu Darmstadt." Neue Schweitzerische Musikgesellschaft, Ortsgruppe Basel. *Bericht über den musikwissenschaftlichen Kongress . . . Basel . . . 1924.* Wiesbaden: M. Sändy, 1969.

Dart, Thurston. "Elizabeth Eysbock's Keyboard Book." *Hans Albrecht In Memorian.* Edited by Wilfried Brennecke and Hans Hasse. Kassel: Bärenreiter, 1962, pp. 84-87.

_____. "John Bull's 'Chapel'," *Music and Letters* 40 (1959):279-282.

_____. "Lord Herbert of Cherbury's Lute-Book." *Music and Letters* 38 (1957):136-148.

_____. "Miss Mary Burwell's Instruction Book for the Lute." *The Galpin Society Journal* 11 (1958):3-62.

De Lafontaine, Henry Cart. *The King's Musick. A Transcript of Records Relating to Music and Musicians (1460-1700).* London: Novello, 1909; reprint edition, New York: Da Capo, 1973.

Delair, Denis. *Traité d'accompagnement pour le théorbe et le clavecin.*   Paris, 1690; reprint edition, Geveva: Minkoff, 1972.

Devoto, Daniel. "De la zarabanda à la sarabande." *Recherches* 6 (1966):27-72.

_____. "La Folle sarabande." *Revue de musicologie* 45 (1960):3-43; 46 (1960):145-180.

Dickinson, A.E.F. "A Forgotten Collection. A Survey of the Weckmann Books." *Music Review* 17 (May, 1956):97-109.

Dickinson, Alis. "Keyboard Tablatures of the Seventeenth Century in the Royal Library, Copenhagen." Ph.D. dissertation, North Texas State University, 1974.

Dieckmann, Jenny. *Die in deutscher Lautentabulatur überlieferten Tänze des 16. Jahrhunderts.*   Kassel: Bärenreiter, 1931.

Dürr, Alfred. "Neues über die Möllersche Handschrift." *Bach Jahrbuch 1954*, pp. 75-79.

Dufourcq, Norbert. "À Travers l'inédit: Nicholas Lebègue, Guillaume-Gabriel Nivers, La Furstenbert et Benaut." *Recherches* I (1960):205-213.

_____. "Une Dynastie française: Les Denis." *Revue de musicologie* 38:2 (December, 1956), pp. 151-152.

_____. "Die klassiche französische Musik, Deutschland und die deutsche Musikwissenschaft." *Archiv für Musikwissenschaft* 22 (1965):194-207.

_____. "Introduction au XVIIe s. musical en France." *XVIIe Siècle* 21-22 (1954):377-382.

_____. *Le Livre de l'orgue français, 1589-1789.* 5 vols. Vol. 4: *La Musique.* Paris: Picard, 1972.

_____. *La Musique d'orgue française de Jehan Titelouze à Jehan Alain.* Paris: Floury, 1941.

_____. *La Vie musicale en France au siècle de Louis XIV: Nicolas Lebègue.* Paris: Picard, 1954.

_____. "Notes et documents sur la capitation payée par les musiciens de Paris en 1695." *XVIIe Siècle* 21-22 (1954):484-494.

_____. "Notes sur les Richard, musiciens français du XVII siècle." *Revue de musicologie* 36 (1954):116-130.

_____. "Pierre Baillon, facteur de clavecins, d'orgues, graveur de musique et organiste français." *Music, Libraries and Instruments.* Hinrichsen Music Book 11. London: Hinrichsen, 1961, pp. 196-200.

Écorcheville, Jules. *Actes d'État civil de musiciens insinués au Châtelet de Paris 1539-1650.* Paris: Fortin, 1907.

_____. "Un Livre inconnu sur la danse." *Riemann-Festschrift, Gesammelte Studien,* pp. 288-293.

_____. "Le Luth et sa musique." *Bulletin français de la Société International de Musique* 4:2 (15 February 1908), pp. 131-164.

_____. *Catalogue des livres rares et précieux composant la collection musicale de feu M. Jules Écorcheville.* Introduction by Henry Prunières. Paris: Émile Paul, 1920.

Eineder. Georg. *The Ancient Paper-mills of the Former Austro-Hungarian Empire and Their Watermarks.* Hilversum: The Paper Publication Society, 1960.

Elling, Catharinus. "Die Musik am Hofe Christian IV. von Dänemark." *Vierteljahrschrift für Musikwissenschaft* 9 (1893):62-98.

Ellis, Meredith. "The Sources of Jean-Baptiste Lully's Secular Music." *Recherches* 8 (1968):89-130; 9 (1969):21-25.

Epstein, Ernesto. *Der französische Einfluss auf die deutsche Klaviersuite im 17. Jahrhundert.* Würzburg: K. Triltsch, 1940.

Ferguson, Howard. [Inventory of Christ Church 1177 MS.] Oxford, Christ Church Library. (Manuscript.)

Festgabe für Hans Joachim Moser zum 65. Geburtstag. Kassel: J. P. Hinnenthal, 1954.

Fischer, Kurt. *Gabriel Voigtländer.* Leipzig: Breitkopf & Härtel, 1910.

Fleischer, Oskar. "Denis Gaultier." *Vierteljahrschrift für Musikwissenschaft* 2 (1886):1-180.

Fournier, P. F. "Le Piédestal de croix de Nébouzat et les bourrés d'Auvergne." *Auvergne et Méditeranée, revue d'Art* 121 (1947):5-30.

France, Ministère de l'éducation nationale. *Catalogue général des manuscrits des bibliothèques publiques de France.* 48 volumes. Paris: Plon, Nourit, 1885-1933.

Frotscher, Gotthold. *Geschichte des Orgelspiels und der Orgelkomposition.* 2 volumes. Berlin: H. Hesse, 1935-1936.

Fuller, David. "Eighteenth-century French Harpsichord Music." Ph.D. dissertation, Harvard University, 1965.

_____. "French Harpsichord Playing in the Seventeenth Century after Le Gallois." *Early Music* 4:1 (January, 1976): pp. 22-26.

_____. Review of *French Baroque Music from Beaujoyeulx to Rameau* by James Anthony. *Journal of the American Musicological Society* 28:2 (Summer, 1975), pp. 374-384.

Furdell, James. "The Klavierbuch of Regina Clara Imhoff." Paper read at the New York State chapter of the American Musicological Society, April, 1969. (Typewritten.)

Gaussen, Françoise. "Actes d'état-civil de musiciens français: 1651-1681." *Recherches* I (1960):153-203.

Gebauer, Curt. *Geschichte der französischen Kultureinflüsse auf Deutschland.* Strassbourg: Heitz, 1911.

Geraklitov, A.A.   *Filigrani 17 veka.* [Watermarks of the 17th Century in Paper of Manuscript and Printed Documents of Russian Origin.]   Moscow: Publishing House of the Academie of Sciences, 1963.

Gustafson, Bruce.   "A Letter from Mr Lebègue Concerning His Preludes."   *Recherches* 17 (1977):7-14.

_____. "A Performer's Guide to the Music of Louis Couperin."   *The Diapason* 66:7 (June, 1975), pp. 7-8.

Haas, Arthur.   "The Chaconne and Passacaille in French Baroque Harpsichord Music." M.A. thesis, University of California at Los Angeles, 1974.

Hamburger, Povl.   "Ein handschriftliches Klavierbuch aus der ersten Hälfte des 17. Jahrhunderts."   *Zeitschrift für Musikwissenschaft* 13 (1930):133-140.

Harding, Rosamund.   *A Thematic Catalogue of the Works of Matthew Locke.*   Oxford: Alden & Mowbray, 1971.

Hardouin, Pierre.   "Notes sur quelques musiciens français du XVIIe siècle."   *Revue de musicologie* 38:1 (July, 1956):   pp. 62-67.

_____. "Quelques Documents relatifs aux Couperin."   *Revue de musicologie* 37 (December, 1955):111-121.

Harley, John.   "Ornaments in English Keyboard Music of the 17th and Early 18th Centuries."   *Music Review* 31 (1970):177-200.

Heartz, Daniel.   *Pierre Attaingnant, Royal Printer of Music.*   Berkeley and Los Angeles: University of California Press, 1969.

Heawood, Edward Ard.   *Watermarks, Mainly of the 17th and 18th Centuries.*   Hilversum: The Paper Publication Society, 1950.

Highfill, Philip H., et al.   *A Biographical Dictionary of Actors, Actresses, Musicians, Dancers, Managers & Other Stage Personnel in London, 1660-1800.*   8 vols. projected.   Carbondale: Southern Illinois University Press, 1973-

Hoffman, Shlomo.   *L'Oeuvre de clavecin de Fr. Couperin.*   Paris: Picard, 1961.

Hotteterre, Mr le Roman.   *L'Art de preluder sur la flûte transversière.*   Edited by Michel Sanvoisin.   Paris: Zurfluh, 1966.

Hubbard, Frank.   "The *Encyclopédie* and the French Harpsichord."   *The Galpin Society Journal* 9 (1956):37-50.

_____. *Three Centuries of Harpsichord Making.*   Cambridge: Harvard University Press, 1965.

Huber, Calvin Raymond. "Life and Music of William Brade." Ph.D. dissertation, University of North Carolina, 1966.

Hunt, Edgar. "Tuning and Temperament." *The English Harpsichord Magazine* 1:7 (October, 1976): pp. 201-204.

Huygens, Constantin. W.J.A. Jonckebloet and J.P.N. Land, eds., *Musique et musiciens au XVIIe siècle; correspondence et oeuvre musicales de C. Huygens.* Leyden: E.J. Brill, 1882.

Huys, Bernard. "Jacques Champion de Chambonnières, Humanist, Klavicinist, en Komponist." *Vlaams Muzektijdschrift* B 24/10 (December, 1972):289-295.

Jacquot, Jean, ed. *Le Luth et sa musique.* Paris: Centre national de la recherche scientifique, 1958.

Jurgens, Madeleine. *Documents du Minutier central concernant l'histoire de la musique (1600-1650).* 2 volumes. Paris: SEVPEN, La Documentation française, 1967-1974.

Kahl, Willi, ed. *Selbstbiographien deutscher Musiker des XVIII. Jahrhunderts mit Einleitungen und Anmerkungen.* Cologne: Stauffen, 1948; reprint edition, Netherlands: Frits Knuf, 1972.

Karstädt, Georg. *Thematisch-Systematisches Verzeichnis der musikalischen Werke von Dietrich Buxtehude.* Wiesbaden: Breitkopf & Härtel, 1974.

Kirchner, Ernst. *Das Papier.* Biberbach: Güntter-Stab'schen Wochenblattes für Papierfabrikation, 1897.

Kirkpatrick, Ralph. *Domenico Scarlatti.* Princeton University Press, 1953.

————. "On Re-reading Couperin's 'L'Art de toucher le clavecin'." *Early Music* 4:1 (January, 1976): pp. 3-11.

Krebs, Carl. "J. J. Froberger in Paris." *Vierteljahrschrift für Musikwissenschaft* 10 (1894):232-234.

La Laurencie, Lionel de. "Les Luthistes Charles Bocquet, Antoine Francisque, et Jean-Baptiste Besard." *Revue de musicologie* 9 (May, 1926):69-77.

————. *L'École française de violon, de Lulli à Viotti.* Paris: Delagrave, 1922-1924.

La Rousselière, Jean-Baptiste-Charles de. *Traité des languettes impérialles pour la perfection du clavecin.* Paris: author, 1679.

La Rue, Jan. "Numerical Incipits for Thematic Catalogs." *Fontes artis musicae* 9 (1962/2):72-75.

_____. "A Union Thematic Catalogue of 18th Century Symphonies." *Fontes artis musicae* 6 (1959/1):18-20.

_____. "Union Thematic Catalogues for 18th Century Chamber Music and Concertos." *Fontes artis musicae* 7 (1960/2):64-66.

Lavallière, Louis-César de La Beaume-le-Blanc. *Ballets, opéra et autres ouvrages lyriques.* Paris: Bauche,   1760.

Le Gallois. *Lettre de Mr. Le Gallois à Mademoiselle Regnault de Solier touchant la musique.* Paris: Estienne Michallet, 1680.

LeMoël, Michel. "Les Dernières Années de Jacques Champion de Chambonnières, 1655-1672." *Recherches 1* (1960):31-46.

Leonhardt, Gustav. "Johann Jakob Froberger and His Music." *L'Organo* 6:1 (January-June, 1968):   pp. 15-38.

Lesure, François, and Thibault, Geneviève. *Bibliographie des éditions d'Adrian Le Roy et Robert Ballard (1551-1598).* Paris: Heugel, 1955.

_____. *Bibliographie des éditions musicales publiées par Estienne Roger et Michel-Charles Le Cève (Amsterdam 1696-1743).* Paris: Heugel, 1969.

_____. "Chambonnières, organisateur de concerts (1641)." *Revue belge de musicologie* 3 (1949):140.

_____. "La Datation des premières éditions d'Estienne Roger (1697-1702)." *Kongress-Bericht Bamberg,* 1953.

_____. "Une Querelle sur le jeu de la viole en 1688: J. Rousseau contre Demachy." *Revue de musicologie* 46 (1960):181-199.

_____. "Réflexions sur les origines du concert parisien." *Polyphonie* 5 (November, 1949):47-51.

_____. "Two Documents from Avignon." *The Galpin Society Journal* 6 (July, 1953):105-106.

Lincoln, Harry B. "I Manoscritti Chigiani di musica organo-cembalistica della Biblioteca Apostolica Vaticana." *L'Organo* 5 (1967):63-82.

Linz.   Wessely, Othmar. "Katalog der Musiksammlung des Oberösterreichischen Landesmuseum Linz." (Typewritten, 1941; revised, 1946.)

Loubet de Sceaury, Paul. *Musiciens et facteurs d'instruments de musique sous l'ancien régime.* Paris: A. Pedone, 1949.

London; British Library, Reference Division [British Museum], L.R. 39a.6 (Sir John Hawkins, *A General History of the Science and Practice of Music*, 5 vols. [London: Payne and Son, 1776], author's exemplar).

London; Guildhouse Library, MS 5038/3 and 5039/1 (All Hallows Church records).

Lüneburg. Welter, Friedrich. *Katalog der Musikalien der Ratsbücherei Lüneburg.* 2nd edition. Lippstadt: Kistner & Siegel, 1955.

Maas, Martha Christine. "17th Century English Keyboard Music; A Study of MSS Rés 1185, 1186 and 1186bis of the Paris Conservatory Library." Ph.D. dissertation, Yale University, 1968.

MacGowen, Margaret. *L'Art du ballet de cour en France, 1581-1643.* Paris: Centre national de la recherche scientifique, 1963.

Machabey, Armand. "La Musique dans les 'Historiettes' de Tallemant des Réaux." *La Revue musicale* 13:126 (1932-33), pp. 350-361; 13:127, pp. 24-30.

Madrid; Bibliteca nacional. Higini Anglès and José Subirá. *Catálogo musical de la Biblioteca nacional de Madrid.* 2 volumes. Barcelona: Consejo superior de investigacionces cientificas, Instituto Español de musicología, 1946.

Massip, Catherine. *La Vie des musiciens de Paris au temps de Mazarin (1643-1661).* Paris: Picard, 1976.

Mélanges François Couperin. Paris: Picard, 1968.

Mellers, Wilfrid. *François Couperin and the French Classical Tradition.* London: Dobson, 1950.

Menestrier, Claude François. *Des Representations en musique anciennes et modernes.* Paris: Guignard, 1681; reprint edition, Geneva: Minkoff, 1972.

Méraux, Amédée. *Les Clavecinistes de 1637 à 1790.* Paris: Heugel, 1867.

Merian, Wilhelm. *Der Tanz in den deutschen Tabulaturbüchern.* Leipzig: Breitkopf & Härtel, 1927.

Mersenne, Marin. *Harmonie universelle.* Introduction by François Lesure. Paris: Centre national de la recherche scientifique, 1963.

Meyer, Ernst Herman. *Die mehrstimmige Spielmusik des 17. Jahrhunderts in Nord- und Mittel-Europa.* Kassel: Bärenreiter, 1934.

Mohr, Ernstwerner. *Die Allemande in der deutschen Klaviersuite.* Basel, 1931.

Moser, A. "Zur Genesis der Folies d'Espagne." *Archiv für Musikwissenschaft* 1 (1918):358-371.

Mráček, Jaroslav. "Keyboard Dance Music of French Origin or Derivation in the First Half of the Seventeenth Century." M.A. thesis, Indiana University, 1962.

_____. "Seventeenth-century Instrumental Dances in Uppsala University Library IMhs 409." Ph.D. dissertation, Indiana University, 1965.

Munich; Bayerische Staatsbibliothek Musiksammlung. Julius Joseph Maier. *Die Musikalischen Handschriften der Kgl. Hof- und Staatsbibl. in München*, Catalogus codicum manuscriptorum bibliotheccaieregia monacensis 7:1. Munich: Palmschen Hofbuchhandlung, 1879.

Nettl, Paul. *Die Wiener Tanzkompositionen in der zweiten Hälfte des 17. Jahrhunderts.* Studien zur Musikwissenschaft 8. Vienna: Universal; Leipzig: Breitkopf & Härtel, 1921.

Nicolai, Alexandre. *Histoire des moulins à papier du sud-ouest de la France, 1300-1800.* 2 volumes. Bordeux: G. Delmas, 1935.

Noack, Fritz. "Die Tabulaturen der hessischen Landesbibliothek zu Darmstadt." *Bericht über den musikwissenschaftlichen Kongress, Basel, 1924.* Reprint edition. Wiesbaden: M. Sandy, 1969, pp. 280-281.

Norlind. Tobias. "Zur Geschichte der Suite." *Sammelbände der internationalen Musikgesellschaft* 7 (1905-06):172-303.

Noske, Frits. "Een apocrief en een dubieus Werk van Sweelinck." *Mededeelingenblad* 20 (September, 1966):27 ff.

_____. [Review of Exempla Musica Neerlandica no. 2] Notes 24:1 (September, 1967), pp. 134-135.

Oldham, Guy. "Louis Couperin; A New Source of French Keyboard Music of the Mid Seventeenth Century." *Recherches* 1 (1960):51-60.

_____. "Musique au soleil (French Music during the Reign of Louis XIV, 1643-1715)." *Music and Musicians* 15:4 (December, 1966), p. 27.

_____. "Two Pieces for 5-Part Shawm Band by Louis Couperin." *Music, Libraries and Instruments.* Hinrichsen's Music Book 11. London: Hinrichsen, 1961.

Oxford. "Catalogue of Music Belonging to the Music School." Oxford: Bodleian Library, 1854. (Manuscript.)

_____. "Catalogue of Music Mss." Oxford: Bodleian Library. (Typescript, in progress.)

_____. [Thematic Catalog of Anonymous Pieces in the Christ Church Library, ed. G.E.P. Arkwright.] Oxford: Christ Church Library, 1935. (Typescript)

Panum H. "Melchior Schild oder Schildt." *Monatschefte für Musikgeschichte* 20:13 (1888), pp. 27-30, 35-41.

Paper Publication Society. *The Nostitz Papers.* Hilversum: The Paper Publication Society, 1956.

Paris; Bibliothèque de l'arsenal. Lionel de La Laurencie and L.A. Gastoué. *Catalogue des livres de musique (manuscrits et imprimés) de la Bibliothèque de l'Arsenal à Paris.* Paris: Droz, 1936.

Paris; Bibliothèque Sainte-Geneviève. Madelaine Garros and Simone Wallon. *Catalogue du fonds musical de la bibliothèque Sainte-Geneviève de Paris.* Kassel: Internationale Vereinigung der Musikbibliotheken, Internationaler Gesellschaft für Musikwissenschaft, 1967.

Paris; Minutier central. (MS) LIII, 104.

Parran, Antoine. *Traité de la musique théorique et pratique.* Paris: Ballard, 1639; reprint edition, Geneva: Minkoff, 1972.

Pearl, Mildred. "The Suite in Relation to Baroque Style." Ph.D. dissertation, New York University, 1957.

Pereyra, Marie-Louise. "Les Livres de virginal de la Bibliothèque du Conservatoire de Paris." *Revue de musicologie* 20 (1926):204-209; 21 (1927):36-39; 24 (1927):205-213; 28 (1928):235-242; 29 (1929):32-39; 37 (1931):22-24; 42 (1932):86-90; 45 (1933):24-27.

Perrault, Charles. *Les Hommes illustres qui ont paru en France pendent ce siècle.* Paris: A Dezallier, 1696.

Petre, Robert. "A New Piece by Henry Purcell." *Early Music* 6:3 (July, 1978), pp. 374-379.

Piccard, Gerhard. *Die Turmwasserzeichen.* Stuttgart: W. Kohlhammer, 1970.

Pirro, André. *Les Clavecinistes.* Paris: H. Laurens, 1924.

_____. "Louis Couperin." *Revue musicale* 1 (1920):1-21.

Pohlman, Ernst. *Laute, Theorbe, Chitarrone.* Bremen: Deutsche Musikpflege, 1968.

Powell, Newman. "Rhythmic Freedom in the Performance of French Music from 1650-1735." Ph.D. dissertation, Stanford University, 1958.

Prodhomme, Jacques Gabriel. *Écrits de musiciens.* Paris: Mercure de France, 1912.

Prunières, Henri. *L'Opéra italien en France avant Lulli.* Paris: Champion, 1913.

_____. *La Vie illustre et libertine de Jean-Baptiste Lully.* Paris: Plon, 1929.

Pulver, Jeffrey. *A Biographical Dictionary of Old English Music.* London: K. Paul, Trench, Trubner & Co., J. Curwen & Sons, 1927.

Quittard, Henry. "Un ancien Claveciniste français: Hardelle." *Revue musicale* 4 (1906):519-521.

_____. "Un Claveciniste du XVIIe siècle, Jacques Champion de Chambonnières." *Tribune de St. Gervais* (1901) 1:1-11, 2:31-44, 3:71-77, 4:105-110, 5:141-149.

_____. "Henry Du Mont." *Tribune de Saint Gervais* 11-12 (1901):297-314.

_____. *Un Musicien en France au XVIIe siècle: Henry Du Mont.* Paris: Mercure de France, 1906; reprint edition, Geneva: Minkoff, 1973.

_____. "Les Origines de la suite de clavecin." *Le Courrier musical et théatrical,* November, 1911, pp. 675-679; December, 1911, pp. 740-746.

Rasch, Rudi A. "Some Mid-seventeenth Century Dutch Collections of Instrumental Ensemble Music." *Tijdschrift voor muziekwetenschap* 22:3 (1972), pp. 160-200.

Rave, Wallace John. "Some Manuscripts of French Lute Music, 1630-1700." Ph.D. dissertation, University of Illinois, 1972.

Ravenel, J., and La Pelouze, Ed. V. de. *La Muze historique.* Vol. 2. Paris: Daffis, 1877.

Reimann, Margarete. "Pasticcios und Parodien in nordeutschen Klaviertabulaturen." *Die Musikforschung* 8 (1955):265-271.

_____. *Untersuchungen zur Formgeschichte der französischen Klavier-Suite.* Regensburg: Gustav Bosse Verlag, 1940.

_____. "Zur Entwicklungsgeschichte des Double." *Die Musikforschung* 5:44 (1952), pp. 317-332; 6:42 (1953), pp. 97-111.

_____. "Zur Spielpraxis der Klaviervariation des 16. bis 18. Jahrhunderts." *Die Musikforschung* 7 (1954):457-459.

Riedel, Friedrich Wilhelm. *Quellenkundliche Beiträge zur Geschichte der Musik für Tasteninstrumente in der zweiten Hälfte des 17. Jahrhunderts.* Kassel: Bärenreiter, 1960.

Ripin, Edwin M. "The French Harpsichord Before 1650." *The Galpin Society Journal* 20 (March, 1967):43-47.

_____. "The Two-Manual Harpsichord in Flanders Before 1650." *The Galpin Society Journal* 21 (March, 1968):33-39.

Roche, Martine. "Un Livre de clavecin français de la fin du XVIIe siècle." *Recherches* 7 (1967):39-73.

Rollin, Monique. "La Suite pour luth dans l'oeuvre de Charles Mouton." *La Revue musicale* 226 (1955):76-88.

_____. "Le 'Tombeau' chez les luthistes Denys Gautier, Jacques Gallot, Charles Mouton." *XVIIe Siècle* 21-22 (1954):463-479.

Rose, Gloria. "Purcell, Michelangelo Rossi and J.S. Bach: Problems of Authorship." *Acta Musicologica* 4:40 (1968), pp. 203-219.

Roth, Bärbel. "Zur Echtheitsfrage der Matthias Weckman zugeschriebenen Klavierwerke ohne Cantus firmus." *Acta Musicologica* 36 (1964):31-36.

Rousseau, Jean. *Méthode claire, certaine et facile pour apprendre à chanter la musique.* 4th edition. Amsterdam: Roger, 1691; reprint edition, University of Rochester Press, 1954.

_____. *Traité de la viole.* Paris: Ballard, 1687.

Rubsamen, Walter H. "The Earliest French Lute Tablature." *Journal of the American Musicological Society* 21:3 (1968), pp. 286-299.

Rudén, Jan Olof. "Ett nyfunnet Komplement till Dübensamlingen." *Svensk Tidskrift för Musikforskning* 47 (1965):51-88.

Russell, Raymond. *The Harpsichord and Clavichord, An Introductory Study.* Second edition, revised by Howard Schott. London: Faber & Faber, 1973.

Sachs, Curt. *World History of the Dance.* New York: Norton, 1937.

Saint-Lambert. *Les Principes du clavecin.* Paris: Ballard, 1702; reprint edition, Geneva: Minkoff, n.d.

Samoyault-Verlet, Colombe. *Les Facteurs de clavecins parisiens, notices biographiques et documents (1550-1793).* Paris: Heugel, 1966.

Schenk, Erich. "Österreichisches im Klavierbuch der Regina Clara Imhoff." *Jahrbuch des Österreichisches Volksliedwerkes* 6 (1957):162-167.

Schierning, Lydia. *Die Überlieferung der deutschen Orgel und Klaviermusik aus der ersten Hälfte des 17. Jahrhunderts.* Kassel: Bärenreiter, 1961.

Schiørring, Nils. *Det 16. og 17. århunderedes verdslige danske visesang.* 2 volumes. Copenhagen: Thaning & Appels Forlag, 1950.

Schmidt, Jost Harro. "Sweelincks Bergamasca und seine Allemande De Chapelle." *Mededeelingblad* 25 (April, 1968):58-64.

_____. "Eine unbekannte Quelle zur Klaviermusik des 17. Jahrhunderts: Das Celler Klavierbuch 1662." *Archiv für Musikwissenschaft* 22 (June, 1965):1-11.

Schneider, Herbert. *Die französische Komponistenlehrer in der ersten Hälfte des 17. Jahrhundert.* Tutzing: H. Schneider, 1972.

Schott, Howard M.   "A Critical Edition of the Works of J.J. Froberger with Commentary."   Ph.D. dissertation, Oxford University (Wadham College), 1977.

Seiffert, Max. *Geschichte der Klaviermusik.* Leipzig: Breitkopf & Härtel, 1899.

Shannon, John R.   "The Mylau Tabulaturbuch, A Study of the Preludial and Fugal Forms in the Hands of Bach's Middle-German Precursors."   Ph.D. dissertation, University of North Carolina, 1961.

Sharp, G. B. "Gaultier and Chambonnières. Two French Tercentenaris." *Musical Times* 1558 (December, 1972):1178-1181.

Silbiger, Alexander.   "Italian Manuscript Sources of Seventeenth-Century Keyboard Music."   Ph.D. dissertation, Brandeis University, 1976.

Smith, Carleton. "Tracking Down Original Scores Missing in the War." *Smithsonian* 6:9 (December, 1975), pp. 87-93.

Snyders, Georges. *Le Goût musical en France aux XVIIe et XVIIIe siècles.* Paris: J. Vrin, 1968.

Somer, Avo. "The Keyboard Music of Johann Jakob Froberger." Ph.D. dissertation, The University of Michigan, 1963.

Starke, David. *Frobergers Suitentänze.* Darmstadt: Tonos, 1972.

Stevenson, Robert. "A Propos de la sarabande." *Revue de musicologie* 47 (1961):113-115.

Straeten, Edmond vander. *La Musique aux Pays Bas avant le XIX siècle.* Brussels: G.-A. van Trigt, 1867-1888.

Tallemant des Réaux, Gédéon. *Historiettes.* Edited by Antoine Adam. Paris: Gallimard, 1960.

Taylor, Thomas F. *Thematic Catalog of the Works of Jeremiah Clarke.* Detroit: Information Coordinators, 1977.

Tessier, André. "Un Claveciniste français, Gaspard Leroux." *Revue musicale* 5:5 (1924): pp. 230-246, supplément.

_____. "L'Oeuvre de clavecin de Nicolas Le Bègue, notes bibliographiques." *Revue de musicologie* 7:7 (August, 1923), pp. 106-112.

_____. "Une Pièce d'orgue de Charles Raquet et le Mersenne de la Bibliothèque des Minimes de Paris." *Revue de musicologie* 32 (November, 1929):275-283.

_____. "Une Pièce inédite de Froberger." *Festschrift für Guido Adler zum 75. Geburtstag*, Studien zur Musikgeschichte. Vienna: Universal, 1930, pp. 147-152.

Thompson, Elisabeth H. *A.L.A. Glossary of Library Terms.* Chicago: American Library Association, 1943.

Tiersot, Julien. "Une Famille de musiciens français, les De la Barre." *Revue de musicologie* 11 (1927):185-202, 12 (1928):1-11, 68-74.

Tilsen, Herta. "Eine Musikhandschrift des Benediktinerklosters Ottobeuren aus dem Jahre 1695." Dissertation, Munich, 1922.

Titon du Tillet, Évrard. *Déscription du Parnasse.* Paris: J.B. Craignard Fils, 1732.

Tollefsen, R. H. "A Fresh Look at the 'Gresse Manuscript'." (Typescript), Utrecht (1975).

Traficante, Frank. "Dispersal of the Cortot Collection: 290 Treatises in Lexington." *Notes* 26:4 (June, 1970), pp. 713-717.

Trichet, Pierre. *Traité des instruments de musique.* Paris: n.p., ca. 1640; reprint edition, Neuilly-sur-Seine: Société de musique d'autrefois, 1957.

Vienna; Minoritenkonvent, Klosterbibliothek & Archiv. Friedrich Wilhelm Riedel. *Das Musikarchiv im Minoritenkonvent zu Wien; Katalog des älteren Bestandes vor 1784, Catalogus musicus I.* Kassel: Internationale Vereinigung der Musikbibliotheken, 1963.

Vienna; Nationalbibliothek, Musiksammlung. *Tabulae codicum manuscriptorum.* Vienna: Akademische Verlag, 1864; reprint ed., 1965.

Vogan, Charles. "The French Organ School of the 17th and 18th Centuries." Ph.D. dissertation, The University of Michigan, 1949.

Voorn, H. *De Papiermolens in de Provincie Noord-Holland.* Haarlem: Papierwereld, 1960.

_____. *De Paiermolens in de Provincie Zuid-Holland.* Womenveer: Drukkerij Meijer, 1973.

Wallon, Simone. "Un Recueil de pièces de clavecin de la seconde moitié du XVIIe siècle." *Revue de musicologie* 38 (December, 1956):105-114.

_____. "Les Testaments d'Élisabeth Jacquet de La Guerre." *Revue de musicologie* 40 (1957):206-214.

Ward, John. *Lives of the Professors of Gresham College.* London: n.p., 1740.

Whitehead, P. J. P. "The Lost Berlin Manuscripts." *Notes* 33:1 (September, 1976), pp. 7-15.

Williams, Peter.   "The Harpsichord Acciaccatura: Theory and Practice in Harmony, 1650-1750."   *Musical Quarterly* 54:4 (1968), pp. 503-523.

Wolf, Johannes.   *Handbuch der Notationskunde.*   2 volumes.   Leipzig: Breitkopf & Härtel, 1913-1919.

Wolffheim, Werner.   "Die Möllersche Handschrift, ein unbekanntes Gegenstüd zum Andreas-Bach-Buche."   *Bach Jahrbuch 1912*:42-60.

_____.   *Versteigerung der Musikbibliothek des Herrn Dr. Werner Wolffheim.*   2 volumes.   Berlin: Breslauer & Liepmannssohn, 1928-29.

Zietz, Hermann.   *Quellenkritische Untersuchungen an den Bach-Handschriften P 801, P 802 und P 803 aus dem "Krebs'schen Nachlass" unter besonderer Berücksichtigung der Choralbearbeitungen des jungen J.S. Bach,* Hamburger Beiträger zur Musikwissenschaft, no. 1.   Hamburg: Verlag der Musikalienhandlung Karl Dieter Wagner, 1969.

Zimmerman, Franklin B.   *Henry Purcell, 1659-1695, an Analytical Catalog of His Music.*   London: Macmillan, 1963.

_____.   "A Thematic Catalogue of Published 17th Century Italian Chamber Music in the Music School Collection, Bodleian Library, Oxford."   (Typescript.)

INDEX

This index includes references to all three volumes, distinguished by Roman numerals. Particularly important references are indicated by boldface, and references which include musical examples are marked by asterisks (*). The concordances to sources which are inventoried in the Catalog are not indexed here, as the Inventories are themselves the indices. Abbreviations are explained in the List of Abbreviations, pp. xviii-xlii.

092954